The Essential
Guide to Living in Mérida

The Essential Guide to Living in Mérida

Edited by Vincent Gricus

The Essential Guide to Living in Mérida, 2011: Including Tons of Visitor Information!

Copyright © 2011 by Hispanic Economics, Inc. Manufactured in the United States of America. All rights reserved. No part of this book may be reproduced in any form or by any means, electronic or mechanical, including photocopying, recording, or by information storage and retrieval systems – except by a reviewer who may quote brief passages in a review to be printed in a magazine, newpaper or on the Web – without permission in writing from the publisher.

Although the author and publisher have made every good faith effort to ensure the accuracy and completeness of information contained in this book, we assume no responsibility for errors, inaccuracies, omissions or inconsistencies herein.

This book is published by Hispanic Economics, Inc., and is strictly intended for educational and informational purposes. It expresses the personal opinions, conclusions and recommendations of the Editor and contributors and does not necessarily reflect the opinions, conclusions or recommendations of the publisher. No liability is assumed for damages resulting from the use of information contained herein.

This book will be updated annually, and subsequent editions will reflect corrections, updates and changes in the opinions, conclusions and recommendations for firms offering goods and services to the public. The Editor welcomes your feedback. Readers are encouraged to forward good faith comments, suggestions, corrections and additions to Vince Gricus. The Editor's email is *MexicoVince@yahoo.com*.

Publication date: June, 2011.

Published by Hispanic Economics, Inc.
P.O. Box 140681
Coral Gables, FL 33114-0681
info@hispaniceconomics.com
HispanicEconomics.com

ISBN 978-0-9791176-4-0

Cover and Interior Design by John Clifton
john@johnclifton.net

Front cover photograph courtesy of Beryl Gorbman

Complete Quick Find

TABLE OF CONTENTS

Editor's Note xiv
Acknowledgments xv

Part I Welcome to the Yucatán! — 1

Where in the world is Mérida? 3

1 The Beauty of Living in the Yucatán — 10

The Beauty of Living in Mérida: The Best Place to Retire in North America 12
Instituto Benjamin Franklin de Yucatán 15
The Mérida English Language Library (MELL) 16

2 The Colonias, or Neighborhoods, of Mérida — 19

The Main Square, or Plaza Grande, or Zócalo 21
Santiago 23
Santa Ana 25
Santa Lucia 27
Mejorada 28
San Juan 30
San Cristobal 32
San Sebastian and Ermita 34
García Ginerés 36
Itzimná 39
Miguel Alemán 40
Centenario 40
Chuminopolis 42
An Important Note about Owning Real Estate in Mérida! 45

Part II Mérida's Amenities — 47

3 The ABCs of MID — 49

Why is Mexico so bureaucratic? 49
Is there is a list of churches? 51

Catholic Church 51
Baptist 51
Jehovah's Witnesses 51
Methodist 51

i

QUICK FIND

Evangelical Christian *51*
Church of Jesus Christ of Latter-Day Saints *51*
Presbyterian *51*
Episcopal *52*
Where can I take cooking classes? **52**
Chef Internacional *52*
Colegio Gastronómico del Sureste *52*
Culinaria del Sureste *52*
MexicaChica *52*
Are there other Expat Communities in Mérida apart from Americans? **52**
Catalan Society *53*
Cuban Society *54*
Centro Cultural José Martí *54*
French Society *54*
Lebanese Society *54*
How do you make sense of the addresses? **54**
Where are the grocery stores and supermarkets? **55**
Drinking Water **55**
Are there blogs or websites recommended to learn more about living here? **56**
Do you have a list of recommended travel books on Mérida, the Yucatán and Mexico? ... **58**
Where can I sign up to take Spanish language classes? **63**
L'Alliance Francaise *63*
Instituto Benjamin Franklin *63*
CIS: Centro de Idiomas del Sureste *63*
ECORA – Instituto de Idiomas y Centro Cultural *63*
Habla: The Center for Language and Culture *63*
Instituto de Lengua y Cultura de Yucatán *63*
Institute of Modern Spanish *64*
MJ International *64*
UNAM: Centro Peninsular de Ciencias Sociales y Humanidades de la UNAM en Mérida *64*
Is birdwatching an avid pastime here? **65**
TOH Bird Festival *65*
Hacienda Chichén *65*
If the floors are made of pasta, can you eat them? **66**
Are there alternative film houses? **66**
Mérida is so close to Cuba – Can I travel to Cuba? **67**
American Citizens and Resident Aliens who wish to travel to Cuba: *67*

4	Museums & Galleries	68

Museum of Anthropology & History *68*

QUICK FIND

Museum of Contemporary Art of Yucatán (MACAY) Museum 68
Casa Frederick Catherwood 68
Casa Museo Montés Molina 69
Museum of the City 69
Tataya Gallery 69
La Luz Gallery 69
Museum of the Yucatecan Song (Museo de la Canción Yucateca) 70
"Juan Gamboa Guzmán" Pinacotea Museum 70
Mérida Gallery 70
Museum of Popular Folk Art 70
City Art Museum (GAMM) 71
In La'Kech Gallery 71
La Clínica - Arte Contemporáneo 71

5 Restaurants in Mérida & Environs   72

Centro (Downtown) - Restaurants 73
Colonia Alcalá- Restaurants 77
Colonia Benito Juárez Norte (Prolongación Montejo Norte) - Restaurants 78
Colonia Buenavista - Restaurants 78
Colonia Campestre - Restaurants 79
Colonia Díaz Ordaz (Most near Paseo de Montejos at Monumento a la Patria) - Restaurants .79
Colonia Emilio Zapata Norte (Prolongación Montejo Norte) - Restaurants 80
Colonia García Ginerés - Restaurants 81
Colonia Itzimná - Restaurants 81
Colonia Jesús Carranza - Restaurants 82
Colonia Mejorada - Restaurants 82
Colonia Mexico - Restaurants 82
Colonia Mexico Norte - Restaurants 84
Colonia Mexico Oriente - Restaurants 85
Colonia Misne - Restaurants 85
Colonia Montecristo - Restaurants 85
Colonia Monterreal - Restaurants 86
Colonia San Antonio Curul – Restaurants 86
Colonia Santa Ana – Restaurants 86
Gran Plaza Shopping Mall 87
Hotel Zone (Paseo de Montejo & Avenida Colón) – Restaurants 88
Mexican Restaurants with various locations 89
"Puertas Cerradas" (Closed Doors) 90
Day Trips from Mérida - Restaurants 90
   Izamal 90

Progreso/Celestun *91*
Haciendas Near Mérida *91*

Part III — The Fundamentals of Moving to Mérida — 93

6 — Getting Here! To Drive, or Not to Drive! — 95

By Air 95
Getting to Mérida by Bus 97
For traveling to other locations from Mérida by Bus 97
By Car 98
Entry of private vehicles into Mexico 99
Regulations for Bringing Your Car into Mexico 101
Applying for a permit at the Mexico Border 102
Requesting Car Import Permits in Advance and Via Internet 104
Applying for a Car Permit Online 104
Insurance 106
 Answers to Commonly Asked Questions *106*
On the road to Mérida! 107
 Military Checkpoints: *107*
 Free Highway Assistance: Green Angels *108*
 The Yucatán's One and Only Toll Road: *108*
Recommendations from the U.S. State Department on Driving in Mexico 109
 Driving and Vehicle Regulations *109*
 Insurance *109*
 Road Emergencies and Automobile Accidents *109*
 Road Safety *110*
Mexican Automobile Insurance 112
Vehicle Registration, or Tenencia and Referendo 112
Car Insurance 115
Moving Your Possessions 115
 Shipping company *116*
 Customs Brokers *116*
Going somewhere? 117
Conversion Chart 118

7 — The Expat Life, or what the Mexicans call "Gringolandia" — 119

The Enigma of Arrival 123
 Democracy, by Joan Didion *123*
 Geography III, by Elizabeth Bishop *124*
 The Good Terrorist, by Dorris Lessing *124*
 Guerrillas, by VS Naipaul *124*

  How German Is It?, by Walter Abish 125
  In a Free State, by VS Naipaul 125
  Life: A User's Manual, by Georges Perec 125
  The Sailor From Gibraltar, by Marguerite Duras 126
  The Sheltering Sky, by Paul Bowles 126
  Speak, Memory, by Vladimir Nabokov 126
 Read Spanish? **127**

8   The Cost of Living in Mérida   129

 Building a Budget for Living in Mérida **133**
  Housing 133
  Utilities: Electricity, Gas, Water and Garbage 134
  Electricity 134
  Gas 135
  Water 135
  Garbage Collection 136
  Internet 136
  Telephone 137
  Food 137
  Transportation 138
 Household Help **138**
  Domestic Workers 140
   Daily wages 140
   Transportation and Meals 140
   Live-In Workers 141
   When to Pay 141
   Room and Board 141
   Health Insurance 141
   Sick Leave 141
   Vacation Pay 142
   Treating Domestic Workers with Respect and Fairness 142
   Gardeners 142
  How to Find Domestic Help 143

9   Settling In: Utilities, Telephone, Gas Stations & Other Necessities   144

 Electricity **144**
 Water **145**
 Telephone **146**
 Internet Service Providers **148**
 Pemex Gas Stations **148**
 Propane Gas **148**

QUICK FIND

| Garbage | 148 |

10 Banking & Financial Affairs — 149

Checking Accounts 151
Checkbooks 151
Checkbook Activation 152
How to Write a Check 152
Accepting a Check 153
Statements and Balances 153
Why so much security? 153

List of Banks (most have English-language versions on their websites) 154
National Associations and Regulators 155

Part IV Making a Home and Building a Life — 157

11 Real Estate — 159

The Curious Case of the Real Estate Market in Mérida's Historic Centro 159
Mérida is for Everyone 162
Buying Real Estate in Mexico 162
Attorneys and Real Estate Agents 162
Rules, Regulations and Restrictions 163
General Process 164
Before you consider buying Real Estate in Mérida, heed these "Lessons Well Learned" 165
Who Can You Trust? 172
The Seven Realities for the Real Estate Market in Mérida's Centro Histórico 174
Buyer, Proceed with Caution! 174
Recommended Real Estate Companies 175
Where Can You Search for "Non-Dollarized" Real Estate? 176
  Here is a list of Mexican Real Estate Companies, by Mexicans for Mexicans 177
  Real Estate Companies Specializing in Progreso and Beach Homes 178
Is Mérida really right for you? 178
A Note about Shorter Stays 179
Here is a list of Bed & Breakfasts, in alphabetical order, that are among Mérida's finest 180
A Note about Renting an Apartment or House 181
New Regulations on the Horizon for 2012? 182
Property Taxes, or Predial 183

12 Contractors, Architects and Designers — 186

Books to Inspire 186
Getting it done 191
  Construction Practices 192

Recommendations	193
Architects	*193*
Contractors	195
Recommended References:	196
Construction Spanish (en inglés y español), by A. P. Scott.	*196*
Constructionary, Second Edition: English-Spanish by the ICC	*196*

13 Furniture, Furnishings & Antiques — 198

Furniture	198
Furniture Stores	199
An Alternative to Furniture Stores: Mom-and-Pop Shops	203
Mexican Antiques	204
Antique shops	206
Decorative Motifs	209

14 Handicrafts, Artists & Books — 211

Handicrafts	211
Artists	213
Books	213

Part V Going Native: The Essence of Mexican and Yucatecan Culture — 215

15 Yucatecans … and Huaches … and Gringos … Oh My! — 217

Fair is Fair Department: Los Muertos de Hambre de la Casta Divina	221

16 Social Expectations and Customs: Being a Good Neighbor — 225

Did you know?	**226**
The Green Revolution began in Mexico	*226*
Blacks outnumbered Spaniards until after 1810	*228*
Many common garden flowers originated in Mexico	*231*
Nineteenth century Mexico map maker first sailor through the Georgia Strait, Canada	*233*
The Thanksgiving and Christmas turkey originated in Mexico.	*236*
Wild Turkey, Meleagris gallopavo	236
Corn	237
Potatoes	237
The first Thanksgiving	238
Pumpkin Pie	238
Christmas Poinsettias	238
Consuelo Velázquez and "Bésame mucho".	**239**
Words of "Bésame mucho" (Consuelo Velázquez)	239

17 Mexican and Yucatecan Holidays & Traditions — 242

Traditional Yucatecan Dishes 242
Día de los Muertos 243
    Day of the Dead nomenclature: 244
Firecrackers 244
Bombas! 245
Mexico's Flag 246
Gremios 248
Mardi Gras – Carnaval 249
Buen Provecho! 250

18   Philanthropy & Non-Profit Organizations   251

Authorized Nonprofit Organizations Operating in the State of Yucatán 251
The Danger of the Hapless Altruist 254
Five Organizations to Stay Away From! (in our opinion) 257

Part VI   Almost Paradise ...   259

19   Attorneys & Public Notaries   261

Dealing with a Mexican Attorney 261
    Mérida 263
    Valladolid 265
    Cozumel, Quintana Roo 267
    Cancún, Quintana Roo 268
    Playa del Carmen, Quintana Roo 276
    Chetumal, Quintana Roo 280
    Campeche, Quintana Roo 281

20   Doctors   283

Doctors listed by Specialties 283
    GENERAL PRACTITIONERS 283
    ALLERGISTS 284
    CARDIOLOGISTS 284
    DERMATOLOGISTS 284
    DENTISTS 284
    ENDOCRINOLOGISTS 285
    GASTROENTEROLOGISTS 285
    GENERAL SURGERY 285
    GYNECOLOGISTS 285
    INTERNAL MEDICINE 285
    NEUROLOGISTS 286
    ONCOLOGISTS 286

QUICK FIND

OPHTHALMOLOGISTS 286
ORTHOPEDISTS 286
OTORRINOLARINGOLOGISTS 286
PEDIATRICIANS 287
PNEUMOLOGISTS.. 287
PSYCHIATRISTS... 287
UROLOGISTS 287
MEDICAL EMERGENCIES..287

21 Schools, Colleges, Universities and Research Centers — 289

Schools, Kindergarten through High School (Preparatorias) 289
American School... 289
Centro Educativo Palmerston.. 289
Centro Educativo Renacimiento (CER) 289
Colegio Americano 289
Colegio Iberoamericano de Mérida, A.C. 290
Colegio Peninsular Roger's Hall 290
Educrea... 290
Escuela Modelo 290
Instituto Cumbres (for Boys) 290
M.J. International 290
Saint Patrick's 290
Centro Educativo Piaget, A.C. 290

These are state institutions offering higher education 291
These are the more important private institutions for higher education 291
Mérida has several national research centers of renown. They include–............291

22 Nutrition, Yoga & Personal Trainers — 293

MyPyramid Tracker 294
Assess Your Food Intake... 294
Assess your physical activity 295

Gyms and Health Clubs..295
Boscos... 295
Exersite Fitness Center 296
Mérida Sports Center.. 296
North Gym Center... 297
SporTec Muscle Factory 297
WW Gym... 297
Xtreme Body Gym 298

Personal Trainer 298
Massages 298

QUICK FIND

Yoga **299**
    Semilla Yoga *299*
    Centro VIRYA 2011 .... *299*
    Yoga Para Ti *299*
    Hotel Macan Ché *299*

23 Health Care & Health Insurance — 300

Private Hospitals **302**
    Clínica de Mérida *302*
    Star Médica *302*
    Centro de Especialidades Médicas (CEM) *303*
    Centro Médico de las Américas (CMA) *303*
    Centro Médico Pensiones (CMP) *303*
    Hospital Santelena *303*

Public Hospitals: **304**
    Hospital Agustin O'Horán *304*
    Cruz Roja Mexicana *304*
    Centro de Salud Pública *304*
    Clínica Materno-Infantil "María José" *304*
    IMSS (Instituto Mexicano de Seguro Social, or Mexican Institute of Social Security) *304*
    Hospital Benito Juárez IMSS *304*

Personal Health Insurance **305**

Health Insurance from American and Canadian Companies **306**
    Expat Global Medical *306*
    American Express (Aetna Global Benefits) *306*
    Expat Financial *307*

Health Insurance from Mexican Companies **307**
    GE Seguros (in the process of becoming HDI Seguros) *307*
    La Peninsular Seguros *307*
    Met Life Mexico *308*

Health Insurance from the Mexican Government **308**
    IMSS (Pensiones) *308*
    IMSS (Serapio Rendon) *309*

Beyond Health Care **309**
    Gym for Seniors *309*
        Seniors Gym *310*
    Adventure Travel and the Elder Expat *310*
    Sex and the Expat *310*
    Plastic Surgery *312*
        Clínica Colón *312*

QUICK FIND

    Sports Facilities 312
        Nationally-Ranked Teams 313

24 Gay and Lesbian Mérida — 314

Gay Mérida 316
    Places to stay 317
    Bars 318
    Cafés and Scenes 319
    Places Favored by Gay Men 320
    Mérida Gay Facebook Community 320
    Mérida Gay Websites 320

Lesbian Mérida 320
    Places to Stay 323
    Bars 324
    Cafés and Hangouts 324
    Places Favored by Lesbians 324
    Day Trips 325
    Mérida Lesbian Blog 325
    Mérida Lesbian Facebook Community 325
    Mérida GLBTQ Community Resources 325

25 U.S. Taxes and Voting — 327

Taxes for U.S. Citizens and Resident Aliens Abroad 327
    When to File 327
    Where to File 327
    Taxpayer Identification Number 328
    Exchange Rates 328
    How to Get Tax Help 328
Voter Registration & Voting for American Citizens in Mérida 329

26 General Services: Emergency, Police, Fire, Post Offices & More — 331

General Contact Numbers 331
    General Emergency Numbers 331
    Utilities 331
    Hospitals 331
    Ambulances 331
    Taxis 332
    Animal Rescue 332
    Visitor Information 332

Post Offices 332
    Mérida Post Offices 332
    Progreso Post Office 333

General Information about Yucatán 333
Air Ambulance & Med-Evac Companies 334
   U.S.-based Companies 334
      ADVANCED AIR AMBULANCE 334
U.S. Embassy, Consulates and Consular Agencies in Mexico: 334
   U.S. Consulates 334
      Ciudad Juárez: 335
      Guadalajara: 335
      Hermosillo: 335
      Matamoros: 335
      Mérida: 335
      Monterrey: 335
      Nogales: 335
      Nuevo Laredo: 335
      Tijuana: 335
   Consular Agencies 335
      Acapulco: 335
      Cabo San Lucas: 335
      Cancún: 335
      Cozumel: 335
      Ixtapa/Zihuatanejo: 335
      Mazatlán: 336
      Oaxaca: 336
      Piedras Negras: 336
      Playa del Carmen: 336
      Puerto Vallarta: 336
      Reynosa: 336
      San Luis Potosi: 336
      San Miguel de Allende: 336
Veterinary Services 336
   Bilingual Veterinarians: 337
   Veterinary Association 337
   Adopt-a-Pet: 337
   Responsible Dog Breeders 337

27   If There Were a "Better Business Bureau" in Mérida ...   338
   MISSION 339
   VISION 339
   AIMS OF THE PROFECO 339
If there were a "Better Business Bureau" in Mérida! 339

28 End of Life Issues: Wills, Assisted Living Options & Caring for an Elderly Parent ... 342
Caring for Elderly Parents ... 343
The Final Adios ... 348

29 Mexican Embassies and Consulates in the U.S. and Canada ... 350
USA ... 350
- *Alaska* ... 350
- *Arkansas* ... 350
- *Arizona* ... 350
- *California* ... 351
- *Colorado* ... 353
- *District of Columbia* ... 353
- *Florida* ... 353
- *Georgia* ... 353
- *Idaho* ... 354
- *Indiana* ... 354
- *Illinois* ... 354
- *Louisiana* ... 354
- *Massachusetts* ... 354
- *Michigan* ... 354
- *Minnesota* ... 355
- *Missouri* ... 355
- *Nebraska* ... 355
- *Nevada* ... 355
- *New Mexico* ... 355
- *New York* ... 355
- *North Carolina* ... 356
- *Oregon* ... 356
- *Pennsylvania* ... 356
- *Texas* ... 356
- *Utah* ... 358
- *Washington* ... 358

CANADA ... 358
- *Alberta* ... 358
- *British Columbia* ... 358
- *Ontario* ... 359
- *Quebec* ... 359

Editor's Note

Every day, somewhere in Mérida, a business opens its doors. Every day, somewhere in Mérida, an establishment closes theirs for good. Every day, someone calls the telephone company to set up service, and others are calling to disconnect their numbers.

In a book this comprehensive something, somewhere will inevitably be out of date, or incorrect. No matter how much care and diligence has been exercised in compiling the information in this book, dear reader, there will be errors and omissions. This is why it's our intention to update this book annually, in order to deliver the most current information available anywhere, and to be the essential guide to visiting Mérida and living in this wonderful city.

So, consider this an invitation. If you have any information, whether it is a correction or any recommendation, to improve this guide, please send me an email and let me know about it. I want to know about it! And remember, in a book this ambitious in scope, there are hundreds of companies and business that were not included. This is, after all, a city of almost one million people! That said, an omission is not to be construed as a negative recommendation!

With that, enjoy this book, and may you find it instructive, illuminating and useful to you.

Vincent "Chente" Gricus
Mérida, Yucatán

Email: *MexicoVince@yahoo.com*

Acknowledgments

This book represents the collaboration, contributions and opinions of many people. Listed alphabetically, as Editor, I would like to thank the following for having contributed, made suggestions, offered information, or provided material quoted about Mérida, which makes this the most comprehensive guide to living in Mérida ever published.

My thanks go to the following contributors, writers, reviewers, and advisors who have enriched this book: Miguel Aguayo de Pau, Karín Alvarez, Ricardo Ancona, Mario Arrendondo, Francisco Arrigunaga, Mark Arbour, Tony Burton, Emilio Guadalupe Chan, George Chehade, Beryl Gorbman, Claudia Guerrero, Vanessa Hernández, Alberto Huchim, Charles Kinbote, Thomas Lloyd, Gerardo Martínez, Concepción May, Hugo de Naranja, Louis Nevaer, Zenaida Pantaleon, Glynna Prentice, Dan Prescher, Diane Provenzano, Reed Robertson, Pete Sigal, and María Luisa Uc.

—V. G.

Part I
Welcome to the Yucatán!

Where in the world is Mérida?

By Louis Nevaer

Mérida, with just under one million residents, is the largest city in the Yucatán, and it is the capital of the State of Yucatán.

It is also one of the oldest cities established by the Europeans in the Americas. Founded by Francisco de Montejo "El Mozo" in 1542, at the time a scant 70 Spanish families formed the "city." It was an ambitious effort, a small European enclave in the heart of a vast wilderness, surrounded by scores of Maya communities, many of which did not know what to make of these foreigners in their midst. It was this uncertainty and precarious nature of their small community that led Montejo to choose this precise location for the city: ruins offered ready-cut stones for building the initial structures of the new settlement.

Mérida was therefore established amid the ruins of the abandoned Maya city of T'ho, which itself was built on the site of an even earlier abandonded Maya ceremonial center, Ichcaanzihó. (When the Spaniards asked the Maya who had built the crumbling temples of T'ho, the answer given was: Who knows?) The name "Mérida" was chosen because it reminded the Spaniards of the Roman ruins found in Mérida, Spain. And so, ruins from one ancient civilization inspired the Spaniards to name their new city in honor of the ruins of another ancient civilization.

From that humble – and audacioius – beginning, Mérida has become what it is today: a cosmopolitan, vibrant city, one of the fastest-growing in Mexico, with a rich history stretching from the 16th century to the present one. Often described as a "colonial gem" and "unspoiled," Mérida has become a "tropical paradise" in the world's imagination, especially since it stands in sharp contrast to glitzy Cancún and the disjointed resorts of the Maya Riviera. Where Cancún boasts beaches and a climate of excess, Mérida boasts opera, museums, symphonies, culture, and the tranquility in which to enjoy it all. It is a community of storied waves of immigrants, and a metropolis of distinctive cuisines that reflects influences from exotic sources, from the Maya to the Middle East.

It also has some of the more riveting history to be found anywhere in the Americas. It is, for instance, the only place in the hemisphere where an uprising of the First Peoples, the Maya, almost led to the complete expulsion of all the Europeans. The War of the Castes in the 19th Century was so ferocious that the Governor ordered the evacuation of the city of Mérida, and Mexico, Cuba, Spain, the United States and the United Kingdom sent ships to help rescue the fleeing refugees. The circumstances that led to this uprising, which are discussed briefly later on this book, itself is a fascinating study of the Maya religious beliefs, and the consequences of the mercantile system imposed under Colonialism.

Mérida is also the place that welcomed Fidel Castro (who resided in Mérida for months) on his quest to foment revolution in his homeland. It is also where Pan Am World Airways built, with CIA money, Mérida's international airport, partly in order to check on Soviet ambitions in the region. Charles Lindbergh surveyed the peninsula from the air, and discovered unknown Maya ruins. Another Charles, Charles Duller, used NASA satellites to penetrate the forest canopy and "see" the remains of Maya ceremonial centers. Louis C. Tiffany made a small fortune designing stained glass windows for the grand homes of Mérida's wealthy. Cuban poet and liberator José Martí spent months here, growing inspired by the Maya. A few decades before his arrival, John Lloyd Stephens and Frederick Catherwood embarked on a grand journey of exploration that resulted in a landmark book, *Incidents of Travel*, which brought the achievements of the Maya civilization to the

State and Federal Officials

Governor (State)
Ivonne Ortega Pacheco

Municipal President (Mayor of Mérida)
Angélica Araujo Lara

Senators (Federal)
Beatriz Zavala Peniche
Alfredo Rodríguez
Cleominio Zoreda

Deputies
- Efraín Aguilar Gongora
- Martín Enrique Castillo Ruz
- Felipe Cervera Hernández
- Jorge Carlos Ramírez
- Eric Rubio Bartell
- Rolando Zapata Bello
- Rosa Adriana Díaz Lizama
- Yolanda Valencia Vales
- Daniel Gabriel Ávila Ruiz
- Liborio Vidal Aguilar

Government Websites
State:
   www.yucatan.gob.mx
City:
   www.merida.gob.mx

consciouness of the world, and launching the field of Maya studies.

The list goes on, and could fill a book. Suffice it to say that Mérida is an oasis of history, and culture, with a distinct set of values, sensibilities and affections that are not quite Mexican, and which set the Yucatán as a region apart. This difference has led to misunderstandings across the centuries, much the same way that the differences between the Maya and the First Peoples from central Mexico led to conflicts between them centuries before any European set foot on this continent. The Maya, after all, saw themselves as a kind of chosen people: the very word "Maya" means just that!

This history of Maya Exceptionalism, in fact, created obstacles to the fledging colony of Spaniards in the Yucatán. Of the Maya settlements within a couple of days' distance from Mérida, some were openly hostile to foreigners settling in the Yucatán. A few welcomed the Spaniards, seeing them both as accomplished in military skills and a people who arrived with astonishing goods; the Maya had never seen horses or hammocks, and they went wild over the Spaniards' foods: Oranges, lemons, cinammon, pork. Most of the Maya, however, were indiffirerent. To them, the Spaniards had as much right to make themselves at home in the ruins of an abandoned city as much as anyone else did!

Montejo, for his part, was careful, having studied the lessons of the Spanish reconquest of the Iberian peninsula from the Muslims. It is not a coincidence that when Mérida was founded, it was dedicated to Nuestra Señora de la Encarnación, Our Lady of the Incarnation. This is the name of a church in Álora, a village in southern Spain, today part of Málaga, which was liberated from the Muslims after several unsuccessful attempts. Montejo saw this isolated outpost of New Spain as surrounded by threats, and he was determined to provide for the safety of families under his responsibility. Since there was no natural protection for the city, such as a river, or cliffs, or outcroppings, a wall would have to be built to protect the residents. More to the point, Mérida was declared a "Ciudad Blanca," a "White City."

I would be willing to bet that somewhere you've read, or someone has told you, that Mérida is the "White City" because the buildings are painted white – very few are, really – or that the name reflects the "cleanliness" of the city. Both of these stories are nonsense, merely myths propagated by tourism officials and the uninformed who repeat what they've been told. Apart from the Museum of Anthropology and the Casa Montes Molina on Paseo de Montejo, what other landmark building is painted white? (And these are painted shades of eggshell, not white!) Indeed, the liming that is widely used to whitewash the buildings was unknown until the mid 17th century. Also, consider the first buildings that still stand today: The Casa de Montejo and the Cathedral, each of which displays its natural stone and were never whitewashed.

The Montejos explicitly sought to make Mérida a "White City" for the safety of Spanish residents. Michel Antochiw Kolpa, a Mexican historian who is an authority on first decades of Mérida's existence, confirms that Mérida was a city where only Europeans could live. Others would visit and work in Mérida proper during daylight hours, but they could not spend the

---

How Safe is Mérida?

Concerned about Safety? Try Living in Yucatán, Mexico

By Thomas Lloyd

Although media images have caused many people to be concerned about safety when considering living in Mexico, statistics, as well as testimonials from Americans living here show that safety is actually a good reason to leave the U.S. and move to Mexico. This is especially true for many of Mexico's favorite tourist areas with significant expat communities, such as the colonial city of Mérida and the surrounding state of Yucatán. If you are considering buying Yucatán real estate, you will actually be improving the level of safety and the resulting comfort in your lifestyle.

Mérida is not only safer than the image people have of Mexico, but it is actually safer than most places in the U.S. According to statistics, aggravated assault, rape, theft, automobile theft, and burglary are all considerably lower in Mexico overall than in the U.S., each rate for Mexico being around 50% of the rate for the U.S., and Yucatán falls well below the national average. In terms of the murder rate (per 100,000 inhabitants), the U.S. was at about 4 for 2009, while Yucatán's rate was 2.5. ...

Besides the stats, Americans who live in Mérida will consistently attest to the fact that they actually feel safer. "Truthfully," says one American, "My wife and I feel safer walking to and from our midtown home in Mérida to parks, restaurants, and evening events than we did in Omaha."

night. This was seen by the Maya as reciprocity: they had restrictions on Spaniards living in their communities, since the Maya believed they were an excitable and dangerous people.

It was this exclusion that created the need to establish "Colonias" – Santiago, Santa Ana, San Sebastian, and so forth, which were designated as residential communities for other peoples. Santiago was established for the Maya who had business in Mérida, and as residential neighborhoods for Europeans who had business in town, primarily Portuguese and Italian merchants. Santa Ana was established for mixed race people, and blacks, who were brought in to augment the labor force and mitigate the Spaniards' fear of skirmishes with the Maya. All the Colonias were considered "extramuros," meaning they were "outside the walls" of Mérida proper. The chapter on the Colonias of Mérida offers a broader discussion, but for now, it's important to note the ambivalence of Spaniard and Maya from the very beginning.

In the early decades, in fact, the same way that Montejo established Mérida as the "White City," the Maya referred to the growing Spanish settlement as "Chak T'ho," meaning, "Red T'ho," or "Red Mérida." Why did the Maya call Mérida the Red City? Well, from the Maya perspective, the Spaniards turned "red" in the tropical sun, much the way native Floridians ridicule snowbirds that arrive every winter and in a few days are red as lobsters for not knowing how to enjoy the sun without getting burned. To the Maya, Mérida was a city of people who turned "red" at the slightest exposure to the sun. (And fear of skin damage is one reason that so many "proper" Yucatecans today are heliophobes!)

It is clear to see that this mutual exclusion and mistrust gave rise to prejudices and misgivings. This is instructive, for it reveals that that the history of Mérida over the centuries has been the struggle for social justice and inclusion.

Mérida is located 198 miles west of Cancún. This is both a blessing and a curse, depending on your perspective. For those who treasure Mérida as a "gem" and "unspoiled" and a "respite" from the world, it is great to be removed from the hustle-and-bustle of Cancún. On the other hand, there are those who lament that Mérida has been eclipsed by Cancún, and that it has been economically marginalized, with most people pointing to the relative difficulty of air travel in recent years as proof of that isolation. A little over a decade ago, Mérida boasted two daily flights to Miami, with regularly scheduled service to Guatemala City, Havana, Houston, New Orleans and Orlando. (Many Yucatecans remember fondly, and proudly, that in the 1980s Eastern Airlines had a direct flight from Mérida to New York City!) In 2011, by comparison, the only commercial international flights are to Havana, Houston and Miami. Local authorities are pushing for increased nonstop service between Mérida and other cities. Maya Air has been encouraged to

In 2011, Canadians Targeted in Progreso

At the height of the winter season, almost 5,000 Canadians usually descend upon the beaches that stretch to the east and west of the Port of Progreso. It is with sadness to report that, as this book went to press, several gangs of thieves had been targeting Canadian residences, breaking into homes and stealing goods. No one has been hurt in the burglaries.

This mini crime wave targeting Canadians prompted Jean Senecal, the First Secretary of the Canadian Embassy in Mexico City and Canada's Consular Agent in Cancún Alie Bourgeois-Charbonneau, to meet with Canadians in Progreso and with Mexican officials during 2010-2011 winter season. The almost 300 Canadians who met with officials requested that a Consular Agent in residence be appointed for the Port of Progreso. The Canadian diplomats also explained the need for Canadian citizens to be more informed about Mexican law, since Canadians were reluctant to assist law enforcement.

Members of one gang of thieves were successfully arrested in January 2011, after dedicated police investigations. For their part, María Alonzo Morales, the Mayor of the Port of Progreso, and Carlos Cantón Magaña, director of the State Judicial Police, indicated that authorities had increased police patrols, and set up neighborhood watch committees.

The Canadian expat community has also been shaken by high profile arrests of Canadian fugitives hiding their midst. The most brazen Canadian extradited back to Canada was Ben Fitznar, who set himself up as a real estate consultant and was living lavishly, was a convicted drug smuggler sentenced to five years prison in Vancouver.

Canadian diplomats made the commitment of providing informational guides to help Canadians understand how to cooperate with Mexican law enforcement, and Mexican officials vowed to continue increased police patrols along the beach resorts. Both Canadian and Mexican officials reminded the public that it's important to be mindful to lock up valuables. Canadian diplomats promised to study the feasibility of establishing a Consular Agency in Yucatan State.

provide daily service to Cancún and Cozumel; it was a major setback when Delta Airlines suspended its flights to Atlanta a couple of years ago.

Whether one considers it good or bad, the result is that Mérida lives in a splendid isolation, a metropolis of tranquility, filled with museums, galleries, exuberant cultural calendars where opera, symphony and concerts take place almost year-round. In 2000, Mérida was designated "American Capital of Culture," which has fostered international conferences and meetings ever since, highlighting the city's unique cultural heritage and vibrancy. That Mérida is a pedestrian-friendly city is an added attraction. Not unlike most colonial cities in Mexico, Mérida affords residents a city where it's possible to enjoy early morning brisk walks, and leisurely strolls in the late afternoons and early evenings. (In no time, new residents learn that it's best to know where you want to be between 11 AM and 4 PM to avoid being caught under the unforgiving sun!) It is a city of Old World charm, yet every park has free Wi-Fi, and youngsters sit on the benches with their elders. Their elders enjoy the afternoons, reminiscing about the good old days, while in the company of their grandchildren – who are busy on Facebook, and Twitter, and whatever youthful folly they are intent on pursuing right then and there.

A tranquil, safe and pleasant metropolis, Mérida feels like a small town, while offering the amenities of a major metropolitan center. Montejo's little colony of 70 or so families has been a successful experiment, one that has flourished across the centuries!

This is Mérida, where you can discover the truth that so often eludes us in our world today: *Life is good.*

1 The Beauty of Living in the Yucatán

Mérida is a splendid city, almost paradise in many ways. But is it right for you?

An even more important question: Are you ready to become an expatriate? Do you have the fortitude to live in a country that is fundamentally different from the United States or Canada? Are you prepared to be a "minority" – a native English-speaker in a Spanish-speaking country?

The truth of the matter is that Americans who move to Mérida (or anywhere in Mexico for that matter) freely choose to become instantly a minority! That seldom occurs to them, and it is a fact of life that affects you in ways that you can only appreciate once you do, in fact, become part of Mexico's English-speaking minority.

It could be liberating – how wonderful to be in a place where there are virtually no expectations of you, other than to abide by the law and to be a good neighbor. No one expects you to form an opinion about what city officials are doing or not doing. No

The Curious Stigma of Being an Expatriate

In Paris, when friends get together and one mentions that he or she is moving overseas to become a "francais de l'etranger," or a "Frenchman in a foreign land," the first reaction is this: *"What are you running away from?"*

To be a stranger in a strange land may sound romantic and adventurous, but it is also fraught with implications. The French are always suspicious of their fellow countrymen they encounter overseas. There is a saying in Paris that the person most likely to swindle you is a fellow Frenchman overseas. Parisians warn each other, with horror stories, about their experiences, or those of acquaintances, when dealing with other Frenchmen living in foreign countries. In France, the stereotype of a French expatriate is of a middle-aged man, who was never too successful in France, who decides to leave France in order to start fresh, in a place where he can reinvent himself.

Often he is also looking for "a less assertive" woman, easily deceived, younger and less experienced in life, with whom to have children. He is also on the prowl for susceptible locals willing to believe in the integrity of a European, or other Frenchmen innocently believing the naive notion that a fellow Frenchman would have his best interests at heart in a foreign land.

Then the story ends in disappointment: the local who was swindled, the fellow Frenchman who was betrayed. The French, in other words, are advised to stay clear of any financial dealings with fellow Frenchmen in foreign lands.

What of Americans in foreign lands? What of Canadians in foreign lands? What are the assumptions that others will make of you?

Will they see you as friend or foe?

one cares to hear what you think about the Governor's position on this or that. No one expects you to volunteer to help the local school with that or the other. No one, really, cares what you think or what you do or what your opinion is about anything.

In many ways, you are invisible, and that affords a certain amount of privacy and the freedom to live life without civic obligations, or responsibilities, or social expectations. It is for many Americans just what they want: the luxury of being left alone so they can pursue their happiness as they see best! This is undoubtedly one of the great pleasures that Mérida affords you as an expatriate that has grown ever so elusive in the United States: *the pursuit of happiness*.

In fact, city officials are so determined to safeguard Mérida's international reputation as a city that is safe and family-friendly that city government is relentless in addressing quality of life issues, regardless of which political party is in charge of City Hall, called the Ayuntamiento. It is as if the "Department of Ambiance" worked round-the-clock to make things even more family-friendly and to enrich the amenities afforded citizens, whether it is closing major thoroughfares on Sundays so families can ride bicycles together, or subsidizing the symphony so anyone can enjoy a world-class concert for the equivalent of a few dollars.

This concern for "quality of life" issues extends to Mérida's disparate expatriate communities, with major overtures being made to the resident Cubans, Lebanese and now Americans residing in the city. It has to be said, however, that the Cubans and the Lebanese have been very successful at integrating themselves into the mainstream life of the Yucatán – a Cuban couple's Yucatecan-born son started the city's largest newspaper mid-twentieth century, the offspring of Lebanese immigrants have successfully entered political office, as is the case with

Should American expatriates have a representative in the U.S. Congress?

The French have a representative in their Parliament, an official elected by the French residing overseas who represents their interests.

In fact, the French have an assembly for French expatriates, the Assemblée des Français de l'Etranger.

The AFE or the "Assembly for French Expatriates" represents the French citizens living abroad. Its members, elected representatives for six years, allow the French expatriates to participate in the national life of their country. They are entrusted with the task of helping and defending the rights of the French citizens regarding social protection, grants, employment and vocational training when dealing with public services.

See: *www.assemblee-afe.fr*

Mérida's former mayor who was of Lebanese descent. The Americans, for whatever reason, have failed to be as successful. Apart from businessman Thomas Kelleher, archaeologist James Callaghan and the family of E. Wyllis Andrews, Americans have not been seamlessly integrated into the social, economic or political life of the Yucatán, and for now remain sidelined on the public stage of civic life.

There are profound reasons for that, which are described when the history of the Colonias is discussed in the next chapter (see the history of the Centenario District). For now, suffice it to say there is beauty in this isolation. It affords a certain degree of anonymity, and it allows you to build a parallel community, one that is not consumed by the demands of the "real world."

Living in Mérida can be as wonderful as it gets: Life is good in a world where many bad things happen.

The Beauty of Living in Mérida: The Best Place to Retire in North America

But we are social creatures, of course, and there is comfort in knowing that Mérida's English-speaking community has reached a tipping point. It can sustain its own social clubs and organizations. It can embark on greater integration, if its members would like to do so. It can collaborate with Yucatecan and Mexicans to work on common causes.

Every year, *International Living* magazine surveys 194 countries around the world, and guess what? Mérida is the best city for Americans to retire to in the whole of North America! And in the entire hemisphere, only Cuenca in Ecuador ranks higher! This is how Glynna Prentice, the Mexico Editor at *International Living* describes Mérida:

> **"Mérida, capital of the Yucatán Peninsula, is a happy combination of old and new: a gracious, historic colonial city with modern conveniences like shopping malls, an international airport, and excellent hospitals. You can enjoy a relaxed life here, with friendly locals, music in the streets almost every night, and several thousand expats to make adjusting easy."** [1]

This is how the editors at "Money Central" on MSNBC.com, in an article titled, "The World's Best Places to Retire," ranked Mérida:

No. 1: Postcard from Cuenca, Ecuador
No. 2: The 4 C's of Mérida, Mexico
No. 3: On the beach in Coronado, Panama

---

[1] See, internationalliving.com/2008/08/08-31-08-Merida/

No. 4: The crowds flock to Punta del Este, Uruguay
No. 5: Secret passages, $15,500 homes in Calitri, Italy

And what does "The 4 C's of Mérida" say about Mérida? Here is Dan Prescher:

> **You may remember my Four C's rating system: Comfort, Convenience, Cost, and Culture. These are the four things I consider when I think about living somewhere. They are completely subjective, and they don't have anything to do with profit potential or return on investment. ... Since I live in Mérida, Mexico, I thought this might be a good time to demonstrate my Four Cs treatment. A rating of 1 in a category is the worst, and a rating of 5 is the best ... so there are 20 possible points. The closer to 20 a place scores, the better it rates with me."**

He then goes on to give Mérida a ranking of 17 out of a possible 20. Mérida gets a perfect score for Convenience and Culture![2]

How *International Living* puts its numbers together:

To rate and rank the 194 countries considered in this year's **Quality of Life Index**, the Editors of *International Living* take into account:

Cost of Living (15% of the final ranking)
Culture and Leisure (10%).
Economy (15%)
Environment (10%)
Freedom (10%)

Health (10%)
Infrastructure (10%)
Safety and Risk (10%)
Climate (10%)

Source: InternationalLiving.com

Almost 25,000 foreign expatriates must agree with Dan Prescher, since they make their home, year-round, in Mérida. That explains the Cubans speaking their rapid-fire Cuban Spanish, and the Arabic-language magazines (published in Mexico City!) with the social goings on of the wealthy Lebanese of Mexico that one finds at the authentic Lebanese restaurants around town.

---

[2] To read Dan Prescher's article, see: *internationalliving.com/2008/08/08-31-08-Merida*

(Did you know more Yucatecans speak Arabic at home than speak English?) It also explains the breathtaking diversity of Mérida's cultural scene, where art exhibitions, festivals and cultural events reflect the interests of the diverse communities. (Did you miss last year's Catalan-language film festival? Or the Korean high tea ceremony? Don't miss the Cuban celebration of Santería next time around!)

You get the idea.

For Americans, there are tremendous opportunities, and city government remains sensitive to certain issues. Officials, for instance, have gone out of their way to discourage a backlash against Americans in Mérida that has arisen not only as a consequence of the situation in Arizona where recent legislation there is perceived as being "anti-Mexican," but also at a number of scams that American expatriates in town have carried out in recent years. This is a far cry from the United States where Mexicans are vilified and, according to FBI statistics, are five times more likely to be the victims of hate crimes as non-Hispanics. Mérida offers civility, and respects the right of all its residents to live their lives in peace.

Quality of Life

The City of Mérida maintains a hotline that anyone can call to report a quality of life issue.

What quality of life issue? Street lights that are burned out, pot holes on city streets, a pile of garbage someone left on the side of the road, excessive noise, a dead animal, fallen tree limbs on sidewalks, and so forth.

The office is **AYUNTATEL** and the number is (999) **924-6962.**

Throughout this book we will discuss wonderful resources available to English-speakers who settle down in Mérida. Two wonderful resources which will whet your appetite, are the centers for English language studies. Mérida is fortunate to have two organizations dedicated to promoting the English language, through courses, library resources and continuing education programs.

The premier resource is the Instituto Benjamin Franklin, which has been in operation for more than four decades, and which dedicates itself to teaching English to Yucatecan and Mexican students, and Spanish to foreigners living here. It also offers courses to young Mexican citizens who need to pass their TOEFL, GRE, GMAT and SAT courses to pursue graduate work overseas. There is no better way to become familiar with the community of English-speaking Yucatecans and Mexicans in town. The other is the Mérida English Language Library, known as MELL, which is an informal social club with a lending library catering primarily to retired expatriates from the U.S. and Canada.

Which is right for you?

Instituto Benjamin Franklin de Yucatán

The Instituto Benjamin Franklin de Yucatán has been operating as a Mexican-North American Binational Center for Cultural Relations for the past 40 years. The center is a non-profit organization promotes cultural and educational exchanges between Yucatán and the rest of the world. Their Spanish-as-a-second language program teaches students from all over the world.

Located in a colonial building in the historic center of Mérida, the Institute's facilities include classrooms with a capacity of 20 students, a library, a video viewing room and snack bar. Staff members are willing to adapt programs to the specific needs of their students.

The Institute offers intensive Spanish courses from as little as a week to as long as a year. Courses begin every Monday the entire year, regardless of the course length. Intensive courses are available for students who have little or no knowledge of Spanish. Intermediate and advanced students may enroll in six or eight-week Spanish classes. Courses feature grammar and conversation classes as well as guided tours to places of historic and cultural interest in the city. Students will be given placement exams upon arrival to determine their appropriate level.

The Institute also offers a number of Mexican history courses, from Pre-Hispanic times to present-day. Students may also enroll in a Mexican culture class with an emphasis on the Maya, Mexican literature classes, and a class on the socioeconomic situation of Mexico.

The Conversation Classes offered are designed jointly by the teacher and students. In lieu of textbooks, students are giving handouts on various topics and current issues they will receive a certificate of program completion. Academic credits can be arranged at student's request.

For Yucatecan and Mexican students, the Institute provides courses for TOEFL (English as a second language), GRE, GMAT and SAT exams. The Institute is certified to administer tests from the College Board (*www.collegeboard.com*). There is an ample library available, and the Instituto Benjamin Franklin is located right downtown.

For more information:

Guillermo Vales Duarte

Director General
Instituto Benjamin Franklin
Calle 57 #474-A, between Calle 52 and 54 Street
Centro
Telephones: (999) 928-0097 and (999) 928-6005
Fax: (999) 928-0097
Website: *www.benjaminfranklin.com.mx*
Email: *franklin@benjaminfranklin.com.mx*

The Mérida English Language Library (MELL)

By Vince Gricus

Some silly resources on the Internet make such flippant declarations as, "When visitors ask us where they can find the heart of the expat community in Mérida, we tell them it's the Mérida English Language Library, of course!"

Well, let's see. There are about 3,500 fulltime Americans, Canadians and other English-speaking residents in Mérida, and only about 600 are members of the Library. That means that, yes, MELL serves about 20 percent of the English-speaking expat community, and of course there are an almost 20,000 expats from non-English-speaking countries who are not served by the Library. (There are almost 6,500 Cubans residing in Mérida, for instance; there are just over 5,000 people from Lebanon, who speak Arabic, and there are 1,500 Spanish-speaking people from Central and South American nations.)

Notice:

On its website MELL claims to be a member of the prestigious American Library Association (ALA), but its membership lapsed in 2007. As this goes to press, it has not renewed its membership. MELL also claims that it is a "Mexican nonprofit institution" and solicits donations on this assertion. MELL, however, has not met the requirements established by Mexico's tax authorities to solicit donations from the public and issue tax-deductible receipts in accordance with Mexican tax laws.

Regardless of statistics, the Library has the potential of being an important resource – but not for everyone. The reason stems from the nature of "expat" communities. In the United States, most libraries are places filled school children, busy doing their homework and studying, with the excitement that comes from learning the wonders of the world – from the mysteries of outer space, to how photosynthesis makes plants grow. They are places filled with hope for the future and the potential of youth. MELL, by comparison, is a place for older people, at times resembling a senior center for lonely Americans – that just happens to have stacks of books.

So here is a "Tale of the Two Expatriates" to show you how everyone's different. A couple from New York, whom I'll call "Mr. and Mrs. R" arrived as guests in Mérida. They loved Mérida instantly, and wanted to buy a house at once. I cautioned them, as I always do, with a straightforward: "First impressions can be misleading. Why don't you spend time here before you decide if this is the place for you to purchase a home?" And I gave them advice on "learning about the community." They decided to take my advice. Every evening they came back, more in love with city. But when they started to drop by MELL, there was a twist to their enthusiasm. They found the place a bit odd, and the people there vacuous. But they loved Mérida. They decided they would buy a home here, with one condition: it could not be *within* walking distance from MELL. They didn't want to be pressured to go there, or have a reason to have anyone within walking distance of MELL to come over to *their* place. They ended up buying a beautiful home a few blocks east of the railroad station, off Mejorada Park.

Then there was the experience of "Mrs. C," a widow from Chicago, who also fell in love with Mérida, and who also took my advice about exploring the city. She instantly was delighted by the company of the regulars she found at MELL. She knew she would only be living in Mérida half the year, and the idea of being within walking distance of MELL was what sealed the deal. She ended up buying a lovely home an easy 15 minute stroll from MELL, and she couldn't be happier.

The moral of the story is obvious: While MELL is not the "heart" of the expat community – by virtue of the fact that most expats in Mérida don't speak English! – it does serve an important segment of the English-speaking expat community.

Is MELL right for you? The only way you'll find out is to drop by, and see for yourself:

Address:
  Mérida English Language Library
  Calle 53 #524, between Calle 66 and 68 Street
  Centro
  Telephone: (999) 924-8401
  Website: www.MeridaEnglishLibrary.com

Hours of Operation
  Monday through Friday – 9:00 am to 1:00 pm
  Monday Evenings – 6:30 to 9:00 pm
  Thursday Evenings – 4:00 pm to 7:00 pm

Saturday – 10 am to 1 pm
Closed Sunday

Membership Dues:
Individual: $250 pesos a year
Family: $350 pesos a year
Student (Mexican student): $100 pesos a year

2 The Colonias, or Neighborhoods, of Mérida

By Louis Nevaer

Now that you have given the matter serious thought and have decided to become an expatriate, or are contemplating becoming one, it's time to understand the "lay of the land," so to speak. What are Mérida's neighborhoods like?

Mérida is a city comprised of neighborhoods, called Colonias, which fan out, encircling the Main Square, or Zócalo. On official maps the Main Square is still the "center" of the city, although so much development has taken place north and northeast that, relatively, the Zócalo is no longer in the middle of the city – it's slightly to the south and west. If you ignore residential neighborhoods built, say, after the 1960s, then, yes, the Zócalo would be the bull's eye of the city. It certainly is the heart of the Colonial district, known as the Historic Center, or Centro Histórico.

One reason Mérida has been able to grow into the metropolis that it is, with about one million residents and Los Angeles-style sprawl, is geography. Unlike other colonial cities, such as Oaxaca, Guanajuato, San Miguel, Cuernavaca, and so forth, which were built in plateaus ringed by mountains and ranges, the Yucatán peninsula, a vast limestone land mass, is flat as a pancake. The Yucatán, in fact, is the "sister" peninsula of Florida – another flat-as-a-pancake land mass.

Another reason Mérida is able to sustain growth is its ample water supply. What water supply you ask? If you look at globe, you will see that all the great cities in the world reside near water – by the sea, adjacent to rivers, on lakeshores. People simply need water, and waterways offer means of transportation: One can travel from London to Venice by vessels; one can journey from New York to Buenos Aires by sea. Mexico City once existed as a series of islands in a vast lake, now almost long gone. And Mérida sits atop what is believed to be one of the world's most extensive underground freshwater river systems. All those cenotes, or sink holes, and all those pozos, or wells, offer an almost unlimited supply of freshwater – and all easily accessible throughout the region.

This continues to fuel ever-growing and ever-ambitious developments. New neighborhoods are announced, groundbreaking ceremonies take place, and the city continues its expansion. And this is the way it has always been. How many times have people mentioned how lovely Colonia Itzimná is, with its charming church around the square surrounding by impressive mansions? Well, that was a town, far removed from Mérida, a couple hundred years ago. But somehow, the distance grew shorter as the vacant land between "Mérida" and "Itzimná" was developed, and today Itzimná resides properly within Mérida's city limits, a once-small town happily incorporated as one of the city's neighborhoods.

Colonel Who?

Did you hear about the Londoner who visited Mérida, fell in love with the place, but shared with a compatriot her reservations about moving here?

"I'm afraid I'm torn," she said. "This is such a lovely place, but I can't see myself living in a place that's so militaristic!"

"Militaristic," a fellow Briton replied.

"Why, yes, all the neighborhoods are named after colonels!"

She had presumed that "Col. García Ginerés" was named after Colonel García Ginerés, "Col. Itzimná" was named after Colonel Itzimná, and that "Col. Santa Ana" was named after Colonel Santa Ana, and so forth.

In Mérida, "Col." stands for "Colonia," or neighborhood, not "colonel," as in a military rank!

With this in mind, consider that as the city "proper" grew, so did the neighborhoods, the first being Santiago, built in the 17th century and named after St. James – Santiago is Spanish for James, by the way – and it was designed to be self-sufficient. It had a Church, a public park, a market and grand buildings for important residents of the neighborhood. Santa Ana, to the north of the Zócalo was first a 16th century plantation and then established in the 18th century as a "colonia," and it was subsequently incorporated into the city proper by official decree.

Unlike other cities which have razed their colonial centers to reinvent themselves in subsequent centuries, the almost limitless supply of vacant land has afforded Mérida the ability to grow without having to tear down what is already there. One result is the absence of high rise buildings, and the other is spread of urban sprawl. Anther result is more charming: Mérida boasts the second-largest declared Historic Center in Mexico. Only Mexico City has more colonial buildings! And when you consider that Mexico City is more than twenty times as large as Mérida, that says something.

Most expatriates still prefer to find something within the "Centro Histórico," although that definition keeps expanding as Mérida is marketed by realtors. If you want to be technical about it, the "colonial" era ended in 1810, when Mexico declared it independence from Spain, meaning that anything built after 1810 is not "colonial." It can be colonial in design, or ambiance, or style. But it is not a colonial building! (The same is true in the United States – after 1776, America's "colonial" era ended!) So anything built during the Victorian or Edwardian times (most of the grand homes along Calle 59, for example, were built to celebrate Mexico's Centennial celebration of its independence, which was commemorated in 1910!) is definitely not a colonial anything. And neighborhoods that, a generation ago no one would have considered "colonial" – such as Paseo de Montejo or Colonia García Ginerés, both of which were considered the height of modernity when they were build in the late 19th and 20th centuries – are now marketed as part of the "Historic Center" filled with grand "colonial" homes.

In broad terms, however, when realtors discuss Mérida, and they speak of the "Historic Center," what they refer to is the series of neighborhoods that immediately radiate from the Main Square, and which are graced with homes that are either from the Colonial period, or were built during the Victorian and Edwardian times. They also refer to areas that are so unlike contemporary suburban living in the United States and Canada that they have an undeniable appeal to American and Canadian buyers, since it excites their imagination about what living in "Mexico" should be, and the kinds of homes in which they envision living.

To understand how these neighborhoods came into existence, it's important to know a few things. Almost every Colonia, or Barrio, within the Historic Center is built around a church. It is each church that is the anchor of the neighborhood, built in the center. There is often a small market adjacent to the church where vendors sell fresh produce and products brought in from neighboring towns and villages. There is often a public gathering place, or playground, across the way. School or government buildings flank the streets around the church. The name of the church is almost always the name of the neighborhood. Santiago is the name of the church in Barrio Santiago, Santa Ana is the name of the church in the Colonia Santa Ana, and so it goes. There are no defined boundaries for the "colonias" in city-center, since they were not designed as formal developments past a dozen or so blocks that radiate from the anchoring church.

The Main Square, or Plaza Grande, or Zócalo

When the Spanish arrived, they decided that the abandoned Maya city of T'ho would be an ideal location for their settlement. It was named "Mérida" because the Maya ruins reminded the Spaniards of the Roman ruins that abound in Mérida, Spain. And in the same way that Europeans had long used Roman ruins as ready-cut building blocks for their own buildings – think how much of the abandoned Coliseum in Rome ended up being used to build palazzos and churches in Rome! The Spaniards set out to use the Maya ruins for their own construction.

The Cathedral of San Idelfonso, for instance, still has Maya carvings on some of the stones visible on its massive walls. The Cathedral, along with the Macay museum of contemporary art, flank the Zócalo on the eastern side. The Governor's Palace is on the northern side, and moving counter-clockwise, the Olimpio Cultural Center and City Hall, or Ayuntamiento, flank the Zócalo on the western side. Moving along, the Casa de Montejo, where the Conquistador Francisco de Montejo lived, is on the south side. The descendants of the Montejo family still lived there through the mid-1980s, until Banamex, today a subsidiary of Citibank, acquired the massive structure for its regional offices. There are numerous business that also ring the Zócalo, from bookstores to video game parlors, pharmacies to coffee shops.

The main square itself is a massive public gathering area. On any given day one finds protestors mounting a sit-in in front of the Governor's Palace, and shoe-shiners buffing clients' boots. Vendors sell elotes – state fair-style corn on the cobs – and balloon vendors add color to the plaza. Children run around after the pigeons, and tourists sit reading up on Mérida from their guidebooks under the shades of the imposing laurels that dominate the park. At night, the Zócalo, unfortunately, takes on an unsavory atmosphere, a place where, not unlike the Ramblas in Barcelona, mostly foreign men scout for sex workers.

Although the Zócalo is a grand, open plaza today, it bears in mind that for much of its life, it was a gated park, and only Europeans – whites – were allowed to enter. It is also interesting to see how much misinformation there is about the Coat of Arms sculptures that flank the entrance to the Casa de Montejo. Depicted, in carved stones, are two conquistadors, fully attired in their battle outfits, standing on the heads of two Maya individuals. In the sixteenth century, the most effective way of communicating that the Spanish were in charge was to use imagery that was familiar to the defeated Maya.

To our sensibilities this comes across as racist, but in the context of it time, it was, in fact, a culturally-sensitive way of conveying vital information to the civic body. In the monumental architecture and bas-reliefs of the Maya, the conquering rulers where always depicted as standing on the heads of the vanquished. Imagine Churchill depicted in a statue as standing on the head of Hitler, or Bush standing on the head of Gore. That's how the Maya made political points. One of the most riveting examples comes from the reconstructed stelae in Copan, where the Maya rulers are depicted as crushing the heads of the defeated rivals. However unfortunate it may seem to us today, those sculptures on the facades convey the message that, henceforth, the guys in the pointy metal headgear are the ones calling the shots.

The last point to consider is that there are few private residences near the Zócalo today. One of the last remaining homes – a home so grand and massive that it has a working elevator! – is owned by the Rosel family. If you walk half a block south on Calle 62, between 61 and 63 Streets, there is a small shop with the simple sign "Joyeria Rosel." To the side is a small passageway, discreet and unassuming. But if you cross to the other side of the street, and look up, you will see how massive the building is in fact. That entire structure is a private residence, with salon after salon, wide terraces and an open air central plaza. The house has not been restored, or updated since electricity was introduced back in the 1910s! And it boasts a series of tunnels, a few of which are believed to be connected to neighboring buildings, and then through passageways to the Cathedral.

Santiago

Barrio de Santiago, one of the most desirable and established Colonias in Mérida, lies five city blocks to the west of the Zócalo. The Church of St. James the Apostle was built in 1637, although it was subsequently damaged during various uprisings. The church that we see today is the one rebuilt in the mid-19th century. It was originally established as a neighborhood where mestizos, people of mixed European and Maya heritage, and the Maya who had business in the city, could live. Mérida, being the "White City," only allowed people who were either European (mostly Spaniards) or their New World-born children (criollos) to spend the night in Mérida proper.

In consequence, Santiago became one of the fastest-growing districts during the 17th century, with artisans, vendors, household help, construction workers and working-class people resided. Many foreigners who had business dealings with Mérida, but who were not able to afford to live in Mérida proper, opted to live in Santiago. One of the more famous families, the Salazars from Portugal, still have descendants in the neighborhood who own small businesses there. And it became a favored shopping area for residents of nearby Colonias of Ermita and San Sebastian, who may not have felt welcome in Mérida proper. Along with Portuguese, the other dominant foreign community was the Germans who arrived in the 19th century, mostly because they supplied machinery to the haciendas, and they introduced pharmaceuticals to the peninsula. The Farmacias Canto chain of pharmacies began when representatives of German manufacturers arrived to expand their sales in Mexico. Around the same time, this was the area where the first Koreans arriving in Mérida lived, before they moved to Colonia Chuminopolis. There is a monument in the northwest corner of the park (across from the Monte de Piedad pawn shop) that commemorates "Chemulpo Street," formerly known as "Calle Incheon," the first community district for Koreans in the Yucatán. Other immigrants last century also have left their mark, and maintained their presence. In the early part of the 20th century, Cuban émigrés settled here, a trend that was accelerated after the Cuban Revolution of 1959. In recent decades, American and Canadian expats have discovered Santiago and it is one of the preferred Colonias in the Historic Center.

With such a curious past, it's no wonder that some of the more noteworthy residents were born, or lived in, Santiago, including Manuel Cepada, one of the more famous governors, who was in office in the 1860s, and who first allowed passage to Americans (and American slaves) fleeing the wreckage of the American Civil War. Other luminaries range the spectrum of life, from composer Guadalupe Trigo to chess Grand Master Carlos Torre Repetto, from Bishop Crescencio Carrillo Ancona to educator Rodolfo Menéndez de la Peña.

A century ago, Calle 59, which runs through Santiago from the Centenario to downtown, was the most fashionable place to live. Many of the grand homes along this boulevard were built between the 1890s and 1910, just in time for Mexico's Centennial. Many of the homes, which were built in the Victorian and Edwardian styles fashionable during the era of Porfirio Díaz, are in the process of being restored. Today Santiago boasts an active little community, with a lively market, filled with cocinas económicas, fresh produce, a section for meats and chicken, and various sellers of everything from tortillas to spices.

There is a small park in front, with a playground for children, and an era that is used for public dances on Tuesday (and skateboarding at all other times!). One legacy of the German presence is the various number of small hardware shops. The Flor de Santiago, one of the oldest cafés in town which itself is an institution, was in fact founded by Cubans, and it is named for Santiago de Cuba! (Yes, there are dozens of Cubans and Cuban-Yucatecan families still in Santiago, and the probably out-number the American residents in the Colonia!)

Across the church, originally opening in 1914 as "La Frontera," was the first "moving pictures establishment" located on the western side of the plaza, and it was adjacent to a hotel, now long-gone. A year later, another movie house, "El Salón," opened on the north side of the plaza. It evolved into the "Apolo," an establishment that specialized in Spanish zarzuela musical theater, and Portuguese operettas. During the Roaring Twenties, it was rechristened as "Cinema Rivoli," and has continued to be a movie house ever since. There are also three large schools in Santiago: Nicolas Bravo, Colegio América and Primaria Vincente Guerrero.

Cultural Activities of Interest

Bailes Musicales, Big Band orchestra music at Santiago Park, on Calle 72 between Calle 57 and 59 Street, every Tuesday at 8:30 PM. It's a very family-oriented event, and it's wonderful to see older couples dancing cheek-to-cheek to the great sounds of the big band era!

La 68, Casa de Cultura Elena Poniatowska, Calle 68 #470-A, between Calle 55 and 57 Street, continues the tradition of Santiago being the cinematic center of the city by showcasing foreign films, documentaries and art house movies. There is a small shop, and they offer a simple supper menu (salads, gourmet pizzas, alcoholic beverages), which is a lovely way to socialize. It's also great to be able to watch a film, open air, while enjoying a drink!

Website: *www.la68.com*

Casa Catherwood, Calle 59 #572, between Calle 72 and 74 Street, exhibits a collection of Catherwood's lithographs of the Maya ruins from 1844, and which were originally published in the legendary book *Incidents of Travel*, by John Lloyd Stephens. There is a small shop with showcases crafts from women's cooperatives around the world, from Kenya to Thailand, Madagascar to Haiti. There is also a small café in the courtyard.

Website: *www.casa-catherwood.com*

Santa Ana

Here's some perspective: Santa Ana is older than Jamestown!

The charming church facing Calle 60 at 45 Street dates back to the 16th century, and was subsequently rebuilt in the 1776 after it was destroyed in an uprising. (Is there a theme going on with anti-clericalism in the Yucatán? No comment!) Excluded from Mérida proper, the residents of Santa Ana were Maya, and blacks, mulattos (people of European and black parentage), and *chinas cambujas* (people of black and Maya parentage).

The area that today comprises Santa Ana was farmland. It extended from Santa Ana to the north and east. These plantations supplied Mérida with most of its produce. Santa Ana park itself (and where the church is built on the north end) is an elevated platform. The reason for this is simple: It's believed to be an ancient Maya platform that once supported an important ceremonial center, probably in the 13th and 14th centuries. It was a sizeable community at the end of the Colonial period, and its believed that just over 10% of the Mérida's population lived in the Santa Ana area.

Today, as is the case with Santiago, Santa Ana is a thriving neighborhood, with a small market filled with fresh produce shops, and others selling condiments. There is a lively set of *cocinas económicas*, and a great deal of businesses. Because Calle 60 is such a busy thoroughfare, and cars headed west on 47 Street are often on their way to Paseo de Montejo, there is less pedestrian activity compared to Santiago. In fact, negotiating the streets can be a bit arduous, and so is parking. Santa Ana's proximity to the wealth of architectural structures along Paseo de Montejo further undermines it as a destination in and of itself, which is unfortunate.

Suffice it to say that on the southeast corner of Santa Ana, adjacent to the market and the tourist-shops is a Pemex gas station, which has detracted from the park's appeal. This is a pity, since most people drive by quickly, or simply don't notice, the Centro Cultural Andrés Quintana Roo, or the Andres Quintana Roo Cultural Center, right on Calle 60, across from the church, which boasts extensive galleries and some rather fine art exhibitions throughout the year.

Good or Bad? You Decide!

Santiago and **Santa Ana** comprise the heart of the American expatriate community within the Historic Center.

English speakers call it "Gringo Gulch," and Spanish speakers informally call it "Gringolandia." This is both good and bad.

It is good because it gives a geographic identity to the growing American and Canadian expatriate community.

But it is bad because, as discussed in the chapter on Real Estate, since 2005 Americans have been their own worst enemies, distorting the housing market and creating a bubble the likes of which Mérida has never seen before.

Also, the Mérida English Language Library, which straddles the "border" between Santiago and Santa Ana, lies dead center between these two Colonias drawing still more Americans to the area.

This is either good or bad, depending on your perspective of things!

Santa Ana, which is roughly defined as the area encompassing Calle 60 to the east, Calle 66 to the west, Calle 45 to the north and Calle 55 to the south, retains a slightly bohemian, artistic sensibility. Many of the expatriates who have moved to the area are artistically inclined – painters, photographers, musicians and writers. The city's impressive Museo de Arqueología is a little more than block from Santa Ana church, draws tens of thousands of visitors to the area, and there are always interesting cafés and small galleries popping up along Calle 60 and the adjacent streets. The Casa de los Artistas, owned by the husband-and-wife couple, Abel Vázquez and Melba Medina are accomplished émigrés from central Mexico who have made a wonderful contribution to the artistic community.

Cultural Activities of Interest

Noche Mexicana, or "Mexican Night," this is a free concert of Mexican music, featuring mariachi sounds and ballads from central and northern Mexico, reminiscent of American cowboy and Western music. It is accompanied by street vendors, in a festive atmosphere, at the foot of Paseo de Montejo, between Calle 47 and 49 Street, every Friday at 7 PM.

100% Mexico, a store located in the lobby of the Hotel Casa San Angel, Montejo #1, by Calle 49 in the Remate. This store operates as a franchise of Fonart, Mexico's federal agency that promotes artisanal excellence throughout the entire country. This shop has museum-quality pieces from every state in Mexico. It is quite simply one of the city's most important treasures!

Website: *www.hotelcasasanangel.com*

Galeria Tataya, Calle 60 #460, between Calle 45 and 47 Street, has one of the city's best collections of contemporary Mexican paintings, selected handicrafts from renowned artisans and an extension offering of contemporary works from Cuba.

Website: *www.tataya.com.mx*

Casa de los Artistas, Calle 60 #405, between Calle 43 and 45 Street, is the home, studio and classroom of Abel Vázquez and Melba Medina. They offer art classes, and have an extensive collection of their work for sale.

Website: *www.artistsinmexico.com*

Following are the other Colonias that comprise the Historic Center.

Santa Lucia

Santa Lucia boasts a special history, one that is invisible to the casual passerby: it is the neighborhood that was populated primarily by Mérida's black community. The Church of Santa Lucia was built as a place of worship for the city's black residents, who were forbidden to set foot in Mérida proper at first, and then, along with the Maya, to spend the night in the city. The courtyard of the church, today covered in cobblestones, was the city's only cemetery for the black community.

Its close proximity to the Main Square, and its rather small geographic area, however, are the two reasons why there are few residences in the Santa Lucia area available. To the west of Calle 60 one finds business and government offices, from Internet cafés to the city's public library, from small hotels and parking lots to the broadcasting offices of radio stations. To the east, similarly, the first two blocks are full of businesses, offices, small hotels, and only then are there a few blocks of residential houses, and most of these are occupied by local families who have lived there for decades, if not generations.

A further impediment to the area, of course, is that the buildings surrounding Santa Lucia Park itself are closed. City officials have struggled for various decades to come up with a redevelopment plan, but for a variety of reasons there has not been much progress. That the Great Recession of 2008 hit many of the smaller business that lined Calle 60 from 47 to 53 Streets has only added to the sense of abandonment one feels along this stretch of Calle 60. Many storefronts are shuttered, and it seems that people briskly walk from past Santa Lucia, which only is active on Sundays, when vendors set up their stalls for "Mérida en Domingo" and Calle 60 is closed off as a pedestrian and bicycle thoroughfare.

Cultural Activities of Interest

Yucatán Serenade is an evening of traditional Yucatecan song and dance, featuring the "Jarana" dance and Trova music, with young Maya ladies dressed in elaborate dresses and Maya gentlemen in traditional costumes. The free concert takes place every Thursday, on the corner of 60 and 55 Streets, 9 PM.

Ki' Xocolatl, Calle 55 #513, between Calle 60 and 62 Street, is the city's premier chocolate shop. Owned by the Master Chocolatier, Mathieu Brees, these award-winning chocolates have found a tremendous following around the world. The chocolates, which are the only bean-to-bar chocolates made from cacao beans grown in the Yucatán, are the most popular Mexican chocolates sold at the Smithsonian in Washington, D.C. and on Amazon.com. That says it all.

Website: *www.ki-xocolatl.com*

Mejorada

To the slight northeast of the Zócalo, running along Calle 59, one enters Colonia Mejorada, anchored by the church located at the intersection of Calle 59 and 50 Street. This church was constructed in 1562, just two decades after the city itself was founded. Why so massive a church so soon after the city's founding?

For two reasons: First, the Cathedral itself would take decades to build. Second, and more importantly, the Spanish had a mandate to Christianize the Maya, and this meant having facilities from which to organize the program of establishing a network of "missions" in every Maya community. At that time, a massive wall was being built around Mérida proper to protect the Spaniards from constant attacks from the Maya. The same year in which construction of the Mejorada church began is also the year when Mérida's first hospital was built across the plaza. The ambivalent nature of Spaniard-Maya relations explains the other structures built in this area: The military fort, or *cuartel*, occupies the entire city block south of the church; and the first Franciscan convent was built adjacent to the church, since nuns were needed to run the hospital, attend to the needs of the Mérida community, and provide administrative support for the Franciscan missionaries.

Many of the first residences in the area were the homes of military officers and high-ranking ecclesiastical authorities, two divergent communities that more often than not were at odds with each other. The political rivalries between the armed forces (state) and the Franciscans missionaries (church) made for an interesting dynamic, particularly in the vast, distant and resource-poor province of Yucatán. It was the backwater of New Spain. The three conquistadors named Francisco Montejo – Francisco de Montejo "El Adelantado" (father), Francisco de Montejo y León "El Mozo" (the son) and Francisco de Montejo "El Sobrino" (the nephew) – were exasperated by the waves of defections among the early settlers. About the same time that Montejo founded Mérida, Francisco Pizarro arrived in Peru, and in short order news spread of vast gold mines in New Granada (South America).

Scores of settlers, realizing that the Yucatán was mineral-poor, left, hoping to find their fortunes in lands further south, made their way to San Francisco de Campeche, seeking passage to Havana, and from there to New Granada (Cartagena). This weakened the Montejos, and it only strengthened the Church in the Yucatán, giving greater prominence to the Colonia Mejorada, since this was the seat from which the early missionary initiatives were launched.

After Mexico's independence, however, the Church's profile diminished, as did the importance of the military in Mérida. The Franciscan convent was relocated elsewhere, and the military was moved to the opposite part of town, where the Centenario Park is presently located. The former convent was donated to the Universidad Autónoma de Yucatán (UADY) by the State government in 1970 and today it is the campus for the School of Architecture. The school houses a research library, incidentally, where the histories of many of the grand homes around town can be located. The campus is open to the public, so feel free to wander and admire the beautiful building, imagining what it must have been like when they was a convent. The barracks is also a public building today, one that houses various educational organizations, the most important of which is dedicated to children's education. The Centro Cultural del Niño Yucateco (CECUNY), or Cultural Center of the Yucatecan Child, is a nationally-recognized educational center that feature classes, workshops and cultural activities to promote childhood development and encourage "classroom skill sets" to less privileged youngsters.

A few blocks to the north and one block west is a vast area under redevelopment – the Victorian railroad station, one of the grandest ones built in Latin America. Portions of the railroad station have been refurbished and house the Escuela Superior de Artes de Yucatán, or ESAY, and it is expected to become a lively community for the visual arts. The railroad tracks themselves remain littered with trains, engines and railcars, a still unorganized "railroad museum" where it's possible to ask permission from the attendants to wander around. As recently as the mid-1980s, trains left the station at sunset and arrived at Palenque at dawn, all in the frayed comfort of antique Pullmans. It was all more romantic that comfortable.

As for Mejorada Park itself, it is one of the more secluded ones in Mérida. There is a large sculpture honoring Mexico's Niños Heroes de Chapultepec. On the western side of the plaza are two time-honored institutions: Los Almendros, a legendary restaurant specializing in Yucatecan cuisine, and El Segoviano, what many considered to be the best Spanish restaurant in the city. To the north one finds a closed movie house, which dates back to the first half of the 20th century, and there are charming buildings on either side, some of which have been recently restored. On the northwest corner is the Museo de Arte Popular, which carries a varied collection of populist handicrafts. On Calle 57 by 48 Street (northeast corner of the plaza) one finds the Museo de la Canción Yucateca, or the Museum of the Yucatecan Song, which honors the trova music of Yucatán and the world renowned Yucatecan musicians, such as Ricardo Palmerín, Guty Cárdenas, Pastor Cervera and Juan Acereto. Both museums are free.

San Juan

Thus far we've discussed the Colonias in the Historic Center that are north of the Zócalo. Now we turn our attention to the ones that lie south of the Zócalo, beginning with San Juan, which is located a few blocks south of the Plaza Grande and a block west. This is one of the older Colonias established once Mérida itself was founded. Its location was rather accidental: It straddles outside the gates that connected Mérida to Campeche.

Campeche was Mérida's lifeline to the rest of New Spain, its link to a seaport where commerce could come and go, and where people could more easily find passage to the other two great colonial seaports of New Spain: Veracruz and Havana. The splendid archway was constructed in 1690, an architectural flourish to the growing importance of Mérida as the Spanish stronghold on the peninsula.

It was here, near the entrance that the Maya, who worked as day laborers in Mérida proper, were allowed to live. In time, ecclesiastical authorities built the Church of San Juan Bautista, St. John the Baptist, in 1769. It was an odd church, since it served two very distinct constituencies. Foremost, it served as a welcome to travelers arriving in Mérida, and it was also here that an extensive campaign to Christianize the Maya who lived to the south of Mérida in the Puuc hills was carried out. The name of the church reflects the mission to baptize the Maya into the Christian faith. As a curious aside, this is the only church in Mérida that bears the influence of Islamic architecture, since the single long corridor speaks of the Muslim legacy.

In recent years, the Church of San Juan has been refurbished, and the park in front of it has been remodeled. It now includes a charming children's playground and the statue – commissioned in Paris and endearingly called "La Negrita," or "the little black one" – that rests at the center of the fountain is back in place. There are plans to make the streets around the church a pedestrian zone, with the focal point being the new statue of Benito Juárez.

Its close proximity to the vast central market – and all the bus routes that ferry people from neighboring communities in and out of Mérida – make it more difficult to carry out plans for a pedestrian thoroughfare, however. Where, city planners wonder, could so many buses be re-routed? Consider that Colonia San Juan is adjacent to the CAME bus station, with buses operating all hours of day and night, making the challenge greater.

But there are civic leaders involved in cultural and urban affairs who want to restore San Juan's history as a center for liberal thinking and European culture. One of the more intriguing historical figures to emerge from this Colonia is Vicente Velasquez, who founded the Sanjuanistas in 1808. Velasquez, who had been educated in Europe,

> ### ! A Caveat about the "Centro Histórico"
>
> In the same way that Miami Beach became a "destination" only after Gianni Versace and Madonna bought residences there, and Tribeca in New York became a "hot" neighborhood solely after John F. Kennedy, Jr. and Robert De Niro moved in, so has Mérida's "Centro Histórico" become an "it" destination after it was profiled in the *New York Times*.
>
> "With its narrow sidewalks, cobblestone streets and chalky colonial buildings painted the color of Easter eggs, Mérida is home to a growing number of expatriates," Kate Murphy reported, in the spring of 2006, setting off a real estate frenzy that has transformed the Centro Histórico from a place to live into a place to plunder.
>
> Not a few American scam artists have set up shop to take advantage of their fellow compatriots, which is a sad commentary on the real estate bubble that still exists in the Centro Histórico.
>
> In your search for value, be mindful of the hype – and those who profit from it.

established a salon in the Hermitage of the Church, where he taught the liberal ideals of European philosophers such as Montesquieu and Voltaire. When the imperial crisis erupted in Spain, it was the Sanjuanistas who voiced their support for the liberal reforms introduced by the Cortés and pledged their support for the Constitution of 1812. A year later, when the first printing press arrived in Mérida, they were at the forefront of printing political literature championing their cause. It is a legacy of the Sanjuanistas that most of Mérida's newspapers are located in the immediate neighborhoods to the south of the Zócalo.

As a Colonia suitable for residences, most of the buildings surrounding the Church of San Juan Bautista have been converted to commercial spaces and offices, with a large Pemex gas station located on the northwest section. Through the southern gates, the cobblestone streets are residential – and among the oldest remaining structures – but, until recently, have been deemed less desirable, since most lack ample backyards on which to build additions, pools or other amenities. Only a few enterprising foreigners have ventured to restore homes in this area, if for not other reasons than given their historical importance, there are strict conservation and restoration laws.

San Cristobal

The Colonias discussed so far reflected the natural evolution of life in Mérida, with the Maya, the arrival of the Spaniards and the introduction of a significant black labor force that was deemed necessary in the 17th and 18th centuries. There is another constituency, however, that has long been overlooked: Indigenous peoples, or First Peoples, from other parts of Mexico.

Why? Divide and conquer. The restlessness of the Maya proved a constant challenge to the Spanish. Montejo resolved that the only way to subjugate the Maya was to bring their traditional enemies to Mérida, and let the ancient animosities between the Maya and the "Aztecs" – the Maya used the derogatory term "uach," pronounced, "watch" for "foreigners" from the Valley of Mexico.

It proved a strategic move, and soon old grudges and rivalries went far in pacifying the Maya. Compared with the conduct of their indigenous peoples from Central Mexico, the Maya found the that Spaniards were "reasonable." For church authorities, on the other hand, the rivalries only made their task more difficult, it was as if old scores that needed settling took precedence over everything else. The Church of San Cristobal – Cristobal means "Christ-bearer" – sought to bring peace to everyone. The Colonia San Cristobal was constructed beginning in 1757, and it was dedicated to the Virgin of Guadalupe, who appeared on the outskirts of Mexico City, and which held special meaning to the indigenous people that Montejo brought from the Valley of Mexico.

As if to underscore the need for cooler heads to prevail, the fortress-like church has an inscription over the nave that reads: "This is the House of God and the Gate of Heaven." That's how people in the 18th century said, "Chill out and sit down."

Although the Colonia is surrounded by shabby buildings, and the inhabitants of the neighborhood are definitely working-class families, the Church of San Cristobal looms large in Mérida's life. As the only church dedicated to the Virgin of Guadalupe, it is the center of the city's life every December 12, the Day of the Virgin of Guadalupe. It seems everyone in town pays homage to the Virgin of Guadalupe, and one would think that everyone wants to do so by physically visiting this one church. If ever there is any doubt about where the passion of the Mexican people lies, forget soccer, it's the Virgin of Guadalupe!

One native of San Cristobal of note was Manuel Crescencio Rejón, who worked for greater social justice and whose family was renowned during Mexico's struggle for independence. If the name sounds vaguely familiar, it should: Mérida's international airport is named after him.

At present, the largest expatriate community in San Cristobal are Europeans – mostly Spanish, Czech and Croatian – and with a certain hipster sensibility. What does this mean? Oh, that their idea of interior design runs more along the lines of graffiti on the walls and Mexican license plates nailed on doorways, and not Talavera tiles in the kitchen. Where Santa Ana affects an artistic flair, the expatriates of San Cristobal, with their trademark complete abandon, are the kind of people who sweeten their espressos with Xtabentun. (If you are not familiar with this liquor, this is how Gary Regan described it in the San Francisco *Chronicle*: "The producers of d'Aristi Xtabentun say that the drink is based on balche, a magical potion said to have been consumed at ancient Mayan rituals, though balche was made from water, honey and tree bark, so honey is the only ingredient common to both beverages. Nonetheless, d'Aristi Xtabentun is a fairly stunning liqueur."[3] Yes, the expatriates here reflect a more Eastern European aesthetics, which is in keeping with the more cultish nature of Christian sects favored in the more superstitious areas of Europe. Think of the ambivalence that surrounds lands where the Roman and the Cyrillic alphabets meet, and now you can image a neighborhood where a few Nahuatl (Aztec) words have intermingled with the indigenous Yucatec Maya.

In some ways, San Cristobal is not unlike the Confederacy in the American South: folks who cling to their liquors and centuries-old grudges, while wrapping themselves in the flag and vowing allegiance to the patron saint, whether it is Robert E. Lee, the Virgin of Guadalupe or the European pursuit of Epicureanism.

---

[3] See: *www.sfgate.com/cgi-bin/article.cgi?f=/c/a/2007/02/02/WIGK9NRPNI1.DTL#ixzz1ATMeeP72*

San Sebastian and Ermita

In keeping with norms of the time, Francisco Montejo "El Adelantado," gave a vast parcel of land to his son, Francisco Montejo "El Mozo," south of Mérida proper. "El Mozo" proceeded to establish a grand estate, with the church of San Sebastian at the center of it. It was a curious development, simply because of a crushing lack of funds. The constant skirmishes with the Maya and the absence of valuable minerals made public finances a constant battle for Mérida.

It would be more than a century later before the present Church of San Sebastian that we see was constructed. Indeed, it took a concerted political effort to finance the 1706 structure, and only after city officials reluctantly extended certain privileges to the Church. During his lifetime, "El Mozo," one has to bear in mind, was only able to build his estate by availing himself to the poorest of the Maya, many from outlying, desolate places. He resettled them in Colonia San Sebastian, almost as indentured servants, with the hopes that their closer proximity to Mérida would afford them greater economic opportunities. This set the precedent, and San Sebastian became known as the "colonia" for the most "desamparados," literally, the most helpless of people. This reputation, throughout the centuries, continued, and seemed a self-fulfilling prophecy: society's most disenfranchised found itself scratching a living in San Sebastian, from destitute Maya in the 17th century to aging American never-do-wells in the 21st century who are making their home here.

Attempts to improve the lot of the residents through education, greater integration with the whole of Mérida's society and recruiting young men for the military did little to reverse the district's reputation. That San Sebastian was the site of the city's first *Rastro Municipal*, or meat-packing district, did little to enhance the area's reputation. Located on the outskirts of Mérida proper, incoming cattle from Campeche was butchered for Mérida's populace, and the sight of vultures circling overhead, which could be seen in the distance from the entire city, was a constant reminder that death was ever-present in San Sebastian. (The *ex-Rastro Municipal* is now a sports complex, with soccer fields and a baseball diamond, adjacent to the Chedraui supermarket, which faces Avenida Itzáes as one travels towards the airport.) For several hundred years, people have avoided the area, and in the popular imagination it is still linked with death; vultures are said to suspend in midflight cognizant of the feeding frenzy that took place here.

If Montejo established Colonia San Cristobal for Central Mexican thugs he brought in to keep the Maya in line, then the nearby Colonia of San Sebastian is the place, long known as the "Barrio Bravo," for home-grown toughs. In fact, in less dramatic terms, the "gangs of Mérida" of the 20th century resided principally in San Sebastian. During the final years of the Porfirio Díaz dictatorship and throughout much of the Mexican Revolution (1910-1917), the fiercest turf wars took place in San Sebastian, with legendary "guerras de barrios" ("wars for the neighborhoods") and "guerras de esquinas" ("wars for the street corners") leaving the place the most dangerous Colonia in Mérida. It is said that from sunset to sunrise, not even the police dared venture into San Sebastian.

The cultural influence of the Maya, however, prevailed, and violence became institutionalized: Rules were established, and the "turf" wars among members came to be supervised by referees who enforced a code of conduct. In other words, Mérida's tradition of *boxing as a spectator sport* emerged from the gritty streets of San Sebastian. As Mérida grew wealthy between the 1880s and 1910s, gentlemen indulged the vicarious pursuit of violence by sponsoring boxing matches. It was not unheard of to have lavish dinner parties in the grand houses of Santiago, Santa Ana or Paseo de Montejo that did not include the spectacle of a boxing match. (In the parlors the ladies would amuse themselves with cards, dominoes and backgammon, while the men smoked cigars, drank liquors and went outside for whatever entertainment the host had arranged for the evening.)

The other saving grace of Colonia San Sebastian is the Ermita de Santa Isabel Church, on the corner of Calle 77 and 66 Street, which is dedicated to Nuestra Señora del Buen Viaje, or Our Lady of the Good Voyage. As attacks against Campeche by English and Dutch pirates intensified in the late 1600s, people in Mérida grew concerned about their safety. The Ermita de Santa Isabel Church, built in the early 1700s on a small grotto overlooking the Camino Real, was established for voyagers to offer one last prayer before embarking on a trip to Campeche. It was also a place to give thanks for those who had arrived safely. Even today, Yucatecans are fond of saying, "Que llegues con toda felicidad," or "May you arrive with complete joy," to those who are about to embark on a journey.

The area of San Sebastian closest to the Ermita de Santa Isabel is currently in the throes of urban renewal. The church itself has been restored, as has the nearby park. The streets are being rebuilt, and the original bricks are being installed. The expatriates moving into the area are primarily Western Europeans, with some Americans. Many intellectuals, artists and hipsters from Mexico City have discovered the area, as have the Spaniards. Occasionally one encounters aging American refugees who fancy themselves being "of the people" – advocating causes as disparate as "ritual" alcoholic enemas (to cleanse your body and mind), or supporting the almost-forgotten Zapatistas rebels. On late afternoons, one can stroll from the Ermita de Santa Isabel up Calle 66 towards San Juan Bautista and it's possible to see the vultures hovering over the intersection of Calle 81 and 70 Street. This is the only Colonia considered dangerous, in that there is street crime, and gangs in the area engage in "turf" battles. It is considered the least desireable area of the Historic Center in which to invest.

The cultural center of the community, however, is **ULE**, located on Calle 64 #560, between Calle 71 and 73 Streets, which is the brainchild of Eugenia Montalván Colón, one of Mérida's leading cultural innovators. The Ermita de Santa Isabela and ULE are the two reasons tourists are making the effort to this Colonia. But the neighborhood remains marginal – and much-hyped. It would be difficult to find a property that was worth more than $200,000 USD in this neighborhood, especially considering the price-per-square-foot of what is available in other parts of town, to speak nothing of the phenomenal retirement home values in Florida, Texas, Nevada and New Mexico.

Cultural Activities of Interest

ULE Centro Cultural
Calle 64 #506, betweeen 71 and 73 Streets
Telephone: (999) 120-4210
Website: *www.unasletras.com*

Summing up the "Centro Histórico, these are the Colonias that constitute the Historic Center proper. They also represent the principle districts where most expatriates long to find a home. It is also the area where, as is amply discussed in the Real Estate chapter, the basic laws of supply and demand have been undermined by a real estate frenzy and hype. With this caveat, what follows is a description of attractive Colonias that ring the Centro Histórico, where value is still to be found, and where more expatriates are discovering splendid residences away from insular world of "Gringo Gulch." These Colonias are all an easy five to fifteen minute drive to the Zócalo, and all are widely served by city buses and commuter vans.

Now we turn our attention to the Colonias around the "Centro Histórico."

García Ginerés

There is a consensus that Colonia García Ginerés, with its stately Avenida Colón, is the most gracious of Mérida's neighborhoods. It is also one of the more storied one. For as long as there are records, the entire area that comprises García Ginerés was part of an "Hacienda" known as Dátil y Limón, or Date and Lemon, which was abbreviated as "Datilimón." The earliest known records date back to the 17th century and they identify this vast estate as bordered by the following properties: Tanlum to the north, Santa Catarina to the south, and San Juan Bautista de Xoclam to the east. It fell within the ecclesiastical jurisdiction of Santiago, and the earliest recorded names as proprietors are the Maya family that was recognized by Mérida as head of the indigenous communities in the northwestern outskirts of Mérida proper: Santiago Euan, and after his death in 1762, his widow, Isabel Ku. In due course, the property passed into the hands of the Lorenzo de Lorra, the Majordomo of Rents for the Nun's Convent.

The entrance to the Hacienda was located on the corner of where today Calle 62 runs into 35 Street, where for many years the Hospital del Niño once stood, and today the Civil Registry is located. But in the intervening years, the residence was home to military, political and religious leaders. Some of the more distinguished names include José Estanisalo del Puerto, a military captain credited with putting down various rebellions, and he built his home there in the 1760s, a grand building named "Nuestra Señora del Loreto;" Manuel Artazo y Barral, who served as Governor (1812-1815), the military leader General Antonio López de Santa Anna, who also served as Governor (1824-1825); and the Bishop José María Guerra y Correa (1834-1863). It was during this time that the Hacienda was called the "Quinta del Obispo," or the Bishop's Quinta. In time, it was sold to Alvaro Peón de Regil, the Count of Miraflores, in the second half of the 19th century.

The Hacienda entered the modern era when Cosme Angel Villajuana y de la Paz, who had served as mayor of Mérida, purchased it in the 19th century, and he renamed the vast estate in honor of his patron saint. The vast stretch of land lay fallow, until Joaquin García Ginerés, a native of Tarragona, Spain purchased it in 1904. He proceeded to develop San Cosme into the first real estate development venture on a modern scale, but encountered resistance. His first attempt had not been as successful as he had hoped, the Colonia Itzimná. (On Calle 17 of Itzimná one can still see some of the buildings he constructed, but which did not convince families to leave Mérida proper for these outskirts so far removed from the Zócalo.) At first, investors were reluctant to share his optimism that a parcel of land, however vast, could prosper, since it was so far removed from the Plaza Grande.

He was adamant: with the "Colonia" San Cosme, he hoped to have more than enough land at his disposal, and build a modern community, one that would rival the Belle Epoque divisions that were being built on the outskirts of major European cities, from Barcelona to Paris. His efforts paid off, and the grounds of the vast Hacienda were urbanized, with modern boulevards, wide streets and generous plots to build gracious residences, obliterating all reminders of the Hacienda's agrarian past. (Today, the last remaining vestige of the original property is located on the grounds of the Jenaro Rodríguez Correa School: A well that was used to water the groves of dates and lemon trees.) Joaquin García Ginerés died in March 1915, and later that same year, by official proclamation, the City of Mérida renamed the district in his honor later that same year: Colonia García Ginerés.

With such pedigree, it is not surprising to learn that many of the notables of the 20th century who made their way to Mérida spent time in the gracious homes of García Ginerés. At the center is Parque de las Américas, or Park of the Americas, which boasts a stela for each nation in the Western Hemisphere, and Puerto Rico.

The architecture of that park is astounding. The fountain at Parque de las Américas is a singular example of the Maya Revival style pioneered by Frank Lloyd Wright and which became associated with the Art Deco movement in the mid-twentieth century. This fountain was designed by Manuel Amábilis in 1946, and a comparable example of a similar style is found in the United States in the Federal Building in Balboa Park, San Diego, designed by Richard Requa in 1935. Manuel Amábilis was a famous architect, his international notoriety having been secured when he designed the Mexican Pavilion for the World's Fair in Seville, Spain in 1929. What is also intriguing is that this park was the center of the cultural links between Havana and Mérida before the Cuban Revolution. The royal palms were a gift of the Rotary Club of Havana in the 1950s and the children's library across from the park is dedicated to nineteenth century Cuban liberator José Martí.

The homes that flank the streets adjacent to the park are filled with history. One home, on the corner of Calle 24 and 23 Street, with its Art Nouveau windows, hosted Gloria Swanson when she was in town, as well as Charles Lindbergh, Joan Crawford, Octavio Paz and Truman Capote. Another house, on the corner of Calle 20 and 17 Street, was built by radio magnate Perfecto Villamil, who hosted just about everyone interviewed on the radio (as was the custom) when they were in town in the 1930s, 1940s and 1950s, including Pedro Infante, Dolores del Rio, Diego Rivera, Frida Kahlo, Louise Nevelson and Gabriel García Márquez. Further afield, the luminaries continue. The house on the corner of Calle 26 and 9 Street hosted Fidel Castro, and two corners away on Calle 26 and 13 Street, that has been a gateway for distinguished intellectuals in the arts and sciences from the world over, everyone from archaeologist Michael Coe to chef Diana Kennedy, from National Geographic's George Stuart to designer Bill Blass, and a list of American and Mexican diplomats, businessmen and politicians too long to enumerate.

It is possible to become dizzy with excitement at the thought of singular families who have been privileged to share this Colonia with so many distinguished men and women from around the world. But, as is often the case, as families of means have left for more contemporary homes, many of the grand mansions along Avenida Colón and the adjoining streets, have come on the market, many of which are corporate offices, but not a few remain private residences.

Itzimná

Colonia Itzimná was a charming Maya village for centuries, an easy horseback ride from Mérida. Although there are scores of Maya towns and villages in the greater environs of Mérida proper, Itzimná held special importance to the Maya. It was a place of pilgrimage to render homage to Itzimná, the Maya deity who ruled over heaven, day and night. Often associated with the points of the compass, and the colors associated with these cardinal directions – east, red; north, white; west, black; and south, yellow – it was a logical place for the Spanish missionaries to build a church to carry out their campaign of converting the Maya to Christianity.

In 1572 they constructed a small fortress-like church, and it was dedicated to Archangel Michael, who is viewed as the "field commander" in the Army of God. The Spanish believed that the pantheon of Maya deities were nothing less than Satan's ploy to deceive humanity, and that the Spaniards would need to enlist guidance from Archangel Michael if they were to triumph and win over the Maya.

That Itzimná resides northeast of Mérida also made it a coveted town, charming and closer to the Gulf's sea breezes, which offered respite during the sweltering summer months. As a rule, the further south one travels from the Zócalo, the hotter it becomes, and the natural growth of upscale communities has been to expand northward, towards the beaches and the sea breezes. Mérida's more privileged families began to build summer homes in the area. The presence of the missionaries had made the area safe from the threat of Maya attacks, and the geography does lend itself to ameliorate the summer heat.

At the end of the 19th century, our illustrious Catalan, Joaquin García Ginerés, envisioned an extensive community with the church of Itzimná at the center, but it was hard to convince investors that people from Mérida would be prepared to live year-round in the *afueras*, or outskirts. What did they mean by this? Simply that there was a reluctance to live *beyond* the newly-installed railroad track! If one had to cross the railroad track, then one was not in a fashionable area.

Many historians credit the success of Colonia García Ginerés to this one simple fact: it resides entirely within the railroad track that then surrounded Mérida, defining "city limits." That was then, of course, and today the gracious, beautiful homes built by Mérida's wealthy are full-time residences, and many comfortable homes (and sought-after schools) are found on the streets that flank the church. It is a very fashionable neighborhood, one where a good number of expatriates are finding homes, and building lives just beyond "walking distance" of downtown.

Miguel Alemán

Directly to the southeast of Itzimná one finds Colonia Miguel Alemán – a place virtually empty of American expatriates. Named after Mexican president Miguel Alemán, this Colonia was the first U.S.-style suburb, and it dates back to 1957.

With broad avenues defining the Colonia, Miguel Alemán boasts one of the most tranquil and family-oriented public squares in town. The center of the Colonia is the vast park, Parque Miguel Alemán, which encompasses an entire city block. In the late afternoons, families gather to socialize, with children playing. There are plenty of teenagers on skateboards, inline skaters and hipsters hanging out, often sharing iPods and texting each other surreptitiously while their grandparents look on, pretending not to see how they are flirting. There is an amphitheater, similar to the one found in Colonia García Ginerés, and on weekends high school bands make a ruckus not far from the children's playground. There are vendors selling all manner of foods, and families coming in and out of the Sacred Heart of Jesus Church, or Iglesia del Sagrado Corazón de Jesús, which has services every morning and evening.

Over the decades, families have bought adjacent plots and today most of the homes are comfortable, two-level residences with enclosed parking and open-floor layouts, very similar to the layouts one finds in Florida and California, with kitchens opened to dining areas and "Florida" rooms. There is no significant business or commercial district, other than pharmacies, corner stores and a few services (dry cleaning stores, sundries shops and small restaurants). There really is no need, since it is a short drive to major shopping malls and supermarkets.

There is a distinct residential feel to the place, and the residents, mostly middle- and upper-middle Yucatecan families like it that way. The park is located on the intersection of Calle 31 and 20 Street. If you go to YouTube.com and search "Miguel Alemán" and "Mérida" you'll find video clips showing teenagers break dancing, skateboarding and carrying on the way the young and hopeful are inclined to do.

Centenario

To the west of the Centro Histórico lies a vast district that really isn't a "colonia" in and of itself, but an area broadly defined as the "Centenario." It's comprised of sections of primarily working-class colonias of Sambula, San Lorenzo and Carrillo Ancona. It's called "Centenario" because at the heart is not a church, but a park, formerly the city zoo, which is bound by Calle 65 to the south, Avenida Itzáes to the west, Calle 59 to the north and Calle 84 to the east. It is also called "Centenario" because the buildings that surround the vast park, "Parque de la Paz," were constructed to commemorate Mexico's centennial in 1910. Before the construction that was carried out anticipating Mexico's Centennial, the area was designated as Santa Catarina.

The Hospital O'Horan, which at the time was en par with any other hospital in the world, also contained an asylum for the insane. The penitentiary was world class, and the broad extension of Calle 59 from the Historic Center to Avenida Itzáes marked a new, formal entry to the city. The grand homes that front that street were built in a real estate frenzy as Yucatecans of means vied with one another for a place along that street, knowing that it would be officially inaugurated when Porfirio Díaz came to Mérida for the Centennial celebrations. (When he did arrive, he also inaugurated state-of-the-art facilities, including the Post & Telegraph offices, which today house the Museum of the City; the Nicolas Bravo school on the intersection of Calle 59 and 72 Street; and the State Department of Health, located Calle 72 and 53 Street.) The grand urban expansion program extended the vast area that fell under the ecclesiastical jurisdiction of "Santiago."

Today, when we refer to the Centenario District, we mean the Parque de la Paz, at Avenida Itzáes and Calle 59, to Calle 76, south to Calle 65 and north to Calle 59-A, which runs into Jacinto Canek at Avenida Itzáes. The homes within this area are in a flux, with some rather modest homes where older people live, their children long moved to other, more prosperous parts of town, and where some grand structures have been rebuilt or refurbished. To give you an idea of the kind of homes located in this area, consider the boutique hotel, The Villa, which, up until a few years ago, was a decrepit structure in a state of near collapse. If you peruse the images at *www.villahotelmerida.com*, you'll understand the wealth that Mérida enjoyed during the Edwardian time.

The Centenario district, however, is also remembered for one of the darkest episodes in Mexican history: It is where Henry Lane Wilson, an American ambassador to Mexico spent considerable time, before taking his post in Mexico City. As is well-remembered, Wilson was implicated in the assassination of Mexican president Francisco Madero on February 22, 1913, and many loyalists came to believe that Wilson had conspired with conservative elements in the Yucatán who were against Madero's liberal reforms. The entire matter festered, particularly when Wilson published his memoirs, *Diplomatic Episodes in Mexico, Belgium and Chile* in 1927, and in which he alluded to his contacts in Mérida and of his admiration for Mérida. This is the primary reason that, even to the this day, Mérida officials are reluctant to accept overtures from American citizens, or to involve them in any official capacity, simply because of the lingering mistrust of their motives, or how associating with American citizens will be interpreted should some untoward event – a *"gringada"* – result as a consequence of any collaboration with U.S. citizens.

The Centenario area is under a slow, but steady, redevelopment. Electric cables are being buried under ground, new lamp posts are being installed, the Centenario has been repurposed as a family-oriented park, several museums, including the Museum of Natural History, or Museo de Historia Natural, located on Calle 59 #648, between Calle 84 and 84-A Street are at the center of activities. In addition to The Villa, there is another boutique hotel a block east, the Casa de las Columnas (www.casadelascolumnas.com) and the tourist-class hotel, the Hotel Residencial (www.hotelresidencial.com.mx). Scattered between are homes, some of which have been restored, and many others that are in need of restoration, or have been repurposed into commercial use.

Chuminopolis

Finally, to the east of the Centro Histórico one finds the Colonia of Chuminopolis, which is a working-class and warehouse district. It is also the site of the city's Korean neighborhood. This is a rich background, made more intriguing by the charming history of Chuminopolis, starting with its ridiculous name! What in the world does it mean? The suffix is easy enough, "polis" is Greek for "city," hence "metropolis." But what of "Chumin"? Well, "Chumin" is a nickname for someone named "Domingo," the same way that "Pancho" is a nickname for someone named "Francisco," and "Nacho" is a nickname for someone named "Ignacio." Mexican revolutionary hero and outlaw "Pancho Villa" was really "Francisco Villa," and "Nacho Figueras," the world-famous polo player, who is the model in the Ralph Lauren Polo advertising campaign, is really "Ignacio Figueras."

"Chuminopolis" is the name given to this Colonia by José Domingo Sosa, a wealthy landowner who was very well-respected during the Belle Epoque. Most of Colonia Chuminopolis occupies lands he owned, and as commerce with farming communities to the south increased, so did the expansion of the Colonia, with massive warehouses and transportation offices. The construction of the railroad in the 19th century further fueled activity, and not just in shipping, but in the diversity of the communities and immigrants living in the neighborhood. It was officially recognized as a Colonia in 1904, after José Domingo Sosa petitioned city officials.

When it was officially established, the Hacienda of Pat San Pedro Noh was annexed into the Colonia. The Hacienda had been a Franciscan monastery, with its renowned House of Christianity, or Casa de la Cristianidad, so named because it lay on the road that led to Valladolid, and it was the last place of prayer before missionaries embarked to their missions that stretched from Mérida to the eastern portions of the peninsula. The Franciscans took their tasks seriously, and were very meticulous about prayer. The Hacienda Pat San Pedro Noh boasts several icons associated with missionary work: In each of the small chapels on the property one finds wooden shelves with several illustrations: Christ of the Blisters, Dedications to the Sorrowful Mother, Our Lady of Fatima, Our Lady of Perpetual Help, and Our Lady of Lourdes.

One of the more colorful characters to move into Chuminopolis was Rafael Quintero, an engineer best remembered for paving the major thoroughfares of Mérida proper. He grew rich, and he indulged in one extravagance: Quinta del Olvido, his "Quinta of Oblivion." It's open to conjecture precisely what Quintero intended with such a peculiar name, but in his "quinta" he built a chapel dedicated to Nuestra Señora del Carmen, Our Lady of Mount Carmel in English, who is associated with the search for inner peace. Historians speculate that the fame and notoriety he received for his work on behalf of Mérida made him weary. Fr. Gabriel of St. Mary Magdalene de' Pazzi, one of the leading authorities on Our Lady of Mount Carmel explains, "Our Lady wants us to resemble her not only in our outward vesture but, far more, in heart and spirit. If we gaze into Mary's soul, we shall see that grace in her has flowered into a spiritual life of incalculable wealth: a life of recollection, prayer, uninterrupted oblation to God, continual contact, and intimate union with him. Mary's soul is a sanctuary reserved for God alone, where no human creature has ever left its trace, where love and zeal for the glory of God and the salvation of mankind reign supreme." Quintero in his later years became a recluse.

In the meantime, other, more urgent, interests were moving into the neighborhood: German brewers. The first brewery had its origin in this area, and it was José Ponce who launched, in 1869, what would become Cervecería Yucateca. And a notorious Juan Martínez is credited with starting Mérida's first "professional" – however that is defined – house of ill repute in this Colonia. German biermeisters, and Yucatecan recluses, beer drinkers and pimps were joined by the arrival of another significant foreign community: Koreans.

Koreans were lured to the Yucatán to work the henequen fields and to build the railroad, and today there is a museum dedicated to their presence in the Yucatán. The Korean Museum, located on Calle 65, between Calle 44 and 46 Street, tells the history of their arrival in the peninsula, and their contributions to Yucatecan society. In a charming event held the last Sunday of each month, the museum holds a children's hour called "Cuentame un cuento, Jalmoni," or "Tell me a story, grandmother." ("Jalmoni" is Korean for "grandmother.") A Korean grandmother tells Korean stories and recounts legends. On occasion the event is also held at the children's library in Parque de las Américas in Colonia García Ginerés.

43

Cultural Activities of Interest

Korean Museum (Museo Coreano)
Calle 65 #397-A, between Calle 44 and 46 Street
Hours: Monday-Friday: 10 AM to 2 PM, and 3 PM to 6 PM
Saturdays: 9 AM to 2 PM
Facebook: *www.facebook.com/pages/Museo-Conmemorativo-de-la-Inmigracion-Coreana-a-Yucatan/153347068015960*

The preceding shares a bit of the history of the more popular Colonias in Mérida. In recent years, however, another number of neighborhoods are becoming destinations for expatriates. Many of these have been "discovered" accidentally: They are on the way to and from the Star Médica medical complex – and medical tourism is a rapidly expanding industry in Mérida!

Be mindful that almost all of these districts were built after 1950, and except for the occasional older structure, these are two-story homes, designed in styles that were fashionable in the 1960s through the 1990s. What they lack in colonial "charm" they more than make up in modern plumbing, family rooms and two-car garages. Most have small, but well tended gardens, and many have high walls, offering privacy, since they lack room for gardens to separate the sidewalks and the actual residence.

Locating the Colonias on a Map

To get your bearings, as a public service, the Mérida Bed & Breakfast Association has a map of Mérida with all the neighborhoods, which can prove invaluable as you look at the various neighborhoods.

The map is in a PDF format, and it is accessible at:
Meridabedandbreakfast.org/movingtomerida/meridaneighborhoods.html

Here is a list of the Colonias, in alphabetical order, which may be worth driving through, and most of these lie northeast of Colonia Miguel Alemán:

Altabrisa	Montecristo
Brisas	Prado Norte
Buenavista	San Antonio Cinta
Chuburná	San Antonio Cucul

THE COLONIAS, OR NEIGHBORHOODS, OF MÉRIDA

Jardines de Mérida	San Esteban
Jardines del Norte	San Lorenzo
La Florida	San Miguel
Los Pinos	Vista Alegre

An Important Note about Owning Real Estate in Mérida!

If you decide to purchase property in Mexico, take note that Mérida resides almost entirely in what is called a "restricted zone," and foreign citizens will need a trust, known as a Fideicomiso, to hold the title.

Q: Why does Mexico have "restricted zones" when it comes to owning property?

A: Once upon a time Mexico made a mistake that it regrets to this day. That mistake was trusting American immigrants. Back in the first half of the 19th century Mexico, like many other countries throughout the hemisphere, encouraged immigrants, simply because there were vast stretches of land that needed to be settled. It was in this spirit that it welcomed Americans who bought land in the northern areas, a vast landscape known as "Tejas." These American settlers proceeded to establish prosperous enclaves, but, in defiance of Mexican law, they insisted on importing America's "peculiar institution" – slavery.

Mexico, aghast that these renegade immigrants were trafficking in human beings, proceeded to put an end to it, and the Americans then declared their independence from Mexico, creating the Republic of Texas.

From that bitter mistake, Mexico has put strict restrictions on the ability of foreigners to own land outright along the borders, and within 50 kilometers of the coastlines. The rationale is to prevent foreigners from conspiring or colluding in the purchase of land along the border or the coastlines for nefarious purposes. Of course, through bank trusts, foreigners can own properties anywhere – from a house in Mérida, or a condo in Cancún – which are protected from expropriation or nationalization through international treaties. But the mere existence of these restrictions is a reminder of Mexico's insistence on taking precautions on the potential threat that foreigners pose to the Mexican nation.

With this in mind, it's amazing to see how many Americans are indifferent to Mexican sensibilities and, either out of ignorance or arrogance, proceed to behave as if they were of political consequence in Mexico. It's an amusing spectacle, for instance, to witness how a couple of Americans can arrive in Mérida, set up a little website where they post articles on, for instance, how to read your electric bill, and then suddenly they think they can assert political rights!

Never forget that, unless and until you become a Mexican citizen, you are a guest of the Mexican nation, and are expected to act accordingly.

Part II
Mérida's Amenities

3 The ABCs of MID

That's enough history and what-not for now. This chapter is dedicated to answering the most often asked questions about Mérida from almost five years' of hosting guests at a B&B. The questions range from: Why is Mexico so bureaucratic? Where are the non-Catholic churches located? Is there a cooking school I can sign up? Are there other expat communities in town? Why do the addresses in Mérida have the letters "x" and "y" in them? Can you recommend a guidebook for the Yucatán peninsula, one that includes the Maya Riviera? Where can I sign up for Spanish classes? Is birding all that popular down here as I've heard? Why are the floors described as "pasta"?

By answering these questions now, you can get a good deal of miscellaneous information out of the way that will give you insights into the peculiar and wonderful aspects of living in Mérida. It also will give you a firm background on culture and society, which will help you understand the chapters that follow – chapters that deal with the more mundane realities involved in everything from opening a bank account, to how to get the CFE to put your name on the electric bill! And, "MID" is the airport code for Mérida – that's how your luggage ended up arriving with you!

It's going to be a fun chapter!

Why is Mexico so bureaucratic?

The one thing that expatriates moving to Mérida, or Mexico for that matter, for the first time find is … exasperation! Why in the world is everything so bureaucratic?! Why is everyone always asking for some paper, receipt, document or whatever?! Why do you find yourself walking around with a folder filled with little papers?!

Little papers!! *Papelitos!*

It makes you want to scream. Really, it does. But there's a reason to this, and it has nothing to do with trying to make your life inconvenient. On the contrary, it is designed to make sure that serious matters are handled in a serious way, and that by being handled correctly, there won't be problems down the road. Mexico, unlike the United States – until recently – has always been adamant about "not trusting and always verifying."

You want to change the name on the electric bill over the phone? No way, José. You have to come down and demonstrate that you are who you say you are, and that you are authorized to change the name on the electric bill. Unlike the U.S., Mexico is very meticulous about its official documents, very demanding with its documentation, and extremely thorough about verifying the validity of paperwork presented for official business.

"All those little papers!"

One of the more exasperating things about Mexico for Americans are all pieces of identification required for just about everything – from setting up an account with the power company to opening a checking account. It seems that "official" papers, identifications, passports, utility receipts are always needed to satisfy requirements for just about anything. This is in stark contrast to the United States where, for instance, in most places all you have to do is call the utility and, over the phone, change billing address or even the name on the account. That's impossible in Mexico, where many transactions require that they be done in person, not over the phone, and with supporting documentation.

Why?

Unlike the U.S. where, for instance, banks sent out pre-approved solicitations for credit cards as if they were confetti on New Year's Eve, Mexico is a place where there are multiple steps, and every step of the way is designed to minimize the possibility of identity theft or fraud. (The research firm of Javelin Strategy reported that identity theft cost American consumers more than $54 billion in 2009.)

The incident of U.S.-style identity theft is almost unheard of in Mexico, but the price is the redundancy built into the system, just to make sure that documentation matches with all the other documentation, but also to make sure that you are who you say you are, and are doing this transaction – whether is setting up a new account with the electric company, or transferring a million pesos to a stranger in Nigeria – is being done of your own volition.

But lest you become flustered, it's good to realize that the annoyance is a one-time deal, for the initial set-up of accounts (and for subsequent changes), but the benefit is that once it is done, you have the peace of mind that comes from knowing your business is well protected, and that you can expect superior customer service, since officials at the bank, tax office, power company, and so on, have met you, and know you. In Mexico, it's almost impossible to be just a name associated with an account number – simply because a real human being is the one who sets up every account!

Is there is a list of churches?

The vast majority of people in Mérida are Catholic, including the sizeable Arab Marist community. Fewer than 10% are Protestant. Another 6% is estimated to be other Christian denominations.

Catholic Church

Website: *arquidiocesisde yucatan.com.mx*

Baptist

"El Mesías"
Calle 28 by 16 Street
Colonia Morelos Oriente

Berea
Calle 35 Diag. #361, between Calle 46 and 48 Street, Centro

Jesucristo es El Señor
Calle 22 #108, Locals 2 and 3, between Calle 29 and 31 Street
Colonia México

First Baptist Church
Calle 62 #538, between Calle 67 and 69 Street, Centro

Jehovah's Witnesses

Salón del Reino de los Testigos de Jehová
Calle 90 #482-B between Avenida Jacinto Canek and 47 Street
Colonia Inalámbrica.

Methodist

La Rosa de Saron
Calle 62 #300-F, corner of Calle 35
Centro

Evangelical Christian

"Emmanuel"
Calle 112 #425-A, corner of
 Calle 59-H
Colonia Bojórquez

"Príncipe de Paz"
Avenida Itzáes, between Calle 71 and 73 Street, Centro

Centro de Fe "Sinai"
Calle 66-B #889, corner of
 Calle 109-D
Colonia Obrera

Centro Cristiano "La Nueva Jerusalén"
Calle 20 #106, between Calle 23 and 25 Street
Colonia Chuburná

Church of Jesus Christ of Latter-Day Saints

Calle 65 #527, between Calle 70 and 72 Street, Centro

Presbyterian

Shalom
Calle 26 #215 by 27 Street
Colonia García Ginerés

El Verbo de Dios
Calle 20, between Calle 21 and 19 Street
Colonia Chuburná

El Divino Salvador
Calle 66 #520 by 63 Street, Centro

Antioquía
Calle 74 #468, Centro

Episcopal

Saint Mark's Anglican Church
Calle 21 #116, between Calle 58 and 60 Street
Progreso

Where can I take cooking classes?

There are a good number of cooking schools in Mérida, and a fair number of tour operators offer cooking workshops – everything from using chocolate in the kitchen, to how to make Mexican and Yucatecan marinades. Here is an alphabetical listing of recommended cooking schools. Bon Appétit!

Chef Internacional

Calle 24 #210-B, by Circuito Colonias
Colonia Mexico Oriente
Telephone: (999) 938-0018
Website:
www.chefinternacional.com

Colegio Gastronómico del Sureste

Avenida Cámara de Comercio
Calle 49 #303, between Calle 46 and 48 Street
Frac. Villas la Hacienda
Website: www.cgscaribe.com

Culinaria del Sureste

Calle 19 #34, by Calle 1-H
Fracc. Montecristo

Telephone: (999) 948-2681
Website:
www.culinariadelsureste.edu.mx/contacto.htm

MexicaChica

(Classes are in English, and part of tour)
Calle 17 #201, by Calle 22
Colonia García Ginerés
In Mérida: (999) 901-5430
Website: www.mexicachica.com
Email: info@mexicachica.com

Are there other Expat Communities in Mérida apart from Americans?

Americans think they are the largest community of expatriates living in Mérida. They are mistaken. There are more Cubans and there are more Lebanese in Mérida than there are Americans. That makes Americans a minority within a minority! And the Americans in Mérida are so conflictive and divisive amongst themselves – as if they were playing out "blue" states versus "red" states about everything all the time – that they have been unable to form a single organization to speak for their community. Other expatriate communities, on the other hand, have been able to set aside their differences and celebrate what unites them.

If you are interested in reaching out to the other expatriate communities, consider doing so:

Canadians in Mérida

Canadian expat Mark Arbour is a stellar example of how moving to another country can be a successful venture, especially with enough planning, appreciation of another culture, and the determination to make it work. Here he shares his perspectives on living and working in Mexico, the businesses he and his business partner are running there, and what he and his wife think are the ups and downs of expat life in Mexico.

Do you have any tips for our readers about living in Mexico?

Embrace the culture and don't try to force your values and beliefs on them. Remember you are a visitor to their country. Most important please do not believe all the negative press in North America about how dangerous Mexico is. Yes, Mexico has a drug war happening. It is the Narcos killing Narcos. It is mostly around the US border where the drugs are destined to go to in the first place.

I was a RCMP (Royal Canadian Mounted Police) for 12 years. I can tell you that you have a 4 times greater chance being murdered in the US than in Mexico. Use common sense, there are bad places in Canada and the US, if you go to those kind of places you risk a violent crime happening. Mexico is no different.

To contact Mark, email him at: *marka@inversafe.com.mx*

Source: *www.expatinterviews.com/mexico/mark-arbour.html*

Catalan Society

Joséph Ligorret Perramon
Director
CASAL CATALÁ
Calle 14 #187, between Calle 23 and 25 Street

Colonia García Ginerés
Telephone: (999) 925-1155
Email: casaldeyucatan@yahoo.com.mx
   The Catalan community operates a Catalan-language

library, the "Biblioteca L'Alba de Ferran de Ral."

Cuban Society

Pedro Juan de la Portilla Cabrera, President
Asociación de Cubanos Residentes en México "José Martí" A.C.
Website: *cuba-mexico.org*

Centro Cultural José Martí

Avenida Colón and Calle 20 (in Parque de las Americas)
Colonia García Ginerés
Hours: Monday to Friday, 8 AM to 7:30 PM; Saturday, 9 AM to 4 PM
Director: Ana Georgina Várguez Pérez
Email: *ana.varguez@merida.gob.mx*

French Society

L'Alliance Francaise
Uptown Location:
Calle 23 #117 by Calle 24
Colonia Mexico
Downtown Location
Calle 56 #476, between Calle 55 and 57 Street
Centro
Telephone: (999) 927-2403
Francophile Website:
www.quoideneuf-merida.com
Email:
quoideneuf_merida@live.com.mx

Lebanese Society

Centro Social & Deportivo Libanés de Yucatán, A.C.
Calle 1-G, #101, between Calle 14-A and 16 Street
Colonia Mexico Norte
Telephone: (999) 948-0408

How do you make sense of the addresses?

Yes, at first it's odd to see an address that goes something like this, Calle 59 #503 x 64 y 66. In Mérida, the addresses are both addresses, and directions. To understand how this nomenclature evolved, you have to go back to language and grade school and the multiplication tables.

In elementary school, kids are taught that 2 x 3 = 6. When read out loud, it's two *times* three *equals* six. In Spanish, it is dos *por* tres *son* seis. But in Spanish, "por" means both "by" and "times," when used to refer to multiplication. This becomes engrained in how we speak throughout our entire lives.

So the mystery of Mérida's addresses is now solved. Calle 59 #503 x 64 y 66 is read: "Number 503 on 59th Street, by 64 and 66 streets." The address includes the direction on how to get there!

On a rare occasion, one will see the address "Calle 59 #503 entre 64 y 66," or "Calle 59 #503 ÷ 64 y 66." In these cases "entre" means "between" and the division symbol is read "divided by" the cross streets.

Where are the grocery stores and supermarkets?

Bodega Aurrera (2 locations)
1. Avenida Itzáes by Calle 90
2. Calle 86-A, #644-E, between Calle 90 and 92 Street, Colonia Los Reyes

Chedraui (3 locations)
1. Paseo de Montejo, by Monumento a la Bandera
2. Avenida Itzáes at Calle 86-B #544
3. Plaza las Américas and Norte (across from Gran Plaza)

Costco
Calle 60 #220, Fracc. del Norte

ISSTEY
Calle 60 #480 between Calle 49 and 51 Street

Mega Comercial Mexicana (2 locations)
1. North Calle 60 and Circuito Colonias
2. Gran Plaza (Ground level)

Mercado Grande (traditional market)
Calle 56 at Calle 65, right downtown

Pacsadeli
Calle 56 #368, between Calle 37 and 39 Street, Centro

Sam's Club
Prolongación Montejo, right before Gran Plaza, on Calle 10 #312

Soriana
Avenida Jacinto Canek, by Calle 12-B #277, Fracc. Yucalpeten

Super San Franciscso de Asis
Calle 59 #646, between Calle 82 and 84 Street

Superama
Prolongación Montejo going north, before the Club Campestre, on Calle 30 #500

Wal-Mart (2 locations)
1. Paseo de Montejo and Avenida Pérez Ponce
2. Plaza Dorada (Ground level)

In addition, San Francisco de Asis operates a chain of Costco-like bulk shopping markets, known as **AKI**, which have great deals on staples, from laundry detergents to soft drinks. There are six scattered around the city, the one closest to the "Gringo Gulch" being in Santiago, on Calle 72, between Calle 57 and 59 Street.

Drinking Water

DO NOT DRINK TAP WATER. Almost everyone in town buys purified water for drinking. It's not that the water is unsafe, but that it's treated and leaves a slight chlorine after taste. The truth of the matter is that there are very few cities in the world where it's perfectly safe to drink the water right out of the faucet. Fortunately, there are plenty of companies that supply purified water. Most peole have 20 liter (5.25 gallon) dispensers in their kitchens, and water is found in every supermarket, or routinely delivered.

Are there blogs or websites recommended to learn more about living here?

Here is an alphabetical list of wonderful blogs and websites that consistently win praise and which will give you a greater understanding about life in the Yucatán.

La Asociación Yucateca de Cactáceas y Suculentas (ASYCS)
www.asycs.blogspot.com

Beryl Gorbman
www.gorbman.com

Bicycle Yucatán
www.bicycleyucatan.blogspot.com

Cairo Cinema Café
www.cairocinemacafe.com

Casa Catherwood
www.casa-catherwood.com

Como un Sueño
www.abelvazquez.wordpress.com

Crazy Gone Native
www.ldorton.blogspot.com

Critica y Punto
www.criticaypuntro.wordpress.com

Diario de Yucatán
www.yucatan.com.mx

Expats Anonymous
www.expatsanon.com

Explore Magazine
http//yucatan.revistaexplore.com

Galeria Tataya
www.galeriatataya.blogspot.com

Inside Mex
www.insidemex.com

Inspiring Expatritism
www.expatify.com

Instituto de Desarrollo de la Cultura Maya
www.indemaya.gob.mx

Jim Conrad's Naturalist Newsletter
www.backyardnature.net/n/11/110313.htm

Johan Normark's Archaeological Haecceities

www.haecceities.wordpress.com/2009/08/31/the-exciting-lives-and-fates-of-sascaberas

Lawsons Yucatán

www.lawsonsyucatan.com

Magnitud Rosa

www.magnitudrosa.wordpress.com

Maya News Updates

www.mayanewsupdates.blogspot.com/

Mérida Hideaway

www.blog.meridahideaway.com

The Mérida Initiative

www.themeridainitiative.blogspot.com

Mérida Restaurants

www.meridarestaurants.wordpress.com

Mesoamérica Foundation

www.mesoamerica-foundation.org

Mexico Bob

www.mexicobob.blogspot.com

Mexico Cooks

www.mexicocooks.typepad.com

Moving to Mérida

www.movingtomerida.com/

On Mexican Time

www.on-mexican-time.blogspot.com/

The Pickled Onion

www.thepickledonion.com

Primera Lluvia

www.primeralluvia.wordpress.com

Proceso

www.proceso.com.mx

Que Comer en Mérida

www.quecomerenmerida.com

La Revista Peninsular

www.larevista.com.mx

Spanish Language Online Magazine

www.algarabia.com

Surviving Yucatán

www.yucalandia.wordpress.com

The Yucatán Times

www.theyucatantimes.com

La 68: Casa de Cultural Elena Poniatowska

www.la68.com/casa-de-cultura-merida/LA68.htm

Do you have a list of recommended travel books on Mérida, the Yucatán and Mexico?

Here is a list of our recommended books. Please note that the description of each book is provided by the publisher.

Moon Yucatán Peninsula (Moon Handbooks)

By Liza Prado, Gary Chandler
Experienced travel writers Liza Prado and Gary Chandler offer up their best advice on Mexico's Yucatán Peninsula, from exploring Mayan ruins and Caribbean beaches to visiting hotspots like Mérida, Cancún, and Playa del Carmen. Prado and Chandler include unique trip ideas for a variety of travelers, such as Pyramids and Palaces, Diving and Snorkeling, and A Family Affair. With essentials on dining, transportation, and accommodations for a range of budgets, Moon Yucatán Peninsula gives travelers the tools they need to create a more personal and memorable experience.

Hidden Cancún and the Yucatán (Hidden Travel)

By Richard Harris
The ultimate beach-to-ruins guide with details on over 40 beaches and 150 Mayan archaeological sites, this edition of Hidden Cancún and the Yucatán is fully updated with dozens of newly added "hidden" spots, like the picturesque coastal village of Xcalak, where small beachfront hotels sit along a pot-holed dirt road. The book also leads readers to authentic eateries from the author's favorite palapa stands to top restaurants, where they can sample dishes unique to the Yucatán. Fully covered are Cancún and the Mayan Riviera, including unusual, fun, and funky alternatives to big resorts.

Yucatán Pocket Adventures (New Pocket Adventure)

By Bruce Conord, June Conord
Need information while you're on the go? Tired of guidebooks that don't fit in your pocket? We hear you. If you're visiting for just a week or two, perhaps you don't need the in-depth history section or geographical details that can make a book cumbersome. Check out this brand new series of portable travel guides designed to be used while you're on the move. Their handy, pocket-sized format means they'll slip into your pocket or fanny pack while you focus on what you came for - whether that's hiking in Belize's rainforest with binoculars in hand, exploring Maya ruins in the Yucatán or taking in historic town sights. Adventures covered are anything from town walking tours and beachcombing to white-water rafting and organized horseback riding excursions. These guides still contain

all the practical travel information you need - places to stay and eat, tourist information resources, travel advice and more. The text is filled with interesting factoids, while town and regional maps make planning day-trips or city tours easy. Best of all, these books are affordable. Maps, index

The Rough Guide to Yucatán 2 (Rough Guide Travel Guides)

By Zora O'Neill, Rough Guides

The Rough Guide to Yucatán is bursting with inspirational ideas for your trip to this balmy Caribbean paradise. The guide covers activities for all travelers, from scuba diving at Cancún to exploring the Mayan ruins at Uxmal. There are detailed entries on the must-see attractions, from the wilds of the Sian Ka'an Biosphere Reserve to Chichén Itzá, one of the New Seven Wonders of the World. There are hundreds of up-to-date reviews for accommodation, restaurants, markets and music venues, and plenty of practical tips for adrenalin seekers. With dozens of user-friendly maps, The Rough Guide to Yucatán will guide you through Yucatán's tumultuous history, pre-Colombian cultures, unique environment and diverse wildlife. Make the most of your time with The Rough Guide to Yucatán.

A Tourist In The Yucatán

By James McNay Brumfield

Journey to the sun washed resort of Cancún and follow a young American couple, Jack and Josephine Phillips, on an adventure into the jungles of Mexico's Yucatán Peninsula. Adventure turns to terror when Josephine disappears and Jack finds himself on the run from mysterious assassins, the Mexican Federales, and possibly even his own government. The Phillips have unwittingly become entangled in the Mexican underworld, a complicated web that stretches from the Caribbean coast line of Quintana Roo to the upper reaches of the United States Government. In a land where the line between the law and the outlaw is blurred, can Jack survive long enough to solve the mystery of his wife's disappearance?

Must Sees Cancún + The Yucatán, 1e (Michelin Must Sees Cancún & the Yucatán)

By Michelin

Cancún is a sun-drenched playground of transparent coastal waters, white-sandy beaches, water sports, vast resorts and golf courses, with bars and nightclubs moving to the sounds of salsa and rumba. Away from the hubbub of the town you head inland to the Mayan relics of the Yucatán, such as mighty Chichén Itzá, offering even the weariest revelers some respite. Sights within must sees Cancún and the Yucatán are grouped according to Michelin's time-honored star-rating system, which for more than 100 years has guided travelers to the best a place has to offer. The Michelin Man symbol represents the top picks for activities, entertainment, where to eat and where to stay.

Lonely Planet Cancún, Cozumel & the Yucatán (Regional Guide)

By Greg Benchwick

Lonely Planet knows Cancún, Cozumel and the Yucatán. This 5th edition helps you build the perfect itinerary, whether it includes visiting ancient Maya ruins, people watching in an open-air café on Mérida's Plaza Grande or heading to Cozumel to dive into the coral gardens of the Great Maya Barrier Reef. Lonely Planet guides are written by experts who get to the heart of every destination they visit. This fully updated edition is packed with accurate, practical and honest advice, designed to give you the information you need to make the most of your trip.

Frommer's Cancún and the Yucatán Day by Day (Frommer's Day by Day - Pocket)

By Joy Hepp

These attractively priced, four-color guides offer dozens of neighborhood and thematic tours, complete with hundreds of photos and bulleted maps that lead the way from sight to sight. Day by Days are the only guides that help travelers organize their time to get the most out of a trip.
- Full-color package at an affordable price
- Star ratings for all hotels, restaurants, and attractions
- Foldout front covers with maps and quick-reference information
- Tear-resistant map in a handy, re-closable plastic wallet
- Handy pocket-sized trim

Pauline Frommer's Cancún & the Yucatán (Pauline Frommer Guides)

By Christine Delsol

Spend less, see more. This is the philosophy behind Pauline Frommer's guides. Written by travel expert Pauline Frommer (who is also the daughter of Arthur Frommer), and her team of hand-picked writers, these guides show how to truly experience a culture, meet locals, and save money along the way.
- Industry secrets on how to find the best hotel rooms
- Details on alternative accommodations, great neighborhood restaurants, and cool, offbeat finds
- Packed with personality and opinions

Fodor's Cancún, Cozumel & the Yucatán Peninsula 2010 (Fodor's Gold Guides)

By Fodor's

Fodor's helps you unleash the possibilities of travel by providing the insightful tools you need to experience the trips you want. Although you're at the helm, Fodor's offers the assurance of our expertise, the guarantee of selectivity, and the choice details that truly define a destination. It's like having friends in Cancún, Cozumel, and the Yucatán Peninsula!

Frommer's Cancún and the Yucatán 2011 (Frommer's Complete)

By David Baird, Christine Delsol, Shane Christensen, Maribeth Mellin
* Hundreds of color photos
* Free pocket map inside, plus easy-to-read maps throughout
* Exact prices, directions, opening hours, and other practical information
* Candid reviews of hotels and restaurants, plus sights, shopping, and nightlife
* Itineraries, walking tours, and trip-planning ideas
* Insider tips from local expert authors

Mexico (Insight Guides)

By Insight Guides
This brand new edition Insight Guide to Mexico features outstanding full-color photography, alongside illuminating explorations of all the places to go in a region-by-region

Buy these books on Amazon.com.

For your convenience, an "iBookstore" has been set up where all these titles are featured – and where you can purchase them, getting whatever discount Amazon.com is offering!

Here is the "iBookstore" addresses:
http://astore.amazon.com/casacathe-20

format, covering everywhere from Mexico City and the Gulf Coast to the less well known tourist areas in the North of the country. Major attractions, such as the Maya ruins and the Copper Canyon are highlighted to help you plan priorities for your trip; all places of special interest are cross-referenced on full-color maps throughout the guide, so they can be quickly pin-pointed as they are mentioned in the text. Additional maps of Mexico and Mexico City can be found within the front and back covers, to provide instant orientation and easy navigation. Clear, color-coded sections include in-depth features on Mexican history and culture, fiestas, art, food and the local people, alongside a detailed look at the Day of the Dead festival celebrated each November. Also included is a section of practical advice covering accommodation for all budgets, transport, eating out and much more. Useful contact information and many other travel tips are also provided. The unique combination of insightful exploration alongside practical advice means that this guide truly is a pleasure to read before, during and after your visit.

The Rough Guide to Mexico (Rough Guides)

By John Fisher, Daniel Jacobs, Zora O'Neill, Stephen Keeling

"The Rough Guide to Mexico" is the essential travel guide to this vast, extraordinarily varied country. From the deserts of the north to the tropical jungles of Chiapas; from ancient pyramids to Mexico City's sophisticated club scene; and, from colonial cathedrals to spring break in Cancún; the Rough Guide provides comprehensive coverage of it all. The guide offers detailed and practical advice on the best places to stay, where to sample some of Mexico's tastiest food and where to go to order the finest margarita for all budgets. The guide is packed with informed description of Mexico's archeological sites and museums and their fascinating historical and cultural background. Readers will find the coverage of hundreds of beaches, excursions and activities indispensable, while richly illustrated color sections explore the wonders of Mexican cuisine and the country's dynamic festivals. Informative and inspirational, with dozens of maps, handy languages tips and site plans, "The Rough Guide to Mexico" is your essential companion to this vibrant, unforgettable country. Make the most of your holiday with "The Rough Guide to Mexico".

Mexico (Eyewitness Travel Guides)

By Marlena Spieler

Recognized the world over by frequent flyers and armchair travelers alike, Eyewitness Travel Guides are the most colorful and comprehensive guides on the market. With beautifully commissioned photographs and spectacular 3-D aerial views revealing the charm of each destination, these amazing travel guides show what others only tell. Includes beautiful new full-color photos, illustrations, and enhanced maps, with extensive information on local customs, currency, medical services, and transportation New "Discovering" feature helps decide which regions are best suited to the trip.

Colonial Mexico 2 Ed: A Guide to Historic Districts and Towns

By Chicki Mallan, Oz Mallan

The intriguing colonial heritage of Mexico is profiled in this detailed and informative guide. Chicki Mallan leads readers through cities such as San Miguel de Allende, Mérida, and Veracruz, revealing 500-year-old churches, Spanish haciendas, and imposing palaces in styles ranging from neoclassical to Mudejar. She also emphasizes distinctive areas to shop in each city. Past and present are celebrated with coverage of festivals, indigenous arts and crafts, and photos taken by Oz Mallan.

Choose Mexico for Retirement, 10th: Information for Travel, Retirement, Investment, and Affordable Living (Choose Retirement Series)

By John Howells, Don Merwin

With information on travel, business opportunities, cost of living, medical care, culture, climate and more, this book will define exciting and different options for retirement.

Michelin Green Guide Mexico Guatemala Belize, 3e (Michelin Green Guide: Mexico, Guatemala and Belize English Edition)

By Michelin

The long-standing Michelin Travel Guides are an ideal travel companion for travelers who really want to connect with the world. Get to know the local way of life through detailed background information on the country, people, and culture. Quickly identify the best places to visit using Michelin's star rating system. The best sites are highlighted on the sites map or you can follow a pre-planned driving tour.

Hola — Where can I sign up to take Spanish language classes?

L'Alliance Francaise

Address: Calle 23 #117 by Calle 24
Colonia México
Ask for: Diana Castillo
Telephone: (999) 927-2403

Instituto Benjamin Franklin

Address: Calle 57 #474-A, between Calle 52 and 54 Street
Centro
Ask for: Rosy Cetina
Telephone: (999) 928-6005
Website: www.benjaminfranklin.com.mx

CIS: Centro de Idiomas del Sureste

Address: Calle 52 #455, between Calle 49 and 51 Street, Centro
Telephone: (999) 923-0954

Address: Calle 11 #203-C by Calle 26, Colonia García Ginéres
Telephone: (999) 920-2810

Address: Calle 14 #106 by Calle 25, Colonia Mexico
Telephone: (999) 926-9494
Ask for: Chloe Pacheco

Website: www.cisyucatan.com.mx

ECORA – Instituto de Idiomas y Centro Cultural

Address: Calle 50 #361, between Calle 53-B and 53-F Street
Colonia Francisco de Montejo
Ask for: Susana Villanueva
Telephone: (999) 953-4974
Website: www.spanishschoolecora.com

Habla: The Center for Language and Culture

Address: Calle 26 #99 B, between Calle 19 and 21 Street
Colonia México
Telephone: (999) 948-1872
Website: www.habla.org

Instituto de Lengua y Cultura de Yucatán

Address: Calle 13 #214, between Calle 28 and 30 Street
Colonia García Ginerés
Ask for: Cecilia Novelo
Telephone: (999) 125-3048
Website: www.ilcymex.com

Institute of Modern Spanish

Address: Calle 15 #520B, between Calle 16-A and 18 Street
Colonia Maya
Ask for: Miguel Ceron
Telephone: (999) 911-0790
Website: www.modernspanish.com

Lengua Alternativa

Address: Calle 37 #539 between Calle 72-A and 74 Street
Colonia García Ginéres
Telephone: (999) 943-9181
Website: www.lengualternativa.com

MJ International

Address: Calle 13 #214, between Calle 28 and 30 Street
Colonia García Ginéres
Ask for: Gabriela Bojorquez
Telephone: (999) 925-4692

UNAM: Centro Peninsular de Ciencias Sociales y Humanidades de la UNAM en Mérida

Address: Calle 43 s/n, between Calle 44 and 46 Street
(Ex Sanatorio Rendón Peniche)
Colonia Industrial
Telephone: (999) 922-8446, Ext. 115

A Note on Language and Accent

Please note that Spanish spoken in the Yucatán is a different and distinct regional accent within Mexico. It is influenced by the Spanish colonial legacy and Yucatec Maya language, which has its own cadence. (Remember, a third of the population of the State of Yucatán speaks Maya!) Yucatec Maya, which is the most-widely spoken indigenous language in Mexico, is harshly melodic, and filled with "sh" sounds (which represented by the letter "x" in the Mayan language).

If you are curious about the emerging "pan-American" standard Spanish, tune in to Univision. Its newscasters are at the forefront of speaking "universal" Spanish, which is fast-becoming the standard for business and news broadcasts. In fact, Univision in Mexico City has courses where broadcasters from other parts of Latin America come to learn this "neutral" speech.

What's the point? Be mindful to ask your instructor to distinguish between a Yucatecan Spanish word or inflection and the "Univision standard Spanish"! After all, you wouldn't want to learn English with a Southern accent if you were in the U.S. – or speak as if you learned in English in Montreal!

THE ABCS OF MID

Is birdwatching an avid pastime here?

Yes, bird watching and birding are a world-class vocation in the Yucatán, and Mérida is the heart of the birding community. But it is Hacienda Chichén, on the outskirts of the ruins of Chichén Itzá that has year-round activities. The annual TOH Bird Festival, by the way, draws birders from the world over.

TOH Bird Festival

www.yucatanbirds.org.mx
Email: *info@yucatanbirds.org.mx*

Hacienda Chichén

Chichén Itzá, Yucatán
Website:
www.haciendachichen.com

Driving directions from Mérida to the Hacienda Chichén: As you stay in the toll Federal highway #180, exit at Piste/Chichén Itzá, it is right at the first toll booth. Make sure you drive to the Chichén Itzá toll booth side of the highway. Once you pay (less than $8 USD) turn right to go towards the town of Piste. In Piste, the road will dead end with the old church on your right near the village's main square. When the road dead-ends, turn left and drive pass the first road sign indicating the archaeological site. Follow the road looking for signs for the "Zona Hotelera" exit. When this road turns to the left towards Xcalacoop, you will see signs indicating the "Zona Hotelera" drive slowly now as you are to take the sharp right turn into the Zona Hotelera road and Chichén Itzá's south entrance; continue on this small rural road until you see the Hacienda Chichén Resort's two ochre-yellow tower entrance.

And here is a listing of organizations of interest to bird watching enthusiasts in Yucatán, most of which have activities in Mérida:

- American Birding Association (ABA): *www.aba.org*
- American Bird Conservancy (ABC): *www.abcbirds.org*
- National Audubon Society: *www.audubon.org*
- Cornell University: *www.cornell.edu*
- BirdLife International: *www.birdlifeinternational.com*
- Programa: Iniciativa para la conservación de las Aves de América de Norte (ICAAN): *www.conabio.org*
- North American Bird Conservation Initiative (NABCI): *www.nabci-us.org*
- CIPAMEX, Organización de Ornitólogos de México:*www.iztacala.unam.mx/cipamex*

If the floors are made of pasta, can you eat them?

If we had a peso every time some idiot referred to the paste tile floors as "pasta" floors, we could retire!

In Spanish, "pasta" means both "pasta" – as in spaghetti or linguine – and it also means "paste," as in a kind of pasty clay. Those beautiful tiles are *paste* tiles, made of *paste* that is colored before it is fired. Talavera tiles are kind of glazed tile, where paint is applied to the clay tile. The origins of the paste tiles so familiar in Spain and Mexico have their origins to the Muslim occupation of the Iberian Peninsula for about eight centuries prior to the discovery of the Americas. Throughout the Middle East beautiful paste tiles, usually with cobalt and turquoise colors, are ubiquitous. *Paahhhstaahhh* tiles? Really? Linguine or angel hair? If you're speaking English, say "paste tiles."

Are there alternative film houses?

Yes, there are three wonderful art film houses in town.

Cairo Cinema Café
Ricardo Ancona, Director
Calle 20 #98A between Calle 15 and 17 Street
Colonia Itzimná
Telephone: (999) 926-5718
Email: *cairocinemacafe@gmail.com*
Website: *www.cairocinemacafe.com*

La 68 Cinema
Paula Haro, Director
Address: Calle 68 #470-A, corner of 55 Street
Centro
To check out schedule:
www.la68.com/casa-de-cultura-Merida/cartelera-documentales.html
Website: *www.la68.com*

El Nuevo Teatrito
Miguel Elenes Inchaurregui, Director
Calle 25 #91, by Calle 14
Colonia Chuburná de Hidalgo
Email for current films:
miguel.elenes@gmail.com

In addition, the State's Instituto de Cultural de Yucatan, known as ICY, sponsors wonderful film festivals throughout the year, and all are free and open to the public. To check out the current cultura programming, visit: *www.culturalyucatan.com*.

Mérida is so close to Cuba – Can I travel to Cuba?

Yes, there are lots of options to travel to Cuba from Mérida, and many Mexican, Canadian and European nationals living in Mérida do travel to Cuba. **But if you are a U.S. citizen or Resident Alien please heed the following warning!**

American Citizens and Resident Aliens who wish to travel to Cuba:

Here is an important notice, so important it's capitalized and in bold letters. Read it!

> **IMPORTANT NOTICE:**
> U.S. CITIZENS AND RESIDENT ALIENS MUST BE IN POSSESSION OF A VALID LICENSE TO TRAVEL TO CUBA. LICENSES CAN BE SECURED BY WRITING MR. JEFFERY BRAUNGER, OFFICICE OF FOREIGN ASSETS CONTROL, CUBA DESK, TREASURY DEPARTMENT, WASHINGTON, D.C. 20220. IT IS A FEDERAL CRIME FOR U.S. CITIZENS AND RESIDENT ALIENS TO TRAVEL TO CUBA WITHOUT A LICENSE FROM THE OFFICE OF FOREIGN ASSETS CONTROL.

4 Museums & Galleries

Museum of Anthropology & History

An extensive exhibition of archaeological, anthropological and ethnographic materials related to the Maya civilization and the history of archaeology in the peninsula.

    Address: Palacio Cantón, Paseo Montejo and 43rd Street
    Hours: Tuesday-Saturday, 8 AM to 8 PM; Sunday, 8 AM to 2 PM; closed on Monday
    Website:*www.inah.gob.mx*
    Admission: $37 pesos for adults, children under 13, senior citizens over 60, students with valid IDs and teachers with valid credentials are admitted free.

Museum of Contemporary Art of Yucatán (MACAY) Museum

A permanent exhibition of work by Yucatecan artists.

    Address: Calle 60, entrance in the corridor flanking the south side of the Cathedral
    Hours: Monday, 10 AM to 6 PM; Wednesday-Thursday, 10 AM to 6 PM; Friday-Saturday, 10 AM to 8 PM; Sunday 10 AM to 6 PM; closed on Tuesday
    Website:*www.macay.org*
    Admission: Free

Casa Frederick Catherwood

This gallery and gift store houses a permanent exhibition of Frederick Catherwood's lithographs of 1844, "Views of Ancient Monuments in Central America, Chiapas & Yucatán," in a beautifully restored Belle Epoque manse. This is the only gallery in town that has won critical acclaim from the international community. A "Fair Trade" gift shop on the first level has an extensive selection of silver by National Geographic Society sponsored Mexican silversmiths and jewelry designers.

    Address: Calle 59 #572 between Calle 72 and 74 Street
    Hours: Monday-Saturday, 9 AM to 2 PM and 5 PM to 9 PM; Closed on Sunday
    Website:*casa-catherwood.com*
    Admission: $50 pesos for adults, children under 12 are admitted free.

MUSEUMS & GALLERIES

Casa Museo Montés Molina

The only mansion in Mérida that retains its original Victorian and Edwardian eras splendor, including its lavish furnishings, which coincide with the "Golden Age" of the Yucatán's sisal/henequen wealth. This is one of the homes that gave Mérida the moniker, "Paris of the West" in the 1900s and 1910s.

Address: Paseo de Montejo #469 between Calle 33 and 35 Street
Hours: English language house tours, Monday-Friday at 9 AM, 11 AM and 3 PM; closed to the public on Saturday and Sunday
Website:*www.laquintamm.com*
Admission: $50 pesos for adults, $25 pesos for children

Museum of the City

Housed in the former Main Post & Telegraph offices, built in 1910 to commemorate Mexico's Centennial, the museum houses a curious selection of historical documents, artifacts and material related to the origins and development of Mérida, some which dates back to when it was T-hó, the original Maya city before the arrival of the Spanish.

Address: Calle 65 between Calle 56 and 56-A Street
Hours: Tuesday-Friday, 8 AM to 8 PM; Saturday-Sunday, 8 AM to 2 PM; closed Monday
Admission: Free

Tataya Gallery

Galería Tataya specializes in contemporary and mid-career Mexican and Cuban painters. They have a constant flow of new works and hold 6 to 8 exhibitions a year. In addition, they sell the highest quality Mexican "*artesanías*" (handcrafts), coming Chiapas, Oaxaca, Michoacán, Sinaloa, Chihuahua, etc., most pieces being "one of a kind."

Address: Calle 60 #409, between Calle 45 and 47 Street
Hours: Tuesday-Saturday, 10 AM to 2 PM and 4 PM to 7 PM and/or by appointment; closed on Sunday and Monday
Telephone: (999) 928-2962
Website: *www.tataya.com.mx*
Admission: Free

La Luz Gallery

A gallery specializing in contemporary Cuban artists. Representing critically-acclaimed Havana-based painters, this gallery in an important source for collectors in Paris, Madrid, Los Angeles and New York.

69

Address: Calle 60 #415 between Calle 45 and 47 Street
Hours: Monday-Friday, 10 AM to 2 PM and 4 PM to 7 PM; Saturday, 10 AM to 7 PM; closed on Sunday
Website: *www.laluzgaleria.com*
Admission: Free

Museum of the Yucatecan Song (Museo de la Canción Yucateca)

A permanent exhibition of photographs, recordings, musical instruments and other artifacts that made Yucatecan music and musicians famous throughout the world. You may not recognize the names of Armando Manzanero, Pastor Cervera, Guty Cárdenas or Ricardo Palmerin, but when you hear their music, you will immediately recognize it from the radio programs and Hollywood films of yesteryear.

Address: Calle 47 #464-A, on the corner of 48 Street
Hours: Tuesday-Sunday, 9 AM to 5 PM; closed on Monday
Website: *www.enjoymexico.net/mexico/Merida-museos-mexico.php*
Admission: $15 pesos, except on Sundays when admission is free

"Juan Gamboa Guzmán" Pinacotea Museum

A permanent exhibition of paintings and sculptures housed in an adjunct entrance to the Church of the Three Orders, whose architecture is of more interest than the works displayed.

Address: Calle 59, side entrance to the church, between Calle 58 and 60 Street
Hours: Tuesday-Saturday, 8 AM to 8 PM; Sunday, 8 AM to 2 PM; closed on Monday
Website: *www.enjoymexico.net/mexico/merida-museos-mexico.php*
Admission: Free

Mérida Gallery

This gallery focuses on emerging Yucatecan artists with a wide following, and has rotating exhibitions approximately 10 times a year.

Address: Calle 59 #452 between Calle 52 and 54 Street
Hours: Wednesday-Monday, 9:30 AM to 6:30 PM; closed on Tuesday
Website: *www.galeriamerida.com/index.htm*
Admission: Free

Museum of Popular Folk Art

A charming exhibition of folk art from the Yucatán and central Mexico.

Address: Calle 50-A #487 by 57 Street
Hours: Tuesday-Saturday, 9:30 AM to 6:30 PM; Sunday, 9 AM to 2 PM; closed on Monday
Website: *www.enjoymexico.net/mexico/merida-museos-mexico.php*

Admission: $20 pesos

City Art Museum (GAMM)

A populist exhibition of local artists, specializing in naïve and outsider works of art.

Address: Calle 65, between Calle 56 and 56-A Street
Hours: Tuesday-Friday, 9 AM to 8 PM; Saturday-Sunday, 9 AM to 2 PM; closed on Monday
Website: *www.merida.gob.mx/capitalcultural/galeria_arte/inicio.htm*
Admission: Free

In La'Kech Gallery

An innovative art space evoking a certain counter-culture perspective, this small gallery features work by some of Mérida's cutting edge emerging artists.

Address: Calle 60 #595-A, between Calle 73 and 75 Street
Hours: Hours not yet set, so please call (999) 242-3948, or if you drop by and ring the bell.
Website: *www.galeriainlakech.com/index_en.php*
Admission: Free

La Clínica - Arte Contemporáneo

A cutting-edge gallery that showcases Mexican and foreign artists under the Alfredo Cruz and Terrence Jon Dyck, La Clínica strives to bring contemporary art to a hipster level.

Address: Calle 62 #367 between Calle 43 and 45 Street
Hours: Visit their website for events, or call (999) 924-0734 for an appointment.
Website: *www.arte-clinica.com/*
Admission: Free

5 Restaurants in Mérida & Environs

Mérida is a city of foodies, but not of great restaurants.

People who love food have long known that. Jeremiah Tower, who along with Alice Waters made Chez Panisse the culinary tour de force that it is, lives here. Martha Stewart swings in to take a cooking class; *New York Magazine* critic Gael Greene spends a month sampling the peninsula's food offerings and restaurants. Gilbert Le Coze, of Le Bernardin, was fascinated by Maya marinades using Seville oranges when he was here. Jacques Pepin has been in town on several occasions, and he has a home in Playa del Carmen. The private chef for Buckingham Palace spent a week not too long ago, anxious to learn about techniques for "enlivening" the offerings for Her Majesty, and years back Julia Child ventured here in search of the "perfect" free range turkey.

Recipes from the Yucatán find their way in the "Slow Food" cookbook, and our region's cuisine caused a sensation in San Francisco in the summer of 2008 when "Tamales Yucatecos" were served at the Slow Food Nation convention, the first time ever, in the United States. That said, we can also say with confidence that international fast food restaurants are consistent around the world. McDonald's, Burger King, KFC, Pizza Hut, Chili's, etc. in Mérida are the same as what you find anywhere else. The same can be said of the kinds of restaurant choices one finds at international hotel chains, from the Marriott to the Hyatt, the Fiesta Americana to the Intercontinental. We are neither reviewing nor listing these restaurants in this section, since they are found in most guidebooks and online resources.

Now, a word about why Yucatecos don't frequent great restaurants. For a variety of reasons, cultural norms encourage home cooking, and many families boast tremendous culinary talents in their families. That is different from having a society, like in Buenos Aires, Barcelona, Tokyo or Paris, where people go out for great meals, whether at a sidewalk café, neighborhood bistro or full-service restaurant. The same can be said of the United States and Canada, where even in New York, the city that pretends it is the city that never sleeps, almost all kitchens take their last orders at 10:30 PM, and if it's 1 AM and you want a meal, you're likely to end up at 24-hour fast-food place. If you notice that our listing differs from what you find in your guidebooks, remember: *Travel writers are seldom restaurant critics, and many concentrate on the familiar paths tourists take while in town.* This is not a criticism; it is reality. Not one guidebook, for example, lists Restaurant Byblos, probably because none is prepared to venture to the Lebanese Social & Sports Club, thinking that it is a private club.

With this background, here is a comprehensive listing of restaurants that we have been to, or our guests have enjoyed, or that friends and colleagues have recommended. They have been arranged by neighborhood. So go out there and have a great meal somewhere in town!

Centro (Downtown) - Restaurants

Amaro
Cuisine: Yucatecan and Vegetarian
Telephone: (999) 928-2451
Address: Calle 59 #507, between Calle 60 and 62 Street
Parking: No (in public parking lots nearby)
Air Conditioned: No
Outdoors: Yes
Drinks: Full bar
Hours: Daily, 11 AM to 2 AM
Website: *www.restauranteamaro.com*

Bella Epoca
Cuisine: Yucatecan
Telephone: (999) 928-1928
Address: Calle 60 #497, between Calle 57 and 59 Street
Parking: 2 doors north of the restaurant is a parking lot
Air Conditioned: No
Outdoors: Yes
Drinks: Full bar
Hours: Daily, 5 PM to 1 AM

Café Alameda
Cuisine: Lebanese
Telephone: (999) 928 3635
Address: Intersection of Calle 58 and Calle 55

Parking: Next door in a public lot
Air Conditioned: No
Drinks: Beer and soft drinks
Hours: Daily, 8:00 AM to 5:00 PM

Café Chocolate
Cuisine: Coffee Shop
Telephone: (999) 928-5113
Address: Intersection of Calle 60 Calle 49
Parking: Yes
Air Conditioned: No
Outdoors: Yes
Drinks: No alcohol is served
Hours: Daily, 7 AM to 12 AM
Website: *www.cafe-chocolate.com.mx*

Café Club Manushan
Cuisine: Café
Telephone: (999) 923-1592
Address: Intersection of Calle 55 and Calle 58
Parking: Next door in the public lot
Air Conditioned: One room is sometimes air conditioned
Outdoors: Yes
Drinks: Beer and soft drinks
Hours: Monday-Saturday from 7:00 AM to 5:00 PM

Café El Hoyo
Cuisine: Café
Telephone: (999) 928-1531
Address: Calle 62 #487, between Calle 59 and 57 Street
Parking: No
Air Conditioned: No
Outdoors: Yes
Drinks: Lattes, soft drinks, non-alcoholic beverages
Hours: Monday- Saturday from 9 AM to 11 PM
Facebook:
www.facebook.com/pages/cafe-el-hoyo/103219969831#!/pages/cafe-el-hoyo/103219969831?v=wall

Café La Habana
Cuisine: Coffee shop, Yucatán-style breakfasts
Telephone: (999) 928-0608
Address: Intersection of Calle 59 and 62 Street
Parking: Across the street in city parking lot
Air Conditioned: Yes
Outdoors: No
Drinks: Full bar
Drinks: 24 hours

Café Peón Contreras
Cuisine: International
Telephone: (999) 924-7003
Address: Calle 60, between Calle 57 and 59 Street
Parking: No
Air Conditioned: Yes
Outdoors: Yes
Drinks: Full bar
Hours: Daily, 7 AM to 1 AM

Café Pop
Cuisine: Coffee, breakfasts and light lunches
Telephone: (999) 928-6163
Address: Calle 57, between Calle 60 and 62 Street
Parking: Street parking
Air Conditioned: Yes
Outdoors: No
Drinks: Coffees, teas and breakfasts
Hours: Daily, 7AM to 12 AM

Café Santiago de Chile
Cuisine: Coffee and breakfasts
Telephone: (999) 154-5565
Address: Calle 59 #572, between Calle 70 and 72 Street
Parking: Street parking
Air Conditioned: No
Outdoors: Yes
Drinks: Coffees, teas and breakfasts
Hours: Monday-Saturday, 7AM to 1 PM
Facebook:
www.facebook.com/pages/Mérida-Mexico/Cafe-Santiago-de-Chile/101782199884142?v=info&ref=ts#!/pages/Mérida-Mexico/Cafe-Santiago-de-Chile/101782199884142?v=wall&ref=ts

Casa Lucia
Cuisine: International, mostly Italian
Telephone: (999) 928 2863
Address: Calle 60 #474 A between Calle 53 and 55 Street
Parking: No
Air Conditioned: Yes
OUTDOORS: Yes
Drinks: Full bar
Drinks: Daily, 7:30 AM to 11:00 PM
Website: www.casalucia.com.mx

El Gallito
Cuisine: Yucatecan
Telephone: (999) 928-6495
Address: Calle 45 between Calle 60 and 62 Street
Parking: Yes, across the street
Air Conditioned: No
Outdoors: Yes
Drinks: Soft drinks, beer and hard liquors
Hours: Daily, 11 AM to 7 PM
Website: *cantinasdemerida.blogspot.com/2006/10/el-gallito.html*

El Trapiche
Cuisine: Tacos and Yucatecan food
Telephone: (999) 928 1231
Address: Calle 62 #491 between Calle 59 and 61 Street
Parking: No
Air Conditioned: No
Outdoors: Yes
Drinks: Beer and soft drinks
Hours: Daily, 7:00 AM to 11:00 PM

Hotel Casa del Balam
Cuisine: Yucatecan and International
Telephone: (999) 924-8844
Address: Calle 60 #488 by 57 Street
Parking: Yes
Air Conditioned: Yes
Outdoors: Yes
Drinks: Full bar
Hours: Daily, 7 AM to 12 PM
Website: *www.casadelbalam.com*

La Blanca Mérida
Cuisine: Yucatecan
Address: Calle 62 and 59 Street
Parking: No
Air Conditioned: Yes
Outdoors: No
Drinks: Soft drinks and beers
Hours: Daily, 7AM to 2 AM

La Casa de Frida
Cuisine: Mexican
Telephone: (999) 928-2311
Address: Calle 61 #526-A between Calle 66 and 68 Street
Parking: No
Air Conditioned: No
Outdoors: Yes
Drinks: Full bar
Hours: Monday-Friday: 6 PM to 10 PM; Saturday: 12 AM to 5 PM and 6 PM to 10 PM; Sunday: 12 AM to 5 PM
Website: *www.lacasadefrida.com.mx*

La Casa de Te
Cuisine: Tea/Coffee House with salads and crepes
Address: Calle 62 between Calle 55 and 57 Street
Parking: No
Air Conditioned: No
Outdoors: Yes
Drinks: Soft drinks, coffees and teas
Hours: Monday – Saturday, 3:00 PM to 11:00 PM

La Chaya Maya
Cuisine: Yucatecan
Telephone: (999) 928 4780
Address: Calle 62 and 57 Street
Parking: In adjacent city parking lot
Air Conditioned: Yes
Outdoors: No
Drinks: Beer and soft drinks
Hours: 7 AM to 11 PM Every Day

La Choperia
Cuisine: Brazilian and Mexican fusion

Telephone: (999) 924-4488
Address: Calle 56 #456 between Calle 51 and 53 Street
Parking: Yes
Air Conditioned: Yes
Outdoors: Yes
Drinks: Full bar
Hours: Tuesday to Saturday: 1 PM to 2 AM; Sunday 1 PM to 7 PM.

La Flor de Santiago
Cuisine: Coffee and breakfast/lunch diner
Telephone: (999) 928-5591
Address: Calle 70 between Calle 57 and 59 Street
Parking: No
Air Conditioned: Yes
Outdoors: Yes
Drinks: Coffees, teas, soft drinks and beer
Hours: Daily, 7AM to 2 AM

La Sabia Virtud
Cuisine: Mexican
Telephone: (999) 252-0380
Address: Calle 55 #504 between Calle 60 and 62 Street
Parking: No
Air Conditioned: Yes
Outdoors: No
Drinks: Soft drinks
Hours: Monday-Wednesday: 7:30 AM to 6 PM; Thursday- Saturday: 7:30 AM to 10 PM; Sunday: 8 AM to 6 PM
Websites: www.lasabiavirtud.com

Los Almendros
Cuisine: Yucatecan
Telephone: (999) 923-8135
Address: Calle 57 #468 by 52 Street
Parking: Yes
Air Conditioned: Yes
Outdoors: No
Drinks: Full bar
Hours: Daily, 12 AM to 6 PM

Los Henequenes
Cuisine: Yucatecan
Telephone: (999) 923-6220
Address: Calle 57 #479 by 56 Street
Parking: Street parking available
Air Conditioned: Yes
Outdoors: No
Drinks: Full bar
Hours: Daily, 11 AM to 7 PM
Website: www.loshenequenes.com

Pan E Vino
Cuisine: Italian
Address: Calle 59 and 64 Street
Parking: No
Air Conditioned: Yes
Outdoors: No
Drinks: Full bar
Hours: Tuesday-Saturday: 7 PM to 2 AM; Sunday: 1PM to 2 AM, Closed on Monday

Pancho's
Cuisine: Mexican &Yucatecan
Telephone: (999) 923-0942
Address: Calle 59, between Calle 60 and 52 Street
Parking: City parking on the corner of Calle 62 and 59 Street
Air Conditioned: No
Outdoors: Yes
Drinks: Full bar
Hours: Daily, 6PM to 2 AM
Website: www.trottersmerida.com

Pizzas Raffaelo
Cuisine: Pizza

Neighborhood: Centro
Telephone: (999) 924-9943
Address: Calle 60 by 49 Street
Parking: No
Air Conditioned: Yes
Outdoors: No
Drinks: Soft drinks
Hours: Monday-Friday, 12 PM to 4 PM and 5:30 PM to 11:30 PM; Saturday-Sunday, 5 PM to 12 AM

Portico del Peregrino
Cuisine: Yucatecan with some international cuisine
Telephone: (999) 928-6163
Address: Calle 57 by 60 Street
Parking: City parking on the corner of Calle 62 and 57 Street
Air Conditioned: Yes
Outdoors: Yes
Drinks: Full bar
Hours: 24 hours

Restaurant San José
Cuisine: Yucatecan
Telephone: (999) 928-6657
Address: Calle 63, between Calle 62 and 64 Street
Parking: No
Air Conditioned: No
Outdoors: Yes
Drinks: Beer and Soft Drinks
Hours: Daily, 7:00 AM to 10:30 PM

Siqueff
Cuisine: Lebanese and International
Telephone: (999) 925-5027
Address: Calle 60 #350, between Calle 35 and 37 Street
Parking: Yes
Air Conditioned: Yes
Outdoors: Yes
Drinks: Full bar
Hours: Daily, 8 AM to 6 PM

Colonia Alcalá- Restaurants

La Tradición
Cuisine: Yucatecan
Telephone: (999) 925-2526
Address: Calle 60 #293 by 25 Street
Parking: Yes
Air Conditioned: Yes
Outdoors: No
Drinks: Full bar
Hours: Daily, 11:30 AM to 6:30 PM

Pimienta
Cuisine: Yucatecan, but only breakfast and lunch
Telephone: (999) 920-2953
Address: Calle 60 #326, between Calle 23 and 25 Street
Parking: Street parking
Air Conditioned: Yes
Outdoors: No
Drinks: Full bar
Hours: Daily at 8 AM to 6 PM

Colonia Benito Juárez Norte (Prolongación Montejo Norte) - Restaurants

Buda Wok
  Cuisine: Chinese/International
  Telephone: (999) 948-3088
  Address: Prolongación Montejo #367, between Calle 47 and 49 Street
  Parking: Yes
  Air Conditioned: Yes
  Outdoors: Yes
  Drinks: Full bar
  Hours: Monday-Saturday: 1 PM to 2 AM and Sunday: 1 PM a 6 PM

Konsushi
  Cuisine: Japanese
  Telephone: (999) 948-1377
  Address: Calle 46-A #485, on the corner of Calle 33
  Parking: Yes
  Air Conditioned: Yes
  Outdoors: Yes
  Drinks: Domestic and International beers
  Hours: Daily, 1 PM to 12 AM

La Recova
  Cuisine: Argentinian steakhouse
  Telephone: (999) 944-0215
  Address: Prolongación Montejo #382 between Calle 33 and 35 Street
  Parking: Yes (Valet)
  Air Conditioned: Yes
  Outdoors: No
  Drinks: Full bar
  Hours: Monday-Saturday: 1 PM to 2 AM; Sunday: 1 PM to 12 AM
  Website: www.larecovamerida.com

Colonia Buenavista - Restaurants

Meyer's
  Cuisine: Deli
  Telephone: (999) 926-0117
  Address: Calle 13 Local #7, between Calle 36 and 38 Street
  Parking: Yes
  Air Conditioned: Yes
  Outdoors: Yes
  Drinks: Full bar
  Hours: Daily, 7AM to 11 PM

Muelle 8
  Cuisine: Seafood
  Telephone: (999) 944-5343
  Address: Calle 21 #142 between Calle 30 and 32 Street
  Parking: Street parking
  Air Conditioned: Yes
  Outdoors: No
  Drinks: Full bar
  Hours: Daily, 12 PM to 6 PM

La Tratto
  Cuisine: Italian
  Telephone: (999) 927-0434
  Address: Avenida Paseo Montejo #479-C
  Parking: Street parking
  Air Conditioned: No
  Outdoors: Yes
  Drinks: Full bar
  Hours: Daily, 6 PM to 2 AM
  Website: www.trottersmerida.com

RESTAURANTS

Rincón Oaxaqueño
Cuisine: Oaxacan
Telephone: (999) 286-9492
Address: Circuito Colonias #151 between Calle 40 and 60 Street
Parking: Yes
Air Conditioned: Yes
Drinks: Soft drinks
Hours: Tuesday to Saturday: 12 AM to 11 PM; Sunday: 9 pm to 5 PM

Trotters
Cuisine: Steak, Fish, Salads, Tapas
Telephone: (999) 927-2310
Address: Circuito Colonias, between Prolongación Montejo and Calle 60 Norte, adjacent to the Renault dealer
Parking: Yes
Air Conditioned: Yes
Outdoors: Yes
Drinks: Full bar
Hours: Monday-Saturday: 1 PM to 2 AM, Sunday: 1PM to 6 PM
Website: *www.trottersmerida.com*

Colonia Campestre - Restaurants

Café La Habana
Cuisine: Coffee shop, Yucatán-style breakfasts
Telephone: (999) 928-0608
Address: Prolongación Montejo #260, across from Club Campestre
Parking: Street parking
Air Conditioned: Yes
Outdoors: No
Drinks: Full bar
Hours: 24 hours

One Burger
Cuisine: Hamburgers and fries
Telephone: (999) 948-2626
Address: Prolongación Montejo #250, across from Club Campestre
Parking: Street parking
Air Conditioned: Yes
Outdoors: Yes
Drinks: Shakes and sodas
Hours: Sunday – Wednesday, 12 PM - 11 PM; Thursday – Saturday, 12 PM t- 2 AM.

Colonia Díaz Ordaz (Most near Paseo de Montejos at Monumento a la Patria) - Restaurants

Cubaro
Cuisine: International
Telephone: (999) 926-6587
Address: Monumento a la Patria and Paseo de Montejo
Parking: Valet or on along the side streets
Air Conditioned: No
Outdoors: Yes
Drinks: Full bar
Hours: Daily, 1PM to 2 AM

Meson del Conde
Cuisine: Spanish

Telephone: (999) 943-2828
Address: Avenida Correa Rancho #370
Parking: Yes
Air Conditioned: Yes
Outdoors: Yes
Drinks: Full bar
Hours: Daily, 11 AM to 7 PM

Nectar
Cuisine: International
Telephone: (999) 938-0838
Address: Avenida 21 #413 between Calle 6-A and 8 Street
Parking: Yes
Air Conditioned: Yes
Outdoors: No
Drinks: Full bar
Hours: Tuesday-Saturday: 7 PM to 2 AM; Sunday: 1 PM to 2 AM, Closed on Monday
Website: www.nectarmerida.com

Slavia
Cuisine: Tapas and International Entrees
Telephone: (999) 926-6587
Address: Monumento a la Patria and Paseo de Montejo
Parking: Yes, valet parking and some limited parking on the street
Air Conditioned: Yes
Outdoors: No
Drinks: Full bar
Hours: Daily, 6 PM to 2 AM

Tobago
Cuisine: Coffees, teas and desserts
Telephone: (999) 926-6587
Address: Monumento a la Patria and Paseo de Montejo
Parking: Valet parking at Slavia
Air Conditioned: No
Outdoors: Yes
Drinks: Full bar
Hours: Every Day: 6 PM to 2 AM

Colonia Emilio Zapata Norte (Prolongación Montejo Norte) - Restaurants

El Argentino
Cuisine: Steak House
Telephone: (999) 926-5444
Address: Prolongación Montejo #116, by Calle 25
Parking: Ample street parking
Air Conditioned: Yes
Outdoors: No
Drinks: Full bar
Hours: Monday- Saturday: 1 PM to 12 AM, Sunday 1 PM to 8 PM

La Rueda
Cuisine: Steak House
Telephone: (999) 912-2387
Address: Calle 37 #352-A by 67-B Street
Parking: Yes
Air Conditioned: Yes
Outdoors: No
Drinks: Full bar
Hours: Daily, 12 PM to 2 AM

Miyabi
Cuisine: Japanese
Telephone: (999) 948-9896
Address: Prolongación Montejo and Calle 34, inside the shopping center
Parking: Yes

Air Conditioned: Yes
Outdoors: No
Drinks: Non-alcoholic beverages, but customers can bring their own liquor.
Hours: Tuesday to Sunday: 1 PM to 11 PM

Tapıoca Joe
Cuisine: Teas and smoothies
Address: Calle 34 #396, between Calle 39 and 41 Street
Parking: Yes
Air Conditioned: Yes
Outdoors: Yes
Drinks: Beverages
Hours: Monday - Thursday, 12 PM to 9 PM; Friday – Saturday, 12 PM to 10:30 PM; Sunday, 12:30 PM to 7 PM.
Website: www.tapiocajoe.com
Facebook: www.facebook.com/people/Tapioca-Joe/100000638496040

Colonia García Ginerés - Restaurants

El Tıo Rıcardo
Cuisine: Steak House
Telephone: (999) 925-2967
Address: Calle 8 #201 and 23 Street
Parking: Street parking
Air Conditioned: Yes
Outdoors: No
Drinks: Full bar
Hours: 24 hours

Los Platos Rotos
Cuisine: Central Mexican
Telephone: (999) 925-3097
Address: Calle 33-D #498, Suite 3, by Reforma
Parking: Street parking
Air Conditioned: No
Outdoors: Yes
Drinks: Soft Drinks and fruit juices
Hours: Monday – Friday, 8 AM to about 3 PM

Colonia Itzimná - Restaurants

Due Torrı
Cuisine: Italian
Telephone: (999) 926-2505
Address: Calle 27 #349 between Calle 10 and 12 Street
Parking: Ample street parking
Air Conditioned: Yes
Outdoors: Yes
Drinks: Full bar
Hours: Daily, 1 PM to 11:15 PM

Entre Tangos
Cuisine: Steak House
Telephone: (999) 938-1838
Address: Ave. Pérez Ponce 118, between Calle 21 and 23 Street
Parking: Yes
Air Conditioned: Yes
Outdoors: No
Drinks: Full bar
Hours: Tuesday -Saturday: 1 PM to 12 AM; Sunday: 1 PM to 6 PM

Wıne House Internatıonal
Cuisine: International
Telephone: (999) 286-8029
Address: Calle 20 #91-A, between Calle 15 and 17 Street
Parking: Yes

Air Conditioned: Yes
Outdoors: Yes
Drinks: Full bar, specializing in rums

Hours: Tuesday – Sunday, 1:30 PM to 12 AM; Closed Mondays

Colonia Jesús Carranza - Restaurants

Hacienda San Antonio
Cuisine: Steak and Tacos
Neighborhood: Colonia Jesús Carranza
Telephone: (999) 926-0480
Address: Calle 27 by 44 Street
Parking: Yes
Air Conditioned: Yes
Outdoors: Yes
Drinks: Soft Drinks and beer
Hours: Daily, 12 PM to 7 PM

Colonia Mejorada - Restaurants

El Café
Cuisine: Breakfast and Lunch
Telephone: (999) 924-0117
Address: Calle 59 #452-A between Calle 52 and 54 Street
Parking: Public parking across the street
Air Conditioned: No
Outdoors: Yes
Drinks: Coffees, teas and soft Drinks
Hours: Daily, 7:30 AM to 4 PM

Colonia Mexico - Restaurants

Acitrón
Cuisine: International, but with a Yucatecan twist
Telephone: (999) 926-0707
Address: Calle 30 #122-A, between Calle 27 and 29 Street, Plaza la Avenida (along Prolongación Montejo)
Parking: Street parking
Air Conditioned: Yes
Outdoors: Yes
Drinks: Full bar
Hours: Tuesday through Saturday, 1 PM to 2 AM; Sunday 1 PM to 6 PM
Facebook: www.facebook.com/pages/merida-Mexico/ACITRON/75112500828

Acqua
Cuisine: International
Telephone: (999) 926-8211
Address: Calle 21 #73, between Calle 12 and 14 Street
Parking: Yes
Air Conditioned: Yes
Outdoors: Yes
Drinks: Full bar
Hours: Monday-Saturday: 1.30 PM to 2 AM; Sunday: 1PM to 5 PM and Monday: 6 PM to 1 AM

BBT Wings
Cuisine: American
Telephone: (999) 254-0909
Address: Calle 27 #98, between Calle 20 and 18 Street

Parking: Yes
Air Conditioned: Yes
Outdoors: Yes
Drinks: Full bar
Hours: Daily, from 6 PM to 2 AM

Bennigan's
Cuisine: American
Telephone: (999) 927-2731
Address: Intersection of Prolongación Montejo and Calle 27
Parking: Yes
Air Conditioned: Yes
Outdoors: Yes
Drinks: Full bar
Hours: Sunday-Tuesday: 1 PM-12 AM; Wednesday-Thursday: 12 PM - 1 AM; Friday-Saturday: 1 PM – 2 AM
Website: www.bennigans.com

Buenos Aires City
Cuisine: Steak House
Telephone: (999) 927-9090
Address: Circuito Colonias corner of Calle 12
Parking: Yes
Air Conditioned: Yes
Outdoors: Yes
Drinks: Full bar
Hours: Daily, 1 PM to 12 AM
Website: www.buenosairescity.com.mx

Campay
Cuisine: Japanese
Telephone: (999) 948-0385
Address: Calle 19 #106 on the corner of 22 Street
Parking: Street parking
Air Conditioned: Yes
Outdoors: No
Drinks: Full bar
Hours: Daily, 1 PM to 11 PM

Go Green
Cuisine: Salad Bar
Address: Prolongación Montejo and 19 Street
Parking: Yes
Air Conditioned: Yes
Outdoors: Yes
Drinks: Soft Drinks
Hours: 24 hours

Guru
Cuisine: Lebanese
Telephone: (999) 252-8400
Address: Calle 20 S/N (in Mexico, "S/N" means "without a number," meaning it's a short street with only one or two buildings, or a sliver of land dissected by major roads; this restaurant is across from the Pemex gas station on Calle 20)
Parking: Yes
Air Conditioned: Yes
Outdoors: Yes
Drinks: Full bar
Hours: Tuesday- Saturday: 1 PM to 2 AM; Sunday 1 PM to 6 PM
Facebook: www.facebook.com/group.php?gid=42910880447

La Nao de China
Cuisine: Chinese
Telephone: (999) 926-1441
Address: Circuito Colonias #13, between Prolongación Paseo Montejo and Chapur Department Store
Parking: Yes
Air Conditioned: Yes
Outdoors: No

Drinks: Soft drinks and beers
Hours: Daily, 11 AM to 9 PM

La Parrilla
Cuisine: Mexican
Telephone: (999) 944-3999
Address: Calle 30 #87 by 17 Street
Parking: Yes
Air Conditioned: Yes
Outdoors: Yes
Drinks: Full bar
Hours: Daily, 12 PM to 2 AM
Website: www.laparrilla.com.mx

Sushi Itto
Cuisine: Sushi
Telephone: (999) 944-3232
Address: Prolongación Montejo #348, between Calle 29 and 31 Street
Parking: Yes
Air Conditioned: Yes
Outdoors: Yes
Drinks: National and imported beers
Hours: Monday-Tuesday: 1 PM to 11 PM; Wednesday-Saturday: 1 PM to 12 AM; Sunday: 1 PM to 10 PM
Website: www.sushi-itto.com.mx

Taquitos PM
Cuisine: Mexican (tacos)
Telephone: (999) 944-0342
Address: Prolongación Montejo #382 on the corner of Calle 35
Parking: No
Air Conditioned: No
Outdoors: Yes
Drinks: Full bar
Hours: Monday-Thursday, 7 PM to 2 AM; Friday-Sunday, 12 PM to 2 AM
Facebook: www.facebook.com/pages/Mérida-Mexico/Los-Taquitos-de-PM/30715198715

Todo Latino
Cuisine: Pan-Latin American
Telephone: (999) 926-8090
Address: Avenida 31 #109, between Calle 22 and 24 Street
Parking: Yes
Air Conditioned: Yes
Outdoors: Yes, a rooftop area with seating
Drinks: Full bar
Hours: Wednesday to Monday, 12:30 PM to 2 AM; Sunday, 12:30 PM to 6 PM

Colonia Mexico Norte - Restaurants

Byblos
Cuisine: Lebanese
Telephone: (999) 899-0141
Address: Calle 1-G #101, between Calle 14-A and 16 Street
Parking: Yes
Air Conditioned: Yes
Outdoors: No
Drinks: Full bar
Hours: Daily, 1 PM to 7 PM

El Postrecito
Cuisine: Desserts and coffee
Telephone: (999) 927-2479
Address: Calle 21 #111 between Calle 22 and 24 Street
Parking: Yes
Air Conditioned: Yes

Outdoors: Yes
Drinks: Soft Drinks
Hours: Monday- Saturday: 12 PM to 11 PM; Sunday from 12 PM to 10 PM
Website: www.elpostrecito.com
Facebook: www.facebook.com/pages/Mérida-Mexico/El-Postrecito/114905387216

Sazón Gourmet
Cuisine: Upscale Mexican dishes, breakfast and lunch
Telephone: (999) 927-8776
Address: Calle 21 #80, between Calle 14 and 16 Street
Parking: Street parking
Air Conditioned: Yes
Outdoors: Yes
Drinks: Full bar
Hours: Monday – Saturday, 8 AM to 4:30 PM

Colonia Mexico Oriente - Restaurants

La Habichuela
Cuisine: Seafood, Pasta, Chicken, Beef
Telephone: (999) 926-3626
Address: Calle 21 #416 by 8 Street
Parking: Yes
Air Conditioned: Yes
Outdoors: Yes
Drinks: Full bar
Hours: Daily, 12 PM to 12 AM
Website: www.lahabichuela.com/merida/merida.htm

Colonia Misne - Restaurants

Hacienda Misne
Cuisine: Yucatecan and International
Telephone: (999) 940-7150
Address: Calle 19 #172
Parking: Yes
Air Conditioned: Yes
Outdoors: Yes
Drinks: Full bar
Hours: Daily, 7AM to 11 PM
Website: www.haciendamisne.com.mx

Colonia Montecristo - Restaurants

Ichi Sushi
Cuisine: Japanese
Neighborhood: Colonia Montecristo
Telephone: (999) 948-0203
Address: Calle 1 #105, between Calle 8 and 10 Street
Parking: Yes
Air Conditioned: Yes
Outdoors: Yes
Drinks: No
Hours: Daily, 1:30 PM to 11 PM

Colonia Monterreal - Restaurants

Sensei
  Cuisine: Sushi Bar
  Telephone: (999) 944-0202
  Address: Calle 37 #202, between Calle 18 and 22 Street
  Parking: Yes

Air Conditioned: Yes
Outdoors: Yes
Drinks: Full bar
Hours: Daily, 1 PM to 12 AM
Website: www.sensei.com.mx

Colonia San Antonio Curul – Restaurants

Vibora de la Mar
  Cuisine: Seafood
  Telephone: (999) 944-9332
  Address: Calle 32 #55, between Calle 55 and 57 Street
  Parking: Yes
  Air Conditioned: Yes
  Outdoors: No

Drinks: Full bar
Hours: Tuesday to Sunday, 1 PM to 11 PM
Facebook: www.facebook.com/group.php?gid=16781836654

Colonia Santa Ana – Restaurants

El Gran Café
  Cuisine: Coffee and Yucatecan
  Telephone: (999) 923 5356
  Address: Remate de Paseo de Montejo and Calle 47
  Parking: Yes
  Air Conditioned: Yes
  Outdoors: Yes
  Drinks: Coffee
  Hours: Daily, 7 AM to 2 AM

Hotel San Angel
  Cuisine: Coffee and snacks, breakfasts and lunch service
  Telephone: (999) 928-1800
  Address: Remate de Montejo #1
  Parking: Yes
  Air Conditioned: Yes
  Outdoors: Yes
  Drinks: No
  Hours: Daily, 7 AM to 10 PM
  Website: www.hotelcasasanangel.com

New York, New York
  Cuisine: Indian and Italian, New York style
  Address: Calle 47 between 58 Street and Paseo Montejo
  Parking: No
  Air Conditioned: No
  Outdoors: Yes
  Drinks: Soft drinks
  Hours: Wednesday – Saturday: 6 PM to 11 PM

La Boheme Café Shop
  Cuisine: Coffees and desserts
  Telephone: (999) 926-6039

Address: Paseo de Montejo #470-B, between Calle 37 and 39 Street
Parking: Street parking
Air Conditioned: No
Outdoors: Yes
Drinks: Coffees, teas and juices
Hours: Monday-Friday 8:30 AM to 8 PM; Saturday: 8:30 AM to 4 PM

Rescoldos Mediterranean Bistro
Cuisine: Mediterranean
Telephone: (999) 286-1028
Address: Calle 62 #366, between Calle 41 and 43 Street
Parking: No
Air Conditioned: Yes
Outdoors: Yes
Drinks: Soft drinks
Hours: Tuesday-Friday 1 PM to 10 PM; Saturday 6 PM to 11 PM

Rosas y Xocolate
Cuisine: International
Telephone: (999) 924-4304
Address: Paseo Montejo #480, by 41 Street
Parking: Street parking, and Valet service
Air Conditioned: Yes
Outdoors: Yes
Drinks: Full bar
Hours: Daily, 7:30 AM to 12 PM, and 1:30 PM to 12 AM
Website: www.rosasandxocolate.com

Gran Plaza Shopping Mall

100% Natural
Cuisine: Vegetarian
Telephone: (999) 948-4590
Address: Calle 8 #306, between Calle 1 and 1-A Street
Parking: Yes
Air Conditioned: Yes
Outdoors: Yes
Drinks: Beer and soft drinks
Hours: Daily, 7 AM to 11 PM
Website: www.100natural.com.mx

Boston's
Cuisine: American
Telephone: (999) 948-3333
Address: Prolongación Montejo #482
Parking: Yes
Air Conditioned: Yes
Outdoors: No
Drinks: Full bar
Hours: Daily, 11 AM to 2 AM
Website: www.bostonsmerida.com

Italianni's
Cuisine: Italian
Telephone: (999) 948-4597
Address: In the Gran Plaza shopping mall
Parking: Yes
Air Conditioned: Yes
Outdoors: No
Drinks: Full bar
Hours: Daily, 8 AM to 2 AM
Website: www.italiannis.com

Lapa Lapa
Cuisine: American
Telephone: (999) 948-0102
Address: In the Gran Plaza shopping mall
Parking: Yes
Air Conditioned: Yes
Outdoors: No

Drinks: Full bar

Hours: Daily, 1 PM to 3 AM

Hotel Zone
(Paseo de Montejo & Avenida Colón) – Restaurants

Chili's
Cuisine: American
Telephone: (999) 925-6346
Address: Hotel Fiesta Americana
Parking: Yes, underground parking at the Fiesta Americana
Air Conditioned: Yes
Outdoors: No
Drinks: Full bar
Hours: Daily, 8 AM to 12 AM
Website: www.chilis.com

Fiesta Americana Restaurant
Cuisine: Buffet and International Menu
Telephone: (999) 942-1111
Address: Fiesta Americana
Parking: Yes
Air Conditioned: Yes
Outdoors: No
Drinks: Full bar
Hours: Daily, 8 AM to 1 PM

La Pigua
Cuisine: Seafood
Telephone: (999) 920-3605
Address: Avenida Cupules and 32 Street
Parking: Yes (Valet)
Air Conditioned: Yes
Outdoors: No
Drinks: Full bar
Hours: Sunday-Tuesday: 12AM to 6 PM; Wednesday-Saturday:12 AM to 10:30 PM
Website: www.lapiguamerida.com

Los Almendros (Fiesta America)
Cuisine: Yucatecan Cuisine
Telephone: (999) 942-1111
Address: Fiesta Americana Hotel
Parking: Yes
Air Conditioned: Yes
Outdoors: No
Drinks: Full bar
Hours: Daily, 12:30 AM to 10:30 PM

Peregrina Bistro (Hyatt Hotel)
Cuisine: International
Telephone: (999) 942-1234
Address: Hyatt Hotel
Parking: Yes
Air Conditioned: Yes
Outdoors: No
Drinks: Full bar
Hours: Daily, 6:30 AM to 6 PM

Spasso
Cuisine: Italian
Telephone: (999) 942-1228
Address: Inside the Hyatt Hotel
Parking: Yes
Air Conditioned: Yes
Outdoors: No
Drinks: Full bar
Hours: Daily, 6 PM to 2 AM
Website: merida.regency.hyatt.com/hyatt/hotels/entertainment/restaurants/index.jsp

RESTAURANTS

Mexican Restaurants with various locations

There are a good number of Mexican chains with multiple locations. These are some that are found in several neighborhoods, and worth a try. Most have a presence in Centro and along Paseo Montejo – and most also have websites, so you can look up their locations in other neighborhoods.

El Fogoncito
Cuisine: Tacos and Mexican traditional foods
Telephone: (999) 944-0315
Locations include: Centro (Calle 62 and 61 Street); Prolongación Montejo; and Altabrisa Mall
Parking: Varies with location
Air Conditioned: Yes
Outdoors: Only at Fogoncito on Prolongación Montejo
Drinks: Full bar
Hours: Daily, 12 PM to 2 AM
Website: www.gruponicxa.com.mx/rest/fog/index.html

Eladios
Cuisine: Yucatecan snack and bar foods
Neighborhood: Various locations
Telephone: (999) 984-0057
Locations include: Colonia Itzimná, Centro, Avenida Itzáes, Colonia Pensiones
Parking: Yes, at all locations
Air Conditioned: Yes
Outdoors: Yes
Drinks: Beer and Cocktails
Hours: Daily, 12 PM to 7 PM
Website: www.eladios.com.mx

Italian Coffee Company
Cuisine: Coffee and sandwiches
Neighborhood: Centro (Calle 62 between Calle 59 and 61 Street) and other locations
Air Conditioned: Yes
Outdoors: No in Centro, Yes for other locations
Drinks: Coffee
Hours: Sunday-Friday: 7:30 AM to 11 PM Saturdays: 7:30 AM to 12 PM
Website: www.italiancoffee.com

Las Jirafas
Cuisine: Tacos
Telephone: (999) 926-4391
Locations include: Paseo Montejo, at Calle 56-A #494
Parking: Street parking
Air Conditioned: Varies with location
Outdoors: Yes
Drinks: Beer and cocktails
Hours: Daily, 7 PM to 2 AM

Los Trompos
Cuisine: Tacos and pizzas
Telephone: (999) 988-4444
Locations include: There are currently 15 locations, so see website
Parking: Some locations
Air Conditioned: Some locations
Outdoors: Some locations
Drinks: Beers and cocktails
Hours: For those located in shopping centers, daily: 11 AM to 10 PM; other restaurants, daily: 6 PM to 2 AM
Website: www.lostrompos.com.mx

Messina's
Cuisine: Pizza
Locations include: Centro
Telephone: (999) 924-9899, or (999) 924-0011
Address: Calle 57 #514-A by 64 Street
Parking: No
Air Conditioned: No
Outdoors: Yes
Drinks: Soft drinks
Hours: Daily, 11 AM to 12 PM, depending on location
Website: www.buscatan.com/directorio/pizza-messinas-pizzerias-Merida-yucatan-505-203.html

Wok to Walk
Cuisine: Asian
Telephone: (999) 944-5866
Address: Various locations, including Prolongación Montejo, Plaza Altabrisa and Plaza Senderos. Check their website.
Parking: Yes
Air Conditioned: Yes
Outdoors: Only at Plaza Mayor
Drinks: No
Hours: Daily, 12 PM to 10 PM
Website: www.woktowalk.com/en/find/index.php

"Puertas Cerradas" (Closed Doors)

"Closed Doors" is a culinary movement in which private dinners are held by renowned chefs, or for special events. Mérida has two "Puertas Cerradas" of renown. To find out about their upcoming events, you have to contact their websites and make reservations. Remixto specializes in coming up with innovative menus for their events, and Casa Catherwood showcases the talents of internationally-acclaimed chefs and mixologists.

Remixto
Cuisine: Underground Sunday Brunch
Neighborhood: Centro
Telephone: (999) 901-5430
Website: www.remixto.com

Casa Catherwood
Cuisine: Underground Sunday Brunch
Neighborhood: Centro
Telephone: (999) 154-5565
Website: www.casa-catherwood.com/puertascerradas

Day Trips from Mérida - Restaurants

Izamal

Hotel Macanche
Cuisine: Yucatecan and International
Telephone: **(998)** 954-0287
Address: Calle 22 #305 between Calle 33 and 35 Street
Parking: Yes
Air Conditioned: No
Outdoors: Yes
Drinks: Wine or beer
Hours: Daily, but call for reservations
Website: www.macanche.com

Sabor de Izamal
Cuisine: Traditional Yucatecan

Telephone: (990) 954-0489
Address: Calle 27 #299, between Calle 28 and 30 Street
Parking: Yes
Air Conditioned: Yes
Outdoors: Yes
Drinks: Full bar
Hours: Daily, 11 AM to 6 PM
Website: www.sabordeizamal.com

Progreso/Celestun

La Palapa
Cuisine: Seafood
Telephone: (998) 916-2063
Address: On the beach
Parking: Yes
Air Conditioned: No
Outdoors: Yes
Drinks: Full bar
Hours: Daily, 11 AM to 6 PM

San Bruno Beach Grill
Cuisine: International
Telephone: (999) 122-5021
Address: On the beach, Km 27.5 on the Carretera Progreso-Telchac
Parking: Yes
Air Conditioned: No
Outdoors: Yes
Drinks: Full bar
Hours: Every Day: 1 PM to 10 PM

Taco Maya
Cuisine: Mexican and American
Telephone: (999) 145-0623
Address: In front of the baseball park in Chelem
Parking: Yes
Air Conditioned: No
Outdoors: Yes
Drinks: Beer and soft drinks

Hours: Saturday – Wednesday, 10 AM to 2.30 PM; Closed Thursday & Friday

Haciendas Near Mérida

Hacienda de Chunkanan
Town/Village: Cuzamá
Cuisine: Yucatecan
Address: In town (where the horse-drawn carriages are hitched)
Parking: Yes
Air Conditioned: No
Outdoors: Yes
Drinks: Not sure, probably beer
Hours: Daily, 10 AM – 6 PM

Hacienda Ochil
Town/Village: On highway towards Uxmal
Cuisine: Yucatecan
Telephone: (999) 924-7465
Address: Km. 27 Uman-Uxmal highway, near Abala
Parking: Yes
Air Conditioned: No
Outdoors: Yes
Drinks: Full bar
Hours: Daily, 10 AM to 6 PM
Website: www.haciendaochil.com

Hacienda San José
Town/Village: East of Mérida, just past Tixkokob
Cuisine: Yucatecan
Telephone: (999) 924-1313
Parking: Yes
Air Conditioned: No
Outdoors: Yes
Drinks: Full bar
Hours: Daily, 7 AM to 12 PM
Website: www.thehaciendas.com

Hacienda Santa Cruz
Town/Village: Santa Cruz Palomeque, south of the Superhighway Periférico, road to Dzununcan
Cuisine: French and Yucatecan Fusion
Neighborhood: Santa Cruz Palomeque
Telephone: (999) 254-0541
Address: Santa Cruz Palomeque Main Street
Parking: Yes
Air Conditioned: No
Outdoors: Yes
Drinks: Full bar
Hours: Daily, 7 AM to 12 AM
Website: www.haciendasantacruz.com

Hacienda Santa Rosa
Town/Village: Maxcanú, on the road to Campeche
Cuisine: Yucatecan
Telephone: (999) 910-0174
Address: In the pueblo of Santa Rosa
Parking: Yes
Air Conditioned: No
Outdoors: Yes
Drinks: Full bar
Hours: Daily, 7 AM to 12 AM
Website: www.thehaciendas.com

Hacienda Temozón
Town/Village: Temozón Sur, on the road to Uxmal, near Temozón village
Cuisine: Yucatecan
Telephone: (999) 923-8089
Parking: Yes
Air Conditioned: No
Outdoors: Yes
Drinks: Full bar
Hours: Daily, 7 AM to 12 PM
Website: www.thehaciendas.com

Hacienda Teya
Town/Village: East of Mérida, on the road to Cancún
Cuisine: Yucatecan
Telephone: (999) 988-0800
Parking: Yes
Air Conditioned: Yes
Outdoors: Yes
Drinks: Full bar
Hours: Daily, 12 AM to 6 PM
Website: haciendateya.com

Hacienda Xcantún
Town/Village: On the road to Progreso, village of Xcantún
Cuisine: International, with a Yucatecan flair
Telephone: (999) 930-2140
Address: Mérida – Progreso Highway, Km. 12
Parking: Parking lot on hacienda grounds
Air Conditioned: Yes
Outdoors: Yes
Drinks: Full bar
Hours: Daily, 8 AM to 11:30 AM and 1:30 PM to 11 PM
Website: www.xcantun.com

Part III
The Fundamentals of Moving to Mérida

6 Getting Here! To Drive, or Not to Drive!

By Air

Mérida has nonstop flights to Cancún, Havana, Houston, Mexico City and Miami, from which connections around the world are possible. Mérida is served by a modern, world-class international airport located a short drive south from the Historic Center. The Manuel Crescencio Rejón International Airport's IATA Code is MID.

Aeroméxico flies to Havana, Mexico City and Miami; United (formerly Continental) flies to Houston; Interjet, Viva Aerobus and Volaris all fly to Mexico City; and Maya Air, a discount airline, flies to Cancún and Cozumel with connecting service on American Airlines to Miami, Chicago and New York. Cubana also flies to Havana.

United (formerly Continental) codeshares with Alliance-member airlines on many flights through Houston. (Continental officially became United in 2011.) Aeroméxico codeshares with Delta on flights through Mexico City. Mexicana Airlines filed for bankruptcy protection in August 2010, when it suspended all service. It is currently reorganizing under court-authorized supervision. In January 2010 be began to prepare to resume service. In 2011 it is expected to begin international service from Mexico City and Cancún, as well as domestic service to certain cities. Mérida is not included in the initial list of cities which will be serviced in 2011, but it is expected to be included for 2012. Stay tuned, but in the meantime, Mexicana codeshares with American on flights through Mexico City. If you are looking for flights, we have found that Orbitz.com, Expedia.com and Kayak.com offer the best schedules and fares.

Aeromar, Aeroméxico Connect, Aviacsa, Interjet, Maya Air, Viva Aerobus, and Volaris offer regional service. Aviacsa is undergoing reorganization and, as this goes to press, has not resumed service.

That said, the truth is that flying into Mérida is relatively expensive, and the schedules are limited. The reason is that, over the past quarter century, Cancún has emerged as a major tourist destination, and it has almost as many flights as Mexico City. Many Yucatecans miss the days when there were two daily nonstop flights to Miami, and regular nonstop flights to Atlanta, New

Orleans and Guatemala City. Maya Air began service in 2009, and it offers nonstop flights to Cancún and Cozumel from Mérida. Cubana, Cuba's national airline, began to fly nonstop Mérida-Havana in 2010.

The good news, of course, is that Mérida is "off the beaten path," a place that is an adventure, a destination that is purposeful. The bad news is that, if you fly from the U.S. or Canada, it can cost around $300 USD more to fly into Mérida than it would to fly to Cancún. One suggestion: Find the cheapest flight to Cancún and connect with the ADO first-class bus to Mérida. It may sound counterintuitive, but the three and half hour bus ride from Cancún to Mérida can save you both time and money. Why? Because many flights via Houston or Mexico City have layovers that last a few hours, and if you are coming from the Eastern Seaboard, flying to Mexico City means you are flying about 700 miles west of Mérida, so your connection will simply fly you back 700 miles east to Mérida.

Business Travel to Mexico: Advice from the State Department

Business Travel: Upon arrival in Mexico, business travelers must complete and submit a form (Form FMM) authorizing the conduct of business, but not employment, for a 30-day period. Travelers entering Mexico for purposes other than tourism or business or for stays of longer than 180 days require a visa and must carry a valid U.S. passport. U.S. citizens planning to work or live in Mexico should apply for the appropriate Mexican visa at the Mexican Embassy in Washington, DC, or at the nearest Mexican consulate in the United States.

And the savings can be substantial: Comparing recent flights from New York to Mérida; and San Francisco to Mérida turned up that flying New York to Cancún was $400 USD cheaper than New York to Mérida, and flying San Francisco to Cancún was $425 USD cheaper than flying San Francisco to Mérida. So it might just be worthwhile to fly to Cancún and then take the bus. It may also be worth the effort to see if you fly into Cancún, take the bus to Mérida, and fly home from Mérida, or the other way around. The preferred websites for finding deals online are Kayak.com, Orbitz.com and Travelocity.com.

Be patient, shop around for a deal online, and consider various options. Once you get there, however, you will be glad you came!

Listed below are the websites for all the airlines that serve Mérida:

Aeromar
www.aeromar.com.mx

Aeroméxico
www.aeromexico.com

Aviacsa
www.aviacsa.com

Click de Mexicana
www.click.com.mx

Cubana de Aviacion
www.cubana.cu

Interjet
www.interjet.com.mx

Maya Air
www.mayair.com.mx

Mexicana
www.mexicana.com

United (formerly Continental)
www.united.com

Viva Aerobus
www.vivaaerobus.com

Volaris
www.volaris.com.mx

Getting to Mérida by Bus

Mérida by bus from Cancún is easy: ADO operates convenient schedules, and has good fares. They even have a shuttle bus from Cancún's airport ($50 pesos, or about $4.50 USD) that takes you directly from the airport parking lot to their bus terminal downton. Depending on the time of day, and the class of service ("Servicio de Lujo" on many Mexican bus lines have seats as wide and comfortable as Business Class on most U.S. airlines; movies, videos and complimentary coffee and teas are included!), one-way tickets to Mérida range from $18 – 36 USD.

Our recommendation? Find the best fare to Cancún, and then give yourself a couple of hours between arrival time and the departing Express Bus to Mérida. The ADO bus line has an English-language website (*www.adogl.com.mx/en/index.htm*). Remember, if you are staying in the Historic Center, you will want to go to Mérida Terminal (CAME) station, which is downtown Mérida.

For traveling to other locations from Mérida by Bus

Once you are here, you'll find that ADO operates convenient schedules and at good prices. Unless you are on a tight budget, or simply want to travel in a more adventurous way, go Primera Clase (First Class). There are fewer stops, the seats are more comfortable, and the service a bit more attentive. ADO is great if you want to travel to Campeche City, Palenque, Villahermosa, Chetumal, or even venture all the way to Mexico City. ADO also has Express buses to Cancún and Playa del Carmen. ADO operates from the main terminal station downtown, as well as from the Fiesta Americana Hotel (Calle 60 and Avenida Cupules).

The Second Class Bus

Terminal Station (Terminal de Autobuses de 2a. Clase) is located at Calle 50 #531 by Calle 67. If you are traveling to the smaller communities throughout the Yucatán, these are the buses that you might want to consider:

Lineas Unidas del Sur Bus Line

Telephone: (999) 924-7565
Service to: Kanasín, Tepich, Tecoh, Telchaquillo, Maní, Oxkutzcab, Sotuta, Cholul, Peto, Homún, Tekit and villages en route to these towns.

Autobuses de Oriente Bus Line

Telephone: (999) 928-6230
Service to: Cancún, Valladolid, Chichén Itzá, Playa del Carmen, Coba and Tulum.

Autobuses de Occidente Bus Line

Telephone: (999) 928-6230
Service to: Izamal, Tizimín, Celestún, Seye, Sotuta, Cenotillo, Dzitas, Cantemaya, Espita, Hunucmá and villages en route to these towns.

Autobuses del Noreste Bus Line

Telephone: (999) 924-6355
Service to: Tizimín, Ría Lagartos, San Felipe, Chicxulub Pueblo, Temax, Cancún, Valladolid, Cholul, Conkal, Motul, Baca, Dzemul, Telchac, San Cristiano, Chabihau and villages en route to these towns.

By Car

If you are driving to Mérida from the United States, it is necessary to point out that currently there are concerns about safety. The continuing conflicts between the Mexican Government and drug cartels have led to some dangerous conditions, particularly at night. It is recommended that you arrive to your point of entry on the U.S. side the evening before, get a good night's sleep and bright and early the following day you enter Mexico and drive as far away from the border as you can reasonably do so. It is recommended that by evening, you arrive at the city where you will be spending the night, get a good night's sleep and continue your journey bright and early the next morning. It has been the experience of many drivers that it is best to enter Mexico at Nuevo Laredo and drive around the Gulf of Mexico.

Here is general advice on bringing your private car into Mexico provided by the State Department:

Entry of private vehicles into Mexico

"Tourists traveling to Mexico by car must have a valid driver's license and a certificate of title or vehicle registration. In the case of a rented vehicle, it is necessary to show a rental agreement in the name of the person driving the vehicle. In the case of a company car, a notarized document proving that the vehicle was assigned to the driver and a proof of employment.

Current government regulations also require you to fill a Temporary Import Permit, a Vehicle Return Promise and to post a vehicle bond to ensure that the vehicle is returned to its country of origin. There are three options for posting a vehicle bond: a credit card, a vehicle value bond, or a cash deposit. All these procedures must be fulfilled at the border before entering the country. When you leave the country you must return the documents that were issued when entering. Sanctions will be imposed to persons who fail to do so.

Requirements for the entry of vehicles into Mexico: On April 1, 1992, the Government of Mexico revised its requirements for the temporary entry (less than six months) of personal vehicles into Mexico. The purpose of these measures is to ensure that illegally imported vehicles do not remain in Mexico. These regulations pertain only to those vehicles which will be driven beyond the approximate 20 kilometer "free zone" south of the U.S.-Mexican border. The Government of Mexico's Ministry of Finance has indicated that these regulations do not affect vehicles which will remain within the "free zone" (note: all of Baja California is considered a "free zone").

Owners of personal vehicles traveling beyond the "free zone" must present the importer's immigration document (tourist card or visa), the original and a copy of the importer's driver's license and vehicle title in the name of the importer. If the operator of the vehicle is other than the importer, the operator must have the same immigration status as the importer and the importer of the vehicle must be present at all times it is being operated in Mexico. If the above documents are in order, the temporary importer of the vehicle has two options for bringing the vehicle into Mexico:

- **Post a bond** based on the value of the vehicle as determined by local customs officials. However, there is no need to pay a bond on the total value of the vehicle. Instead, licensed Mexican bonding agencies on both sides of the U.S.-Mexican border provide this service for a fee of up to 1 or 2 percent of the value of the vehicle.

- **Make a sworn statement** at the Mexican Army and Air Force Bank (Banco Nacional del Ejercito Fuerza Aerea y Armada S.N.C.). A fee of $10 is required and can only be paid with a credit card (Visa and Mastercard) issued by a bank in the importer's country of foreign residence (e.g., the United States for U.S. citizens). American Express and Diners Club cards are not considered to be bank issues cards and therefore cannot be used to pay the fee (payment may not be made in cash). Offices of the Banco Nacional del Ejercito are located in all customs offices at ports of entry and their hours are reportedly the same as those of the customs offices. The bank will provide the appropriate forms for this service. All vehicle importation documents should be in the vehicle when it is operated. When leaving Mexico, these documents should be returned to the Mexican customs office at the border.

When vehicle importation documentation is lost or stolen, replacement documents can be issued by regional Mexican customs offices to the importer after he or she obtains a certified document from the U.S. Embassy or one of its consulates attesting to the loss.

In the "free zone," foreign vehicles can only be operated by the owner or (if the owner is present but not driving the vehicle) by a citizen or permanent legal resident (LPR) of the vehicle's place of registration.

For additional information, individuals traveling to Mexico by personal vehicle should (prior to their travel) contact the Mexican Embassy in Washington, DC, or the Mexican Consulate nearest their residence.

Thousands of U.S. citizens travel throughout Mexico each year using both privately owned and rental vehicles. U.S. citizens planning to drive in Mexico may do so on a current U.S. driver's license but should confirm that their current U.S. insurance will cover driving in Mexico or purchase additional insurance to cover the period of their travel in Mexico. While Mexico has an extensive primary and secondary road system, driving conditions are crowded and often hazardous to the uninitiated driver. Drivers in Mexico should exercise particular care and should not drive after nightfall outside urban areas. Night time driving can be particularly hazardous because of slow moving unlighted vehicles even on primary roads. In addition, some Mexican roads, particularly in isolated regions, have at times been targets for robbery by bandits who operate primarily after dark.

Driving restrictions in Mexico City: In an effort to reduce air pollution in Mexico City, Mexican authorities restrict all vehicular traffic including vehicles of tourists in Mexico City. For vehicles of non-Mexican registration, the restriction is based on the last digit of the license plates. The schedule is as follows:

> Monday - no driving of vehicles with license plates with final digit of 5 or 6.
> Tuesday - no driving of vehicles with license plates with final digit of 7 or 8.
> Wednesday - no driving of vehicles with license plates with final digit of 3 or 4.
> Thursday - no driving of vehicles with license plates with final digit of 1 or 2.
> Friday - no driving of vehicles with license plated with final digit of 9 or 0.

Also, no driving of vehicles with temporary license plates or any other plate that does not conform with the above.

Saturday and Sunday – all vehicles may be driven.

Failure to comply with Mexican laws governing temporarily imported vehicles can result in vehicle confiscation and/or fines.

A publication entitled "Tips for Travelers to Mexico" with additional useful information is available through the Office of Mexico's Flash Facts system at (202) 482-4464 by requesting document #8112. The nearest Mexican Consulate can also provide current information on safety and recommendations."

There are certain procedures for the "temporary" importing of your U.S.-purchased vehicle into Mexico. The process normally takes about an hour to complete at the border, and it can be considerably less if the paperwork has been completed beforehand, either online or by going to the nearest Mexican Consulate in your area. Following is an explanation of the process provided by MexConnect.com:

Regulations for Bringing Your Car into Mexico

"Here are a couple of steps you need to take when you decide to drive across the border into Mexico. If you abide by these rules, you'll be making sure you can legally take your trip to Mexico by car.

If your travel is within the **Border Zone** (usually up to 20 kilometers south of the U.S.-Mexico Border) or the **Free Trade Zone** (including the *Baja California Peninsula* and the *Sonora Free Trade Zone*) there are no procedures to comply with. However, if you wish to pass these zones, the following procedures will apply. You must secure a permit by following the next few steps.

Applying for a permit at the Mexico Border

Step One

To acquire a permit, simply drive your vehicle (including RVs) to a Mexican customs office at the border and present an original plus two (2) copies of the following documents:

Valid proof of citizenship (passport or birth certificate)

In the case of dual citizenship, the solicitant must present his or her Mexican passport or proof of Mexican nationality

The appropiate immigration form (FMT or "tourist card")

The valid vehicle registration certificate, or a document, such as the original title that certifies the legal ownership of the vehicle. It must be in the driver's name.

The leasing contract (if the vehicle is leased or rented), which must be in the name of the person importing the car. If the vehicle belongs to a company, present the document that certifies the employee works for the company.

A valid driver's license, issued outside Mexico.

If the documentation shows the vehicle is registered in the name of the spouse, the importation can be done as long as the marriage certificate (and one copy) is presented.

An international credit or debit card, also issued outside Mexico (American Express, Mastercard or Visa), in the name of the driver of the vehicle.

Note: If you do not possess an international credit card, you will be asked to post a bond, payable to the* Federal Treasury, *issued by an authorized bonding company in Mexico.

> As an alternative to posting a bond, you may make a cash deposit at Banco del Ejército in an amount equal to the value of your vehicle according to the "Table of Vehicle Values for Bonding Companies" (see table on the next page for an idea of the cost).

> Banco del Ejército now has a website (see on next page) wherein you can obtain the most recent rates and regulations. In addition, you may now apply in advance via Internet, but you will still need to have all the copies (as above) when you arrive at the border.

Step Two

Once you have the originals and a set of photocopies of these documents, present them to the Vehicular Control Module located in Customs to process the importation permit.

All documents and the credit card must be in the name of the owner, who must also be in the vehicle when crossing the border.

Step Three

Your international credit card will be charged an amount in national currency equivalent to $27.00 USD at the Banco del Ejército.

If you do not have an international credit card or debit card, Banco del Ejército will accept a cash deposit in an amount equal to the value of your vehicle (see table). Your deposit plus any interest it may earn will be returned to you when you leave Mexico. Or, you may choose to obtain a bond through an authorized Mexican bonding company located at all the border crossings. The authorized bonding companies will require a refundable deposit equal to the value of the vehicle, according to the table below. The bonding company will also assess taxes and processing costs for this service.

Step Four

Upon your departure from Mexico, and if the vehicle is not going to be driven back into Mexico, the permit for temporary importation must be cancelled at Customs. That's all there is to it. Follow these simple steps and you shouldn't have any problems. **However, please remember, if your car is found in Mexico beyond the authorized time limit, or without the appropiate documents, it will be immediately confiscated.**

GETTING HERE! TO DRIVE, OR NOT TO DRIVE!

 Amount of Bond in U.S. Dollars

2001-2010	1996-2000	1996 and older models
$400.00	$300.00	$200.00

The car permit can be requested at the following border crossing points

Arizona Border Points	**California Border Points**	Ciudad Miguel Alemán
Agua Prieta	Mexicali	Columbia
Naco	Otay Mesa	General Rodrigo M.
Nogales	Tecate	Quevedo
San Luis Río Colorado	Tijuana	Matamoros
		Nuevo Laredo
Sonoyta	**Texas Border Points**	Ojinaga
	Ciudad Acuña	Piedras Negras
	Ciudad Juárez	Reynosa

Requesting Car Import Permits in Advance and Via Internet

If you wish, you can apply for the import permits up to 6 months before the vehicle enters Mexico. This can be done through any of the following Mexican consulates in the United States:

Chicago, Illinois
Austin, Dallas, Fort Worth and Houston, Texas
Los Angeles, San Bernardino and Sacramento, California
Albuquerque, New Mexico
Denver, Colorado
Phoenix, Arizona

By presenting all the documentation and requesting the import permit from Banjercito you will then be charged the equivalent of $36.00 USD plus tax (I.V.A. 15%), and this will need to be billed to an international credit/debit card issued inside the U.S.

 ### Applying for a Car Permit Online

You may now apply for a car permit in advance, online. The request can be made between 20 and 60 days prior to the vehicle crossing the border. By using the Internet service, your temporary

permit will be sent to you by mail. This service is to help speed up the permit process. If you would like to apply online, the English-language website is:

www.banjercito.com.mx/site/imagenes/iitv/instruccionesIITV_ing.html.

- You must electronically accept the terms agreement
- You then register all your personal information
- You must input the vehicle data as well
- Your credit/debit card will be charged an amount in national currency equivalent to $45.00 USD plus taxes (I.V.A. 15%)

You will then receive confirmation electronically as well as a limit date by when you must have sent copies of all the required documents. There are three ways this documentation can be sent:

> Electronically via email to:
> CIITEVAduanaMexico@sat.gob.mx.
>
> The subject must include the applicant's name and the folio

> Via certified mail to:
> Avenida Industria Militar #1055 Colonia Lomas de Sotelo
> Delegación Miguel Hidalgo
> 11200, México, D.F.
>
> The remittent must be the applicant and the folio.

You can also personally deliver the copies at any of the CITEV modules in the customs offices at any border.

Upon electronic confirmation, Banjercito will send the import permit to the address requested on the application in less than 20 days.

When you arrive at the border crossing, you will need to provide the Folio number assigned to you during the on-line process, and there is a charge of 27.00 USD at the border modules (or $39.60 USD at the consulate modules).

In addition, the same documentation must be presented, the original and two photocopies:

Valid proof of citizenship (passport or birth certificate) In the case of dual citizenship, the solicitant must present his or her Mexican passport or proof of Mexican nationality.

The appropiate immigration form (FMT or "tourist card")

The valid vehicle registration certificate, or a document, such as the original title that certifies the legal ownership of the vehicle. It must be in the driver's name.

The leasing contract (if the vehicle is leased or rented), which must be in the name of the person importing the car. If the vehicle belongs to a company, present the document that certifies the employee works for the company.

A valid driver's license, issued outside Mexico.
If the documentation shows the vehicle is registered in the name of the spouse, the importation can be done as long as the marriage certificate (and ne copy) is presented.

An international credit or debit card, also issued outside Mexico (American Express, Mastercard or Visa), in the name of the driver of the vehicle.

> ### Pemex Gas Stations
>
> Mexico's state-owned oil monopoly is Pemex, which operates or franchises all the gas stations throughout the country. The price of gas is set by the government, and as such, there is no need to drive around looking for the cheapest gas: it is the same everywhere. But because gas stations are Pemex franchises, there are fewer than in the U.S. and Canada: Make sure you fill up before heading for a long trip! Please note that Mexico's gas stations are staffed with attendants who pump the gas, wipe your windshields (and check your oil upon request). These attendants should be tipped. The best way to handle yourself is to say, "*$195 pesos, por favor,*" while holding a $200 peso note in your hand.

Insurance

U.S. and Canadian auto insurance is **NOT** valid in Mexico. Mexican auto insurance is mandatory in many states and cities and you should **NOT** drive without it. If you are in an accident or other vehicle-related problems and you do not have insurance, you may be arrested and your vehicle impounded until the authorities can figure out the situation. A list of insurance companies that can provide the coverage you need appears later in this chapter. Most allow you to buy insurance over the phone, fax or Internet.

Answers to Commonly Asked Questions

1) The temporary authorization for the importation of vehicles is valid for any type of vehicle weighing less than three tons for periods up to six months (180 days).

2) The temporarily imported vehicle may be driven across the border multiple times during the authorized period.

3) Always carry with you the importation permit when driving your car in Mexico. Do not leave this document in the vehicle; it is indispensible in the case of damage, theft, or accident.

4) The sale, abandonment, or use of the vehicle for financial gain will result in its confiscation.

5) The vehicle temporarily imported by the owner may be driven in Mexico by the spouse or adult children, as long as they have the same immigration status. Other persons may drive the vehicle as long as the owner is in the vehicle."

> **Know Before You Go!**
> Before you take your car into Mexico, we recommend that you check the State Department Travel Advisories in effect concerning driving conditions in Mexico. International Travel information is available at:
>
> www.travel.state.gov/travel/cis_pa_tw/tw/tw_1764.html

On the road to Mérida!

Once you are well on your way, take time to enjoy the ride. Most of the highways are modern, and some have tolls, so be prepared. It is best to drive carefully and cautiously, taking time to rest at the Pemex gas stations, stretch your legs, be hydrated. Never drive if you are tired or sleepy. Try to avoid driving with the sun in your face. As you approach the Yucatán peninsula, the geography changes quickly, and you soon realize you are entering a tropical environment.

Military Checkpoints:

It is probably not news to you, but there's a drug problem in the world out there, and it just so happens that, geographically, Mexico is in the middle of it. What you probably don't know, however, is that the U.S. doesn't control the export of firearms. As a result, as you drive around the peninsula, you may encounter military checkpoints. There is nothing to fear, and if they wave you to stop, simply comply. If you are traveling away from the U.S. (east or south) they are probably looking for firearms. If you are traveling towards the U.S. (west or north) they are probably looking for drugs. In either case, the young soldiers are polite and we know of no one who has found them to be anything other than respectful and courteous while doing their jobs.

No matter what you have seen in Hollywood films, nothing untoward is going to happen, and they are there for your protection, since you are a guest in this country.

Free Highway Assistance: Green Angels

The Secretariat of Tourism (a federal agency) operates "Angeles Verdes," or "Green Angels." This is a public service that helps motorists who are distressed along the road. As you drive the highways, you will probably see them helping motorists. They are there to help you with flat tires, drivers who ran out of gas, motorists experiencing general car problems (overheated radiators, dead batteries), and they will even tow you to the nearest gas station or town. There is no charge for their help, but the young men and women who work for them won't turn down a tip if offered ($50 or $100 pesos, depending on how much they helped). If you are in trouble, you can contact them by dialing 078 983-1184.

The Yucatán's One and Only Toll Road:

When you arrive in the Yucatán, you will find that there is only one toll road between Mérida and Cancún (*Autopista de Cuota*) is fast and safe, but not cheap. The toll between Mérida and Cancún is $319 pesos, one way. (The toll between Mérida to Chichén Itzá (Kantunil exit) is $67 pesos. The toll between Mérida to Valladolid (Kantunil exit) is $117 pesos). There is only one gas station and rest area, about halfway between Mérida and Cancún. Take a break, stretch your legs, go to the restroom, or buy a soda or water. If you are hesitant to pay the hefty toll, you may want to consider that the Toll Road avoids 43 towns and villages, so that's a lot of school crossings and 146 speed bumps ("topes") along the way. (Yes, we have counted them!) If you are making a roundtrip, you might want to consider using the Toll Road one way, and the take the secondary road (marked "Libre," meaning "Free"), which will add about an hour to your travel time, but then again, it meanders through scenic Maya villages.

From the State Department, general overview of health insurance questions for Americans overseas:

What's the difference between Travel Insurance and Travel Medical Insurance?

- Travel Insurance insures your financial investment in your trip. Typically it covers such things as the cost of lost baggage and cancelled flights, but it may or may not cover costs of medical attention you may need while abroad.

- Travel Medical Insurance covers costs of medical attention you may need while abroad.

Recommendations from the U.S. State Department on Driving in Mexico

Driving and Vehicle Regulations

U.S. driver's licenses are valid in Mexico. Mexican law requires that only owners drive their vehicles, or that the owner be inside the vehicle. If not, the vehicle may be seized by Mexican customs and will not be returned under any circumstances. The Government of Mexico strictly regulates the entry of vehicles into Mexico.

Insurance

Mexican insurance is required for all vehicles, including rental vehicles. Mexican auto insurance is sold in most cities and towns on both sides of the border. U.S. automobile liability insurance is not valid in Mexico, nor is most collision and comprehensive coverage issued by U.S. companies. Motor vehicle insurance is considered invalid in Mexico if the driver is found to be under the influence of alcohol or drugs.

Road Emergencies and Automobile Accidents

Motor vehicle accidents are the leading cause of death of U.S. citizens in Mexico. Motorists should exercise special caution on the heavily-traveled expressway south of Cancún, particularly the two stretches between Cancún/Playa Del Carmen and Playa del Carmen/Tulum.

If you have an emergency while driving, the equivalent of "911" in Mexico is "066", but this number is not always answered. If you are driving on a toll highway (or "cuota") or any other major highway, you may contact the Green Angels (Angeles Verdes), a fleet of trucks with bilingual crews. The Green Angels may be reached directly at (01) (55) 5250-8221. If you are unable to call them, pull off to the side of the road and lift the hood of your car; chances are that they will find you.

If you are involved in an automobile accident, you will be taken into police custody until it can be determined who is liable and whether you have the ability to pay any penalty. If you do not have Mexican liability insurance, you may be prevented from departing the country even if you require life-saving medical care, and you are almost certain to spend some time in jail until all parties are satisfied that responsibility has been assigned and adequate financial satisfaction received. Drivers may face criminal charges if injuries or damages are serious.

Road Safety

Avoid driving on Mexican highways at night. Even multi-lane expressways in Mexico often have narrow lanes and steep shoulders. Single-vehicle rollover accidents involving U.S. citizens are common, often resulting in death or serious injury to vehicle occupants. Use extreme caution when approaching towns, driving on curves, and passing large trucks. All vehicle occupants should use seatbelts at all times.

Please refer to *Road Safety Overseas* for more information.
The website is: *www.travel.state.gov/travel/tips/safety/safety_1179.html*

For additional information in English concerning Mexican driver's permits, vehicle inspection, road tax, mandatory insurance, etc., please telephone the Mexican Secretariat of Tourism (SECTUR) at 1-800-44-MEXICO (639-426).

For detailed information in Spanish only, visit Mexican Customs' website *Importación Temporal de Vehículos* ("Temporary Importation of Vehicles"). The website is: *www.aduanas.sat.gob.mx/aduana_mexico/2007/A_Body_Vehiculos.htm*

Travelers are advised to consult with the Mexican Embassy or the nearest Mexican consulate in the United States for additional, detailed information prior to entering Mexico.

In recent years, moped rentals have become very widespread in Cancún and Cozumel, and the number of serious moped accidents has risen accordingly. Most operators carry no insurance and do not conduct safety checks. The U.S. Embassy recommends avoiding operators who do not provide a helmet with the rental. Some operators have been known to demand fees many times in excess of damages caused to the vehicles, even if renters have purchased insurance in advance. Vacationers at other beach resorts have encountered similar problems after accidents involving rented jet-skis. There have been cases of mobs gathering to prevent tourists from departing the scene and to intimidate them into paying exorbitant damage claims."

State Department Advice on Bringing U.S. Cars into Mexico:

Vehicle Permits: Tourists wishing to travel beyond the border zone with their vehicle must obtain a temporary import permit or risk having their vehicle confiscated by Mexican customs officials. At present the only exceptions to the requirement are for vehicles entering through the Nogales port of entry and traveling in the Baja Peninsula and in most of the state of Sonora. To acquire a permit, one must submit evidence of citizenship, title for the vehicle, a vehicle registration certificate, a driver's license, and a processing fee to either a Banjercito (Mexican Army Bank) branch located at a Mexican Customs (Aduanas) office at the port of entry, or at one of the Mexican consulates located in the U.S. Mexican law also requires the posting of a bond at a Banjercito office to guarantee the export of the car from Mexico within a time period determined at the time of the application. For this purpose, American Express, Visa or MasterCard credit card holders will be asked to provide credit card information; others will need to make a cash deposit of between $200 and $400, depending on the make/model/year of the vehicle. In order to recover this bond or avoid credit card charges, travelers must go to any Mexican Customs office immediately prior to departing Mexico. Regardless of any official or unofficial advice to the contrary, vehicle permits cannot be obtained at checkpoints in the interior of Mexico.

Travelers should avoid individuals who wait outside vehicle permit offices and offer to obtain the permits without waiting in line, even if they appear to be government officials. There have been reports of fraudulent or counterfeit permits being issued adjacent to the vehicle import permit office in Nuevo Laredo, Cuidad Juárez and other border areas. If the proper permit is not obtained before entering Mexico and cannot be obtained at the Banjercito branch at the port of entry, do not proceed to the interior. Travelers without the proper permit may be incarcerated, fined and/or have their vehicle seized at immigration/customs checkpoints. For further information, contact Mexican Customs about appropriate vehicle permits.

Mexican Automobile Insurance

The following companies specialize in providing comprehensive automobilie insurance for those driving from the U.S. to Mexico.

ADA-VIS Global

Full service insurance agency by phone or fax.
Website: www.mexicoinsurance.com

Adventure Mexican Insurance

Complete insurance services.
Website: www.mexadventure.com

Baja Bound

Mexican insurance online.
Website: www.bajabound.com

DriveMex

Purchase and print online policy.
Website: www.drivemex.com

Instant Mexico Insurance

Complete auto/car insurance.
Website: www.instant-mex-auto-insur.com

Lewis and Lewis Insurance Agency

Mexican auto insurance, Mexican home insurance, international boat insurance, international medical insurance
Website: www.mexicanautoinsurance.com

MexBound.com

Purchase and print online policy.
Website: www.mexbound.com

MexicanInsurance.com

Purchase and print online policy.
Website: www.mexicaninsurance.com

Mexico Insurance Professionals

Serving all of Mexico.
Website: www.mexicanautoinsurance.com

Sanborns Mexico Auto Insurance

Full coverage auto insurance in Mexico.
Website: www.sanbornsinsurance.com

West Coast Insurance Services

Standard and special lines auto insurance for your vehicles in Mexico.
Website: www.westcoastri.com

Vehicle Registration, or *Tenencia* and *Referendo*

Once you move to Mérida, at some point, you'll end up buying a car (or legally importing the car you drove from the U.S.) When you do buy a car in Mexico, here's how the annual vehicle registration works. Remember, if you are delinquent in paying your vehicle registration fees, your car can be seized by the police. That's never a pleasant experience, in Mexico or anywhere else in the world.

Vehicle registration fees are comprised of two categories. The first is the *Derecho Vehicular*, simply referred to as *referendo*. This is a fixed amount, regardless of the value of your vehicle.

Now comes the peculiar tax: *Tenencia*. The *tenencia* applies to motor vehicles that are less than 10 years old. What's the *tenencia* all about, many people ask. Well, the *tenencia* is a lot like the toll on the Florida Turnpike. And it's a lot like what governments around the world are accustomed to doing: Once they see a source of revenue, it's hard to shut it off.

So, here's the story. In Florida, the toll on the turnpike was supposed to be a *temporary* fee to pay for the construction of the toll road. But it generates so much income for the State of Florida that, although tolls collected have paid in full for the turnpike (back in 1989), the tolls continue to this day – ostensibly to have a fund for road improvements! (That's funny, but doesn't the State of Florida impose a $2.50 a day tax on all car rentals to defray highway maintenance expenses?)

Here in Mexico, the *tenencia* was enacted in 1962, when Adolfo López Mateo was president, for the purposes of paying for the 1968 Summer Olympic Games! Eleven years later, when the law was due to expire, Congress reauthorized it, giving 30% of all funds raised to the respective states for general funding purposes. And so it has gone forth.

Regardless of its history, its important simply to note that the *tenencia* is levied on cars less than 10 years old, and it is based on the value of the car. If you have an inexpensive vehicle, you pay considerably less than if you have Rolls Royce.

It's possible to pay for your dues online, but most people prefer to go in person to the *Módulos de Vialidad y Padron Vehícular*. There are two convenient locations. The least crowded one is located across from Gran Plaza, in the parking garage where Chedrahui Supermarket. The other, in the *Centro Histórico*, is adjacent to the Military Hospital, on the south side of the *Parque de la Paz*, which fronts the Centenario on Avenida Itzáes and Calle 59.

To expedite matters, here is what you will need to pay your vehicle fees and get your new license plates:

- *Comprobante domiciliario*: This is a utility bill, such as electric (CFE) or water (JAPAY). It must be in your name, and you have to show the original and a copy, which they will keep
- Photo identification, again the original and a copy to leave behind. If you are a foreign citizen, you will need to show your passport and FM3, along with copies of each, including the section listing your current status and renewals (*prorrogas*)

- The old license plates
- Money, preferably cash, to pay the corresponding fees (and outstanding fines) on the vehicle
- To find out what the current *tenencia* and *referendo* on your vehicle is, there is a website that, with your plate number and car serial number, will calculate what is due.

The address is: *https://srvshyweb.yucatan.gob.mx/reemplacamiento/solpagreem.htm*

If you are sending someone on your behalf, in addition to the above, you will have to provide a *Carta de Poder*, or Power of Attorney, with your signature and the signature of the designated person acting on your behalf. The letter has to be in Spanish, and you will need to show the original and have a copy to leave behind.

A simple Power of Attorney consists of:

> A quién corresponda:
>
> *Por medio de la presente se autoriza a (*name of the person you acting on your behalf*) quien ampara su personalidad moral con su (*list identification used, a IFE card, a driver's license, a passport*), para tramitar el pago de la tenencia, el referendo y cambio de placas, del vehículo (*list car manufacture and make of vehicle, such as a Volkswagen GTI*), número de serie (*vehicle ID number*), y número de placas (*license plate number*).*
>
> Atentamente,
>
> (*Your name*)

Make sure you sign the letter – exactly as your signature appears in your passport and FM3 – and that you print your name below.

You will need the original, and a copy. The person you are sending on your behalf will need to produce his or her official identification, and have a copy to leave behind. The person will also have to show official identification, and have a copy to leave behind.

As with everything else, the sooner you do this, the shorter the lines since it's human nature to procrastinate!

In 2011, Yucatán State announced that it would end the tenencia tax for vehicles valued at $300,000 pesos (about $24,000 USD) or less. Vehicles valued at more than $300,000 pesos will still have to pay the tenencia, and vehicles used for commercial purposes, regardless of their value, are still subject to the tenencia.

Oh, yes, one more detail: The *tenencia* ceases to exist as a federal tax on December 31, 2011. What's the bad news, you ask? On January 1, 2012 it's up to each state to decide whether or not to enact its own version of the tax! This, of course, makes as much sense as the State of Florida "ending" the toll tax on the Florida Turnpike, only to say that it's now up to each individual county to decide whether to continue imposing the toll ... what do you think the answer to that little question would be? So get ready for a whole new set of rules and procedures for the state-imposed *tenencia* come January 2012!

Car Insurance

Now that you have a car, you need insurance. Here are reputable insurance agencies that can provide all kinds of automobile coverage.

GNP
Calle 16 #97, between Calle 17 and 19 Street, Colonia Mexico
Telephone: (999) 944-6333

Inbursa
Paseo de Montejo #497, between Calle 45 and 47 Street, Colonia Santa Ana
Telephone: (999) 928-0629

ING Insurance
Calle 21 #117-D, between Calle 24 and 24-A Street, Centro
Telephone: (999) 926-3343

Interacciones
Calle 31 #170, between Calle 20 and 22 Street, Colonia Alemán
Telephone: (999) 938-2218

Seguros La Peninsular
Calle 47-A #501, between Calle 66 and 64 Street, Centro
Telephone: (999) 928-1187

Moving Your Possessions

It's one thing to drive, or fly, to Mérida ... but if you're moving here, how do you get your stuff into town?

If you are driving across the border, you will have to do all the shipping and Customs work at that time. If, as most people end up deciding, you will have your household goods shipped to

Mexico, then this will be done through the Port of Progreso. The most reliable company is Linea Peninsular, Inc., which ships from the Port of Panama City, Florida to the Port of Progreso, Yucatán. The cost of shipping, of course, depends on the amount of furniture being shipped, and the distance from your home in the U.S. to Panama City, Florida.

Once it arrives at the Port of Progreso, you will need a Customs Broker to handle the paperwork to import legally your furnishings and household goods. There are two Customs Brokers that are extraordinary: María Luisa Uc Varguez of Agencia Aduanal Del Valle Sureste, and Hiram Cervera of Agencia Aduanal Cervera. Each continues to win praise for their selfless, thorough and professional work, and each has vast experience helping expatriates get their household goods safely and quickly through Mexican Customs.

Here is the contact information to ship to Yucatán and clear Mexican Customs:

Shipping company

Linea Peninsular, Inc.

US Address:
  5323 W. Highway 98, Suite 215
  Panama City, FL 32401
  Telephone: (800) 858-4280 or (850) 522-4500
Email: *usoffice@lineaships.com*
Website: *www.lineaships.com*
Mexico Address:
  Calle 25 #151-A, between Calle 80 and 82 Street, Centro
  Progreso, Yucatán
Telephone: (969) 935-5519
Website: *www.lineaships.com*
Email: *mexicooffice@lineaships.com*

Customs Brokers

Agencia Aduanal Del Valle Sureste

Lic. María Luisa Uc Varguez
Calle 27 #168-A, between Calle 84 and 86 Street, Centro
Progreso, Yucatán
Telephone: (969) 934-30-55, Ext.127
Email: *malu@aadelvalle.com.mx*
Website: *www.aadelvalle.com.mx*

Agencia Aduanal Cervera

Hiram Cervera
Calle 84 #127, between Calle 27 and 29 Street, Centro
Progreso, Yucatán
Telephone: (969) 935-3535
Email: *Agencia@cervera.com.mx*
Website: *www.cervera.com.mx*

Going somewhere?

We are a sparsely populated peninsula, with long stretches of road between towns. Before you head out, head to a gas station. Fill up the tank, have the attendant check the tires, the oil and clean your windshield. Make sure you have water, sunscreen and a hat. Taking a map is a good idea. Here are the distances:

Distance from Mérida to:

Destination	Miles	Kilometers
Campeche City	158	253
Cancún	199	318
Ceiba Club de Golf	9	14
Celestún	58	93
Chetumal	285	456
Chichén Itzá	75	120
Cobá	145	232
Dzibilchaltún	10	16
Ek Balam	111	179
Holbox Island	218	350
Isla Mujeres	206	330
Izamal	44	72
Kabah	63	102
Labná	74	118
Lol-Tún Caves	70	113
Mexico City	969	1550
Motul	28	45
Ochil, Hacienda	16	26
Oxkutzcab	60	100
Petac, Hacienda	13	20
Playa del Carmen	240	386
Progreso	22	35
Ría Lagartos	165	263
Sayil	79	126
Sisal	33	53

Destination	Miles	Kilometers
Telchac Puerto	39	62
Temozón, Hacienda	21	34
Teya, Hacienda	8	12
Ticul	53	84
Tizimin	132	212
Tulum (via Coba)	171	274
Uxmal	50	80
Valladolid	100	160
Xcanatún, Hacienda	8	12
Yaxcopoil	14	22

Conversion Chart

Kilometer-Mile Conversion

1 kilometer = 0.60 miles

So if you multiply kilometers by 0.6, you'll end up with miles.

Example: 10 kilometers (10 x 0.6) is equivalent to 6 miles.

And if you multiply miles by 1.6, you'll end up with kilometers.

Example: 10 miles (10 x 1.6) is equivalent to 16 kilometers

7 The Expat Life, or what the Mexicans call "Gringolandia"

Americans call it "Gringo Gulch," and Yucatecans and Mexicans refer to it as "Gringolandia." These are the Colonias of Santiago and Santa Ana in the heart of Mérida's Historic Center. But what does this mean?

The self-effacing ways of thinking about the American (and Canadian) presence in Mérida speaks to the nature of our presence: At all times, foreigners are *guests* of Mexico. Until you become a Mexican citizen, or marry a Mexican citizen and have a child born in Mexico, your presence is that of a *guest*. It's possible to own entire city blocks of buildings, or have millions of dollars invested in businesses, but that does not detract from the tenuous nature of every foreigner's presence in Mexico.

This is important to remember: Mexico's hospitality is generously extended, but it can also be withdrawn.

Why are so few permanent rights extended to foreigners? Because history has taught Mexico that it must be cautious of others' intentions. Mexico, throughout its history, has been besieged. It was the target of an unprovoked war by the United States, it has been occupied by Napoleon III (who sent over Maximilian I to serve as "Emperor"). It has been the subject of intrigue during World War I with the notorious and infamous Zimmerman Telegram.

As a result, Mexico is wary of the political influence of foreigners in Mexico, and it imposes significant restrictions on the right of foreign citizens residing in Mexico to engage in the political process. Foreigners are forbidden to join political parties, attend political rallies, make political statements in public, or engage in public debate on all political issues. This is both *liberating* and *humbling*.

Liberating: It is liberating because you can forget any ideas about attending political rallies, becoming involved in one or another candidate's campaign, or even walking door-to-door gathering signatures on any petition.

Humbling: It is humbling because it makes you realize that, in the political life of the Mexican nation, foreigners have no power whatsoever. In a city like Mérida, with almost a million people, the American expat community, comprised of about 3,500 permanent residence, is, in one word: Insignificant.

How insignificant?

Consider this: Of the hundreds of thousands of Americans who have resided in Mérida over the past 200 years, only *four* have entered the consciousness of Yucatecan society! Who are they? John Lloyd Stephens, an attorney and diplomat, who came down here in the 1830s and 1840s and produced two bestselling books, *Incidents of Travel*, which brought to the attention of the world the magnificent architectural and archaeological accomplishments of the Maya. Edward Thompson, the American Consul in Mérida who supervised the archaeological excavations at the Sacred Cenote at Chichén Itzá – and who remains notorious for having shipped untold treasure to Harvard's Peabody Museum. Alma Reed, who was invited to Mexico by President Alvaro Obregón, hailed a "Hero of Mexico" for saving the life of a Mexican teenager sentenced to death by the State of California, and who carried out a tawdry, impossible affair with Felipe Carrillo Puerto, Governor of

Expats in the Yucatán

Nationality	Number
Cubans	6,500
Lebanese	5,250
Americans	5,000*
Chinese**	1,700
Canadian	1,550***
Spanish	900
Argentine	550
Italian	450
Korean	425
German	375
Guatemalan	225
South American	625
Other European	875
Other Asia	375
Africa	125
Total	**24,925**

Please note that this excludes Cuban-Mexicans and Lebanese-Mexicans, which number in the scores of thousands.

*American fulltime residents are 3,500 and 1,500 additional part-time residents

**Chinese from Taiwan, not mainland China

***Canadian fulltime residents are 425 and 875 are part-time residents

These figures are compiled from various sources, including foreign embassies in Mexico City and data from INEGI (Instituto Nacional de Estadística Geografía e Informática), as of November 2010.

Yucatán. And Joann Andrews, who has dedicated decades of her life to building and nurturing an environmental consciousness on the Yucatán Peninsula, and is cherished by generations of Yucatecans as one of their own – "una joya del Mayab," meaning, "a jewel of the land of the Maya."

There are, of course, other expatriates who have become legends. Antonio Menéndez who, along with his wife, Angela González, arrived in the Yucatán in the 1860s from Cuba, fought for social justice, and established schools for women and the Maya, both believing that education for women and the less privileged was necessary for progress. (Their son, Carlos R. Menéndez went on to found the *Diario de Yucatán*.) Joaquin García Ginerés, a native of Catalonia and who worked to modernize Mérida along the lines that the great cities of Europe were expanding during the Edwardian age. He was so instrumental in the growth of Mérida that the Colonia García Ginerés is named after him, by official proclamation in his honor. In our time, Miguel A. Bretos, another Cuban, who has had a distinguished career as a historian, scholar and was the first director of the Hispanic department at the Smithsonian in Washington, D.C. is much beloved. His intellectual contributions to Mérida continue to astonish, from the first history of the colonial churches of the Yucatán (*Iglesias de Yucatán*, 1992), to the most comprehensive history of Mérida's cathedral (*Mérida: Biografía de una Catedral*, 2011).

And how political sensitive is Mexico to foreigners interfering in the political process of the Mexican nation? Consider this: Article XXX of the Mexican Constitution empowers the president to expel, immediately and without recourse, any foreigner deemed "inconvenient." The last time this was used widely was by president Ernesto Zedillo who expelled hundreds of foreigners who supported the Zapatistas in Chiapas. Current president Felipe Calderon has used it sparingly, primarily against foreigners involved in drug trafficking and money laundering activities.

What does this "political insignificance" mean? It means

> **Advice from the State Department:**
>
> "**The Mexican Constitution prohibits political activities by foreigners**; such actions may result in detention and/or deportation. Travelers should avoid political demonstrations and other activities that might be deemed political by the Mexican authorities. Even demonstrations intended to be peaceful can turn confrontational and escalate into violence. U.S. citizens are urged to avoid areas of demonstrations, and to exercise caution if in the vicinity of any protests."

that you are absolutely free to come here and enjoy yourself, delight in this beautiful city, make lifelong friends with other expats, Mexicans and Yucatecans, build a wonderful life for yourself without any political or civic questions entering your life. It also means that you can forget about bringing down a clipboard and to collect signatures for a petition in front of City Hall!

The moral of the story is that only if you think otherwise – that you can become an active agent in a country that really doesn't want your input about anything unless you are working for an accredited international agency on official business – will you be disappointed.

There is wisdom to this advice, since Mérida's recent history is littered with well-meaning and well-intentioned foreigners who arrive here, think they can contribute significantly to the city's life, who then find out that, although they are received politely, their overtures are ignored, and they are, if not turned away, then at least relegated to the sidelines.

Remember: Mérida has much to offer you, but there is little that you can offer Mérida.

After all, if you are an entrepreneur and start a business, that's great. But no one forgets that business ventures exist to make the entrepreneurs money. And if you come here thinking you can donate your time and skills to a worthy cause, just go to Chapter 18 and you will see an overwhelming list of bona fide nonprofit organizations duly authorized to work in fields from helping children with autism to saving endangered sea turtles, from protecting women in abusive relationships to improving the city's urban planning. In addition, there are hundreds of "civil associations" – "asociaciones civiles" – that are involved in all manner of things, from rescuing abandoned pets, to providing support groups for caregivers of people with Alzheimer's.

Many Americans, unfamiliar with how Mexican society is organized, embark independently and start initiatives that are doomed to failure, as they are seen as working *outside* established norms. Why create a parallel organization to duplicate work that is already being carried out by Mexicans? Why insult the people of Mérida by coming across as thinking you are better qualified to do this or carry out that?

It's a curious place, this "Gringolandia," this "Gringo Gulch." But it is a welcoming place.

The "Expat Life" is one of measured leisure, and careful overtures to the community at large. The Cubans and Lebanese have been very successful at integrating themselves into the fabric of Yucatecan life. There is much that American and Canadian expatriates can learn from them.

And in the spirit of learning what it means to be an expatriate, here are Hugo de Naranja's recommendations for becoming a Good Expat!

The Enigma of Arrival

The Ten Must-Read Works of Fiction for Anyone Living Abroad

By Hugo de Naranja

Lonely Planet and *Rough Guides* and the CIA's *World Factbook* may give you extremely useful practical information, but the project of long-term displacement, the demands of living outside your country of origin for extended periods of time, often requires a different order of *know-how* and an approach that hard facts alone can't explain.

Fiction is invaluable for learning to see yourself and what you're up to more clearly, and understanding how other people see themselves and what they're up to. The very finest fiction also takes you where you didn't know you wanted to go. What follows is a list of ten books, in alphabetical order, who we consider among the best for taking you there:

Democracy, by Joan Didion

Inez Victor gets around.

The Vietnam War nears its disastrous end. Post-colonial discontent convulses Southeast Asia. Inez travels a lot with her pompous husband Harry, a senator aspiring to the presidency, and takes some side-trips with Jack, her tight-lipped intermittent soul mate who shares her uncanny knack for "interesting times."

Saigon falls to the North Vietnamese. The American evacuation dissolves into anarchy. Inez loses patience with her countrymen's faith in their specialness — an insight that ushers her story toward its ineffably sad, almost hopeful, conclusion.

This is perhaps the funniest work in all of American 20th century literary fiction, and after turning its last page, you'll forever miss Inez, Janet, Harry, Jack, Billy, Dwight, Ruthie, and, yes, even Frances.

Geography III, by Elizabeth Bishop

Bishop's father died eight months after she was born. Her mother lost her mind a few years later. Bishop spent her life wandering — Europe, North Africa, Latin America — staying the longest, twenty-six years, in Brazil.

She was never ambitious about her career as a poet. She spent years, sometimes decades, reworking a single poem. Her humility was uncompromising: she refused to use her work for confession or self-disclosure. She took a dim view of poets who thought they were prophets and of poems that smacked of oracular self-importance. Bishop wrote about what she'd directly observed in the world outside herself, and referred to her personal life, her emotions, only rarely, and with a diamond cutter's precision.

Small, witty, a frequent hostage to asthma and alcohol, Bishop wondered what travel meant and why she never felt at home in the world. And she was always dazzled by nature's ability, through its beauty and oddness, to lift her above the loneliness that followed her everywhere. She's now regarded as one of America's greatest poets, and *Geography III* represents her finest work.

The Good Terrorist, by Dorris Lessing

Lessing seems to be coolly examining a group of politically minded misfits who coalesce long enough in London to dream up and execute a fatal plan.

But she's less interested in politics than in the specific deficiencies that make a person so despise and reject his own country's liberal democracy that he'd do it harm.

Ticking away at the heart of this novel is an ingenious technique so covert and subversive in its cunning that you may never quite figure out just why *The Good Terrorist* haunts and unsettles you long after you've read it.

Guerrillas, by VS Naipaul

The English-speaking world's most famously merciless writer fixes his eye on moth-to-the-flame characters drawn to a revolutionary movement on a Caribbean island.

Dread, doom, and folly are as thick in the air as the bauxite dust covering the island's roads. Something sinister announces its approach with flashes of surprising violence.

Pay close attention to the game Harry introduces to his guests after brunch at his beachfront home. It's a booby-trap Naipaul has set for his characters, but you, the reader, are an intended target, too.

How German Is It?, by Walter Abish

The past is a slow-acting venom that causes dreamy stupor leading to moral paralysis.

Abish had never visited Germany before writing *How German Is It?,* but readers and critics agreed that he captured the essential essence of post-war Germanness better than any native-born German.

His characters, including the son of a German officer involved in the 1944 plot to assassinate Hitler, can't wake themselves from the nightmare of history. Terrorism and its origins flicker throughout the story until the unforeseeable revelation at its end.

> **Buy these books on Amazon.com.**
>
> For your convenience, an "iBookstore" has been set up where all these titles are featured — and where you can purchase them, getting whatever discount Amazon.com is offering!
>
> Here is the "iBookstore" addresses:
> http://astore.amazon.com/casacathe-20

In a Free State, by VS Naipaul

The novella's pretext is a road-trip through troubled East Africa.

But Bobby and Linda aren't just hapless characters Naipaul has set up to take a fall. With a light touch and singular economy, Naipaul makes the two live and breathe as much as Flaubert does Emma Bovary.

And just as Flaubert set out to describe and indict mid-19th century France, Naipaul, with far fewer words, makes the entirety of Western colonialism his target and, with a ruthlessness and speed that will leave you gasping, pulls the trigger.

Life: A User's Manual, by Georges Perec

To live abroad successfully, you ought be able to pay close attention to the fine details of how other people live their lives — their habits, customs, histories, pretensions, and vulnerabilities. But this attention must also be the sort that can be focused quickly and remain acute despite frequent, and arbitrary, interruption.

Life: A User's Manual moves forward and backward in time, in fits and starts, in 99 chapters, as it obsessively scrutinizes the fascinating inhabitants of a fictional Parisian apartment block.

Since the novel's clever puzzle-like structure doesn't march orderly from beginning to middle to end, you can open to any random chapter, or read them all in their given sequence, with equal pleasure. Which makes *Life: A User's Manual* perfectly suited for reading while traveling, and for the distractions and disruptions of living abroad.

The Sailor From Gibraltar, by Marguerite Duras

The French often think of travel as pure escape, and find whatever's exotic in the foreign to be elegant, as opposed to alienating.

In *The Sailor From Gibraltar*, Marguerite Duras gives us a sun-struck narrator who, while on vacation in Italy, abandons everything to follow Anna, a seductive American who plies the Mediterranean in her gorgeous yacht, perpetually searching for her lost great love, a sailor from Gibraltar. The sunshine. The sea. Life at sea. Pleasure. All the necessary romantic elements appear to be in place. Yet Duras isn't handing you romance, but mystery.

The Sheltering Sky, by Paul Bowles

A friend once described *Without Stopping*, Bowles' globe-trotting name-dropping memoir, as a "very meaty *People* article." You wish there was more to it, but what you have is satisfying enough that you're willing to accept it on its own terms.

Bowles makes a similar demand of his readers in *The Sheltering Sky,* the story of a well-heeled intellectual couple, Port and Kit, who wander into North Africa, incautiously looking for answers to some unstated questions they have about their lives.

Yes, of course, self-absorption can be addictive and dangerous. Had Kit been less distracted, however, she'd have never drifted away in the amazing "vision quest" that makes up the final third of the book.

Speak, Memory, by Vladimir Nabokov

Nabokov said he never wanted to return to Russia because he'd kept everything worth keeping from his homeland in his memory and in his heart.

If you've ever wondered what you might take with you from the places and people who formed you, long after those places and people have vanished, *Speak, Memory* will show you how the world's greatest connoisseur of the irretrievable past guarded his treasures against the predations of time.

His pretty mother returning home after a morning of mushroom hunting. His handsome father returning home after a close-call with an assassin. Biarritz in the summer. A lovely little girl rolling a hoop through a Parisian park. It's all there. All of it. Luminous, distinct, and eternal.

Read Spanish?

If you are fluent in Spanish, here is a list of the best books available in the Spanish language. These titles were compiled by a survey of critics in Mexico and Spain and are the best 20 books (29 in reality since a few were tied for various rankings) for 2010.

1. **Verano**, de J. M. Coetzee (Mondadori)
2. **Poesía reunida**, de William Butler Yeats (Pre-Textos)
3. **Blanco nocturno**, de Ricardo Piglia (Anagrama)
4. **El sueño del celta**, de Mario Vargas Llosa (Alfaguara)
5. **El amor verdadero**, de José María Guelbenzu (Siruela)
6. **Retratos y encuentros**, de Gay Talese (Alfaguara)
7. **Algo va mal**, de Tony Judt (Taurus)
8. **Dublinesca**, de Enrique Vila-Matas (Seix Barral)
9. **Tarde o temprano**, Poemas 1958-2009, de José Emilio Pacheco (Tusquets)
10. **Esencia y hermosura**, Antología, de María Zambrano (Galaxia Gutenberg/Círculo de Lectores)
    Tiempo de vida, de Marcos Giralt Torrente (Anagrama)
    Tierra desacostumbrada, de Jhumpa Lahiri (Salamandra)
11. **El mundo bajo los párpados**, Jacobo Siruela (Atalanta)
12. **Visión desde el fondo del mar**, Rafael Argullol (Acantilado)
13. **Hojas de Madrid**, Con La Galerna (1968-1977). Blas de Otero (Galaxia Gutenberg/Círculo de Lectores)
    Libro de los muertos. *Apuntes 1942-1988*, Elias Canetti (Galaxia Gutenberg/Círculo de Lectores)
14. **Notas al pie de Gaza**, Joe Sacco (Mondadori)
15. **Correr**. Jean Echenoz (Anagrama)
16. **Autobiografía sin vida**, Félix de Azúa (Mondadori)

Del lado del amor. Poesía reunida 1994-2009. Juan Antonio González Iglesias (Visor)
Nunca fue tan hermosa la basura. José Luis Pardo (Galaxia Gutenberg/Círculo de Lectores)
Todo lo que tengo lo llevo conmigo. Herta Müller (Siruela)
17. **Brillan monedas oxidadas**, Juan Eduardo Zúñiga (Galaxia Gutenberg/Círculo de Lectores)
18. **Hoy no es ayer**, Ensayos sobre la España del siglo XX. Santos Juliá (RBA)
    La experiencia totalitaria, Tzvetan Todorov (Galaxia Gutenberg/Círculo de Lectores)
    Leviatán o la ballena, Philip Hoare (Ático de los libros)
    Una saga moscovita, Vasili Aksiónov (La otra orilla)
19. **La idea de la justicia**, Amartya Sen (Taurus)
20. **La muerte del adversario**, Hans Keilson (Minúscula)

8   THE COST OF LIVING IN MÉRIDA

How much does it cost to live in Mérida? What do you need to know in order to come up with a realistic budget? What are "unexpected" expenses that you can "expect" to encounter once you make the move?

The answer, of course, is that it depends on your lifestyle. If you are accustomed to drinking champagne every evening with dinner, and you have a lavish home that requires a full-time staff, then that's a far different budget than if you are retired, living on a fixed income, and are more frugal in your ways.

Consider that most people in Mérida manage to live decent, honorable and comfortable lives on about $325 USD a month, excluding rent or mortgage. But also consider that most Yucatecans do not own cars, have air conditioners or expect to make one or two trips back to the States every year. On the other hand, there is at least one residence in Mérida that is equipped with a heliport, and which has a household staff of 37 full-time employees, so you can imagine the expenses in maintaining that lifestyle.

In Mérida, as in the world over, the sky's the limit!

But to get down to the matter of figuring out a realistic budget, let's start at the beginning. Every year UBS in Switzerland surveys the most important cities in the world and then ranks the cost of living in them, using New York City as the benchmark. Out of the 70 cities surveyed, Mexico City ranked 64th **least expensive**. That means that when, 122

> **Cost of Living for a Retired Couple**
> Based on a U.S. dollar exchange rate of 12.50 pesos the cost of living in Mérida can be as little as $1,989 USD a month to as much as $4,765 USD. These figures are based on expenditure on housing, food, education, transportation, clothing, recreation, health, furniture, appliances and personal use
>
> For expatriates often the most important starting references upon arriving in a foreign country are expatriate clubs and associations. Some of the most important are the American Society along with the DAR, the International Friendship Club, and Rotary International. American Society acts as a large umbrella organization harboring smaller clubs and associations that are based on particular fields of interest.
>
> Source: *SolutionsAbroad.com*

goods and services (including housing) were taken into account, what costs $1 USD in New York, costs only $0.40 USD in Mexico City! That means that Mexico City is about 60% cheaper than New York.

That's step one, because it gives you an idea of where Mexico ranks relative to other cities, from Miami to Los Angeles, Tokyo to Dubai. The second step, of course, is figuring out how cheaper or more expensive it is to live in Mérida than in the nation's capital. Fortunately, the Mexican government does a great job of analyzing and monitoring costs of living throughout the country. Most people don't know this, but Mexico classifies the country into three economic zones, "A," "B," and "C." Zone A, which includes Mexico City is the most expensive area. Zone C, which includes Mérida, (and the entire Yucatán peninsula) is the least expensive area to live.

The National Commission on Minimum Wages, CONASAMI, for "Comision Nacional de Salarios Minimos," and INEGI, Mexico's Census Bureau, estimate that it is about 25% less expensive to live in Mérida than it is in Mexico City for everything, excluding energy (the prices for gasoline and electricity these products are set at the federal level and are the same for the entire country).[4]

That means that when you discount the cost of living from Mexico City's UBS ranking, Mérida is one of the more affordable places to live in Mexico. (It's about one third of what one would expect to pay for a comparable lifestyle in New York City.) This, of course, gives you a perspective with which you can start to set a budget for living in Mérida.

---

[4] For information on Mexico's Commission on Minimum Wages, see: *www.conasami.gob.mx/*. For information on Mexico's Census Bureau, see: *www.inegi.org.mx/*.

There are two other factors to consider. First is your housing. If you own your place (as most expatriates do), then you don't have a mortgage. The annual Predial tax is rather insignificant, usually the cost of an elaborate birthday dinner at one of the fancier restaurants or hotels in town. If you rent, then you have to consider whether your "renting like an expat," or "renting like a Yucatecan."

The difference is considerable, and well worth pondering. In the chapter on Real Estate, we discuss the "artificial" real estate market that has emerged around the Historic Center, and the shameful role that American expatriates working in the real estate business have played in making this once-affordable part of town into an almost unbearable place in which to rent. Colonial houses that have been refurbished, remodeled and upgraded have been "dollarized" – priced to fetch prices as if this were exclusive neighborhoods of Miami, Ft. Lauderdale or Boca Raton.

Mexico Cost of Living Report: Autumn 2010:

Living Costs and Detailed Price Table of Food, Groceries & Pharmaceuticals

The Autumn 2010 Mexico Cost of Living Report is published by MexExperience to help anyone who is considering a move to Mexico, whether to live here full time or part time, to work, study, take a sabatical or retire and who wants to better understand the cost of living in Mexico today.

The report will enable you to get a good understanding of current living costs in Mexico and create a financial budget tailored to your specific lifestyle choices and requirements.

This report offers readers a detailed analysis of the real costs of day-to-day living in Mexico. The report has been compiled from data gathered during October 2010 and is fully up-to-date with the latest prices and cost trends in Mexico.

The report highlights prices and costs across a range of products and services most foreign expatriates will seek when they live in Mexico. It also includes a number of overlooked costs which people forget to include when they compile their budgets, sometimes with significant consequences when the actual costs are compared with the estimates after having lived in Mexico for a while.

To order the report, go to:
www.mexperience.com/liveandwork/mexico-cost-of-living.php

Many American and Canadian expatriates are told to "expect" to pay ridiculous prices. "For approximately $900 to $1,600 USD per month, furnished homes with swimming pools, in desirable neighborhoods, are available," Jane McCarthy and Bruce Kelley advise would-be expatriates. For those prices you can rent a wonderful, two story home with three or four bedrooms, as many bathrooms, a two-car garage, with staff in residential neighborhoods where Yucatecan professional live with their families! To pay that much for anything in the Historic Center – where there probably isn't parking, the "pool" is so small one would be challenged to swim a lap, and the décor is in all likelihood what was on-sale at some discounted "rustic Mexican" operation defies reason.

To find value in renting an apartment or house, you have to go "native" – use the "Avisos Económicos" of the *Diario de Yucatán* to understand what the fair market price is for renting in various neighborhoods. Here's a benchmark: The average rent for a two-bedroom, one-bathroom dwelling (apartment of single-family house) in an average neighborhood in Mérida, unfurnished (except for stove and refrigerator) is $3,000 pesos, or about $240 USD. That's what Mexicans pay, and that's what you can also pay.

The other factor to consider is that energy is as expensive in Mexico as it is in the rest of the world. Depending on where you moving from in the U.S., electricity can be a bit more expensive than what you are used to paying. Mexico's state-owned oil monopoly, Petroleos Mexicanos, or Pemex, sets the price for gasoline (unleaded, super unleaded) and diesel. The prices are uniform throughout the country, and the only gas stations are operated by, or franchises of, Pemex. For almost the entire country, the electric power company is the Comision Federal de Electricidad, known as CFE. The CFE sets the price of electricity, through complicated formulas, for the various economic "zones," and then depending on whether it is residential, government, industry and other categories (hospitals, etc.). If further allow for subsidies applied during various times of year, and there are formulas that increase rates for "above-average" residential use. The bottom line is that no matter how you look at it, electricity is one of the most expensive commodities in Mexico. People really try their best to conserve power, and it is almost unheard of for a landlord to include the price of electricity in any rental agreement. This is one reason why there are more fans in Mérida than air-conditioners!

So, it's settled: Housing will be very inexpensive, but energy costs require that you be more frugal than you are probably accustomed to back in the United States or Canada.

But how do you go about building a budget? Simple: Item by item. This is how to go about it in a comprehensive way.

 Building a Budget for Living in Mérida

The first step, of course, is to consider your current lifestyle. How much do you already spend? Whatever that figure is, you should expect to pay considerably less for basic staples, and perhaps a bit more for luxuries.

Why? Because things like fresh fruit, utilities (except electricity), household help, and taxes are considerably lower in Mexico than in the U.S. or Canada. On the other hand, many luxuries in Mexico are subject to import taxes. For the most part, for instance, luxury goods, such as fine wines and high-end electronics are a bit more expensive. If you are accustomed to enjoying a case of French wine throughout the month, you may be better off finding some wines you enjoy from countries (such as Chile and Spain) that enjoy preferential trade agreements with Mexico.

It's also important to keep in mind that items you find at familiar places, such as Costco, Sam's Club and Home Depot can be a bit more expensive: Mexico has a 16% sales tax, called IVA, for Impuesto al Valor Agregado, which is familiar to Canadians and Europeans as the "Value-Added Tax"). It's possible to rationalize this consumption tax by realizing that Mexico has, for all intents and purposes, no real income tax – unless you make a considerable income. Most expatriates in Mérida are retired, and not working, and very few have permission from Immigration authorities to be engaged in income-generating activies, whether it comes from either working as an employee or from money from renting homes.

Housing

If you own your home in Mérida, the only expenses are the Predial tax, which, as discussed in Chapter 11, is a nominal fee, hardly the equivalent of the onerous property taxes levied in the United States. On the other hand, since almost all of Mérida and its environs are within the Restricted Zone, you own your property through a Fideicomiso, usually administered by a bank.

These trusts levy an annual fee, which run into several hundred dollars. An average Fideicomiso tax for foreigners in Mérida is about $5,000 to $7,500 pesos, or between $400 USD to $600 USD. When the Predial tax is added, the costs of maintaining your home in Mérida is well under $750 USD for most people.

If, on the other hand, you are renting, then you know outright how much your housing expenses will be. For most expatriates, the average cost of renting a 2 bedroom, 1 bathroom house is about $42,000 pesos a year, or $3,360 USD. Of course, there are privileged individuals who live in lavish homes that cost them upwards of $750,000 USD, and there are residences that rent for about $2,750 USD a month, but considering the options, housing is a very reasonable

133

expense, far less than homeowners' association fees, or monthly maintenances on condominiums or co-ops in the U.S., and a mere fraction of the property taxes levied by local governments.

Utilities: Electricity, Gas, Water and Garbage

These are the basics of life, and in Mérida they are, except for electric power, more than economical. In the next chapter, how to set up service for basic utilities is addressed. For now, however, as you go about creating a budget for yourself, keep these guidelines in mind.

Electricity

The state-owned Comision Federal de Electricidad, or CFE, provides electric power to Mérida. Energy throughout Mexico is owned by the government, both electric and petroleum. Electric power is supplied in 110V, 60 cycle which is consistent with the U.S. and Canada; whatever appliances anyone brings from the U.S. or Canada will work in Mexican outlets. Mexico's economic growth, however, has outpaced the ability of the CFE to build new plants and expand service as necessary. Electric rates are high, and there is a great civic effort to conserve as much electricity as possible. In fact, on a globalized basis, Mexico's electric bill is about 20% higher than the median electric bill in the U.S.

Electricity will be the most expensive utility on your budget without a doubt, and yet, it is not a deal breaker. The CFE has a bimonthly billing cycle, and you will receive a bill every other month. The rate you pay, however, reflects prior usage, over the previous six billing periods (an entire year). If your consumption falls in relation to what you consumed around the same time the previous bill, and this is a consistent trend, your rate will decline. If, on the other hand, your consumption rises over the same period, and this is a trend, your rate will increase – and effort to get you to conserve.

The average residential bill for a home where there are two air-conditioners in use, is about $3,500 pesos, or about $280 USD. This may sound high, but the billing cycle is for two months, so the monthly bill for the average home in Mérida is about $140 USD. For Yucatecans and Mexicans, this is an extravagant expenditure. For most Americans and Canadians, it is steep, but not unreasonable. Many expatriates (and Yucatecans and Mexicans) become compulsive about conservation – preferring ceiling fans, and turning on their air-conditioners only at night. Did we mention that rates at night are lower than during day-time hours? Yes, it is a complicated system.

Overall, frugal expatriates can expect to pay about $80 USD a month for electricity, and those who have a swimming pool and run air-conditioners habitually, can expect to pay about twice that much or more.

Gas

There is no natural gas in Mérida. Propane tanks are used, and most residences can fill their gas tanks for about $2,000 pesos, or about $160 USD. This should last about six months, so the annual expenditure that the normal expatriate household can expect to spend is about $320 USD a year, or just under $27.00 a month. Unless you're taking hot baths every day, or doing laundry daily, or are cooking for an army, there's no reason to use more than this in propane gas.

Water

At the beginning of this book it was mentioned that Mérida is built over what is believed to be one of the largest underground river systems in the world. Water is plentiful, and very, very inexpensive. Water is provided by the Junta de Agua Potable y Alcantarillado de Yucatán, known as JAPAY, and pronounced, "Hah-Pie." How cheap is cheap? Consider this: Few people pay more than the minimum, and this is determined by neighborhood. In most of

Sample Prices in Mérida, 2011

Renting a house or an apartment, 2 bedroom, 1 bathroom in an average neighborhood:
3,000 Pesos

Renting a room in a private home:
1,200 Pesos

Bus fare: **6 Pesos**

A cappuccino, café latte or espresso in a café:
20 Pesos

Lunch at an average sit-down restaurant:
60 Pesos

Dinner at an average sit-down restaurant:
80 Pesos

A bottle of beer at a bar: **15 Pesos**

A drink at a nightclub: **40 Pesos**

A pack of cigarettes: **32 Pesos**

A soft drink (from a vending machine):
7 Pesos

A newspaper: **8 Pesos**

A cab ride, within Historic Center: **30 Pesos**

Ticket to the movies (weekday performance):
15 Pesos

Roundtrip airfare to Mexico City:
1,800 Pesos

Mérida's Colonias, the bill is $72 pesos, or less than $6 USD – for two months! Unless you are filling an Olympic-size pool every week or running the washing machine every day, average Yucatecan household budgets the equivalent of $35-40 USD for water for an entire year.

Garbage Collection

Here again, expect to pay a minimal amount. In the older Colonias in poor neighborhoods, the garbage collection fee is $17 pesos a month – less than $1.50 USD. In the more affluent neighborhoods, the fee is an average of $42 pesos – or under $3.50 USD. This means that the Christmas tip you give the garbage man will probably amount to most of the annual cost of garbage collection. And let's face it, you do have to give the garbage man a Christmas bonus, right?

Internet

Apart from utilities, there are other "essentials" of modern life: Internet, Cable television and telephone service. Here again, given the global nature of the world and the fact that Carlos Slim, who is, according to *Forbes* magazine, the richest man in the world, and he made his fortune in telecommunications. That means, there are no bargains to be found. There are, happily, no major rip-offs, either!

Cable television is now so intertwined with the Internet that it's almost impossible to separate the two. The two largest cable television companies serving Mérida are CableMAS and CableRED. Each offers competitive packages that allow unlimited Internet along with a broad selection of cable channels for about $1,200 pesos a month, or about $96 USD. If you are a fan of certain programming channels, such as HBO, CNN, Bloomberg, Showtime, Cinemax, TLC, Discovery, E! and Fox, you can get them in Mérida. SKY offers a comprehensive package for about $650 pesos a month, which is about $52 USD. (SKY offers a less comprehensive selection for about $450 pesos, or $36 USD, but you have to check with them to see if the channels you want are or are not included.) As you can see,

---

Cash vs. Credit

Mexico's consumer protection agency encourages stores to pass along savings to consumers who choose to pay cash instead of credit cards for two reasons. Since merchants have to pay fees to the banks when they accept credit and debit cards, it's only fair that consumers who pay cash enjoy a 1-3% discount. Also, the government wants to discourage consumers from getting into credit card debt.

What this means is that many retailers – from Sam's Club to Comercial Mexicana – will offer a discount if you pay cash. Take advantage of this by going to an ATM before heading out to shop.

however, CableMAS, CableRED and SKY offer packages that are somewhat less expensive than in the U.S.

Telephone

If there's one area where "globalization" is evident, it has to been in the sheer number of telephone calling plans and options available. It would fill a small book. You can choose between Telmex, Telcel, Iusacell, Telefonica and Axtel. You can choose calling cards, or almost-disposable cell phones that can be recharged at any convenience store. You can use Skype or Magic Jack, or you can even try two Dixie cups and a string. OK, perhaps the last option is not really an option. The bottom line is that for standard land lines, a regular telephone that you plug into the wall, the basic rate is about $200 pesos a month, and that includes 100 free local telephone calls. After that, there's a $5 peso charge for additional calls. There are plans that include all manner of options, but be mindful that for about $1,100 pesos per month, which is about $88 USD, Telmex has a "Telmex Sin Limites," or "Telmex Without Limit" which allows you to enjoy all the local and domestic long distance service you can use, and it includes 2 MB of broadband Internet connection with wireless router. Bottom line, telephone could cost you as little as $200 pesos a month ($16 USD) or as much as $1,100 pesos ($88 USD), Internet included, unless you're doing something wrong.

Food

What kind of diet do you have? If you eat locally, then your groceries in Mérida can be reasonable. A diet that consists of seasonal fruits bought at the local market, along with standard vegetables (from onions to carrots, potatoes to celery) will run you about a third of what you can expect to pay in the U.S. Seasonal fruits are an even better deal. In Mérida it's possible to pull up to a street vendor and purchase 100 oranges for $50 pesos, which comes out to four cents of a US dollar per orange! By the same token, if you eat local meats – chicken, turkey and pork – you will be surprised at how far your money goes. On the other hand, if you insist on having kiwis from New Zealand, grapes from Chile and apples from Vermont, you can expect to pay a premium. If you insist on beef (hardly a head of cattle is found in the Yucatán!), or other meats like lamb, then it will be a bit more expensive. Many expatriates insist on shopping at Costco and Sam's Club, while forgetting that if you go local – Aurrera, Chedraui, Comercial Mexicana and San Francisco de Asis – you are likely to get deals. The same applies to beverages: Tequila and rum drinkers save more money than those who insist on whiskeys and European vodka. Wines from Chile and Spain are a bargain, whereas wines from France and Italy can be a bit pricey. California and Oregon wines are no bargains, but they are not unreasonable either. If you cultivate a taste for Mexico's excellent beers, you will be better off than if you insist on American brands, such as Budweiser and Miller. Soft drinks are a bargain, as are the basic staples which are price-controlled by the government through a series of subsidies and ceilings: eggs, flour, and cornmeal. Most expatriates find that their average grocery bill is about 25% less than it is in the U.S., and a full 45% less if they go local – and shop for produce, poultry, fish and pork at local markets.

Transportation

What do you include in transportation? The cost of maintaining your car? The amount you spend on taxis? Bus fare? Round-trip airfare back home two or three times a year to visit friends and family? It's all up to you. But getting around town should cost no more than $30 or $40 pesos per taxi ride, which comes out to somewhere between $2 or $3 USD per ride. Bus fare in Mérida is $6 pesos, or about half a US dollar. If you own your car, then how much do you budget for car maintenance, gas and insurance? It all depends on the state of your vehicle, its value (which affects the insurance premium), and how much you drive. In other words, these are all variables that more or less duplicate your expenses back home – with the exception of taxis and public transportation, which are considerably lower in Mexico. The price of gasoline you ask? Once upon a time gas in Mexico was very cheap; today it approximates prices in the least expensive markets in the U.S. Many expatriates who live in the Historic Center walk, take taxis and will rent a car only when they need to drive somewhere. (Roundtrip cab fare from downtown Mérida to Costco, or Sam's Club or Home Depot runs under $150 pesos, or $11 USD, so doing a biweekly run for staples fits easily into anyone's budget.)

So now you can build a budget. There are some expatriates who own their own homes and can live comfortably just on the Social Security checks. There are others who are more privileged and spend money with abandon. It's possible to live very comfortably in Mérida on $1,000 USD per person per month, and comfortable enough on about $850 USD a month.

What does the average expatriate couple in Mérida spends? According to educated guesses from city officials and the U.S. consular personnel, a typical American retired couple in Mérida lives on a budget of $1,850 USD a month. This is seen as extravagant by Mexican standards, but reflects what it costs to live in a very comfortable manner, enjoying meals out, seeing movies, having drinks with friends, and not counting every *centavo*.

And speaking of extravagance, let's talk a little about household help.

Household Help

One reason many Americans retire outside the U.S. is because getting household help is much cheaper than in the U.S. Unless you are very privileged, almost no one in the U.S. or

Canada has full-time servants. Yes, there are professional maid services in the U.S. – Merry Maids, Maid Services of America, Maid Brigade and so on – but these are by-the-hour services that are not inexpensive, and the scope of services they provide are very limited, and dictated by the agencies for which they work.

By contrast, in Mexico, there are vast numbers of middle-aged women who, because they are raising their children alone, or need to supplement their families' income for a variety of reasons, are available to work a few hours a day, or a few days a week, to supplement their incomes. A quarter century ago it was not uncommon for middle class families in Mérida to drive to a nearby village, find a young woman to work for them for the entire week or longer, and then return to their families for a few days off. That's one reason so many homes in the Centro Histórico have a "maid's quarter," usually a small bedroom with a utilitarian bathroom. That's seldom the case nowadays, simply because the government does a better job of making sure that young people stay in school longer, and there are other opportunities for employment in nearby villages. (Is it necessary to comment on the thousands of employees that the resorts of Cancún, Playa del Carmen and Isla Mujeres require to keep tourism industry churning away?)

It's odd to find a *young* woman working as a full-time maid in anyone's house nowadays. But habits die hard, and many still think of "maids" as "young" women from villages. In the same way that it has taken Americans an entire generation to resist the derogatory and demeaning practice of calling black men "boys," in the Yucatán there are still some Yucatecan families that use the degrading term "muchachas" to refer to women in their 30s, 40s and 50s who help around the house. What's worse, of course, is when expats arrive and, with an inexplicable sense of entitlement and arrogance, think that it's appropriate to refer to a grown woman as a "girl." How would an American or Canadian woman react if a fellow expat walked up and said, "Hey babe, nice tits!"

Well, that's how Mexican women feel when they are referred to as "muchachas" by their employers – so please refrain from using this derogatory term. And if you find yourself in the company of *anyone* who refers to domestic workers as "muchachas," "muchachos" or "mozos," you'd be well advised to find yourself a better class of acquaintances, unless you came to Mexico to surround yourself with American low-lifes as seen on "The Jerry Springer Show"!

The same applies for handimen who work for you. The term "mozo" is a carryover from Victorian times, when households consisted of several full-time live-in help. The "mozo" was the man who, unlike the gardener or watchman, was allowed inside the house, usually to carry out more difficult work, moving furniture, scrubbing terraces, handling the dogs, cleaning windows and chandeliers, and doing basic repairs, from fixing toilets and sinks, to replacing doorknobs and broken tiles.

In 2011, the correct way of referring to people who are employed as household help is by their given name, and to establish the relationship to you, by their job. "Elena, the lady who helps around the house," or "Juan, the man who helps us with chores" will suffice. (In Spanish, "Elena, la señora que nos ayuda en la casa" or "Juan, el señor que nos ayuda con las diligencias.") Now that it's clear there are no "muchachas" or "mozos" and that the only person who calls household help their "muchacha" or their "mozo," is, in one word, an asshole, how do you go about getting help around the house?

Domestic Workers
Daily wages

Domestic workers are usually contracted by the day. They are expected to work no more than 10 hours in a day, have their duties spelled out, and have all the supplies they will need provided for them. They are not expected to bring supplies with them, unless one of their responsibilities is to do the shopping, they have a list of items to buy, and they are given money beforehand.

The wage depends on the level of work, the hours expected and the price negotiated. It depends on many factors, including the size of your house and the duties involved. A person who has a one-bedroom house and needs someone to come dust has a different requirement than someone with a four-bedroom house, two terraces, a swimming pool and throws dinner parties every night for friends and family and hangers-on. A family with children is a different client than a mostly sedentary retired couple. In 2011 for a full day's work, it is common to pay between $200-$400 pesos.

Transportation and Meals

Roundtrip bus fare is expected to be provided. Lunch is to be provided. The bus fare should reflect the cost of your worker's round trip cost from their home to yours, and back to theirs. Lunch is handled one of two ways: They can be served a ration of the same lunch that you yourself will be having, or you can give them enough money $30-$50 pesos to buy lunch at the nearest Cocina Económica. It's not acceptable for you to have a lunch of lobster bisque and serve your employee soda crackers and a glass of water.

Live-In Workers

The employer-worker situation changes dramatically if you have live-in help. If you are privileged enough to have a maid or a handyman live in your home full-time, then you are privileged enough to formalize the business relationship so that each employee enjoys the benefits of health insurance, vacation time, and all the other amenities that full-time workers are entitled to expect.

When to Pay

For live-in help, they are expected normally to work Monday through Saturday morning. They are to be paid for the week in full, including bus fare to return home. They are expected to return on Monday. It is always a good idea to have them sign a receipt for the wages they received, which is almost always in cash. Remember that in December it is customary to pay the Christmas bonus, known as the *Aguinaldo*, which is an extra two weeks' salary or an entire month if someone has been working for you for five years or more. Of course, this is to be paid no later than December 15, since most people in Mexico use this money for Christmas expenses.

Room and Board

It is expected that you provide room and board for live-in domestic help. This means a room of their own, preferably with their own bathroom, and they are to be fed three meals a day. In Mexico, it is expected that this includes two soft drinks a day, but alcohol is strictly forbidden. Many employers provide a small television set as well.

Health Insurance

The easiest way to fulfil the expectation that you provide health insurance for live-in domestic help is to have each person sign up with the Instituto Mexicano del Seguro Social (IMSS), which has a *Seguro Voluntario* program for individuals who are not employed by formal employers. (Your home is a residence, not a place of business.) The monthly premium varies, depending on the person's age, health, and other details, but it usually runs $350 to $450 pesos a month. It is expected that you provide the money for their premium, thus making sure that if they become ill, you won't have to worry about their health, or their ability to pay their doctor's bills and medicines.

Sick Leave

It is expected that you are to accommodate medical requests. If a person has a doctor's note to justify days off, these are honored ordinarily. If a request is made to take care of ailing relative or a sick child, reasonable accommodation of such requests are expected.

Vacation Pay

As with everyone else who works for a living, federal holidays are days off, and you should negotiate a two-week paid vacation that accommodates their needs and your schedule as well.

Treating Domestic Workers with Respect and Fairness

Remember that even the rich and famous and powerful get into trouble if they treat their household staff poorly. Remember Caroline Kennedy? How could she have "forgotten" to pay her nanny's Social Security taxes for years? There's no doubt her mother Jackie Kennedy Onassis taught her better. And what happened to Caroline? When her ethical lapse became known, she had to withdraw from consideration for being appointed U.S. Senator from the State of New York. In Mérida, a number of prominent socialites have faced social scorn for how they treat their help. And among expats, some have been ostracized for their callous behavior, thinking that workers in Mexico can be treated like plantation workers in "Gone With the Wind." The last thing you want is to be whispered about behind your back by the proper Yucatecan ladies from the International Women's Club. Or worse yet, the last thing you want is to be served notice that you've been ordered to appear before the labor board!

Gardeners

Unlike maids and handymen, gardeners are a rare and coveted breed. Often equipped with their own tools, the lush, tropical environment in Mérida makes it a pleasure to have wonderful gardens. But they require much attention, and finding a reliable gardener is a difficult challenge. Why? Simple: There are more gardens than there are gardeners! And this is exacerbated by the fact that, believe it or not, friends *steal* gardeners from one another by enticing them with – higher pay! Friendships have ended over gardeners that changed clients, and there is always a peculiar subtext to conversations about gardeners. Of course there are gardening care services, but these charge market rates comparable to the U.S. And a word of advice: Once you find a gardener whose work you like, try to build a great relationship with him on a personal level. Why? If you don't, remember that there are many of others in need of gardening services! Expect to pay between $250 and $600 pesos for a gardener (for larger gardens, they often have an assistant or apprentice).

How to Find Domestic Help

Word of mouth and personal referrals are always the best, of course. And then there are the "Avisos Económicos" in the *Diario de Yucatán*. It's possible to post notices at places like the Mérida English Language Library and on the Main Square, City Hall has a "Jobs Available" listing. Always check a person's references before you let them into your home, and always exercise prudence with your cash and valuables. This applies in Mexico the same way it applies everywhere else on earth!

Advice from the U.S. State Department on Mexican Labor Laws:

U.S. citizen property owners should consult legal counsel or local authorities before hiring employees to serve in their homes or on their vessels moored in Mexico. Several U.S. citizen property owners have faced lengthy lawsuits for failure to comply with Mexican labor laws regarding severance pay and Mexican social security benefits.

---

9 Settling In: Utilities, Telephone, Gas Stations & Other Necessities

The previous chapter covers most utilities in planning a budget. In Mexico, unlike the United States, electric power generation and the petroleum industry are state-owned and state-run, with prices set on a federal level through a complicated system of rules. In Yucatán, state government provides potable water. What follows is a general orientation into basic utilities and related services.

Electricity

The Comision Federal de Electricidad, known as CFE, is responsible for almost all of Mexico's electricity production. Their website is *www.cfe.gob.mx* and here is how they describe their Mission:

"The Federal Electricity Commission (CFE) is a company created and owned by the Mexican government. It generates, distributes and markets electric power for almost 34.2 million customers. This figure represents almost 100 million people. The CFE incorporates more than a million new customers every year.

The infrastructure to generate electric power is made up of 178 generating plants, having an installed capacity of 51,571 megawatts (MW). 23.09% of its installed capacity stems from 22 plants which were built using private capital by Productores Independientes de Energía (PIE).

The CFE creates electric power using various technologies and various primary energy sources. It has thermoelectric, hydroelectric, coal-fired, geothermal and wind powered plants and facilities, as well as one nuclear power plant.

In order to take the power from its generating plants to the household of each one of its customers, the CFE has more than 745,000 Km. of power lines that transmit and distribute electric power.

Electricity reaches almost 137,000 communities (of these, 133,390 are not cities, while 3,356 are). Also, 96.85 % of the population uses electricity.

During the last decade, 42,000 solar modules have been installed in small communities very distant from large population centers. In the future, this technology will be the most widely used in the villages that do not have access to conventional electric power.

As to total sales volume, 99 % and the remaining 1 % is for export purposes.

Even if the household sector makes up 88.23% of CFE's customers, sales in this area represent 26.69% of total sales to the general public. Inversely so, in the industrial sector, less than 1% of the customers make up more than half of the sales volume.

The CFE is also the government agency in charge of planning the national electrical system. Said plan is set forth in the Works and Investment Program of the Electrical Sector (POISE), which describes the evolution of the electrical market, as well as the expansion of the generation and transmission capacity, in order to satisfy the demand for electricity in the next ten years. This plan is annually updated.

CFE's commitment is to offer excellent service, and as it guarantees high quality standards in all its processes, it rivals the best electrical companies in the world.

The CFE is a decentralized government agency, duly incorporated and which controls its own assets."

If you're wondering what the CFE means by "exporting" electricity, it sells some to U.S. utilities across the border, and more importantly, it provides free electric power to northern Belize as part of Mexico's foreign aid program to that nation.

Water

Junta de Agua Potable y Alcantarillado de Yucatán, known as JAPAY, is responsible for potable water throughout Yucatán State. It is very reasonable, with the average bill being about $3 USD a month! Japay operates several offices around town to serve the public. All are open 8 AM to 3 PM, Monday-Friday. Most are open 8:30 AM to 1 PM on Saturdays. All are closed on Sundays.

These are located:

Centro

Calle 60 #526, between Calle 65 and 67 Street

Colón
Avenida Colón #503, by Avenida Reforma, Department 5

San Benito
Interior of the San Benito Market, Third Level, Department 9, Block C12

Plaza Dorada
Interior of Plaza Dorada, adjacent to Coppel

Colonia Miguel Alemán
Calle 27 s/n, between Calle 24 and 26 Street

Chedraui Norte
Calle 60 #301, Colonia Loma Bonita (Interior of Centro Comercial Chedraui, Department 1)

Chenkú
Calle 43 #229, between Calle 28 and 32 Street, Casco Hacienda Chenkú

Xoclan
Calle 71-B s/n, by Avenida 128, Colonia Bosques de Yucalpetén

Vergel
Avenida Universidad Pedagógica, by Calle 25 D, Fracc. Vergel II

Their website is: *www.japay.yucatan.gob.mx.*

Telephone

What can be said about telephone services around the world? What a plethora of choices – some dismal, others fantastic, but always complicated. In Mexico, suffice it to say that Teléfonos de Mexico, to Telmex, made Carlos Slim a billionaire! Basic service runs about $160 pesos (about $13 USD) a month for 100 telephone calls. Then there are the "disposable" cell phones which cost about $300 pesos ($24 USD) for the phone itself, and which you can buy air time from most convenience stores in increments of $20, $50, $100 or more pesos. Most cable companies also now provide telephone service.

In addition, many expatriates use SKYPE or Magic Jack or have "Mexico plans" for their iPhone or Blackberry service, usually on AT&T or Verizon.

With so many choices, knock yourself out finding out which plan works best for your needs and budget:

Alestra (ATT)

Call 800-288-000 and they will set you up with a plan that allows you to call the US for one monthly fee.
Website: *www.att.com.mx*

Axtel

Paseo de Monetejo #473, Colonia Santa Ana
Website: *www.axtel.com.mx*

Cablemas

Call (999) 942-7900, and they will set you up with cable TV, Internet and phone service
Website: *www.cablemas.com*

Skype

Skype has great plans that many expatriates find wonderful for their needs, especially those who have home offices and work on their computers.
Website: *www.skype.com*

Telmex

Call 800-123-000 and they will set you up.
Website: *www.telmex.com.mx*

Verizon

Verizon Wireless has plans that many expatriates find excellent for their needs in Mérida. They are found under the "Nationwide Plus Mexico Plans."
Website: *www.verizonwireless.com*

Vonage

This is another company that has great plans for expatriates. If you sign up during one of their on-going promotions, they will wave the initial set up fee (about $30 USD).
Website: *www.vonage.com*

Internet Service Providers

Telmex, Axtel and Cablemas are the leading Internet service providers in Mérida. They all have comprehensive and competitive plans, and you are sure to find one plan that meets all your needs. The standard plans will run you about $1200 pesos, just under $100 USD a month, and this should include a cable television plan.

Pemex Gas Stations

Petroleos de Mexico, known as Pemex, operates or franchises all the gas stations throughout the country. The price of gas and diesel is set by the government. There are no self-service stations in Mexico: all gasoline must be pumped by an attendant, who also will wipe your windshield, and if requested, check your oil and tires. A tip for these services, of course, is expected and $5 pesos, about forty-cents USD, is expected.

Be mindful that because the government operates retail gasoline service stations, there are far fewer gas stations in Mexico than there are in the U.S. or Canada. What does this mean? That you should always fill up whenever your tank is about one-quarter full!

Propane Gas

Gas Imperial
Telephone: (999) 982-2222

Delta Gas
Telephone: (999) 943-5050

Gas Peninsular Telephone
Telephone: (999) 946-1241

Gas de Yucatán, S.A.
Telephone: (999) 983-4232

Garbage

Servilimpia
Carretera Mérida-Susula, Tablaje Catastral
Telephone: (999) 945-1213

Pamplona
Calle 66 #720, between Calle 99 and 101 Street
Telephone: (999) 984-479

10   Banking & Financial Affairs

As recently as the mid-1980s if you wanted to open an account at J. P. Morgan on Wall Street in New York, you were required to maintain a minimum of $5,000 USD. In today's money, that's the equivalent of just over $12,000 USD. That's a considerable sum of money to have in a non-interest bearing account, just to say your bank was J. P. Morgan.

We forget that until the era of deregulation ushered in by Ronald Reagan, most Americans were excluded from the formal banking system – and phrases such as "Bankers' Hours" referred to a business culture where banks opened at 9:30 AM and closed for the day at 1:30 PM. Few Americans understand that the "arbitrary" rule among banks that no wire transfers are executed after 1 PM isn't arbitrary at all. It is a legacy of the tradition that banks closed for business at 1:30 PM, and it was considered "bad form" to do actual work a half hour before finishing business to the public for the day! (Of course, just because banks closed their doors at 1:30 PM, bankers kept working on behalf of institutional investors and clients, often late into the night.)

Reagan, however, wanted to democratize banking and financial services, and make checking accounts and bank loans accessible to virtually everyone. Today, with the advent of ATMs (introduced in the mid-1980s as well), there are banking services around the clock, and some banks, most notably TD Bank, even open on Sundays.

It's therefore not surprising that in 2010 Citibank was given an award for its pioneering work in helping Americans from all economic backgrounds open and maintain checking and savings accounts. "The award we are receiving is for fifteen years of work," Vikram Pandit, Chief Executive Officer of Citibank, told John Cassidy, a reporter for the *New Yorker*, at the awards ceremony. "It was work that was pioneered by Citi to get more financial inclusion. And it's part of a broader reform effort we are involved in under the heading of responsible banking."

Banking in Mexico, similarly, has long been seen as something for the privileged, and achieving greater "financial inclusion" remains one of the nation's top priorities in banking. Before Nafta, many banks required a minimum of the equivalent of $1,500 USD to open an account, and only a small number of Mexicans were able to have access to formal banking services. It was only after Nafta – and the 1994 devaluation of the peso – that Mexico's banking system embarked on an accelerated program of globalization and transnational integration. In 1994 the top ten Mexican banks were Mexican-owned; today nine of the top ten banks are owned by foreign banks.

As a result, there is a mixed legacy, and banking in Mexico, compared with banking in the U.S., remains a *more* formal activity. That means that banking in Mexico is accomplished in a more meticulous manner, characterized by ritualized procedures and has double-safeguard measures at every step.

In Mérida, banking culture is even more reverential to old traditions. Why? With the peninsula so far removed from Mexico City, it was up to wealthy families in the Yucatán to establish the first banks in town. José Castelló, whose Banco de Campeche, was a major force on the peninsula, merged his bank with the Banco Yucateco, owned by Eusebio Escalante, his son Nicolás Escalante Peón and his wife's brother Manuel Peón Contreras to form the Banco Peninsular de Yucatán, an institution where coffee on porcelain was served when one came to cash a check.

These Old World customs prevailed throughout the 20th century. It was only after World War II, when the Yucatán became more connected to Mexico

---

A Message on Banking from Glynna Prentice, editor of "Mexico Insider" magazine:

"Long-term, most expats end up opening a Mexican bank account. You can wire in much larger amounts, which you can then access with a local ATM card or by check. However, here are a few things to keep in mind:

- Like many other countries, Mexico requires you to show proof that you *need* an account in Mexico. Banks likely will require some evidence that you actually plan to live in Mexico, such as a residence visa, a property title, or at least a utility bill in your name, before they'll open an account for you. So keep in mind, when you buy property in Mexico, that you may not be allowed to open a peso-based account until *after* you've taken title — and make your payment arrangements accordingly.

- International wire transfers can be costly—at both ends. Be sure to ask what your home country bank charges to wire the money internationally *and* what the Mexican bank charges to receive it and convert it to pesos. For the home-country end, check if you can lower the fee by doing the transfer yourself over the Internet. (You may want to check into this anyway.) At the Mexico end, ask other expats in the area for their recommendations on banks and on transfer methods.

- Mexican bank fees are exorbitant, so be sure you check what they are. Overdraft fees, for instance, are a whopping $1000 per overdraft (about $85 USD plus tax).

And, of course, you can also use a home-country credit card. I know some expats who manage perfectly well in Mexico with just a home-country ATM card and credit cards (and never have to risk those high Mexican overdraft fees)."

Source: www.MexicoInsider.com

City (think highways, civilian aviation) that "Mexican" banks came in and began to acquire independent Yucatecan banks. Established Yucatecan families, however, saw Bancomer and Banamex as interlopers that brought crass commercialism to banking. Many Yucatecan families switched to banks to those in Miami, Houston and New York. After Nafta, the arrival of Citibank (which acquired Banamex) and the Spanish banks (one of which, BBVA, acquired Bancomer) arrived on the scene the city's banking culture changed once again, effectively ending the traditions of Yucatecan banking completely.

Today, banking is far more "democratic" than it once was, but nonetheless, by American standards, banking is still too formal. Patience, in other words, is required.

So now that you understand the formal and ritualized bankground of banking in Mexico and you have taken Glynna Prentice's advice, here's how it works:

Checking Accounts

For a checking account, or *cuenta bancaria*, the paperwork is in Spanish, which means that if you are not fluent in Spanish, you should bring along a friend who can help with the translation and any questions you may have. Bring your passport, along with three copies, which will probably be needed to adhere to various forms. (If you plan on opening a business account, you will also need a copy of your FM2 and FM3 visas, along with four copies.) When you fill out the signature card, your signature must be signed exactly the same as it appears in your passport. Every check you sign must be signed as it appears on the signature cards as well. If there is a variation, the check will be refused.

Checkbooks

Checkbooks, or *chequeras*, are considered important legal documents, and are treated as such. Each check has to be accounted for, so if you make a mistake, you can't simply write "void" across it, or rip it up. If this happens, you have to keep the check and report it as "cancelled" to invalidate it – which is different from stopping payment. Upon opening an account, you will receive temporary checks, usually three or five, until your regular checks are ordered. As in the United States, your checks will have your name printed on them. But in Mexico, when your checks are ready, you will have to pick them up at the bank. When you do, you will be asked to show the same identification that you did when you opened the account, and you will have to sign receipt for it (and the banker will sign receipt of delivery for the branch manager).

Checkbook Activation

When you have your checkbook in hand, there's one additional security measure: The checks have to be *activated*. This can be done with at the bank when you pick-up the checks (each branch has to call the customer service office to initiate the process), or you can call the toll-free number when you are ready to use the checks. If you call the bank there are two security codes that will be requested of you to verify your identity over the telephone. First is the "key," or *clave*, which is a secret code given to everyone upon opening a bank account. The second is your PIN number, referred to as "NIP" in Spanish. When you activate your checkbook you can activate the entire series of checks, or just the one you plan to use. Why do the banks do this? This is simply an additional layer of protection against fraud. If you only plan to use the first five checks, you have the peace of mind of knowing that no one can use the subsequent ones until you call the bank to "activate" those checks.

How to Write a Check

Everyone knows how to write a check, which is why it's well worth reviewing how to write a check for the Mexican banking system!

1. Any error will render the check void. Nothing can be crossed out, nothing can be misspelled.
2. The name of the person must be correctly spelled out. The quantity must be clearly written in numbers and spelled out (in Spanish).
3. You must write out "pesos" and "centavos" after the written amount, and you must write out "M.N." after the written amount. ("M.N." stands for "Moneda nacional," or national currency).
4. Be careful to make sure that the month is written in Spanish, and remember that in Spanish, the names of the months are written in lower case! (If you write "Febrero" for "febrero," the check may be returned unpaid!)
5. Your signature must match exactly as it appears when you opened your account, which is why it is a good idea to sign your name exactly as it appears in your passport – you can refer to your passport to see if you are "John Smith," of "John A. Smith" or "John Anthony Smith." Many people sit at a desk, turn off all distractions, have their passports in hand and set about writing out their checks to make sure everything is correct.
6. Please remember that checks written over $100,000 pesos must be cleared through the Central Bank. Mexico is enacting a series of laws to combat money laundering and this is one necessary measure, even though it has become quite burdensome for business. Remember, anything that approximates more than $10,000 USD is checked and double-checked!

Accepting a Check

The lesson is that if this is what you are required to do when you *write* a check, then it follows that these are the details that you need to look for when you *receive* a check!

If there is *any* error or discrepancy, the bank will refuse to process the check. That's the bad news. The good news is that, unlike the U.S., Mexican banks operate throughout the entire country, and it is common for people simply to deposit funds into each other's account. Someone in Mexico City can deposit into your account cash rather than send you a check, and you can verify the deposit online or by calling the toll-free number. Similarly, you may be asked to deposit money into someone else's account rather than giving him or her a check. This, of course, depends on the level of trust.

Another practice that is common is to write the check payable to "Al Portador." No, Al's not a person. It means "To the bearer," roughly the equivalent of writing a check payable to "Cash" in the U.S. and Canada.

Remember Glynna Prentice's advice: Banking fees are exorbitant in Mexico. Bounce a check, and you are in for a $100 USD penalty! Don't do it. And if you bounce a check to a merchant, you will be blacklisted for a minimum period of five years! Why? The merchant is also assessed a fee, and their own banking credit history is negatively impacted. Even if you offer to pay the penalty the merchant was assessed, they will still have a blemish on their record with the bank for having accepted a check that bounced!

Statements and Balances

Your bank statement will be sent to the address provided when you opened your account. If you move or want to change the mailing address, you cannot do it over the phone. It has to be done in person, face to face with an officer, and you have to provide proof of your new address, such as a utility bill (CFE or JAPAY), known as a *comprobante*, in your name with the new address listed. Note: The only exception is if you have someone go on your behalf who is a Power of Attorney, a *carta de poder*, along with his or her official identification (IFE card or passport) and three copies the identification. They will also need originals and copies of *your* utility bill.

Why so much security?

As mentioned when we discussed all the "papelitos" Mexican bureaucracy requires, we noted that Identity Theft is almost unheard of in Mexico, and the reason for that is the layer upon layer of safeguards enlisted every step of the way. Yes, it is tedious, but you can have peace of mind knowing that your banking account is safe!

List of Banks (most have English-language versions on their websites)

Banamex (Banco Nacional de Mexico)
www.banamex.com.mx

Banco Azteca
www.bancoazteca.com.mx

Banco del Bajio
www.bb.com.mx

Banco de Comercio Exterior
www.bancomext.com

Banco de Mexico (Central Bank of Mexico)
www.banxico.org.mx

Banco Nacional de Credito Rural (Banrural)
www.banrural.gob.mx

Banco Nacional de Obras y Servicios Públicos
www.banobras.gob.mx

Bank of America Mexico
www.bankofamerica.com.mx

BanRegio
www.banregio.comBBVA

Bancomer
www.bancomer.com.mx

Bansi
www.bansi.com.mx

Consultores Financieros (Confia)
www.comfia.com.mx

Grupo Financiero Banorte
www.banorte.com

HSBC Mexico
www.hsbc.com.mx

Nacional Financiera/Banco de Desarrollo
www.nafin.com

Santander Serfin
www.santander.com.mx

Scotiabank Inverlat
www.scotiabank.com.mx

National Associations and Regulators

Asociación de Bancos de Mexico

www.abm.org.mx

Comision Nacional Bancaria y de Valores

www.cnbv.gob.mx

Scam Warning

There is absolutely, positively no reason whatsoever why anyone in Mexico would request your Social Security number, with the exception of a bank officer opening a bank account. Mexican law now requires that bank accounts opened in Mexico by U.S. citizens and residents be reported to the IRS, which is part of efforts by the U.S. and Mexican governments to combat money laundering and tax evasion. This is the only legitimate reason for disclosing your Social Security number.

A number of Americans have set up companies in Mérida to provide "expatriate services" to other Americans moving to Mérida. In the process of providing these "services," individuals are being asked to disclose their Social Security numbers.

This is a scam that works one of two ways. First, they use your Social Security number to run a credit report on you with the U.S. credit agencies. Then they have an idea of your financial worth – and how much they can charge or bilk you for their services. Second, by compiling that much financial information about you, and knowing when you are in Mexico, you are exposed to identity theft. If you're out of the country, and they have so much confidential information, it can be used in ways that are unauthorized by you.

Never, ever give anyone in Mexico your Social Security number who is not a bank officer, and then only at the time you are opening a bank account. The only other exception is for official business with the IRS at the American Consulate. **Be especially wary if one of these so-called "expatriate services" companies asks for your Social Security number!**

Part IV
Making a Home and Building a Life

11 REAL ESTATE

The Curious Case of the Real Estate Market in Mérida's Historic Centro

Since the 1970s there has been a steady exodus of residents from Mérida's historic center. There are several reasons for this migration. The most important one has to do with the rise of Mexico's middle class. As educational opportunities grew for more Mexicans in the 1950s and 1960s, expectations changed. Whereas before, people in Mérida were unable to get college degrees, their financial independence was limited. Most were resigned to living with their parents in multi-generational households.

As Yucatecan families in Centro were able to send their kids to college, suddenly their adult children, once they started to form their own families, could aspire to their own homes and to different lifestyles. The rise of Mérida's middle class created demand for new suburbs that were built around the city, on the periphery of the "Circuito Colonias." Whether it was the lower-middle class Colonia Pensiones or the more affluent middle class Colonia Miguel Alemán, suddenly two-story homes, with gardens and garages, some with swimming pools and basketball courts were accessible. American suburban life as seen on "Bewitched" and "I Dream of Jeannie" was possible. Through this process, Yucatecans have moved out of the Historic Center, leaving elderly grandparents, many of whom resisted leaving the homes in which they lived most of their lives, behind. When elder relatives were no longer able to live independently, they moved in with their adult children, and the houses were closed down, some virtually abandoned. As time passed, the heirs often bickered over what to do with their parents' former home, or didn't care enough to do anything about it, simply because the homes were deemed to have little value, and the legal fees for getting titles changed and paying overdue *predial* taxes offered even more disincentives to do anything about it.

In the 1980s, when American expatriates began to "discover" Mérida's center, a good number of the homes in downtown Mérida were occupied by senior citizens, and a surprising number were closed up, or just abandoned, by their owners. It was possible to buy a colonial home in the Historic Center for $12,000 USD to $25,000 USD. A good number did, and this was the beginning of a demand for something in which Mexicans saw little value: colonial buildings in a congested city center that had none of the modern conveniences. Again, up until the mid-1990s, the owners of those old homes are primarily occupied by elderly people whose adult children lived elsewhere in town, or were houses that had been closed up.

Mérida's experience was radically different from other Mexican cities. When people bemoan that other cities – Guanajuato, Puebla, Oaxaca, San Miguel de Allende – boast vibrant colonial city centers, with European-style cafés and bars, lively restaurants and an exuberant night life, and wonder why Mérida's historic center becomes silent as cemetery come sundown, there's a reason.

The obvious one is flight to the suburbs, where most Yucatecans under the age of 50 live. But there is another one that is seldom mentioned: Geography. Most of Mexico's colonial cities are in the highlands, surrounded by mountains or ravines. Mérida is flat as a pancake, with cheap land all around. If you wanted to build a golf course in Guanajuato, it simply cannot be done because there is no land for it. But in Mérida, there is the possibility of dreaming up an ambitious project, and carrying it out.

Consider Mérida's entire real estate market:

Average days on the market for a colonial home in the "Historic Center": **1,342**

Average days on the market for an existing home outside the Historic Center: **53***

Average days on the market for a new subdivision: **15**

Average days on the market for a home financed through Infonavit, Mexico's federal agency for residential real estate: **0****

This figure excludes properties outside the Historic Center that are listed with American-owned real estate firms that are pricing in U.S. dollars and marketing primarily to foreigners. These homes are usually found in Colonia García Ginerés, Colonia Itzimná, Colonia Alemán and Colonia Mexico.

**For homes financed by Infonavit, there's a waiting list!*

A new gated community with an enormous community center that boasts tennis courts and swimming pools? Why not?

A Jack Nicklaus-designed golf course with a Mark Spitzer swimming academy, with million dollar homes throughout? Why not?

A new division for working-class people that has easy access to highways? Why not?

An L.A.-style shopping center with lots of parking and American anchor stores? Why not?

A new university campus for 5,000 students? Why not?

A shopping mall that has an ice skating rink? Why not?

A private subdivision minutes from the golf practice range? Why not?

A state-of-the-art medical facility with its own hotel? Why not?

And the "Why not" scenarios continue, creating a vast city of breathtaking sprawl.

Days (or Years) on the Market

Each area of any geographic location or subdivision in residential real estate has what is called an "average number of days on the market." This indication shows home sellers in any particular area how long most homes remain on the market prior to a sale. In some places, like Texas, certain areas average a very impressive 30 days on the market prior to the property being sold. In other areas, like Nevada, average time on market could peak at 542 days on the market prior to a successful sale.

Days on market and cumulative days on market can be a death sentence for most home sellers. The longer a home stays available, the more buyers will wonder what is wrong with it and why it hasn't sold. While in reality the home might be perfectly sound and in good condition, homes that have not sold quickly can earn a stigma that is less than desirable, and could kill a potential deal before an offer is ever even made.

Source:
www.ehow.com/about_5347814_long-can-house-listed.html

It is the abundant supply of choices – and cheap land – that fuels the growth of the city. Mexicans from other areas of the country – from Mexico City and Cancún – delight in the options open to them, from gated communities to U.S.-style suburban sprawl, and continue to flock to the numerous developments that ring the northern and northeastern areas of the city. Few Mexicans have any interest whatsoever in the Historic Center as a place to live, and fewer still have the desire to live out a "tropical" version of Mexican colonial living.

The result is the very odd fact that, if you review the offerings on the websites for real estate companies like Tierra Yucatán, Mexico International or Hacienda Mexico, you will see that there are properties that have been listed there for *years*!

In a **healthy** market, an average house is for sale between 45 and and 90 days. If you are dealing with a market where houses remain unsold for more than 90 days, you should start asking a simple question: **What is going on in this market?**

Mérida is for Everyone

For about a decade a small group of expatriate realtors have worked very hard to give Mérida an "upscale" image, setting up elaborate Internet sites that feature beautiful homes that are the stuff of fantasy: infinity pools, soaring ceilings, exquisite Victorian and Edwardian paste tile floors, lush gardens and decadent living spaces. That's great, especially since Mérida is a city filled with unique and splendid properties. But the number of people who can call their private bankers and give instructions to wire half a million dollars first thing tomorrow morning is few.

What about the majority of people? What about people who want to find an affordable retirement home in a charming, mid-size city? What about people who are weighing the options of living in a retirement community in Florida versus a bit more adventurous retirement in Mexico or Costa Rica?

The fact of the matter is that most American expatriates in Mérida live on fixed incomes, and rely on their Social Security checks every month. There are many people who would like to have a higher standard of living in Mexico than they could otherwise afford back in the U.S., not a lower one!

Buying Real Estate in Mexico

By Inspiring Expatriatism

If you set out to buy real estate in Mexico, you usually must deal with a real estate company, a buyer's lawyer, a bank and a public notary. Though there are legal regulations, keep in mind that Mexican real estate agents do not have to be licensed or certified; anyone can set up a real estate company.

Attorneys and Real Estate Agents

You should have a Mexican attorney involved in this process so they can draw up contracts, and review the conditions and terms of sale. An attorney can also perform background research on real estate agents. It is a good idea to have your own attorney, not one appointed by a real estate company. Attorneys must be licensed, and are the only ones who can give you real legal advice. Make sure your attorney can present you a "cédula professional." Attorneys can also take care of some bureaucratic procedures in their behalf, and save you money this way.

Notary publics are also important in this process. Unlike in other countries, being a notary public is highly regulated; one must be at least 35 years old, have a degree in law, at least 3 years of experience at a notary public office, and pass an exam. They are the ones who officialize all of your documentation and permits in this process. You are allowed to choose your own notary public.

Most real estate deals in Mexico are done in cash, but financing is becoming more common.

Rules, Regulations and Restrictions

According to the law, the Mexican nation owns all land and water in Mexico, along with minerals, salts, ore deposits, natural gas and oil. That ownership can be assigned to individuals, however.

There are also restricted zones, which Mexico prohibits foreigners from legally owning. They include land within 100 kilometers of the Mexican border and 50 kilometers within a Mexican coastline. However, a foreigner can invest in such lands under a real estate trust, known as "fideicomiso." A Mexican bank is to be assigned as the trustee, has title to the property and owns

Fideicomiso

To own property in the restricted area which includes Mérida and some areas of the Yucatán, you engage a Mexican bank to execute and hold title to the property using a contract known as a fideicomiso. With this, you and the bank are both listed on the title papers.

The fideicomiso creates a trust contract for the benefit of the foreign buyer. The bank has a fiduciary obligation to the owner. The owner has all the benefits of ownership and retains the legal right to lease, sell, and/or will the property to his heirs. Fideicomisos are currently 50 years documents. They can be renewed at the end of the term for an additional 50 years. There is no limit to the number of times the fideicomiso can be renewed.

The renewal fee is currently about $900 USD.

The cost for initiating a fideicomiso is approximately $2,800 USD. There is an annual fee to the bank for maintaining the contract. The annual fee is based upon a percentage of the value of the home. An estimated figure for a home in the $100,000 range is about $600 USD a year. Current law does not allow a fideicomiso for properties larger than 2,000 square meters (approx. 21,520 square ft.).

From: www.realestate-yucatan.net

the records. Foreigners can have unrestricted use of the lands under this loophole, but not officially own that land.

Real Estate Developments are companies that buy large quantities of land, and then develop it with creating a residential community, and putting in some facilities.

General Process

First, you should find a property that you like and agree a price verbally, and then set it up in a document, "Convenio de Compra/Venta." You must set up a trust if this property is within restricted zones. Then you must seek permission from the Foreign Secretary's office to buy land, followed by signing a "Calvo Clause." If you are buying property from a Real Estate Developer, have your notary public invesitage them.

Next, you should get a copy of the Land/Property Deeds from whoever is selling you your property, and have it investigated by your notary public. You must have the land appraised, which can also be organized by a notary public.

You must obtain a permit, and you'll have to submit the following documents:

- Passport
- Birth Certificate
- Marriage Cerificate (if necessary)
- Visa (could be a tourist visa)

Your notary public will probably assist you in this process. They must also get the following documents from the property seller:

- Original property deed
- Tax receipts
- Public utilities bills
- Details of land service fee

Your seller must pay a Capital Gains Tax. Then your payment of the property will take place when the deed is signed over to you, at the notary public's office. You must also pay any other fees and taxes."

For more information, see *www.expatify.com*.

Before you consider buying Real Estate in Mérida, heed these "Lessons Well Learned"

By Vince Gricus

It will come as no surprise to anyone that the world is still recovering from the real estate bubble that burst in 2008.

Not all countries, however, were affected in the same way. In Mexico, the government has programs administered through an agency known as INFONAVIT that regulates the majority of housing construction, mortgages and purchases. It is intended to make home ownership possible for Mexico's working and lower middle classes. This, which represents the majority of Mexico's housing market, was insulated from the excesses of the market excesses and speculation that led to the worldwide collapse in housing.

But when it comes to the *unregulated* real estate – which is where almost all expats buy and sell their homes in Mexico – Mérida was not immune to excesses. I say that from my own experience, which illustrates the bust-and-boom cycle of what occurs in Mérida now that more and more people from around the world are discovering this gem in the heart of the Yucatán Peninsula.

When I arrived in Mérida for the first time, I came here as an ordinary tourist. I had recently retired from a long career working in the aviation industry, and one of my unfulfilled dreams was to own a Bed & Breakfast. I was staying at a Bed & Breakfast, and I mentioned this to my hosts. One of them indicated there was a suitable business for sale, and I inquired about the asking

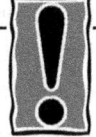

Expatriates who Prey on Expatriates
(Yes, there are many!)

Acting on a hunch, I later gave a taxi driver 50 pesos to answer my questions honestly. When I asked him if Mérida taxi drivers kept tabs on gringos for local real estate agents, he just slapped his chubby thighs and laughed and laughed and laughed.

"Oh, it's not only taxi drivers," he chortled. "It's everyone. Look, it's easy to follow what you guys do and where you go. You've been around a lot of the city. How many other gringos have you seen?"

Although Mérida may seem like a city of almost one million, you, as a gringo, will move almost exclusively within the confines of a very, very small demographic, namely Mérida's middle- and upper-classes. They will watch you like a hawk.

Almost everyone has a vested mercantile interest in the what, when, where, why, and how of everything you do, say, eat, drink, wear, and buy.

By Hugo de Naranja, writing in **ExpatsAnon.com**

price. "It's $349,000 dollars," I was told, which seemed reasonable to me. My reference was the greater real estate market in St. Louis, Missouri. I mentioned that I had a partner, and I would have to discuss it with him. In my absence, the realtor met with my partner. My partner disclosed that he was an attorney with his own practice. In the morning, I asked for a confirmation of the asking price and I was told it was a "bargain" at $399,000 USD. The asking price shot up by $50,000 USD overnight, once they found out my partner's ability to pay! Properties are priced all over the place! For example, one property, "Casa del Panadero" was simultaneously listed for "$259,000 dollars" on RealestateYucatan.com, "$325,000 dollars" on mexintl.com, and "$299,000 dollars" on other sites (including Tierra Yucatán, Casa Blanca Real Estate and Hacienda Mexico real estate). The house eventually sold for $225,000 dollars – furnished!

When it comes to real estate agents, my best advice is to do your homework. There is no need to rush into any market – especially Mérida's Historic Center where the same houses have languished for sale **FOR YEARS**! Trust me; there isn't a list of eager buyers standing in line with cashier's checks in hand!

Let me share with you my personal experience with Tierra Yucatán. Perhaps others have had different experiences, but I can only speak for myself. When I arrived in Mérida, I spoke no Spanish and I knew no one in town, and neither did my partner. As a result, we wanted a turnkey property, ready to move in. We explained this to the agent at Tierra Yucatán. Our tour of several properties began with an Agent and his Assistant. The Assistant looked displeased to be even driving around with us, as the Agent asked all kinds of questions. Our request was to be shown a property that was move-in ready, had three or four bedrooms which could be suitable for a Bed & Breakfast, with a swimming pool, and hopefully a garage as well. The first property we were shown was on the corner of Calle 57 and 72 Street, a very busy intersection. One of the rooms was being used as a TV repair shop. And when we walked inside, we could see the sky. Why? Because some of the rooms had no roof! It was in shambles. (That property, five years later is still for sale.) The next property was equally unsuitable, but for different reasons – it was next to "bath house," and we could imagine just the kind of people who would be knocking on the door at all hours of the night asking for a room! The third property was equally unsuitable, with all the bathrooms needing to be remodeled and updated.

It was clear that they were interested in showing you what they wanted to show you, and not what you asked to see.

We then went for lunch at a nearby restaurant. I was ready to scrap the whole project. The restaurant owner came by, and we discussed the waste of a morning we'd had with the folks from Tierra Yucatán. Then he offered, "Why didn't they show you Tom's place? It's for sale." After lunch, we were off to see this place, right in the heart of Santiago. It was exactly what we asked for: Up and running as a Bed & Breakfast, it had four bedrooms, a pool and parking. It was just a question of settling on a price, and the paperwork was handled by another real estate company, with minor delays or headaches!

What $250,000 USD gets you around the world?

One of the more curious aspects of the real estate market in Mérida's Historic Center is the notion that you can buy a decrepit property on the verge of collapse for $50,000 USD, spend another $200,000 USD and walk away with a "bargain." Or that you can look at completely remodeled, rebuilt or refurbished homes listed for $250,000 and get that fantasy Mexican home – and it's a deal.

Mérida is a wonderful city, but it is not Barcelona or Milan or Chicago or Buenos Aires. There is no reason why anyone can't move to Mérida and find a wonderful home for more than $75,000 USD or $100,000 USD.

But if you look at most real estate listings, you'd think that the "average" property in Mérida cost a quarter million dollars! To put things in perspective, in 2011, what does $250,000 USD buy you?

In **Taos**, New Mexico you can get a 3-bedroom, 3-bathroom house.

In **Barcelona**, Spain, you can get 2-bedroom, 2 bathroom apartment on Paseo de Borne, one of the more fashionable avenues in the city.

In **Miami**, Florida you can get a 3-bedroom, 2.5 bath condo overlooking Biscayne Bay.

In **Dubrovnik**, Croatia you can buy a ten-room hillside villa on two acres of land overlooking the Adriatic Sea.

In **St. Croix**, U.S. Virgin Islands, you can buy a three-bedroom, 2.5 bathroom ranch-style home on an acre of land.

In **Paris**, France you can buy a 1-bedroom, 1-bathroom pied-à-terre in the Marais neighborhood.

How is it possible that in Mérida you'd have to settle for second-rate properties, such as the claustrophobic "Casa de la Virgen" or "Casa del Angel," which are located on one of the busiest streets in Centro, with buses careening down the street all hours of the day and night, have no parking, and whose "pools" are little bigger than most hot tubs? Absolutely ridiculous!

As a general rule, the less informed you are about the local market and the options available to you, the more likely you are to run into trouble. There are untold horror stories of uninformed foreigners being bamboozled into make decisions they subsequently regret. "Had I know X, I would have done Y," is a familiar refrain among many expats. Over the past five years or so, there's been an explosion of "Buy Owner" signs ("Trato Directo" in Spanish) that have appeared around town. Many Yucatecans who do want to sell their houses are fed up with the empty promises of "dollars" made to them, and are happy to get "pesos" for their properties.

Lesson #1

It's a very fluid market, and one of the curious things is that the realtors in question are expatriates!

One reason for it being such a fluid market is that there are no regulations for being a real estate agent. And it's become quite easy for anyone to come to Mérida, learn the basics of buying and selling, and set up shop – using their ability to speak English as a competitive advantage to sell to other expatriates! Forget that stereotype that Mexicans will take you for a ride. That has not been the case, at least in my experience. In fact, it's been the opposite: foreign expats in business down here are more likely to think in terms of dollars, and not in pesos.

Lesson #2:

During the 2000s as more and more Americans have been discovering Mérida, the local market has been "dollarized"!

What do I mean by this? That during the height of the real estate frenzy that engulfed the world – think 2002 through 2008 – here in Mérida, foreigners arrived, set up shop as "realtors" and went around knocking on every door that had a "Se Vende" – "For Sale" – sign and promised the owners that they could get dólares for their house.

In no time, Yucatecans living in these glorious but often neglected and outdated homes in the *Centro Histórico* could only think in terms of dollars.

And it worked: For Americans, the real estate was "a bargain," even when they took into account the expense of remodeling and upgrading their homes. Some wanted all the modern conveniences, others wanted to transform their homes into a "Frida Kahlo Mexican Fantasy," still others wanted a luxurious home with infinity pools and gracious terraces for outdoor living that they could never afford back in the States.

Is it any wonder that Mérida's Historic Center became "dollarized"? If you didn't offer to pay in dollars, local sellers were not impressed.

Consider this anecdote. A local friend tells me this story. His granduncle, who lived out of town, wanted his grandsons to study in Mérida, and to do so, they needed a local address. A colleague mentioned to him that a neighbor was selling his house. It was a small house, and it would need major renovations to bring it up to date, but it was structurally fine, and, while modest, would meet the needs of two teenage brothers who would be visited by their mother on the weekends. Best yet, the price was right: $600,000 pesos, or about $48,000 USD. A few months later, the granduncle was in Mérida, and went by to see the house. It still had a "Se Vende" sign on it, but now it was listed with a realtor. During that time, an American real estate agent, driving around town, saw the "Se Vende" sign and called up the seller. The American realtor convinced the Yucatecan owner that $48,000 USD was not enough to ask for. "We can get you $67,000 USD!" the American real estate agent promised, and that's the price it was listed for. The granduncle was somewhat discouraged when he heard that the price had jumped from $48,000 USD to $67,000 USD, but was willing to be patient. Time passed, and the house, listed for $67,000 USD languished on the market. Months later, the granduncle, back in town, went to see the seller.

"How much do you want for this property?" he asked.

"It's $67,000 American dollars," was the reply.

"This is Mexico! The currency is the *peso*! Don't talk to me about American *dollars*," the granduncle protested.

Pause.

"I think your house is worth $600,000 pesos, and that's what I'm willing to offer you right now."

The Yucatecan was silent, probably thinking that the house had been on the market for more than 10 months without a single offer, and that he was now being offered what he originally wanted for the house in the first place.

"That's what I can offer you, and the offer is good until I hear back from another seller where I made an offer earlier this morning," the granduncle added.

"It's yours," the seller said, extending his hand.

A property that had been "dollarized" – and remained unsold – was now brought back to the "real world" of Mexican pesos and Mexican prices.

The Global Recession of 2008 is taking care of a great deal of the "dollarized" properties in Mérida's Historic Center, although this is often news to the American real estate agents who contributed to dollarizing and inflating Mérida's real estate market!

So with these experiences under my belt, I cannot in good conscience recommend three of the most popular real estate agencies in town that have contributed much to creating a speculative bubble here in Mérida, and which have sold properties at far above their market value in recent years.

This is not to say that there are no American real estate companies in Mérida that I would recommend, or who have demonstrated their professionalism and integrity. Jim Mann of Mérida Yucatán Properties is one agent whose praise many people continue to sing. (For the sake of full disclosure, Jim Mann was not the agent who sold us our Bed & Breakfast, and neither I nor my partner have bought or sold real estate properties through Mérida Yucatán Properties.) Of the real estate agencies in Mérida founded and run by Americans, Mérida Yucatán Properties is the one that, to my knowledge, has the highest customer satisfaction, and it is the one that has tried to "rationalize" the market by pointing out that in 2011, the U.S. dollar continues to fluctuate against the Mexican peso in an unpredictable way, and that the market in Mérida is still recovering from the Global Recession. But remember, like Jim Mann there are scores of reputable, honest and ethical realtors in Mérida, American and Yucatecan alike, who will look out for you and your interests.

Lesson #3

There are lots of neighborhoods that offer wonderful values, and which are almost always ignored by expatriate real estate companies that are obsessed with the "Centro Histórico" or the beaches near Progreso. The third lesson to consider is that Mérida is blessed with many neighborhoods where there are exceptional values. For those on fixed incomes, there are lovely houses in Colonia Pensiones, which is close to the Historic Center, the highway to the beaches near Progreso, and which is often overlooked. For those who are more willing to live among "locals," Colonia Miguel Alemán, which was designed and built in the 1960s, has wonderful homes, in a solidly middle class neighborhood with wonderful amenities and a terrific "small town" feel. Consider that each afternoon it seems that all the families are out in the neighborhood park, with kids on their bicycles and multi-generational families enjoying the late afternoon and early evening sense of community by being out with neighbors.

Is Mérida's "Historic Center" a Rip-Off? You decide.

What has happened to Mérida's Historic Center?

In 2006, Kate Murphy, writing in the *New York Times*, reported this: "Most of the plaster buildings in the historic district are from the early 19th century and have high ceilings, Moorish ironwork and colorful, patterned floor tiles called mosaico. They are also bargains, at around $40,000 for a four-bedroom, two-bathroom colonial home."*

This described a colonial home in downtown Mérida that would need an equal amount of "remodeling" and "upgrades." The total cost of a lovely, colonial home with all the modern conveniences would cost absolutely, positively no more than $80,000 USD, about the same price as a simple, one-bedroom retirement condo just about anywhere in Florida!

Now consider Mérida's Historic Center in 2011:

In January 2011, there were 43 properties listed on the real estate website, "**Hacienda Mexico**," which is by an American realtor catering primarily to other Americans. **The average price: $433,350 USD!**

That same month, a survey of "**Renta y Ventas**" website, which is by Mexicans primarily for Mexicans, yielded an **average price of $88,000 USD** (or $1,100,000 pesos, at an exchange rate of 12.50 pesos to 1 dollar), for a 3-bedroom, 2.5 bathroom home, with a garage in any of the Colonias outside the Historic Center.

Have Americans become their own worst enemies in their relentless marketing and hype surrounding Mérida's Historic Center?

How did a retirement home that should cost no more than $80,000 USD in 2006 become an over-the-top extravagance of excess, now presented as a "deal" at an average price that exceeds **twice** the average price of a residence in the U.S. in 2011? (The median price of a home in a metropolitan area in the U.S.: $172,000 USD.**)

Don't believe the hype!

Mérida is for everyone, not just rich Americans!

*Sources: *"Mérida: Finding a Home (Cheerios Included) in Mexico," by Kate Murphy, New York Times, March 12, 2006. **The price of a median home in a metropolitan area, for the third quarter 2010, is provided by www.Realtor.org.*

These are just two neighborhoods that are often overlooked, and which a real estate agent who has your interest at heart, and is willing to do a little legwork will find suitable places for you to consider.

Keep these three lessons in mind, and you will be a smart buyer in Mérida's real estate market.

Who Can You Trust?

There is no doubt, if you've read this far, that this is the saddest chapter in the book. And it is the saddest chapter with good reason. What was only a few years ago a charming, sleepy historic district, became a frenzied, hyped area where rapid-fire marketing sought to present to foreign retirees and foreign investors as a "golden opportunity" for real estate investment.

Americans living in Mérida, presenting themselves as "licensed real estate professionals" – an oxymoron since there are no licensing requirements for real estate agents in Mexico at present– established real estate companies. Enlisting Mexican nationals, who by virtue of being fluent in Spanish and more familiar with real estate norms in Mexico, could canvas door-to-door trying to get the residents of the Centro Histórico to put their houses up for sale, with the promise of being paid in dollars, new properties were brought to the market faster than buyers could be found for them.

Most of the residents, being elderly Yucatecans, whose adult children had moved to other parts of the city, were torn. Yes, it would be wonderful to make enough money to secure their old age, but what about the emotional ties they held for the houses that had been their homes for their entire lives?

The power of economics, however, began to prevail, and soon houses that had seen few, if any, "updates" since electricity had been installed, were on the market. A quarter century ago, a "fixer-upper" could be had for $12,000 USD to $25,000 USD. These were lovely, comfortable homes that would, of course, require new bathrooms, remodeled kitchens and window panes installed (built before air-conditioners were invented, these homes had screens, wooden shutters and wrought iron). They were, in one word, a bargain.

As recently as 2006, the average price of a four-bedroom house in Mérida's Historic Center that needed to be refurbished could be bought for about $40,000 USD!

It is a shame that, in 2011, $40,000 USD would only buy you a little more than a pile of rubble! Of course this is an exaggeration, but it also reflects the **unspeakable damage that a small group of expatriates have havocked upon the Historic Center**. The relentless hype of Mérida as a "tropical paradise" has seduced many into thinking they had better act fast, and at any price, in order to secure a place in the Yucatán's sun. Nothing could be further from the truth. Unless you are determined to live within at the confines of Colonia Santiago and Colonia Santa Ana, in Mérida the sky is virtually the imit. There are splendid homes that can be purchased anywhere in town. In this section we mention that the median price of one of the real estate websites owned by expatriates which target expatriates is more than $433,000 USD. For that much money, you could buy a lifetime membership in the exclusive Yucatán Country Club, a plot of land adjacent to the Jack Nicklaus Golf Course and build the house of your dreams. Or you could buy TWO median-priced residences in the United States!

What has occurred in Mérida defies disbelief, and it is embodies the greed of expatriates who have descended upon Mérida, with nothing less than the intention of taking advantage of other expatriates who are looking for comfotable retirement homes. It is something that mystifies the people of Mérida, and one that undermined the entire promise that Mexico is something different from the U.S.

To be sure, the real estate market in Mérida' Centro Histórico has been "ruined" by a select, few expatriate real

A Bubble About to Burst?

As 2011 began there were indications that the artificial real estate bubble that characterizes Gringolandia was about to burst. The bellwether – Casa Panadero – sent shockwaves when it sold *a third less* than the original asking price! If this isn't a reality check, then what is?

Other properties with signs that read "Reduced" or "Motivated" have begun to appear. The hardest hit Colonias in the Historic Center were the more marginal and least desirable ones: **San Cristobal, San Sebastian & Ermita**, and **Chuminoplis**. Expatriates who invested in those neighborhoods had best be planning to be around for quite a while. **Good luck to anyone living in those "Colonias of the Deluded."**

Of course, given the unsustainable run-up on prices, it's only natural for some "reality" to set in. This is especially true now that many more expatriates are savvy – there are exceptional values in the Colonias that lie on either side of Avenida Miguel Alemán from Itzimná towards Star Médica.

Is it any wonder that dreadful places like "Casa de la Virgen" and "Casa del Angel" have languished, unsold, for years and years? And the only properties that are selling are the ones that are deeply discounted, such as "La Casita," which was originally listed for $149,000 USD, but finally sold for $95,000 USD, indicative of how inflated and unrealistic the "listed" prices are in the current real estate market.

173

estate agents. But that is a broad brush with which to describe all the expatriates, most of whom are honest and sincere, who are working to make a life for themselves in Mexico, and who champion the best of Mexico. What's the point? That, in the same way the French are taught to be wary of their respective expatriates in foreign lands, one should not make the natural assumption that their fellow countrymen in Mérida has *their* best interests at heart. They most likely don't.

The Seven Realities for the Real Estate Market in Mérida's Centro Histórico

1. This is an area where there is little demand for residential real estate by the people who are from Mérida.

2. Mexicans moving in from other areas of Mexico have also shown little interest in this district as a place to live.

3. Yucatecan owners are seldom in a hurry to sell these properties since they were mostly inherited from their parents or grandparents, meaning there is little interest in lowering asking prices once an asking price is set, and this makes the real estate market price inelastic.

4. Demand for these properties is generated primarily by foreigners moving to Mérida.

5. Demand is cultivated principally by foreigners who are working in the real estate business in Mérida and sell almost exclusively to other foreigners.

6. Mérida's real estate market in the Historic Center operates like a localized market bubble, with little, if any, relation to the forces of supply and demand that shape the real estate market in other areas of Mérida.

7. Given the peculiar circumstances of local demand, or lack thereof, the principal market for homes in the Historic Center are other expatriates, meaning that once you buy a property in Mérida' Historic Center you are almost exclusively limited to selling to other foreigners.

Buyer, Proceed with Caution!

Want to know about perhaps the most shocking example of what's happened?

A property named "Quinta Alicia" which has been for sale for almost **AN ENTIRE DECADE**!

Originally listed as a **one-million-dollar-fixer-upper**, the price has been lowered – by a whopping one thousand dollars! Yes, you read correctly: For only $999,000 USD you can own a fixer upper that has been on the market since the time when, for instance, you could make reservations for dinner at "Windows on the World" at the World Trade Center in New York! That poor owner is going to become a little old man sitting in his rocking chair still waiting for his $999,000 USD pay day!

Now that you have been forewarned, the question now becomes: **Who can you trust?**

There are two choices. There are a select number of real estate companies that have worked very hard to keep the Centro Histórico "sane," by which we mean, "reasonable." There have been a few real estate companies that have resisted the temptation to promise "limitless dollars" to the Yucatecan families who live in the Centro Histórico. There are real estate agents who have cautioned expatriate sellers that tripling their investment is "unrealistic." These stand in sharp contrast to those who make slick videos, post them on YouTube, and pretend that Mérida is Paris or Rome or Barcelona, where – of course – one can't expect to find a "fabulous" home for under half a million dollars.

That said, there are two options: You can choose to work with realtors who, in my opinion, have shown integrity and decency, striving to be fair to both sellers or buyers; or you can choose to work with Mexican realtors who primarily work with Mexican buyers, who are completely outside the "Gringolandia Bubble" of real estate self-delusion and swindle.

If you speak little or no Spanish, you may feel more comfortable dealing with an expatriate realtor in Mérida. If you are confident that your can manage in Spanish (or that your Yucatecan or Mexican realtor's English is good enough for you), you may want to look for real estate "like a local" and eschew the Gringolandia Bubble altogether.

These are the expatriate realtors who have worked diligently to contribute to a healthy, sustainable real estate market in Mérida. They have avoided the frenzied rush to sell to American (and Canadian and European) investors who are solely interested in "flipping" properties, or have made unrealistic promises to Yucatecan and Mexican property owners about how the value of their homes. Although you are primarily responsible for looking out for your own best interests, it's good to be guided to realtors whose integrity has been proven time and again.

Recommended Real Estate Companies

Jim Mann	Gabriela Cornelio
www.Meridayucatanproperties.com	www.casayucatanrealestate.com

REAL ESTATE

Oscar Cruz	Rupert Millautz
www.luzrealestate.com	www.buenavidarealtors.com

Jorge Cáceres
www.casablancayucatan.com

Where Can You Search for "Non-Dollarized" Real Estate?

If there is one mantra about Mérida in this book, is that to get a "fair market value" for just about anything, it is best to search the "Avisos Económicos," or the Classified Section, of the

The Challenges of Real Estate: A Slightly Cynical Perspective
By Professor Charles Kinbote

The interaction between your *average* Mérida real-estate agent and your *average* gringo client is one of **absolute mutual contempt** for reasons you *must* inscribe upon your mind and heart if you've any hope of surviving your whirl through the Mérida real-estate market, not to mention **the hair-raising plunge** into the actual purchase of a home.

This **absolute mutual contempt** arises from the fact that:

* Your average gringo client is of the dirty-fingernail knuckle-dragging racist type who secretly or vocally believes that Mexicans are stupid, lazy, subhuman dupes.

* Your average Mérida real estate agent has an enormous chip on his or her shoulder due to such things as the Mexican-American War, the outrageous mistreatment and exploitation of Mexican migrants by American agribusiness, and Arizona's barking-mad legislators who shamelessly terrorize and vilify utterly powerless and vulnerable Mexican immigrants for cheap political gain.

* Your average Mérida real estate agent therefore believes that average gringo clients are either dirty-fingernail knuckle-dragging racists, or willfully gullible self-deluded bleeding-hearts possessed of a toilet-trained kind of bigotry that makes them flatter themselves on their own open-mindedness, regard Mexicans as guileless simpletons, and betray themselves as easily victimized by the shame they feel for their gringo prosperity.

From the website: ExpatsAnon.com

Diario de Yucatán. From guitars to bookshelves, hammocks to rental houses, if it's out there, it's probably listed in the *Diario*'s classified section. This will give you a basic understanding of what people in Mérida expect to pay for just about anything.

So how do you shop for real estate as if you were a Mexican citizen?

When it comes to real estate, there are ample offerings, from two-bedroom houses in the Historic Center, to four-bedroom homes in the outlying Colonias. Once you peruse the "Avisos Económicos," then you are in a position to search for real estate as if you were a Mexican! And fortunately, there are Spanish-language sites that cater to Mexicans looking for real estate in Mérida. The advantage, of course, is that everything is priced in pesos, and that the entire market has not been distorted by expatriate realtors selling real estate in Mexico.

The disadvantage, on the other hand, is that almost everything on these websites is in Spanish. But then again, there lies the "authenticity" of the offerings – these are companies that are designed *by* Mexicans *for* Mexicans. There are other websites, of course, but these seven, listed alphabetically, will give you an idea of what's out there, what's available, and what's reasonable.

Here is a list of Mexican Real Estate Companies, by Mexicans for Mexicans

Some of these are national companies, meaning that they have classified listings for the entire country, and you should be confident in your Spanish, at least confident enough to make the initial inquiry.

Enormo

www.enormo.com.mx

InmoMexico

www.inmomexico.com

Three Real Estate Companies Not Recommended

It is important to point out several expatriate realtors who have contributed to the "hyping" of Mérida, and who have skewed their offerings towards properties that exceed the price of a median home in the U.S. If you are in a position to have your bank execute a wire transfer for about half a million dollars, simply because you have that much money, or all you want to do is be handed the keys to a property that's move-in ready, there's nothing wrong with that. As editor of this book, however, I would not recommend these three realtors to anyone thinking of purchasing a retirement home on a budget, or who is interested in getting value for his or her money.

www.MexIntl.com

www.tierrayucatan.com

www.haciendamexico.com

Quality Yucatán

www.qualityyucatan.com

Rentas y Ventas

www.rentasyventas.com

Semerena Properties

www.semerena.com

Trovit Mexico

www.asas.trovitmexico.com.mx

2 Casa Realty

www.2casarealty.com

Real Estate Companies Specializing in Progreso and Beach Homes

Kab Yucatán

www.kab-yucatan.com

Mayan Living

www.mayanliving.com

Is Mérida really right for you?

Mérida is a great place to visit, but do you really, truly, madly want to live here?

Mérida, the Schvitzing Capital of the World
By Beryl Gorbman

The yenta does not understand why so many foreigners move to Mérida. Sometimes she doesn't understand why she herself moved to Mérida. It is so awfully hot most of the time. In May, we had nearly a month of consecutive days over 105 degrees F and humid. You couldn't leave your house, except to run to the a/c car and drive to the a/c store and return to your a/c house. That is, IF you can afford a/c.

Sweating is a constant state of the human body here. Schvitzing, as it's called in the Yiddish vernacular. You can be sitting perfectly quietly watching TV and the sweat will roll down your face and neck.

Schvitzing is okay once in a while, but when there's an extended period of days of 100 degrees F and high humidity, it makes me crazy (er). I rebel and keep the a/c on starting at around 4 PM and then all through the night. I worship the god of a/c. Electricity costs more here the more you use, so our bill in the hot months is a major expense.

We have at least three groups of house-guests coming in the next few months and they will think this place is just fabulous. Lots of North Americans come in the winter and have a great time. They fall in love with the place because it is so gorgeous and gracious and then immediately buy houses because "the houses are so cheap." Many of these buyers sell the following year, or retreat back up north from late April until October. That's most of the year.

So if you're thinking of moving here, try visiting in May or August.

Source: www.yucatan-yenta.com

Only you can answer that question! That's why, in all fairness to you, it is important for you to consider that question thoroughly and thoughtfully. Yes, Mérida is a tropical paradise, but it is not paradise. The greatest obstacles are the summer heat, and the mosquitoes. Everyone who lives here full-time has to cope with both.

It's not difficult to understand why: Look at the globe. Yucatán lies along the same parallels as does the Arabian peninsula! And the median temperature in Yucatán is hotter! Why? Because the Arabian peninsula is desert, so at night, it cools down. Yucatán is covered by forests, which keep the sun's warmth during nighttime. The result? The average temperature is higher here than it is in Mecca!

It's not impolite to burst out laughing

Should you find yourself in the company of a real estate agent who is trying to convince you that any home in the Historic Center priced at more than $200,000 USD is a "value," ask him or her one question.

"How long has this been on the market?"

If the answer is measured in **YEARS** and not fewer than six months, it's not impolite to burst out laughing.

There's nothing more pathetic than having your time squandered by some clown who thinks that telling you all about how a place has been "restored" and "refurbished," and you walk around and see nothing but fixtures from the "Sale" aisle of Home Depot all over the place!

That is the reason you are advised to spend some time here, before you decide this is where you want to live. Mind you, there are thousands of expatriates from the world over living here, and there are thousands more who spend a portion of the year here. It is a wonderful place, but it isn't for everyone.

The best way to find out for yourself, one way or the other, is to spend a few weeks here. Beryl Gorbman, who's been here for almost a quarter century, recommends spending the months of May or August here. Then again, bear in mind that the city, like Rome, Italy, is virtually abandoned in August – everyone it seems is at the beach towns that spread east and west of Progreso! But her point is well taken, even if Mérida seems like a ghost town in August. If you are only going to come here between Christmas and Easter, you won't have a problem with the heat. But if you plan on being down here year-round, take note of the weather patterns that exacerbate summer's heat.

A Note about Shorter Stays

Renting an apartment or house is, as is common in the United States and Canada, usually done on a year contract. But what if you want to explore Mérida, and check out the city for several weeks, or several months, without signing a year-long contract?

One solution is negotiating a long-term stay at one of the better Bed & Breakfasts in town. It's possible to get a deal for a two-week, three-week or month-long stays. Many visitors who are in Mérida on "medical tourism" – and require several visits to doctors, dentists or other health professionals, rent by the week, or month. A good number of would-be expatriates, likewise, rent for a month to decide if, indeed, Mérida is the right place for them, or to have a comfortable "base of operations" while they search for the ideal property.

> Here is a list of Bed & Breakfasts, in alphabetical order, that are among Mérida's finest

Angeles de Mérida
Calle 74-A #494-A, between Calle 57 and 59 Street
Centro
Website: www.angelesdemerida.com

La Casa Lorenzo
Calle 41 #516-A between Calle 62 and 64 Street
Centro
Website: www.lacasalorenzo.com

Casa Mexilio
Calle 68 #495, between Calle 57 and 59 street
Centro
Website: www.casamexilio.com

Casa Santiago
Calle 63 #562, between Calle 70 and 72 street
Centro
Website: www.casasantiago.net

"In Ka'an"
Calle 15 #527 between Calle 24 and 26 Street
Colonia Maya
Website: www.inkaan.com

Los Arcos
Calle 66 #448-B, between Calle 49 and 53 Street
Centro
Website: www.losarcosmerida.com

In addition, there are two splendid boutique hotels, one run by a gracious husband-and-wife team from the United Kingdom and the other by a refined Yucatecan gentleman. Both hotels accommodate stays for individuals checking out the real estate market in Mérida.

Hotel Zamná
Calle 53 #547, between Calle 70 and 72 Street
Centro
Telephone: (999) 924-0103
Email: zamna.merida.centro@gmail.com
Website: www.casazamna.webs.com

Hotel Casa Nobel
Calle 72 #403-C, between Calle 39 and 41 Street
Centro (Avenida Reforma)
Telephone: (999) 920-0369
Email: reservaciones@hotelcasanobel.com
Website: www.hotelcasanobel.com

A Note about Renting an Apartment or House

Many expatriates find it prudent to rent while remodeling a home. This, of course, makes perfect sense. As with realtors, be forewarned, there are currently no licensing requirements for "property management" in Mexico. Anyone can set up a rental and property management company. And if you purchased a "fixer-upper" it might make sense to live down here for the 6, 9 or 12 months that a renovation, reconstruction and building takes place. It's difficult to deal with architects, contractors and designers about a house in Mérida if you happen to be thousands of miles away!

Renting a house or an apartment is much the same as it is in other countries, with the exception of the attorney fees and the contract. You will be responsible for the fee to prepare the contract, which is one month's rent. The attorney will prepare a lease contract and 12 promissory notes. The rest is standard, with first and last month's rent. Often you can avoid a security deposit if you have a Mexican citizen sponsor (co-sign) you. This is often difficult to do with casual acquaintances, since the Mexican citizen will be legally responsible to pay the rent should you default on the rental agreement.

It is also important to remember that, once again, the rental market has been "dollarized." If someone quotes you rent in dollars, what's the matter with them? This is Mexico!

Your best bet is to check out the "Avisos Económicos" to know what the fair market value of a rental apartment or rental house goes for in the different Colonias around town. And of

If You Rent ... Protect Yourself!

Another necessary warning: If you rent from a Mexican citizen, every adult Mexican has two numbers, one is the IFE (Instituto Federal Electoral), which is issued as a national identification number. The other is an RFC, or Registro Federal de Causante, which is used for tax purposes. Renting from a Mexican citizen requires no other tax formalities on your part.

But if you are renting from a foreign national – an American or Canadian or European citizen in Mérida – please protect yourself by asking for a "Recibo Fiscal." This means that the person renting you the apartment or house is authorized to be a foreigner engaged in the business of renting properties in Mexico.

In recent years, some Americans and Canadians have been deported for renting out apartments and houses without authorization. (This is a form of tax evasion.) And as a consequence, renters – that could be you! – have been forced to find other housing. **Always ask for a Recibo Fiscal if your landlord is not a Mexican citizen!**

course you can rent a comfortable, but modest home in the Historic Center (2 bedroom, 1 bathroom for about $2,500 pesos, or $200 USD per month), or you can rent a more contemporary and comfortable home (a 3 bedroom, 2.5 bathroom, split level house with a garage in Colonia Buenavista goes for $5,000 pesos, or $400 USD per month).

Furnished, luxury rentals can go much higher, whether priced in pesos or dollars, but as a general rule, the same Mexican real estate companies that cater to Mexicans have the best deals. For a reference point, check out Rentas y Ventas (*www.rentasyventas.com*) simply because they have hundreds of listings, ranging from $1,800 pesos to $25,000 pesos per month.

> **Please note**: Many Spanish websites list prices with an "MN" at the end of a price, such as $5,000 MN. "MN" stands for "Moneda Nacional," or "National Currency." It means pesos. $5,000 MN is read as "Five thousand, national currency."

New Regulations on the Horizon for 2012?

If it seems as if the Historic Center's real estate market is in disarray, there's comfort in knowing that Mexican officials have taken notice. Miguel Ángel Aguayo de Pau, president of the Asociación Mexicana de Profesionales Inmobiliarios, or Mexican Association of Professional Realtors, who took office in early 2011, has gone the record for establishing regulations on realtors and how real estate companies operate in Yucatán State. Noting that there are "around 100" foreigners acting as real estate agents – and only about 300 properties in the Historic Center or Progreso beach are registered in the names of foreigners. Mr. Aguayo de Pau, wants tighter regulation. He pointed out that although real estate companies are not currently regulated by the state, real estate agents are expected to have certifications issued by INFONAVIT to prove that they meet the minimum standards of training in order to be considered bona fide real estate agents. Mr.

> 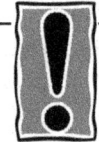 **May I see your Certificate from INFONAVIT?**
>
> If your real estate agent cannot produce a copy of his or her Certificado from INFONAVIT, ask yourself this: Does this person know the rules and regulations governing real estate in Mexico, or is this a con artist?
>
> Protect yourself: **Always use a real estate agent who has been certified by INFONAVIT!**
>
> Source: Asociación Mexicana de Profesionales Inmobiliarios (AMPI)

Aguayo de Pau expressed his concern that under current conditions, it is too easy for real estate agents who have not been certified by INFONAVIT are more likely to commit fraudulent real estate transactions, or be themselves defrauded because of their ignorance of real estate norms. He has expressed concern that members of his industry organization are becoming alarmed at the trends in pricing – and lack of sales – in the city's Historic Center, creating an unsustainable situation for both buyers and sellers in this area.

Bottom line: If your realtor cannot show you his or her Certificate from INFONAVIT, find yourself another agent!

Property Taxes, or *Predial*

Finally, once you have purchased a home in Mérida, there's the matter of the annual "property tax," which is really not a property tax, but a jurisdiction fee, and it's nominal.

Known as the *predial*, this annual tax is assessed on all real property. The word *predial* – which is pronounced, PREH-dyahl – is the equivalent of the property tax assessed in the United States, but with an enormous difference.

To understand the difference, it's necessary to review its origins. *Predial* is an adjective for *predio*, and *predio* is a parcel of land. Mexican law is derived from the Napoleonic Code, which in turn is based on Roman law. Throughout Latin America, Roman law forms the basis of the legal institutions. Where property is concerned, the biggest difference between Roman law and Common law (which is the basis of English law, and American legal principles) concerns subsoil resources. Under Roman law everything under the ground belongs to the state (Caesar). And under U.S. law, everything under the ground belongs to the property owner. That's why if you have a ranch in Mexico and, in the course of digging a well you strike oil, well, that's not your oil. It belongs to the federal government, which reserves the right to exercise eminent domain. In the U.S., on the other hand, John D. Rockefeller was able to keep the oil he discovered in Texas, and went on to become the world's richest man.

This idea, that you own the property (and everything on it, but nothing beneath it), gave rise to the question of government authority and state jurisdiction. Do you acquiesce to the idea that your property is located within the jurisdiction of the government?

The *predial*, or tax on terrains, is based on the principle that by paying a nominal tax you are acknowledging that you are subject to the jurisdiction of the government that imposes this fee. This idea is so engrained in the legal system inherited from Spain that, for instance, the

Constitution of Ecuador explicitly states that any communal property held by a recognized community of First Peoples (indigenous populations) is automatically exempt from any *predial*. The rationale behind this is that, symbolically, the sovereignty of the First Nations is recognized, and they are not, technically, required to acquiesce to the authority of the modern nation-state under whose jurisdiction their communities reside.

Over the years, the concept has evolved, simply out of fairness. If you own a piece of land that has a high rise hotel on it, you should pay more than someone who owns a parcel of land where they have a simple one-bedroom home. On the other hand, the *predial* has never been viewed as a source of "substantial" income, but merely a formal mechanism of establishing jurisdiction and validating the social contract between the government and those governed. This is the reason, relative to U.S. property taxes, which are used to fund an array of government services, in Mexico the *predial* is a nominal fee, one that seldom creates financial hardship on property owners. In contrast, it's no uncommon to hear stories of Americans who decide to sell their homes because they can no longer bear the burden of property taxes!

Now comes two important factors. First, because Mexico is loath to create homelessness, failure to pay the *predial* is never used to seize a property, or evict people from their homes. Unlike the United States where governments are empowered to put liens on properties, or seize a property for back taxes owed, that simply doesn't happen in Mexico. Second, it's easy to see why, since there are no real, immediate sanctions for failing to pay the *predial*, there is a very high incidence of noncompliance. Folks just don't pay, and as a result, government offers incentives to pay the tax. If you pay in January, you will probably receive a 10%-15% discount, depending on what city government approved for the year in question. If you pay within the first trimester of the year, you're automatically entered to win a prize, like a house or a car.

You can imagine what happens where there is no real penalty for failing to comply with paying a tax. That's right! Many people go years, or even decades, without paying it. But, of course, in the end government finds a way to get its due. For the *predial*, there is an enforcement mechanism at the end of the day: The law prohibits the sale of property or changing the name on a deed if there are unpaid *predial* taxes that are outstanding.

When it comes time to sell a property, or you inherited a property and you want the title in your name, the Notario Público is required to square all pending taxes with the Catastro. This is one of the important tasks that real estate agents are supposed to provide, and it is one that is often burdensome to individuals who, upon inheriting a property, realize that their beloved old grand-aunt had been a scofflaw for years!

With this in mind, remember that because the city continues to grow so rapidly, the *predial* is now a significant source of discretionary income for the city of Mérida, and that it is used for funding general functions of the city government services, from school lunch programs to repairing the facades throughout the Centro Histórico. And, unless you plan to be in your home until you die and are content to let your heirs deal with back taxes, interest and penalties, it's best just to do the right thing, and enjoy the generous discount offered if you pay your *predial* in January – and you might even win a lovely gift, such as a brand new car!

Final Word on Rental Housing Prices in 2011
Don't let yourself be bamboozled into paying way too much for a rental!
Heed these price guidelines:

- A 2 bedroom, 1 bath house or apartment in a perfectly decent, safe Mexican neighborhood (unfurnished, possibly no appliances): $250 USD to 300 USD

- Want to go more upscale? The rental of a 2 bedroom, 2 bathroom house or apartment, with a yard, in a professional, middle-class neighborhoods north of Centro: $500 USD to $600 USD

- Need luxury living? Upper-class homes and apartments in newer, north of Mérida neighborhoods from with two-car garages, an ample garden and many with small pools, and even a maid/guest quarters: $800 USD and higher

Rental Procedures in Yucatán:

Home and apartment rental conventions vary from state to state in Mexico. In Yucatán, because tenant eviction is difficult for landlords to obtain through the courts of law, rental requirements often include the following:

1) An "Aval" or guarantee secured by real estate property

2) The signing of financial obligations such as "Pagarés" (IOUs) in lieu of a rental contract, and/or

3) A security deposit in the amount of one month's rent or more.

Furthermore, the renter must pay the landlord's attorney the equivalent of one month's rent for preparing and legalizing the various documents. In reality, the process is less onerous than it sounds, but renters should be aware in case they opt for renting from Mexican landlords. Often certain requirements are waived or modified. For example, instead of the "aval," an additional amount towards the security deposit can be requested. Renters who speak little or no Spanish: We recommend using their own local attorney to represent them in the negotiations, as the landlord's attorney represents only the landlord's interests. A list of attorneys is provided in Chapter 19.

12 Contractors, Architects and Designers

One of the great things about living in Mérida is that you get to live in a great city, filled with wonderful architecture and a rich history. Mérida's Cathedral, for instance, celebrates its 450th anniversary in 2011 – and it was the first Cathedral built on the mainland of the Americas! With a history so rich, it is difficult to decide where one will be inspired when it comes to architecture and design.

To get your creativity going, here are 15 great books that everyone should check out from the library (or better yet, buy) that will offer inspiration on what can be done, and how it should be done. The descriptions for each book are from Amazon.com and there are links provided to two iBookstore pages have been set up to allow you to read more about each book, and to get whatever discount Amazon.com offers should you decide to purchase any of these books.

After these brief descriptions of these books, there's a discussion on the Contractors, Architects and Designers who can help you make your home everything you want it to be. Look over these books, then we'll get on to making recommendations on who can make your dream home in Mérida a reality!

Books to Inspire

Here is a list of our recommended books. Please note: The description of each book is provided by the publisher.

Casa Yucatán
By Karen Witynski and Joe P. Carr

A dazzling photographic journey, *Casa Yucatán* focuses on architectural elements, water spaces, and open-air living in houses both colonial and contemporary, including haciendas and coastal retreats. The Yucatán has undergone a remarkable restoration renaissance of late: ancient pyramids now share the dense jungle landscape with revived haciendas, and colonial homes boasting high-beamed ceilings and cool tile floors posture amidst elegant plazas and renovated nineteenth-century mansions.

 ### Hacienda Style

By Karen Witynski and Joe P. Carr

Invite the rich colors, natural textures, and romantic beauty of Mexico into your home.

 ### Hacienda Courtyards

By Karen Witynski and Joe P. Carr

Explore the architectural elements and water havens that will inspire your own courtyard paradise.

 ### Traditional Mexican Style Interiors

By Donna McMenamin and Richard Loper

There is charm and character in a Mexican home like no other architectural style. It is a classic, timeless style that remains in constant demand. All who enjoy looking at beautiful interiors and want new ideas for their own home will find this book irresistible. Over 280 color photographs of some of the most beautiful new, old, and remodeled Mexican-style homes are compiled here. Color is everywhere vibrantly painted walls offer a rainbow of hues, hand painted talavera tiles cover every available surface, and traditional Mexican folk arts adorn walls and furnishings. Twelve chapters illustrate beautiful entryways, living rooms, kitchens, dining rooms, bedrooms, bathrooms, ceilings and floors, stairways, niches, fireplaces, lighting, and arts. Having specific rooms and architectural details divided into separate chapters is a format sure to please decorators, designers, architects, builders, and homeowners looking for new and exciting ideas.

 ### Casa Mexicana Style

By Annie Kelly and Tim Street-Porter

Acclaimed architectural photographer Tim Street-Porter vividly captures this enduring passion for design in *Casa Mexicana Style*, the follow-up to his best-selling *Casa Mexicana* (more than 100,000 copies sold). In this gorgeous new book featuring more than 250 photographs, Street-Porter takes us on an insider's tour of 30 stunning homes, from urbane city apartments and modernist beach houses to stately rural haciendas and lovingly restored colonial townhouses.

Mexican Country Style
By Karen Witynski and Joe P. Carr

Now in paperback, *Mexican Country Style* is the classic that helped launch the popular Mexican design revival. Authors Karen Witynski and Joe P. Carr navigated coastal villages and old colonial mining towns by bus and burro, bumping down narrow cobblestone streets in search of simple and utilitarian elements like country tables, workbenches, storage trunks, corral gates, and heavy old doors. Intrigued by the diversity they encountered, the authors documented the wide variety in style, design, and shape of each object they encountered. Weathered coffee mortars, milking stools shaped like animals, and sculptured sugar molds reflect a rich local history as well as the ingenuity of the hands that crafted them. *Mexican Country Style* is the result of those fascinating journeys and boundless discoveries, a celebration of a rugged, romantic beauty and magical antiquity that continues to make its way into the contemporary interiors, gardens, and commercial settings across the country.

In A Mexican Garden: Courtyards, Pools, and Open-Air Living Rooms
By Gina Hyams and Melba Levick

The team behind the best-selling *Mexicolor* and *Mexicasa* has unlocked the gates to Mexico's patios, courtyards, and walled gardens. From private homes to luxurious resorts, *In A Mexican Garden* celebrates Mexico's hidden oasis where lovers meet for margaritas at sunset and families gather for spirited fiestas. The dazzling array of featured properties includes rustic coastal hideaways, elegant Spanish Colonial mansions, rural haciendas, and Modernist architectural masterpieces. Melba Levick's stunning photographs capture page after vibrant page of bold Mexican design elements: swirling mosaic floors, elaborate frescoes, hand-carved stone fountains, and lush native plants. Gina Hyams' informative text explains the historic roots of these uniquely Mexican outdoor spaces. Garden design enthusiasts, fans of Mexico, and anyone who appreciates a siesta in

Buy these books on Amazon.com

For your convenience, an "iBookstore" has been set up where all these titles are featured – and where you can purchase them, getting whatever discount Amazon.com is offering!

Here is the "iBookstore" addresse:
http://astore.amazon.com/casacathe-20

the sun need only open this book to hear the quiet babble of fountains and glasses clinking to toast another beautiful sunset.

Adobe Details
By Karen Witynski and Joe P. Carr

In their fourth book, authors/designers Karen Witynski and Joe Carr forage through the American Southwest and mountains of Mexico in search of the furnishings, accents and architectural elements that reveal its time-honored beauty and character.

The New Hacienda
By Karen Witynski and Joe P. Carr

The New Hacienda looks at the ways in which designers and architects have integrated the visual culture of the hacienda and blended Mexican elements in new homes on both sides of the border. From ancient stone walls and arcaded portals to cobbled courtyards and grand salons, hacienda style comes alive with a spirited mix of once-forgotten objects and contemporary furniture.

Mexicocina: The Spirit and Style of the Mexican Kitchen
By Betsy McNair and Melba Levick

In the tradition of the popular *Mexicolor*, photographer Melba Levick captures the bright colors and bold shapes of the kitchens of Mexico, this time touring private historic homes, resorts, and cooking schools. Here, priceless collections of indigenous pottery sit side-by-side with sleek appliances, Frida Kahlo's wooden spoons are right where she left them, and San Pasqual Bailón, the patron saint of cooks and kitchens, blesses every last handmade copper kettle, Talavera tile, and neon sign. *Mexicocina* tantalizes more than just the eyes, featuring mouthwatering recipes for innovative Mexican dishes at the end of each chapter, from appetizers to dessert. Inspiration abounds in these Mexican kitchens, whether the reader is redecorating, making travel reservations, or just dreaming of the scent of café de ollas.

Mexicolor: The Spirit of Mexican Design
By Tony Cohan, Masako Takahashi and Melba Levick

Basking in sunlight and coursing with energy, Mexico enjoys a unique relationship with color-inspired, intrinsic, inseparable from life itself. This vibrance sings forth in the pages of *Mexicolor*, the collaborative project of an artist, a photographer, and a writer all in love with the brilliant displays of color seen everywhere in Mexico. Walls washed flamingo pink on top, deep matte blue on the bottom. A green flatbed truck heaped with orange marigolds. A sea of colorful skeletons at a Day of the Dead fiesta. The radiant reds, yellows, purples, and greens of the fruits and vegetables at *el mercado*. *Mexicolor* explores Mexico high and low, from colonial towns to dazzling beaches, from traditional workshops to contemporary interiors, from open markets to extraordinary homes and inns, uncovering the colorful artistry that permeates everyday life across this vast nation. *Mexicolor* is an ideal resource for anyone looking to brighten a home, and a beautiful picture book brimming with imagination, creative ideas, and pure pleasure.

Casa San Miguel: Inspired Design and Decorations

By Annie Kelly, Tim Street-Porter and Jorge Almada

San Miguel de Allende, one of the prettiest destinations in Mexico, has become a fabulous source for stylish decorating ideas as many international designers are flocking to this artistic mecca. Acclaimed architectural photographer Tim Street-Porter and style writer Annie Kelly take us on an insider's tour, from stately rural haciendas and villas to renovated colonial townhouses. Featured are more than 250 glorious photographs of residences that show a blending of local crafts and handiwork with antiques and contemporary furnishings. Beautiful outdoor entertaining and garden areas enliven many of the houses. With a foreword by Jorge Almada of Casamidy, a design company based in San Miguel, *Casa San Miguel* is a unique inspirational design resource. It provides a vicarious look at daily life in this picturesque Mexican town that is attracting many international trendsetters.

Traditional Mexican Style Exteriors

By Donna McMenamin and Richard Loper

Beautiful, classic, and timeless architectural details of Mexican style are shown in over 300 color photographs of new, old, and remodeled traditional homes and gardens. From Spanish Colonial facades in San Miguel de Allende, Guanajuato, Mexico, to the best of the Mission and Spanish Eclectic homes, this volume is a must for everyone interested in Mexican architecture and outdoor charm. This book excites the readers imagination through nine chapters, including facades, doors, gates, portales & patios, columns, fountains, pools, cantera stonework, and gardens. Arcades support massive tiled roof overhangs and bring shade to the outdoor sala an affirmation for outdoor living at its best. Sparkling pools and spouting fountains bring tranquility to flower-filled gardens and courtyards. The pictures will inspire decorators, designers, architects, builders, and homeowners looking for traditional and exciting ideas. Everyone who enjoys looking at beautiful facades, outdoor living areas, and gardens will covet this book.

 ## Santa Barbara Style

By Kathryn Masson and James Chen

This book showcases Southern California's most historically significant and beautifully preserved Spanish-revival houses of this century. Twenty-one private homes built between 1922 and 1991 are featured in stunning color photography that captures exterior and interior architectural details, Spanish and Mexican antique furnishings and folk art, and lush landscaping and tiled fountains. Among these are the Adamson House in Malibu, with its extraordinary collection of custom tile from Malibu Potteries; the contemporary Greenberg House in Brentwood, by Ricardo Legorreta; The Andalusia Courtyard Apartments in Hollywood; and Casa Pacifica, the former home of Richard Nixon, overlooking the ocean in San Clemente. Brief narratives highlight the history of each building and its design influences on the Spanish-revival movement in California.

 ## Mexicasa: The Enchanting Inns and Haciendas of Mexico

By Gina Hyams and Melba Levick

Perched on a rugged coastline, set in verdant ranch land, or tucked away in a picturesque colonial town, the magnificent inns and haciendas of Mexico spring to life in the pages of *Mexicasa*. Historically and culturally important, these living museums contain wondrous collections of Mexican arts and crafts as well as enchanting gardens and courtyards. Acclaimed photographer Melba Levick captures the stunning architecture and colorful folk art that draws admirers from all over the world, while author Gina Hyams reveals the tradition and unique story behind each retreat. An extensive directory listing the contact information for each of the 21 featured inns makes this an indispensible resource book as well as a celebration of the spirit of Mexico.

Getting it done

Now that you have settled on a house, or at least have whittled down the multitude of options to a few, it's time to think about what you want to do. The wonderful books featured in this section should inspire anyone, and the great thing about Mérida is that a good number of the architects whose work is featured in these books happen to live in town. There are also excellent contractors, some of whom have worked on restoration projects of the most important buildings in Mérida.

Construction Practices

Construction Managers in Mexico are responsible for all the employees who work for them. The client is responsible to pay the Construction Manager, and the Construction Manager pays wages, and taxes (health insurance, payroll deductions, etc.) that are applicable. Construction Managers are also expected to carry personal liability insurance. Construction Managers normally procure all the materials needed for the project, and hire subcontractors who will do specialized work, such as pool design or solar panel installation.

As the Client, however, your responsibility is to make sure that the Construction Manager is complying with the law. This is rather easy to do by simply requesting to see, for instance, proof of insurance, receipts for health insurance payment, and payroll signed by the employees. (Most employees in Mexico are paid in cash, and they are required to sign receipt of their cash wages every time they are paid.) As the Client, you are entitled to the receipts for all the materials purchased and for copies of all the payroll sheets indicating that the workers were paid for their labor.

As is the case in the U.S., it is customary to follow the "30" percent rule – have a reserve of about 30% because unforeseen problems are bound to arise, causing original budgets to increase, and expect such delays to add about a third of the initial projected time. A $30,000 USD renovation that should take three months, might end up costing $40,000 USD and take four months. That's well within the norm, in Mexico as it is in the U.S.!

Where things are a bit different in Mexico than in the U.S. is one very important – and fortuitous aspect: Architectural firms enlist a staff of contractors and designers who can marshal resources to complete the entire project. In the U.S., by contrast, an architect will design a building and that's that. The rest is up to the Client. In Mexico, the architect also has a contractor, or works with contractors, to make the design a reality. What's better is that the entire project is seen as an organic endeavor. This means that architects often work with a number of designers who can flesh out the vision in its entirety.

This is a blessing for expatriates, since working with an architect one has available an entire team of contractors and designers at his or her disposal. There have been many instances when, for instance, a specific dining room set was designed to match the vision for the kitchen, and the wrought iron used throughout was then used to inspire bathroom fixtures and bedroom furniture.

In other words, architects more than design, they carry out the project through all the steps necessary to make it a reality.

One final caveat: If you are purchasing a historic building, be aware that the National Institute of Anthropology and History, known as INAH, has jurisdiction over what can and cannot be demolished. Often times the integrity of the original design has to be respected, plans have to be submitted for approval to INAH and permits have to be issued. If you think that a "gratuity" will solve any lingering questions about whether a room can be knocked down to build a luxurious bathroom, think again. Many a homeowner has been forced to restore rooms and walls that were modified in violation of approved plans. This is one reason so many architects recommend that Clients purchase houses with ample – and they mean ample – backyards. Why? If you must restore the original structure with little modifications, remember, there's no limit to the fantasy kitchen, extravagant bathrooms and luxurious bedrooms that can be added on from where the *back terrace opens onto the backyard*. Yes, there are master bedroom suites that open onto swimming pools.

A word of caution: Having lived in Mérida for years now, and being the host of a Bed & Breakfast, I have seen a good number of things about the people who are here. I know of a guest from Great Britain who was swindled out of $20,000 USD by an American "contractor" who just took her money and ran. I know of others who've had larger amounts taken, and recently a friend was ripped off in the amount of $5,000 USD by the same guy – he was back in town. Trust me, in my experience, you are well advised to **be more careful from a fellow expatriate than from a local contractor**. Why? Because expatriates can leave anytime, whereas local contractors are from here, have their family here, and live here!

Recommendations

Here is a list, although it is not comprehensive, of professionals who continue to win praise from expatriates. The person ultimately responsible for looking out for your best interests is, of course, you. All these architects, however, have relationships with contractors and designers. Two additional contractors are listed, simply because they are the crème del a crème when it comes to expertise, skills and reputations in Mérida.

Architects

Salvador Reyes

The Reyes Rios + Larrain Studio of Architecture and Design.

Located in Mérida, Yucatán, Mexico, this firm was founded by Architect Salvador Reyes Rios and Josefina Larrain Lagos. Their award-winning work has established the standard for colonial remodeling and hacienda restoration in Mexico. Many of the former colonial mansions and haciendas in the state of Yucatán and elsewhere in Mexico have been converted to luxury hotels and private homes under their supervision.

Email: *info@reyesrioslarrain.com*
Website: *www.reyesrioslarrain.com*

Alvaro Ponce

Alvaro Ponce Arquitectos

An award-winning architect, Alvaro Ponce's work has been featured in *Casa Yucatán*, which is reason enough to consult him if you are engaged in major undertaking. His work on the haciendas in the area, as well as important *casonas* – mansions – in Mérida harks back to a time when excellence was demanded and expected.

Calle 45 #172, between Calle 38 and 40 Street
Colonia Benito Juárez Norte
Telephone: (999) 943-3075
Website: *www.aponce.com.mx*

Note: Salvador Reyes and Alvaro Ponce are the "superstars" of architects in Mérida. Why? Because so many of their projects end up being photographed and showcased in design books and architectural magazines. But there are other architects who work on more modest scale, and whose work is exceptional. Some of the works of the architects listed below have appeared in the pages of the most prestigious magazines, including *Architectural Digest*.

Banish Mosquitoes!

Not quite paradise! The most annoying thing about living in Mérida are the mosquitoes. There's nothing that can be done about it, since it's their planet as much as it is ours, and they love the tropics. Every year health officials warn about them, and report on outbreaks of dengue fever in poorer neighborhoods, so it is a perennial concern.

But there is a solution! A natural, organic and sustainable solution: **Colibri incense**.

Imported from Auroville, India this is the only all-natural incense made of scents that scare them away. Ideal for indoor and outdoor use, many Hacienda resorts and local restaurants and bars use them for patio and terrace seating.

In town, only Casa Catherwood sells them, although if you are in Celestun or near Uxmal there are resorts that have them in their gift shops. You can't have a gracious home if you have mosquitoes buzzing around!

More information at:
www.casa-catherwood.com/colibri

Victor Cruz

ESTILO Arquitectura
   Telephone: (999) 738-9089
   Website: www.estiloyucatan.com

Arturo Campos

Campos Architects
   Telephone: (999) 926-9080
   Website: www.camposarquitecto.com

Mercedes Sánchez & Alvaro Cervera

Cervera & Sánchez Arquitectos
   Telephone: (999) 958-0961
   Website: www.architectsinyucatan.com

Rubén Portela Rodríguez

Ambientes Diseño Arquitectónico
   Telephone: (999) 928-7488
   Email: ambientesda@prodigy.net.mx

Miguel Rojanes

Miguel Rojanes Arquitectos
   Telephone: (999) 101-0060
   Website: www.miguelrojano.com
   Email: m_rojano@yahoo.com

Contractors

José Luis Cáceres

The Cáceres family is synonymous with executing masterful renovations and restorations. Much of the work done at Palacio Cantón and the Teatro Peón Contreras was supervised by this family, which has been in Yucatán for generations. At present, apart from world-class contractors, the firm has arguably the best carpentry services in Mérida. Many of the woodwork done in galleries and museums around town was done by this firm, and the same applies for upscale resorts and hotels in Cancún, which are regular clients for custom work.

Construcción de la Península, S.A. de C.V.

Calle 59 #530 by Calle 66
Centro
Telephone: (999) 314 1566
Website: *www.construcciondelapeninsula.com*
Email: *caceres@construcciondelapeninsula.com*

G. Fernando González

Fernando González spent years working in the United States, and is both fluent in English and he is with the expectations of American clients. His no-nonsense professionalism exudes confidence, and his authoritative familiarity with labor norms in Mérida proves exceptional. In recent years, Fernando González has become the "go to" resource for English-speaking expatriates who want a reputable, honest and conscientious firm for their projects.

Sistemas a Mano, S.A. de C.V.

Calle 15 #80, between Calle 23 and 25 Street
Dzitya, Yucatán
Telephone: (999) 176-2154 and (999) 101-0878
Email: *ggonz98294@aol.com*

Recommended References:

If you are engaged in a hands-on manner in the design, construction or rehabilitation of your property, it might a good thing to get a copy of either of these reference books:

Construction Spanish (en inglés y español), by A. P. Scott.

Over 1,000 words and terms both English/Spanish and Spanish/English make this book a real help on any construction project. The right term for the tools and equipment make a safer and more efficient jobsite. The book saves time and money and it will also help teach English or Spanish. Tools, equipment, safety, landscaping and more are covered in this pocket sized, 116 page book.

Constructionary, Second Edition: English-Spanish by the ICC

The International Code Council Constructionary is a handy, on-the-job English-Spanish, Spanish-English dictionary containing more than 1,000 construction terms, as well as pronunciations, useful phrases, and conversion tables. This resource will help you improve communications, creating a safer and more efficient job site. The International Code Council (Whittier, CA) is the organization that produces the International Building Code — the most widely adopted building code in the world. They offer unmatched technical, educational, and informational products and services, including code application assistance, educational and certification programs, plan reviews, monthly magazines and newsletters, and training and informational videos. They have more than 16 locations throughout the U.S. and Latin America.

> ### Americans Scamming Americans?
>
> "In reflecting on our experience [building our dream home], we are chagrined to find that it wasn't the locals that misrepresented themselves or took advantage of us, as many *norteamericanos* might fear when undertaking a project like this. It was [David Sterling] a fellow expatriate. Do we think he did it on purpose? We hope not. Giving him the benefit of the doubt, we think he bit off more than he could chew and couldn't admit it," James and Ellen Fields.
>
> *Source: "Building Our House IV," in "Yucatan Living"*

13   Furniture, Furnishings & Antiques

Furniture

If you are making the move to Mérida, many people take advantage of the one-time opportunity to ship your household goods from abroad into Mexico. This provision in the law is designed to let people bring their furniture, kitchen wares, household items, art, books and whatever one normally finds in a home without having to pay taxes. There are, of course, shipping fees, but that depends on the shipping line or moving company, and there are fees that are charged by the Customs Brokers who take care of all the paperwork.

Of course, there are restrictions: whatever you find in a pantry or a medicine cabinet is not allowed. (What's the point in bringing a half-used bottle of ketchup, or an open tube of toothpaste?) And the items have to be used – if you want to import six ceiling fans in their unopened boxes that you got for a bargain off the Internet, you're going to have to pay a duty on that, since the fans, obviously, weren't in use in the home you're vacating.

Some people want a fresh start, and sell their furniture before moving to Mexico. Others find that their furniture, at some point, will need to be replaced. That old sofa from the 1980s? The dining room set that really doesn't fit in with your Mérida home? The bookcase that you forgot to treat for termites and is falling apart?

You get the idea. Chances are you will be buying furniture at some point. If you want to find a few antiques, that subject is discussed later in this chapter. Bear in mind that the best Mexican antiques are in Mexico City and Guadalajara, and that Mérida is better known for having antiques from Spain, France and Italy, although most of these remain in private homes, and seldom come on the market.

Two things to consider as you choose furniture for your Mérida home. First of all, make sure that the wood is treated for termites, and think about choosing light colors. Yes, there is tremendous beauty in the dark, rich mahogany, but as a matter of maintenance, it's important to be able to spot evidence of termites, or other bugs, and there are a lot of critters in the Yucatán!

Second, be mindful of the balmy evening air – as charming as it is, the breezes carry mold, which grows on leather, especially in rooms where the air doesn't circulate. Leather furniture needs to be cleaned regularly. Always follow the manufacturer's instructions. As a general rule, most leather furniture can be cleaned with lukewarm water and a very mild soap. (Never use alcohol, cleaning solvents, oils, varnishes or polishes on leather. Always avoid extreme temperatures. For more information, see *www.ehow.com/how_2086289_care-leather-furniture.html*) If you will be leaving for more than a couple of weeks, you will have to cover all your leather furniture with cotton sheets.

The following furniture stores are listed in alphabetical order, not in any preference. It is recommended that you visit a variety of stores to comparison shop, and to get a better understanding of the options around town. Following are a listing of furniture stores.

Furniture Stores

Azcué

Gran Plaza, second floor
www.azcuemuebles.com

One of the more economical furniture options in town, this is the Mérida store of a national chain well-known for its customer service. Its principal market is the emerging middle class, which is one reason it has both a wide selection of futons and also children's furniture. Often this store has a wide selection of discontinued models, which means they are on sale at great prices. This store is a must-see for value, especially if you have guest bedrooms to furnish, or expect to have kids visiting you – bunk beds are always in stock.

Casa Italia

Prolongacion Montejo #99, between Calle 19 and 21 Street
Telephone: (999) 948-0551

This store primarily sells from a catalog, since the furniture takes about three months to deliver. It has to first be made in Italy, then shipped to Progreso, and then trucked to you. It operates much the same way that Luminare, in Coral Gables, Florida and Chicago, Illinois sells high-end Italian design furnishings (*www.luminaire.com*). But there are a few pieces on hand, which is a great way to appreciate the design, quality and workmanship of the pieces. If you are wondering where all those mansions being built in the Yucatán Country Club are going to get their exquisite furniture, well, now you know.

Colomer

Calle 20 #99, between Calle 19 and 21 Street, Colonia Itzimná
Telephone: (999) 926-9977
www.colomermuebles.com

This is another company that specializes in furniture for institutions – hotels, resorts, government offices – and does a great job of it. Its residential line is very much in keeping with contemporary Mexican aesthetics and the needs of the modern family. Their dining room sets are very comfortable, and make great use of combining woods, fabrics that complement the paste tiles of Mérida. They also excel at bookcases and cabinets, almost like a high-end version of Restoration Hardware in the U.S. Best yet? Yes, they can reproduce whatever piece of furniture you saw in a magazine and ripped out the page!

D'Europe Muebles

Calle 60 #370, between Calle 39 and 37 Street, Centro
Telephone: (999) 925-3086
www.deurope.com.mx

The furniture store for the Europhile! Fast approaching the half-century mark, this furniture store (founded in Mexico City and with locations in Puebla, Hidaldo, Morelos and Mexico State as well as Yucatán), offers a vast selection of contemporary European design. They operate two locations (the other is on Calle 21 #321, adjacent to Plaza de las Américas), and their staff is knowledgable about finding pieces that fit your own individual aesthetics. With prices in the mid-range of what is available in town, this is a terrific resource, especially for dining room and bedroom sets. They have built a reputation for customer service, and when they have a sale, some sets are reduced as much as half off.

Gringo Furniture

Calle 20 #99, between Calle 19 and 21 Street, Colonia Itzimná
Telephone: (999) 926-9977
www.gringofurniture.com

What do you get when enterprising Americans set up shop to cater to the Mexican fantasies of other Americans? Gringo Furniture. And that's a good thing. It takes special skill to be able to channel the aesthetics of the Founding Fathers, Mexican colonial aesthetics, Frank Lloyd Wright and a certain neo-Colonialism, but it works. While one can question the political sensibilies of a "Plantation Dining Set," there are no arguments to be made with a "Safari Sectional with Wood

Arm Rests." No one gets it 100% right all the time, but Gringo Furniture has some homeruns with their Rattan, Designer and Rustic Contemporary series.

Luna del Oriente (antique Asian imports)

Calle 65 #541-A, between Calle 66 and 68 Street
Telephone: (999) 247-2953
www.lunadeloriente.com

This store, run by an American husband-and-wife team, carries the best Chinese and Indian antiques and architectural elements anywhere outside Mexico City! Really, they do. The taste, selection and aesthetics are exquisite, and it is one of the few shops in Mexico that carry Mongolian furniture, and Chinese antiques from the Gansu region. If Asian furnishings capture your imagination, and didn't bring some with you, an appointment to this store will give you a vast selection of extraordinary pieces from which to choose.

Marbol

Gran Plaza, Second Floor
Telephone: (999) 948-3048
www.marbol.com.mx

Marbol specializes in a resort aesthetic. If you see any of those alluring brochures for the fancy hotels and resorts from Cancún to Playa del Carmen which boast furniture that is slightly colonial in nature and definitely laid-back resort in feel, then you already know the spirit of their offerings. It is certainly a favorite among Mexicans living in Mérida who hail from the Valley of Mexico and futher north (think of the triangle formed by Monterrey, Guadalajara and Mexico City). Their principal clients are resorts, and that means you are sure to find tasteful designs in dark wood and fine rattan.

MID Muebles

Calle 18 #66 between Calle 5 and 7 Street, Colonia San Antonio Cinta
Telephone: (999) 286-4477
www.midmuebles.com

A bit off the beaten path, this is one of the most innovative furniture stores around. They offer contemporary and sleek designs, excellent craftsmanship and exceptional value. Aimed at Mérida's middle class families, the prices are quite something – and because they are also manufacturers, they can custom built to your specifications. They have an extensive selection for all rooms in their online catalog. One of the wonderful services they offer is re-upholstery, which can save you a significant amount, especially for pieces that have sentimental value and just need to be refreshened up. And if you have a home office, they offer one of the most extensive selections of furniture for home offices anywhere on the peninsula.

Nasström

Calle 31 #104, between Calle 20 and 24 Street, Colonia Mexico
Telephone: (999) 927-2354
www.nasstrom.com.mx

This company is a manufacturer for Ikea. As a result, you have a line of Scandanavian-inspired furniture that is manufactured just south of the airport in the town of Uman. Who would have thought? But there it is! You can select from an overwhelming selection of styles and fabrics, and it will be made-to-order in Uman. The prices are reasonable (think of the higher end items at an Ikea store), and when they have their sales, then you can get sofas and club-style chairs at an exceptional value. The staff is bilingual, and although they don't offer designer services, they are quite knowledgeable about appointing colonial homes that have been recently remodeled.

Paladium

Calle 30 #76-B between Calle 11 and 13 Street, Prolongación Montejo
Telephone: (999) 944-9782

This is a one-stop furniture and furnishings store. It carries living room sets, dining room sets, bedroom sets and every imaginable accessory, from side tables to lamps. The designs are contemporary, with slick lines and lots of glass. There is a small design staff on hand that can assist in designing a room, or selecting individual pieces to complement what you have. The staff is pleasant and helpful, and it merits a visit to see what's out there on the market.

Triunfo

Paseo de Montejo at Calle 39

What can be said about this place? It's a madhouse. This is a Mexican company that buys containers full merchandise that has been seized by Mexican Customs, auctioned off by U.S. Customs and sold, often as discontinued merchandise, primarily by Indian and Chinese companies. It is a bazaar of the bizarre. It's certainly worth a look, especially if you are in the market for utilitarian tableware, eclectic outdoor and garden furniture, or want to have some items in your home that are camp or kitsch, or a bit of both. The only thing that's missing is popcorn, since this place is such a carnival.

Tropical Cocoon

www.tropicalcocoon.com

This is another one-stop online resource that is truly a no-brainer. The two more successful lines, especially for the Yucatán peninsula, are the Caribbean Furniture and Contemporary Furniture collections. It's definitely not for everyone, but if you have confidence in your taste (and know how to use a tape measure expertly), then this may just be the simplest solution to outfit your home without any hassles.

Yucatán Custom Furniture

Telephone: (999) 286-3427
www.yucatancustomfurniture.com

The husband-and-wife team (she is Yucatecan and he is Canadian) behind Yucatán Custom Furniture strive to provide a one-stop online resource, with one exception: they offer the ability to customize woods, colors and tones, finishes at various price ranges. Their collections reflect both the physical requirements of the Yucatecan climate with the aesthetics of the local architecture. Their line of platform beds, modern canopy bed frames and colonial bed frames continue to win lavish praise, as does their customer service.

An Alternative to Furniture Stores: Mom-and-Pop Shops

Along Calle 67, between Calle 58 and 64 Street

Many of the furniture stores found along this street have "Rustic" lines, meaning furniture that resembles very utilitarian pieces found in many Mexican homes. That's great, and there's something to be said for having a few pieces of "authentic" Mexican furniture, and along Calle 67 you will see a good number of stores selling dressers, beds, cabinets, shelves and wardrobes that are found in many homes of working and middle class Yucatecans. These are terrific values, and with sandpaper you can distress the paint, or select several shades of stain. Not only will you have a unique piece, but it certainly will have the cachet of authenticity – at bargain prices.

Caoba/Tropical Mahogany Furnishings

In recent decades tropical mahogany furniture (caoba) that is made from sustainable forests from Campeche has been in much demand. One of the most successful manufacturers and distributors is based in Spain. **Rustic Ross** has developed several lines that are so favored by Europeans – whose aesthetics differ strikingly from those of Americans and Canadians – that various models of furniture (Queen Anne cabinets, Holland display case, Ortega cabinets, Jonker wine racks) are now made in Mexico for export to Europe and South America. For more information, just contact them at: Ross_Systems@terra.es

Mexican Antiques

No matter what your style, it's always wonderful to have a few old pieces in your home. Let's face it, you're getting better every day, and there's something about a piece of furniture, architectural piece or artwork that's been around for a while and, like you, has been getting better every day. Even if you live in a house inspired by the modern minimalism of Philippe Starck, it's always a good idea to have one vintage or antique object to provide a focal point to a room in a way that reflects your personality.

In the section above on furniture we noted the wonderful shops, Luna del Oriente. This foreign-owned company, however, specializes in objects from India, the Subcontinent and Far East. In this section, we provide a list of local companies that offer antiques from Mexico, the United States and Europe. This means that now is a great time to look through those design books we recommended and to get inspired!

But first, of course, a digression to explain the unique character of the antiques found in Mérida. The Yucatán's historic isolation from the rest of Mexico is a constant theme that has shaped the peninsula's culture, society and tastes. When it comes to antiques, Yucatecans usually brought furniture from Havana, and from Europe. During the height of the henequen wealth a century ago, Yucatecans imported the finest antiques from Europe, the United States and central Mexico. To give you an idea of the sheer variety that was prevalent one, consider the following anectdotes.

It's a little known fact that many of the antiques found at the Napoleonic Museum in Havana, Cuba have a Mérida connection. Housing one of the most important collections in the world of Napoleonic and French Revolutionary memorabilia outside France, this museum is located in a mansion named the *Dolce Dimora*, a structure designed in the style of a Florentine Renaissance villa. It was built by the Italian-Cuban politician Orestes Ferrara in 1928. The current museum opened in 1961 and it features thousands of items from the personal collections of Cuban tycoon Julio Lobo, who had shipped several important pieces to Mérida, as they made their way to Cuba. Bought over a period of almost two decades at auctions and from antiques dealers around the globe, Lobo had a number of representatives and buyers search the world for pieces connected to

Napoleon. The collection on exhibit – Lobo fled the Cuban Revolution – includes paintings, engravings, and a library with over 5,000 books, hand-written notes, glassware, porcelains and weapons. One of the most riveting pieces is the Emperor's death mask, which Francesco Antommarchi, Napoleon's personal physician made, in order to have the sculptor Antonio Canovas cast several copies in bronze. Other notable pieces include Napoleon's pistol used at the Battle of Borodino and the spyglasses he used while in exile at St. Helena. This, of course, is an extraordinary story, and the Mérida connection is both superfluous to this great collection, but intriguing nevertheless.

The point is that in the same way that wonderful antiques have landed in Mérida and been sent elsewhere, the reverse has happened. Important collections of Cuban antiques were surreptitiously shipped to Mérida in the 1960s. The Pantaleon family sent what would be a container of furnishings in the early days of the Cuban Revolution for safekeeping in Mérida.

Similarly, important pieces of American memorabilia from the Civil War have found their way to Mérida. Several **carte-de-visite photographs of General** Robert E. Lee are in Mérida, which range in price from $12,000 to $17,000 USD! American collectors over the years have acquired several Audubon drawings – which today fetch astronomical prices. A cachet of letters from Louis C. Tiffany caused quite a stir a decade or so ago when they were found in an old trunk of an established family.

Mérida's own history is also found in antique shops. When the legendary Hotel Itzá, on the intersection of 59 and 58 Streets, closed downtown, the Arts & Crafts furniture in the lobby was sold at a bargain price. If you venture to Centro del Paseo, on Paseo de Montejo and Avenida Pérez Ponce, enter from the main entrance of the original house. Where the utilitarian (read: ugly) stairs go to the second floor, there used to be a

Warning!

You may have noticed that in discussing "antiques" we have stayed away from mentioning "antiquities."

There's a reason for that and here is a very important note: **All pre-Columbian art and antiquities belong to the Mexican State.** If you have any pre-Columbian art, it must be registered with the National Institute of Anthropology and History (Insituto Nacional de Antropología e Historia, or INAH). Buying and selling pre-Columbian art without a license is a **federal offense**. Be aware that many Yucatecan families own stunning pre-Columbian ceramics, engravings and sculptures that have been inherited over several generations, which should have been registered with officials.

Furthermore, U.S. federal law makes it a crime to import or export Mexican pre-Columbian artifacts without a license from INAH. **Go for reproductions instead!**

magnificent stained glass window depicting a pastoral scene in an hacienda. When the building was remodeled, the glass was carefully removed, and stacked, and then removed by the original owners. That stained glass window was designed by Tiffany in New York!

Treasures are everywhere. Indeed, the most important pieces today remain with local families, or have been bought and sold among Yucatecans directly. Only after the economic crisis of 1982 and then the peso devaluation of 1994 have some families sold objects through "antique shops" in town. Those with significant holdings prefer to deal with Mexico City dealers, and Mexicans moving to Mérida often prefer to deal with reputable dealers with whom they are familiar – in Mexico City or Guadalajara or wherever they came from. One rare exception are the contemporary Virgin of Guadalupe images of Enrique Salazar which remain in great demand, particularly since John F. Kennedy, Jr. had one in the loft in Tribeca he shared with his wife, Carolyn Bissette. If you see them in a gallery around town, buy one – and hoard it!

What does this history mean? Well, it means that while Mérida is awash in antiques and antiquities, there are few dealers who have generations-old traditions of being in the antique business. This doesn't mean that you can't find hidden treasures, but it means that you have to be diligent about it. And if you have not been able to befriend Yucatecan families of a certain level, chances are that the best bet is to avail yourself to one of the shops listed alphabeticlly below, which just might help you find something extraordinary.

Antique shops

Antiguedades Jorge

Calle 21, Local 4-Bis, between Calle 38 and 38-A Street,
   Colonia San Pedro Uxmal Chuburná
Mérida, Yucatán
Cell Telephone: (999) 163-6596

Jorge Vázquez, who speaks a little English, owns this delightful business. The "shop" is actually two adjacent warehouses packed with all manner of stuff located behind his home. He spends most of the morning running errands and seeing clients. If you want to catch him, the best bet is to show up at Santa Lucia Park downtown on Sundays, where there is an open-air flea market. The varied selection of objects he offers gives you a glimpse into what he **Specializes in:** old photographs; lots of various kinds of bottles and glasses; 19th and early 20th century cast irons; religious objects and artifacts; ceramic tiles; and personal objects from lives long past. If anything catches your eye, do make an appointment to visit him, and there you will see the furnishings where these objects were kept: tables, drawers, wardrobes, dressers, with chairs and tables and fancier table settings and mirrors. It's a place to find something special and unique that speaks to you, and will bring Yucatecan history into your home.

Candiles & Decoración

Calle 59 #530, between Calle 64 and 66 Street
Mérida, Yucatán
Telephone: (999) 928-6321
Website: *www.candilesydecoracion.com*

Mario Cáceres, who is bilingual, is the manager of this family-owned business. It is, technically, a chandelier and lighting fixture company, but they are antiquarians and they carry an extensive selection of antiques. The company was founded by Mario Cáceres Bernés, and he was one of the leading voices in Mérida for reclaiming the historic center. In the 1970s, the Peón Contreras Theater on the corner of Calle 60 and 57 Street was in such a state of disrepair that authorities feared it was on the verge of collapsing. It was only after the government bought it that repairs began, and it was Mario Cáceres Bernés who spearheaded the interior restoration. That grand chandelier in the theater, you ask? Yes, it was restored by Candiles & Decoracion, and so have the chandeliers in scores of homes along Paseo de Montejo, Avenida Colón and Calle 59. In Yucatecan society, the Cáceres are the go-to family for restoration work, and they are also the go-to family for specific, hard-to-find colonial furniture and furnishings. An advantage that Mario Cáceres has is that, by virtue of being part of Mérida's social scene, he is familiar with the families, family histories and family holdings behind many of the mansions in town. Chances are that if you are interested in, say, a portrait of a pope painted in the 17th century, they know who has such an object. Interested in some religious artifacts from a cathedral in Havana that somehow made its way to Mérida? They probably can direct you in the right direction. At present, they are remodeling their location to include a showroom with antiques, but this is one resource that can answer your questions, and work with you to find what you are looking for. And when you need your antique Swarovski crystal chandelier cleaned, this is the place up to the task.

El Bazar

Calle 19 #201-D, between Calle 22 and 24 Street, Colonia García Ginerés
Mérida, Yucatán
Cell Telephone: (999) 157-6636

Roberto Guzmán, who is bilingual, is the proprietor of this shop. A physician by profession – he grew tired of seeing sick people all day, he says. So he changed professions. It seems like every foreigner meanders through this shop, and often times, Guzmán will be sitting, smoking a cigarette and sipping a soft drink in the company of another Yucatecan. (Yes, doctors smoke.) The folks he entertains are usually the owners of the objects for sale. Most of the inventory is on consignment from Yucatecan families who want to discreetly liquidate a few items. Sometimes you will find an exceptional piece at a terrific value, and at other times it's obvious that now that both dear great-grandmothers have passed away, it is no longer necessary to have so many wardrobes or dining room tables, especially since most homes now have closets, and everyone is either eating in the kitchen, or the family room. There are also several tables overflowing with the detritus of privileged lives: souvenirs from trips to Tokyo, ashtrays from France, knick-knacks from Africa, tschostskes from Disney World, Niagra Falls and a charming souvenir Statue of Liberty from the 1950s. Guzmán is often authorized to offer a discount, so if you see something you like for $2,000 pesos but think it's worth $1,600 pesos, make an offer. He might be authorized to grant it, or will call the owner and get back to you.

J&K Antiques

Calle 66 #470, between Calle 55 and 57 Street, Centro
Mérida, Yucatán
Telephone: (999) 244-0065 (English)
Telephone: (999) 154-7142 (Spanish)
Website: *www.yucatanantiques.com*

The first American to venture into the Mexican and European antiques market in Mérida, Jim Mann has done quite a job. Specializing in American and West European pieces, Mann has managed to assemble a respectable collection of objects. This store is the one that has the most feeling of an American antique shop of any in town, which is one reason American and Canadian expats feel so comfortable shopping there. The prices are reasonable, and the objects reflect the exciting nature of a new busieness: New pieces seem to arrive all the time, and if you wait too long, something you had been thinking about will invariably have found a home by the time you return. It's clear that "Jim" is the "J" in "J&K. The key to the company's success, however, rests with the "K" – "Kio." The Yucatecan partner is the one with the linguistic and cultural ties to the local community, and increasingly one is finding a few pieces from Yucatecan homes. Why is this important? Because these are antiques that have long resided in Mérida, and whose prices reflect savings from shipping and customs. And because Kio is from Mérida, he can more easily gain the trust of some Yucatecan families who have splendid pieces that may no longer be suitable for their current lives. Without a doubt, this is one resource that cannot be overlooked as you find antiques and collectibles for your new home in Mérida.

Julio Alfaro

Calle 75, at the intersection of 72 Street, Centro
Mérida, Yucatán
Cell Telephone: (999) 151-9030

Julio Alfaro, who is not very familiar with English, has quite a set-up. The actual building is jam-packed with all kinds of furniture – mostly dining rooms, bedroom furnishings and hallway closets and stands. There are a good number of mirrors. The outside terrace and yard, on the other hand, are different creatures. Doors and chairs in all states of repair and disrepair are stacked on top of each other, or leaning against the wall. The yard is strewn with all manner of carved stones, fountains, wrought iron doors, distressed doors, mechanical engines. It is a mess! And tucked in the northwest corner of the compound, well, there's a workshop where restoration takes place. When it comes to a vast selection of objects that are truly authentic in their history, this is the place! It's easy to envision seeing several doors being refurbished and be transformed into glass-topped tables, and there is a great selection of carved stones or artifacts that will enhance any garden. Alfaro is hard to reach at times, and it's unfortunate that his kids mind the shop when he's not there. They are not very helpful: they are more engaged watching television or playing games on their cell phones than they are in answering questions, or even know the asking price on anything. You might as well drop by, and if anything catches your eye, then call to see when you can see Alfaro directly.

Decorative Motifs

There will come a time when you realize you might need a decorative object here or there, or need to find something for a friend – a fellow expat, another foreigner, a Yucatecan or a Mexican – as a housewarming gift. These are stores that offer a wide selection of decorative objects.

AJ Arte Objeto

Calle 20 #87, between Calle 15 and 17 Street, Colonia Mexico
Mérida, Yucatán
Telephone: (999) 948-4563

Arte di Firenze

Calle 26 #115-A, between Calle 13 and 15 Street, Colonia San Antonio Cinta
Mérida, Yucatán
Cell Telephone: (999) 129-5114

Decoración Inn

Calle 7 #186-A, Colonia García Ginerés
Mérida, Yucatán
Telephone: (999) 925-0302

Inex

Calle 10 #321, between Calle 27 and 29 Street, Colonia San Esteban
Mérida, Yucatán
Cell Telephone: (999) 183-5052

RC Arte & Decoración

Calle 42 #360, between Calle 13 and 15 Street, Colonia San Pedro Uxmal Chuburná
Mérida, Yucatán
Telephone: (999) 944-0483

14 Handicrafts, Artists & Books

Handicrafts

Visitors and new residents alike often express disappointment in the lack of handicrafts in Yucatán. This is a valid complaint, and there is a reason. Historically, the traditional crafts of the Maya people in Yucatán have centered on red and black coral, and tortoise shell. Since the 1970s, consistent with concern for protecting our planet, strict laws have transformed contemporary practices: Coral reefs are protected habitats and marine sea turtles are endangered species under federal protection. Coral and tortoise shell handicrafts are illegal, and it takes generations for new traditions to emerge.

That said, there are other products that are in abundance: honey, chocolate, anise liqueur, henequen (sisal) goods, silver (filigree) jewelry, men's *guayabera* shirts and women's embroidered sun dresses *(huipiles)*, and fine Panama hats *(jipis)*.

But that doesn't mean that there are not wonderful handicrafts from *other* regions of Meixco!

Whether you are visiting or establishing a residence in Mérida, one of the pleasures is acquiring Mexican handicrafts. Nelson Rockefeller and Frida Kahlo are largely credited with bringing to the world's attention the vitality, integrity and beauty of Mexican handicrafts.

And good news! Mérida has three authorities with breathtaking knowledge, refined tastes and sweeping resources that can help you appreciate – and acquire – handicrafts that are museum quality. The Mexican government recognizes that the artisanal arts are part of the world's cultural heritage, and it nurtures its development. Through the Fondo Nacional para el Fomento de las Artesanías, or National Fund for the Development of Arts and Crafts, and every ethnic group is represented in its program.

Why is this important? Because in Mérida there is only one place where you can find handicrafts from each of Mexico's 32 states and the Federal District. It's 100% Mexico, located in the lobby of the Casa San Angel Hotel, where Paseo de Montejo begins. It's proprietor is Homa Abhari, a Persian immigrant to Mexico, who is a true connoisseur with refined taste and she can guide you. For instance, the great Sonoran desert is home to many Native Americans on both sides of the U.S.-Mexico border, and some of the pottery from Chihuahua is as exquisite as the finest Hopi pottery found in the U.S. Homa Abhari is one of Mérida's living treasures, a resource where visiting dignitaries and celebrities shop.

There are two other connoisseurs in town. Francois Valcke, from Belgium, and his partner Gerardo Martínez, from Venezuela, who together own Tataya Gallery. After decades on the Continent and London, they settled in Mérida, where they showcase exquisite handicrafts that they source from around the country. Each year they close shop and embark on pilgrimages of discovery, often tracking down the very artisans that contributed to the famed Nelson Rockefeller Collection of Mexican arts and crafts. Their Gallery – with two locations, one in Santiago downtown, and the other on Calle 60 across the street from Santa Ana church – reflects their connoisseurship of pottery from Oaxaca, Chiapas and Puebla, along with sculpture. Tataya Gallery also represents established Cuban artists, which are coveted primarily by European collectors, and long-established Mérida families.

Whether you want to spend $25 USD or $2,500 USD, between Homa Abhari, Francois Valcke and Gerardo Martínez you are sure to find something exceptional.

100% Mexico
   Homa Abhari
   Paseo de Montejo #1, Remate
   Centro
   Mérida, Yucatán
   Telephone: (999) 928-1800
   Hours: Monday – Saturday 10 AM to 1 PM and 4 PM to 7 PM; Closed Sundays

Galeria Tataya (Santiago)
   Gerardo Martínez
   Calle 72 #478, between 53 and 55 Streets
   Centro
   Mérida, Yucatán
   Telephone: (999) 928-2962
   This location is By Appointment Only.

Galeria Tataya (Santa Ana)
   Francois Valcke
   Calle 60 #409, between 45 and 47 Streets

Colonia Santa Ana
Mérida, Yucatán
Telephone: (999) 287-0685
Hours: Monday – Saturday, 10 AM – 2 PM and 4 PM – 7 PM; Closed Sunday

Artists

In addition, there are a few living artists who are in town whose work is exceptional. If you have the chance to purchase something from any of these artists, by all means do so. One, Karen Clarke, spends considerable time in Mérida and has a studio here, but she is represented by Mercury Gallery in Boston. The others are gracious and can accommodate your request to see their work – Ariel Guzmán, whose work is often on view at the MACAY, and Marcela Díaz, whose beautiful henequen sculptures are in the lobby of Rosas & Xocolate. Katrin Schikora has a wonderful studio in Cholul, and Enrique Salazar, whose work became highly sought after when John F. Kennedy, Jr. purchased one of his "Virgin of Guadalupe" paintings for his loft in Tribeca, has a studio in town. No sophisticated residence in the Yucatán is complete without the work of these artists!

Karen Clarke

Website: www.mercurygallery.com/KarenClarke.html

Marcela Díaz

Email: marceladiazmdeoca@hotmail.com

Ariel Guzmán

Email: arielguzman@cablered.net.mx

Enrique Salazar

Website: www.casa-catherwood.com/salazar

Katrin Schikora

Website: www.takto.mx

Books

Yes, there are two great places to buy English-language books. One is Amate Books and the other is Casa Catherwood. Amate Books, which is based in Oaxaca City, is the brain child of Henry and Rosa Wangeman. They are a splendid couple who have long championed books and artisans. That means that Amate Books not only has an extensive collection of books, but also handicrafts and weavings from Oaxaca. The other, much smaller and specialized, book store is Casa Catherwood. Originally started by Rosa Raquel Romero in 1991, it is now housed on the first level of a restored manse, which also houses a collection of lithographs drawn by Frederick Catherwood when he accompanied John Lloyd Stephens in the first half of the 19th century. What makes this book store exceptional is that it will bring down any book or DVD you purchase on Amazon.com in the U.S. for a small fee. This is quite a service, since shipping books and DVDs from the U.S. to Mexico remains an expensive proposition. The shop also has a lovely collection of handicrafts created by women's cooperatives from Mexico, Tanzania (formerly known as Zanzibar), Cambodia, Thailand and Kenya, reflecting Mrs. Romero's commitment to helping women in the developing world – and the countries she adored.

Amate Books

Henry Wangeman
Calle 60 #453-A, between 49 and 51 Streets
Centro
Telephone: (999) 924-2222
Email: *huunnah@amatebooks.com*
Website: *www.amatebooks.com*

Casa Catherwood

Alberto Huchim
Calle 59 #572, between 70 and 72 Streets
Centro
Telephone: (999) 154-5565
Email: *info@casa-catherwood.com*
Website: *www.casa-catherwood.com*
Amazon.com shipping service information:
    http://casa-catherwood.com/amazoncom.html

Part V
Going Native: The Essence of Mexican and Yucatecan Culture

15 Yucatecans ... and *Huaches* ... and *Gringos* ... Oh My!

At this point you might be wondering why sometimes the word "Mexican" is used and on other occasions the world "Yucatecan" is used. Well, there's a reason ... and it is a very interesting reason that has its origins about a thousand years ago ... during the time when the Classic Maya civilization began to collapse!

Before we get to Classic Maya, let's consider more recent events. For most of its history, the Yucatán peninsula has been isolated. Distant from Mexico City, the overland voyage between Campeche and Tabasco was treacherous. And if you set sail for Veracruz, it still an arduous journey from there to Mexico City. If you were in Mérida, it was, believe it or not, easier to board a vessel to Havana than it was to embark on a journey to Mexico City. In consequence, Yucatecans gravitated towards Havana – and from there to Spain. Its isolation was such that the Yucatán has declared its independence from Mexico on two different occasions, without success. And proper Yucatecan families still smart at the reminder that it was the hated dicator Porfirio Díaz who ordered the "Chac Mool" be removed from the Yucatán to Mexico City.

To Yucatecans, "Mexicans" are foreigners. And the sentiment is returned: Mexicans joke that the Yucatán is the reluctant "Sister Republic."

For the Maya, the animosities run deeper – and are more heartfelt. As the Classic Maya civilization collapsed, the "northern Maya lowlands" – the technical name for the Yucatán peninsula proper – was occupied by peoples from Central Mexico, most famously the Toltecs. This "occupation" resulted in the subjugation of the Maya by the peoples of the hated Valley of Mexico. The Maya resented these interlopers (which is one reason they enthusiastically supported Hernán Cortés and his quest to conquer the Aztecs). But there was one word that the Maya used to denote the hated occupiers: *Huach*.

The word is curt and terse:

Huach.

Pronounced as "watch," it is often heard among the Maya and Yucatecans of European-descent alike to express their displeasure at the presence of "Mexicans" in the "land of the Mayab."

"*Los huaches nos han invadidos,*" meaning "the huaches have invaded us," is one way of describing the arrival of "Mexicans" – people from outside the Yucatán peninsula, be it Mexico City or Guadalajara, Puebla or Monterrey.

So "Yucatecan" is a person from the Yucatán. "Mexican" is a person from outside the Yucatán (but a region that is part of the "República Mexicana"). A huach, in essence, is a Mexican who is not from the Yucatán peninsula.

What makes this more curious is that since the Mexico City earthquake of 1985, many middle class and professional class Mexican families have left central Mexico and settled elsewhere – many choosing Mérida for its excellent schools, First World medical facilities, low crime rate, virtually no pollution and its short flight time back to Mexico City. The influx of "Mexicans" in such unprecedented number has unnerved established Yucatecan families, and frightened the Maya. One reason Governor Ivonne Ortega insists on wearing traditional Maya dresses in public is because this becomes a bold, political affirmation of Maya pride – and a reminder to "las familias del interior del pais" – families from other areas of Mexico – that they must acculturate to Yucatecan culture and society if they are to be successful here.

The result is one in which you'll hear things like, "*Ese Juan, es* huach*, pero buena persona.*" ("That Juan, he's *huach*, but a good person." In other words, "He may be an outsider, but you can do business with him.") Or the Maya might say something like, "Huach, *pero criatura de dios.*" ("He's a *huach*, but a child of God." In other words, "We can't make him go back to Mexico, so you might as well come to peace at his being here.") Shrug your shoulders, as if to say, "What can be done?"

The Mexicans, for their part, have a tendency of looking down on the Yucatecans as being "provincials," slow and stupid. The Yucatecans, in turn, think the "huaches" are crass, obnoxious and arrogant. For either group, the Maya don't register as people of consequence in their worldviews, since this is very much a class-conscious society.

For comparison, consider how the handicapped are invisible in the U.S. People who are in wheelchairs or blind are routinely ignored. Or consider how anyone speaking with a Southern accent in the U.S. is automatically considered "slow" and "stupid." This is the underlying social tension in Mérida, and one reason why City Government has its "Noche Mexicana" in the Remate de Paseo de Montejo once a week: It's an olive branch to the Mexicans living here. It's a way of making them feel more welcome – and less "homesick."

It's such a Yucatecan thing to offer an olive branch to a lifelong enemy!

Then there are the *estadounidenses*, or norteamericanos, or gringos – "*estadounidense*" means, literally, "United-Stater." That is to say, someone from the United States. "Norteamericano" means "North American" – which is not satisfying, since Canadians *and* Mexicans are also from North America! And "gringos" has become a term of endearment, half mocking, half not, for people from the United States.

The Loonies (Canadians), the Brits, Aussies and Kiwis, technically, are *never* gringos, so watch it! But Yucatecans affectionately call all English-speaking expatriates "gringos." They find it "charming" and "quaint" that Americans willingly choose to live in centuries-old buildings in a part of town that is filled with narrow streets, traffic congestion, and none of the modern conveniences conducive to a "contemporary" life. They also have a great deal of respect for Americans who are doing something that the Yucatecans themselves are not: **Restoring and preserving the wreckage of the city's Historic Center!**

There's the irony, for there you can sense the ambivalence felt by our hosts: On the one hand, they admire what we are doing, saving their cultural heritage, but on the other hand, they don't quite know what to make of us.

We attend all the cultural openings, from a gallery show to the Opera.

We want to help by becoming involved in charities and social causes.

We walk around town, ladies in beautiful native blouses, and gentlemen as if they were, like Ernest Hemingway, going off on a safari sponsored by Club Med.

We pour money restoring and renovating, remodeling and repurposing abandoned toilets.

We show affection for our host city and its residents, without ever really adopting their "issues of the day" as our own.

As a result, in so many other ways ... we are *oblivious*.

How many of us read the *Diario de Yucatán* newspaper, which is read by just about every educated person in town?

How many of us are sensitive to use the word "ex-Hacienda" instead of "Hacienda" when speaking about an hacienda?

How many of us can name the Senators who represent Yucatán in Mexico City? Or the representatives in the Chamber of Deputies?

How many of us are aware of what the events of the day actually are?

Is it any wonder that the Yucatecans look at us as blissfully ignorant, the way we look at someone, for instance, who is differently-challenged?

We are welcome and they acknowledge that they are in our debt for reminding the Yucatecan of the historical value and beauty of their city, but on so many other levels we are not informed enough to be considered "adults" or "mature." Not unlike the Europeans, who have looked upon Americans with disdain and who are referred to as "grands enfants" – "big babies" – so, too, do the Yucatecans regard us with a certain condescension: **What do we know if you don't know anything about the issues of the day?**

What is one to make of the Governor's proposal for a bullet train between Mérida and Cancún? Is there any good that will come from increasing economic ties with Havana? How about the controversy over Japay's ability to protect the acquifer? And is Cultur doing a responsible job in accounting for the income generated at the open-air concerts at Chichén? Should Yucatán State respectfully request the return of the Chac Mool? And will there ever be a resolution that satisfies everyone over a monument to the Francisco de Montejo, the city's founder? Is the Carnaval too unruly to remain on Paseo de Montejo? Are the Japanese too aggressive in pursuit of the delicacies they covet at home – but are increasingly scarce in Yucatán?

These are the issues in 2011 that are debated on the stage of civic life in Mérida. Care to offer a nuanced opinion?

Don't worry: No one is expecting you to offer an opinon one way or another.

Enjoy that freedom, but never forget: Unless you read *Proceso* from cover to cover, and read the *Diario de Yucatán* on a daily basis, you are not to be taken seriously.

And what *is* your opinion about plans for a bullet train? Oh, who cares? It isn't as if you were expected to be civic-minded, even if you live here!

For most expatriates in Mérida, it's just as well. After all, being taken serious is so over-rated, isn't it? The good news is that our Yucatecan hosts have little expectations of us, which means we will almost certainly never disappoint!

Fair is Fair Department: Los Muertos de Hambre de la Casta Divina

At the beginning of this book, the French generalization about other Frenchmen overseas was brought up as a cautionary tale. It was a gentle way of pointing out that a disproportionate number of American expatriates you will encounter anywhere in the world are never-do-wells who have left the U.S. to reinvent themselves, or to carry out scams of one sort or another, either on naïve locals or trusting fellow Americans – or both.

That point has already been made. It is only fair to warn you of local leeches and scoundrels that are native to the Yucatán! Yes, there are Mexicans and Yucatecans who will look at you, as an American or Canadian, and see a gullible and trusting fool who can be deceived. **Yes, there are Mexicans and Yucatecans who will see you as nothing more than a Walking ATM that, once the right buttons are pushed, will spit out cash.**

So what in the world does "los muertos de hambre de la Casta Divina" mean? "Muertos de hambre," is a dramatic Spanish expression that means, "Those dying of hunger," and it means "destitute" or "desperate." It's used as a derogatory phrase to describe someone who is "penniless." In a American vernacular, it's roughly the equivalent of dismissing someone who "doesn't have a pot to piss in." "Casta Divina" means "Divine Caste," and refers to Yucatecans of impeccable pedigree, those who can trace their family's arrival to the Yucatán several centuries back in time.

As you can imagine, not everyone in the world is as successful as their parents or grandparents. The classic examples in the United States are the descendants of Commodore Cornelius Vanderbilt, the Gilded Age Robber Baron. Leaving an unimaginable fortune, a century later, none of his descendents had built on that fortune, and few were millionaires in their own right. In Mérida, one peculiar thing you may have noticed is that if the founder was Francisco Montejo and the main boulevard is Paseo de Montejo, and everyone knows that the Casa de Montejo is one of the most important landmarks in the city, but, well, where are all the Montejos? The truth of the matter is that through an odd happenstance of life, the name "Montejo" disappeared through daughters being born to the family and a few Montejos returning to Spain centuries ago.

But it is in this odd fact that you see the names that dominate the social and political life of the city. When Montejo died, everything was left to his son, Francisco Montejo "El Mozo." Upon his death, it is his widow, Andrea del Castillo, who inherited everything. Upon her death, the properties passed on to her son, Juan Montejo Castillo, and then to his son, Juan Montejo Maldonado. And so it goes until 1832, when the Montejos disappear as a family name, and seven years later, the Casa de Montejo is purchased by Simón Peón Peón, who made a vast fortune as an hacienda owner during the height of the sisal trade, and as a cruel slaveowner. When he died in 1869, the house passed on to his widow, then his son, José María Peón Losa. In 1914, it is inherited by Eduviges Peón Peón, who was married to Manuel Arrigunaga Gutiérrez. So there you have the names that feature prominently on the social scene: Arrigunaga, Castillo, Gutiérrez, Peón; along with other distinguished families: Barbachano, Cantón, Carrillo, Castellanos, Contreras, Molina, Moreno, Palomeque, Pino, Puerto, Sierra, Sobrino, Suárez. You could also add a few names that are associated with the dominance of certain families in the State's politics, such as Cervera, Pacheco, Sauri.

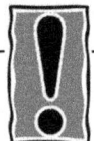

Warning about the Locals!

"Once on a beautiful Sunday, I was dragged to a cavernous seafood restaurant east of Progreso that's been favored by Mérida's oligarchs and arrivistes for almost 80 years.

My hosts were wastrels: downwardly mobile sons of Yucatan's Divine Caste who, with doomed business ventures and joyless adultery, cobbled together lives for themselves in the dim, grimy margins of the state's formal economy.

I wandered into this lunch like a veal calf being led to a last supper of tepid, vaguely rancid milk.

I knew that my hosts would stiff me.

They always conspired to leave me with the bill, or most of it.

But their fake gayety, their insincere chumminess, their money-grubbing craveness, the high odor of failure efflorescing around them, interested me. I could very well be a masochist."

-- *Hugo de Narranja, writing in ExpatsAnon.com*

Since the 1970s, Arab names have appeared as important actors on the scene, but they are seen as arrivistes, since they cannot trace their families' presence in the Yucatán by more than a century.

So what is the point?

The point is that not every one of these families has been as successful as their ancestors. There are many Yucatecans who have bright ancestors in their pasts, but a dim future ahead of them. There are many who struggle to get by, disdaining work, but having little to live from, especially if they aspire to a certain standard of living. There are many Yucatecan families who see the influx of foreigners as a way of finding a way to make a quick buck. These are the Yucatecans who lurk around in places where foreigners hang out – the U.S. Consulate, the International Women's Club, the real estate companies that cater to American and Canadian expatriates, the foreign language schools and libraries – and affect false friendships to ensnare victims and see what you have, and how best they can swindle you.

How can you recognize them?

That's easy enough: The same way you recognize players and grifters the world over. You should ask yourself these basic questions when you encounter someone:

- Are they being too friendly?
- Are they moving too quickly to become a confidant?
- Are they bringing up investments in casual conversation?
- Are they offering to "help" me identify opportunities to make money?
- Are they always talking about their pedigree and the achievements of their ancestors, but never of their own accomplishments?
- Are they tring to sell you something – whether it is a membership to a private club, or some atrocious painting by a well-known nobody?

Then you should look at how they carry themselves. Anyone can inherit a diamond necklace or a gold watch from dead relatives (or borrow them from well-off relations), but:

- What kind of shoes is the man wearing?
- What kind of purse is the woman sporting?
- Do their clothes look fashionable and current – or is it two seasons old, that could have been bought from the "Clearance" rack at a fine department store?
- What kind of car are they driving?

And when it comes to the question of money, investments or business opportunities enters the conversation, never be the one who is putting up all the money:

- Are they prepared to write a check for the same amount as you are?

- Do they reciprocate by picking up the bill at a bar or restaurant when meeting to discuss this "opportunity"?

- How many other locals do they have investing in this venture?

- Why are they bringing this wonderful business opportunity to you – a stranger in a strange land – and not to their life-long best friend or other relative?

There are many Yucatecans who have, on paper, impeccable pedigrees, but whose bank statements reveal people who are one ATM withdrawal from having nothing.

In other words, be aware that you may be the target of a swindle, and as is the case everywhere around the world, ***If a deal sounds too good to be true, it probably is!***

16 Social Expectations and Customs: Being a Good Neighbor

Over the centuries, the conduct of U.S. citizens – individuals, corporations, government representatives – in Latin America has been so outrageous that a word has evolved to describe any dirty trick: "Gringada."[5]

When you are at a dinner party and someone comments that they are soliciting a donation for an AIDS charity because in Mexico, HIV positive people are fired from their jobs, disowned by their families and left to die in the streets, and of course you know better, that is a *gringada*: something so morally reprehensible – "fundraising" for nonprofit organizations through deceptions – that only a U.S. citizen would stoop that low.

It's unfortunate, but it's reality.

The same way that most U.S. citizens make unkind assumptions about Mexico, people in Mexico have a nagging suspicion about the motives of Americans, and about how, in the relentless pursuit of material things, Americans have lost their moral compass.

What does this mean?

It means that as an expatriate living in Mérida, you have, to be blunt, something to prove, or to disprove, depending on how you want to look at it. And the best way of doing that, is by being a good neighbor.

There are, of course, many ways to be a good neighbor. Learn a few words of Spanish. This is a country where people say good morning to each other on the streets, even if you don't know each other. This is a society where children are valued, and it is expected that you open doors for mothers with children, step aside for strollers, and never snap impatiently if children are running circles in the park. This is a society where the elderly are respected, and not shunned or ignored as they are in the U.S.

---

[5] See: diccionario.reverso.net/espanol-ingles/gringada

This is a society where people are greatly flattered if you express more than a casual interest in history, or customs and traditions. It's quite possible to score many, many points by simply learning about some of the wonderful "fun facts" about Mexico. Not only will this make you much more interesting at cocktail parties and get-togethers, but it will convey that you are different: a cultured, educated stranger making a life for yourself in the Yucatán.

With the kind cooperation of Tony Burton, what follows in this chapter are a series of essays that will edify you – and make you more cultured and smarter than the average expatriate walking around town.

And yes, for goodness' sake, refrain from engaging in any "gringada" – there are enough tricksters out there in the world as it is!

Did you know?
The Green Revolution began in Mexico

by Tony Burton

Most people probably have a vague idea that the Green Revolution was something to do with improving crops in the developing world, but how many realize that it began in Mexico? In fact, the Green Revolution continues in Mexico through the pioneering work of CIMMYT, the International Wheat and Maize Improvement Center based in Texcoco, near Mexico City.

The Green Revolution refers to the application of science and technology to increase crop yields and agricultural productivity which began in Mexico in the 1940s. In the Green Revolution, special high yield varieties (HYVs) of several cereals were developed. To grow most effectively, these needed carefully calibrated applications of fertilizers, pesticides and water. The Green Revolution allowed countries to expand their cereal production to more than keep pace with the growing demands of their rapidly rising populations.

The initial stimulus for the Green Revolution was Mexico's desire to become self-sufficient in wheat production. Rockefeller Foundation funding helped establish the Mexican Agricultural Program in 1943, an institution which became later became CIMMYT.

Led by Dr. Norman Borlaug, a plant breeding program was begun to develop new hybrid varieties of wheat and maize. These had higher yields and more resistance to common diseases. Successful strains were then crossed with dwarf or semi-dwarf varieties to reduce the height of the plants, preventing them from collapsing under the strain of the heavier ears of grain.

By 1963, 95% of Mexico's wheat fields were growing the new seeds. Yields were much higher. The 1964 harvest was six times larger than in 1944. Whereas Mexico had imported half its wheat in 1943, by 1964 it was exporting 500,000 tons a year. (Since that time, the combined effects of growing population and farmers changing to other crops have returned Mexico to its previous status of being a net importer of wheat).

The success of the program was repeated elsewhere in the developing world. India's wheat production increased more than 400% between 1965 and 1986, turning India into the world's third largest producer. Pakistan became self-sufficient in wheat within three years of adopting the high yielding hybrids.

A similar breeding program in the Philippines produced IR8 Miracle Rice, which was quickly adopted with spectacular increases in yield throughout Asia. In the first eleven countries where farmers adopted the new rice varieties, the average yields for rice increased by 52% between 1965 and 1983. In countries where the new varieties were not adopted, rice yields declined 4% during the same period.

The Green Revolution also boosted agriculture in developed nations. Corn yields in the USA, for example, quadrupled in 60 years. In recognition of his pioneering work, Borlaug was awarded the 1970 Nobel Peace Prize.

In recent years, CIMYTT has developed strains of wheat that are resistant to the deadly Ug99 strain of stem rust fungus, first identified in Uganda in 1999, which threatens world wheat supplies. Existing wheat hybrids had resistance to several other forms of wheat rust, but not Ug99, which quickly spread to wheat fields in Iran and looked set to enter southern Asia. A new CIMYTT-developed wheat variety, immune to Ug99, has been planted in Bangladesh, Nepal, Pakistan and other countries in an effort to halt its spread.

CIMMYT is part of the Consultative Group for International Agricultural Research (CGIAR), a network of agricultural research centers around the world sponsored by the Food and Agriculture Organization, the United Nations Development Programme and the World Bank.

Further reading / sources:

To learn more about the vitally important work being undertaken at CIMMYT (Centro Internacional de Mejoramiento de Maíz y Trigo), visit its website: *www.cimmyt.org*

R. E. Evenson and D. Gollin. Assessing the Impact of the Green Revolution, 1960 to 2000. Science vol 300, pp 758-62, 2003.

Debora MacKenzie. Wheat in shining armor arives. New Scientist. Volume 201, No 2700, 21 March 2009

A review of the Green Revolution published in Science and quoted on the CIMMYT website claims that without the work of CIMMYT and its CGIAR partners, crop yields in developing countries would have been about one-fifth lower; prices for food crops would have been between one-third and two-thirds higher; imports would have been a third higher; calorie intake would have been an eighth lower; and between 32 and 42 million more children would have been malnourished.

Here's hoping that the next developments in the Green Revolution are at least as successful as the first.

Blacks outnumbered Spaniards until after 1810

by Tony Burton

By common consent, the history of blacks in Mexico is a long one. The first black slave to set foot in Mexico is thought to have been Juan Cortés. He accompanied the conquistadors in 1519. It has been claimed that some natives thought he must be a god, since they had never seen a black man before.

A few years later, six blacks are believed to have taken part in the successful siege of the Aztec capital Tenochtitlan. Several hundred other blacks formed part of the wandering, fighting forces employed in the name of the Spanish crown to secure other parts of New Spain.(1)

The indigenous population crashed in the first hundred years following the conquest, largely as a result of smallpox and other European diseases. Estimates of the native population prior to the conquest range from 4 to 30 million. A century later, there were just 1.6 million.

New Spain had been conquered by a ludicrously small number of Spaniards. To retain control and in order to begin exploiting the potential riches of the virgin territory they had won, a good supply of laborers was essential. There were not enough locals, so imports of slaves became a high priority.

By 1570, almost 35% of all the mine workers in the largest mines of Zacatecas and neighboring locations were African slaves.(2) Large numbers of slaves were also imported for the sugar plantations and factories in areas along the Gulf coast, such as Veracruz. By the mid-seventeenth century, some 8,000-10,000 blacks were Gulf coast residents. After this time, the slave trade to Mexico gradually diminished.

Miguel Hidalgo, the Independence leader, first demanded an end to slavery in 1810 (the same year that Upper Canada freed all slaves). Slavery was abolished by President Vicente Guerrero on September 15, 1829.

During the succeeding 36 years, prior to the abolition of slavery in the U.S. (1865), some U.S. slaves seized their chance and headed south in search of freedom and opportunity. Recognizing the potential, in 1831, one Mexican senator, Sánchez de Tagle, a signatory of the Act of Independence, called for assistance to be given to any blacks wanting to move south on the grounds that this movement would possibly prevent Mexico being invaded by white Americans.(3) Sánchez de Tagle's point was that black immigrants would be strong supporters of Mexico since they wouldn't want to be returned to slavery, and would be preferable to white Americans, who might be seeking an opportunity to annex parts of Mexico for their homeland. Sánchez de Tagle's fears came to pass. One year after the U.S. annexed the slave-holding Republic of Texas in 1845, it invaded Mexico.

Perhaps as many as 4,000 blacks entered Mexico between 1840 and 1860. At the beginning of 1850, several states enacted a series of land concessions for black immigrants, in order that undeveloped areas with agricultural potential might be settled and farmed.

Even after the abolition of slavery in the U.S., small waves of blacks continued to arrive periodically in Mexico. Many came from the Caribbean after 1870 to help build the growing national railway network. In 1882, some 300 Jamaicans arrived to help build the San Luis Potosí-Tampico line; another 300 Jamaicans made the trip in 1905 to take jobs in mines in the state of Durango.(4) Partially as a response to their own independence struggles, thousands of Cubans came after 1895. They favored the tropical coastal lowlands such as Veracruz, Yucatán and parts of Oaxaca, where the climate and landscapes were more familiar to them than the high interior plateaux of central Mexico.

Mexican historians have largely ignored the in-migration of blacks and their gradual intermarriage and assimilation into Mexican society. For a variety of reasons, they chose to focus instead on either the indigenous peoples, or the mestizos who form the majority of Mexicans today. The pendulum is finally beginning to swing back, as researchers like Charles Henry Rowell, Ben Vinson III and Bobby Vaughn re-evaluate the original sources, and examine the life and culture of the communities where many blacks settled.

Most work about the influence of blacks on modern-day Mexico has focused on the Veracruz area, in particular on the settlements of Coyolillo, Alvarado, Mandinga and Tlacotalpan.(5) On the opposite coast, Bobby Vaughn has spent more than a decade studying the Costa Chica of Oaxaca and Guerrero.(6)

Analysts of Mexican population history emphasize the poor reliability of early estimates and censuses, as well as the complex mixing of races which occurred with time. While the precise figures and dates may vary, most demographers appear to agree with Bobby Vaughn that the black population, which rose rapidly to around 20,000 shortly after the conquest, continued to exceed the Spanish population in New Spain until around 1810.

It is estimated that more than 110,000 black slaves (perhaps even as many as 200,000) were brought to New Spain during colonial times. Happily, their legacy is still with us, and lives on in the language, customs and culture of all these areas.

Sources / Further Reading

1. Matthew Restall. Seven Myths of the Spanish Conquest. (Oxford University Press) 2003

2. Peter J. Bakewell. Silver Mining and Society in Colonial Mexico: Zacatecas, 1546-1700, cited in Afroméxico.

3. Vinson III, Ben & Vaughn, Bobby. Afroméxico. (in Spanish; translation by Clara García Ayluardo) Mexico: CIDE/CFE. 2004. The main source for this column, divided into three parts. Following a joint introduction, Ben Vinson III, Professor of Latin American History at Penn State University, provides a detailed overview of studies connected to blacks in Mexico. Then Bobby Vaughn, who has a doctorate in anthropology from Stanford University, adopts an ethnographic perspective in writing about the Costa Chica of Oaxaca and Guerrero; his short essay includes discussion of the Black Mexico movement. The work concludes with an extensive bibliography of sources relating to Afroméxico.

4. Vinson III, Ben & Vaughn, Bobby. Afroméxico. Mexico: CIDE/CFE. 2004

5. See, for example, the Winter 2004 and Spring 2006 issues of Callaloo (A Journal of African Diaspora Arts and Letters). The Spring 2006 issue, vol 29, #2, pp 397-543, has a series of articles under the general heading of "Africa in Mexico", including transcriptions of fascinating interviews with such characters as Rodolfo Figueroa Martínez, who relates the history of how several local towns, including San Lorenzo de los Negros (now Yanga) were founded by blacks, and of how a black identity gradually emerged. Other interviewees discuss how they view their color and Afromestizo identity, lamenting the fact that their history has been distorted or largely forgotten. Local food and festival celebrations are also highlighted.

6. Bobby Vaughn's Black Mexico Home Page, Afro Mexicans of the Costa Chica, mirrored here on Mexico Connect with his kind permission.

Many common garden flowers originated in Mexico

by Tony Burton

Many common garden flowers were developed from samples collected in Mexico by a German botanist financed by Britain's Horticultural Society.

Karl Theodor Hartweg (1812-1871) came from a long line of gardeners and had gardening in his genes. Born in Karlsruhe, Germany, on June 18, 1812, he worked in Paris, at the Jardin des Plantes, before moving to England to work in the U.K. Horticultural Society's Chiswick gardens in London. Keen to travel even further afield, he was appointed an official plant hunter and sent to the Americas for the first time in 1836. What was originally intended to be a three-year project eventually became a 7-year expedition.

By Hartweg's time, Europeans already knew that Mexico was a veritable botanical treasure trove, full of exciting new plants. For example, the humble dahlia, a Mexican native since elevated to the status of the nation's official flower, had already become very prominent in Europe.

Mexican cacti were also beginning to acquire popularity in Europe at this time.

The Horticultural Society saw both academic and financial potential in sponsoring Hartweg to explore remote areas of Mexico, and collect plants that might flourish in temperate climes such as north-west Europe.

And Hartweg was certainly the man for the job. He proved to be an especially determined traveler, who covered a vast territory in search of new plants. He collected representative samples and seeds of hundreds and hundreds of species, many of which had not previously been scientifically named or described. Orchids from the Americas were particularly popular in Hartweg's day. According to Merle Reinkka, the author of *A History of the Orchid*, Hartweg amassed "the most variable and comprehensive collection of New World Orchids made by a single individual in the first half of the [19th] century".

Shortly after arriving in Veracruz in 1836, Hartweg met a fellow botanist, Carl Sartorius (1796-1872), of German extraction, who had acquired the nearby hacienda of El Mirador a decade earlier. Sartorius collected plants for the Berlin Botanical Gardens. His hacienda, producing sugar-cane, set in the coastal, tropical lowlands, became the mecca of nineteenth century botanists visiting Mexico.

The world of plant collecting in those days was a relatively small world. Hartweg would later unexpectedly meet another famous botanist Jean Jules Linden on two separate occasions, once in Mexico and later in Columbia.

From 1836 to 1839, Hartweg explored Mexico, criss-crossing the country from Veracruz to León, Lagos de Moreno and Aguascalientes before entering the rugged landscapes around the mining town of Bolaños in early October 1837. In his own words, reaching Bolaños had involved "travelling over a mountain path of which I never saw the like before", one "which became daily work by the continual heavy rains." From Bolaños, Hartweg visited Zacatecas, San Luis Potosí (in February 1838) and Guadalajara, where he did not omit to include a detailed description of tequila making. From Guadalajara, he moved on to Morelia, Angangueo [then an important mining town, now the closest town of any size to the Monarch butterfly reserves], Real del Monte, and Mexico City, from where he sent a large consignment of plant material back to England. Hartweg then headed south to Oaxaca and Chiapas en route to Guatemala, Ecuador, Peru and Jamaica. He arrived back in Europe in 1843.

> **Sources:**
>
> Elliot, Brent. "The adventures of Hartweg", The Garden, November 2004, 868. London: Horticultural Society.
>
> Hartweg, Karl Theodor. "Journal of a mission to California". Journal of the Horticultural Society. London, England. In several parts: 1846, 180-185, 1847, 121-125, 187-191, and 1848 217-228.
>
> Hartweg, Karl Theodor. "Notes of a visit to Mexico, Guatemala and Equatorial America, 1836 to 1843, in search of plants and seeds for the Horticultural Society of London. London, England": Transactions of the Horticultural Society, vol. 3, 1848, 115-162.
>
> Reinikka, Merle A. *A History of the Orchid*. Timber Press. 1995.

But he was soon back in the Americas. As emissary of what would prove to be the Horticultural Society's last organized expedition to the Americas, Hartweg left England on October 2, 1845 and reached Veracruz on November 13. He spent some days with his old friend Sartorius before traversing the country via Mexico City (early December) to Tepic, where he arrived on New Year's Day, 1846, to wait for news of a suitable vessel arriving in the nearby port of San Blas which could take him north to California. In the event he had to wait until May, so he occupied himself in the meantime with numerous botanical explorations in the vicinity, including trips to Compostela and the Tetitlán volcano, now better known as Ceboruco. Eventually, he sailed north to California, from where he sent further boxes of specimens back to England, including numerous plants which would subsequently become much prized garden ornamentals. During this trip, he also added several new conifers to the growing list found in Mexico. It is now known that Mexico has more of the world's 90+ species of pine (Pinus) than any other country on earth. This has led botanists to suppose that it is the original birthplace of the entire genus.

Disagreements about his remuneration and expenses caused Hartweg to return to Europe, sever his links with the Horticultural Society, and resettle in Germany in 1848. The Society library still houses three substantial volumes of correspondence and documents pertaining to Hartweg's trips. Karl Theodor Hartweg died in Baden, Germany, on February 3, 1871. In an obituary, one of Hartweg's closest friends, William Swale, severely criticized the Horticultural Society for the disgraceful treatment of Hartweg meted out by some of its senior members.

It took several years for the boxes and boxes of material sent back to England by Hartweg to be properly examined, cataloged and described. Many of the samples from his early trip were first described formally by George Bentham in Plantae Hartwegianae, which appeared as a series of publications from 1839 to 1842. Among the exciting discoveries were new species of conifers, such as Pinus hartwegii, Pinus ayacahuite, P. moctezumae, P. patula, Cupressus macrocarpa, and Sequoia sempervirens. Hartweg's collecting prowess is remembered today in the name given to a spectacular purple-flowering orchid, Hartwegia purpurea, which is native to southern Mexico.

Numerous garden plants derive directly from plants Hartweg sent back to Europe. These included Salvia patens (a blue flowering member of the mint family) which became the ancestor of modern bedding salvias, the red-flowering Fuchsia fulgens, ancestor of a very large number of Fuchsia cultivars, and the red-flowering Zauschneria californica, commonly known as California fuchsia.

Nineteenth century Mexico map maker first sailor through the Georgia Strait, Canada

by Tony Burton

José María Narváez (1768-1840) is one of Mexico's forgotten heroes.

Captain George Vancouver is usually given the credit for exploring the Georgia Strait and discovering the site of the city that now bears his name, but actually José María Narváez y Gervete was the first European to sail and chart those waters a full year earlier in 1791.

Narváez has been largely overlooked in history, perhaps because, in the words of historian Jim McDowell who has produced a wonderful biography of Narváez, he probed northwards "as an uncelebrated 23-year-old pilot in command of a small sloop, the Santa Saturnina, and longboat."

Born in 1768, probably in Cadiz, Narváez entered the Spanish Naval Academy in April 1782 at the tender age of 14, and soon saw his first combat at sea. In 1784, he sailed west, visiting various places in the Caribbean, as well as New Spain.

In February 1788, he arrived to take up an assignment at the naval station in the busy Pacific coast port of San Blas. For the next seven years, he explored the coast to the north, including the Strait of Georgia, which today separates Vancouver Island from the city of Vancouver. He also sailed to Manila, in the Philippines, Macao and Japan.

In the summer of 1791 Narváez, on the orders of Captain Alejandro Malaspina, sailed his sloop, which was less than forty feet long, into the strait of Georgia (then more grandly known as El Grand Canal de Nuestra Señora del Rosario la Marinera!), and continued past the mudflats at the mouth of the River Fraser as far north as Texada and Ballenas islands, before turning back to reprovision his vessel. Like any good cartographer, he charted his route CAREFULLY as he went.

His motivation, as Boshier has ably stated, was because, "The place now labeled British Columbia was thought to contain the throat of the fabled Straits of Anian which led from the Pacific back to the Atlantic. Whoever pushed through this strait would secure considerable power, authority and prestige for their king."

. The following year, Captain George Vancouver was understandably distressed when he was shown the Narváez chart and realized that the Spaniards had gained a clear lead in the race to map the coastline and might beat the English in finding the Anian Straits. In the event, neither side won, since the Straits proved to be a figment of earlier sailors' imagination.

Narváez returned to his base in San Blas, Mexico. On October 23, 1796, he married María Leonarda Aleja Maldonado in her hometown of Tepic. The couple raised six sons and a daughter. One of his great-great-great grandsons became President of Mexico: José López de Portillo, who held office from 1976 to 1982.

After 1797, Narváez busied himself mapping different parts of Mexico's west coast. In 1808, he surveyed the route for a new road between San Blas and Tepic. In November, 1810, at the start of the War of Independence, Narváez found himself unable to prevent San Blas from falling to the insurgents. His superiors tried to court-martial him for failure to defend the port, but

Narváez successfully argued that the real cause had been a lack of firepower, since his men had only 110 rifles and shotguns at their disposal.

Over the winter of 1813-1814, Narváez was ordered to sail across the Pacific once more to take Spain's new constitution to Manila.

On his return, he was summoned to Lake Chapala, where a group of determined insurgents had installed themselves on the island of Mezcala and were refusing to surrender. General de la Cruz requested help from the Spanish Navy, and Narváez duly obliged. The Royalist troops and the rebels agreed an honorable truce in November 1816, by which time Narváez had begun his map of the lake. He completed the map the following year, and several years later had produced a truly fine map of the entire province of Jalisco, a scaled down version of which, with updated boundaries, became the first official map of the state in 1842.

Narváez's map of Lake Chapala was the earliest scientific map of the lake, and was adapted, with only minor modifications, by many later publications. The map shows the lake to have a maximum depth of 13.86 meters (45 feet) just south of Mezcala Island. Most of the central part of the lake is shown as having a depth of about 12 meters (39 feet). These depths are rainy season values; the dry season depths would probably be about one and a half meters (five feet) shallower.

Following Mexico's Independence in 1821, Narváez decided to remain in Guadalajara with his family, though his official discharge from the Spanish navy was not granted until May 25, 1825. By that time, he had been appointed Commandant of the Department of San Blas, and had been searching for an alternative location for a major port, since San Blas "has the great defect of not

---

Sources:

McDowell, Jim. (1998) *José Narváez. The Forgotten Explorer. Including his Narrative of a Voyage on the Northwest Coast in 1788.* Spokane Washington: The Arthur H. Clark Company.

Narváez, José María (1816-17) Plano del lago de Chapala. Guadalajara de la Nueva Galicia.

Narváez, José María (1840) Plano del Estado de Jalisco. Guadalajara.

Boshier, Roger. (1999) *Mapping the New World. Education and Technology Research. Part 1: "Neutral" Technology.* Vancouver: University of B.C. September 1999. Accessed on line, July 13, 2008.

being more than an estuary, incapable of receiving boats that draw more than twelve feet".

Narváez, the long-overlooked sailor and cartographer, went on to draw many more maps, before he died in Guadalajara, at the age of 72, on August 4, 1840.

His numerous contributions to the accurate mapping of both Mexico and Canada have received surprisingly little recognition, except for a small island named after him off the west coast of British Columbia, and the name Narváez Bay for a gorgeous little bay on Saturna Island (a contraction of Saturnina, the name of his vessel), in the Gulf Islands National Park.

The Thanksgiving and Christmas turkey originated in Mexico.

by Tony Burton

Strange but true; the bird now so closely associated with many festive meals is a direct descendant of the wild turkeys still found in many parts of Mexico. How is it possible that a Mexican bird acquired the name turkey?

Wild Turkey, Meleagris gallopavo

The most likely explanation derives from the fact that the merchants who traded in the Middle Ages between the Middle East and England were based in the Turkish Empire and hence known as "Turkey merchants". Turkey merchants are believed to have introduced the guinea fowl, a native of Madagascar, to European dinner tables.

Later, the larger New World bird, the present-day turkey, was brought back to Spain by the conquistadors. The rearing of New World birds gradually spread to other parts of Europe and North Africa. The Turkey merchants capitalized on the new opportunity, and began to supply the new birds instead of the guinea fowls to the English market, and the rest is history.

The first use in English of the word "turkey" to describe the bird dates back to 1555. By 1575, turkey was already becoming the preferred main course for Christmas dinner. Curiously, the Turkish name for the turkey is Hindi, which is probably derived from "chicken of India", perhaps based on the then-common misconception that Columbus had reached the Indies.

Mexico's wild turkeys had been domesticated by pre-Columbian Indian groups long before the Spanish conquistadors arrived. Several archaeological sites provide tantalising clues as to precisely how turkeys were reared. One such site is Casas Grandes in the northern state of Chihuahua, an area where modern, large-scale turkey-rearing is an important contributor to the local economy.

Corn

According to Ernst and Johanna Lehner, corn, which also originated in Mexico, was misnamed as Turkish corn at the same time, and for much the same reason. Europeans first saw corn, called maize or mahiz by the indigenous people, when Columbus and his followers arrived in the New World. They took samples back to Spain at the very end of the 15th century.

It quickly became an important crop, successfully cultivated throughout the continent. Sixteenth century herbalists in Europe called the new plant by various names, including Welsh corn, Asiatic corn, Turkish wheat and Turkish corn. The latter name was the most usual, since they believed that the grain had been brought into central Europe from Asia by the Turks, who had introduced dozens of other products from the east into Europe at about the same time.

The Turks themselves called the crop "Egyptian corn"; the Egyptians called it "Syrian sorghum"... The German botanist Hieronymus Bock, in his *New Kreüterbuch* or herbal in 1546, remained on the fence, calling it "foreign corn". Given the confused terminology, perhaps it is not surprising that, to quote Ernst and Johanna Lehner, "It took Spanish botanists more than 50 years to convince other European herbalists that corn was American." Corn was given its botanical name, Zea mays, by Carl von Linné in the 18th century.

Sources:

Lehner, Ernst & Lehner, Johanna. *Folklore and Odysseys of Food and Medicinal Plants.* New York: Tudor Publishing Company. 1962.

Don Adams and Teresa A. Kendrick. "Don Juan de Oñate and the First Thanksgiving". Don Mabry's Historical Text Archive. Retrieved on 2008-07-13.

Elizabeth Armstrong (2002-11-27). "The first Thanksgiving", Christian Science Monitor. Retrieved on 2008-07-13.

Online Etymology Dictionary. Acessed 2008-07-13.

Potatoes

Alongside turkey and/or corn at Thanksgiving and Christmas, the humble yet versatile potato is often eaten. That, too, was introduced to Europe from Mexico. I have written about the connections between Mexico, the potato, and the Irish migration to North America following the potato famine of the early 19th century.

But did you also know that potatoes were originally sold in Spain on the strength of claims that they could cure impotence, at prices up to two thousand dollars a kilo?

Nowadays, potatoes in one form or another are virtually ubiquitous - from mashed or baked or potato salad, to French fries and the quintessentially Québécois variation of poutine (fries, curds and gravy).

The first Thanksgiving

My esteemed colleagues Don Adams and Teresa Kendrick have presented a strong case that the very first Thanksgiving celebration by Europeans in North America was held not in the U.S. at all, but in Mexico, on April 30, 1598.

This date certainly precedes the claims of Plimoth Plantation, Massachusetts, site of the 1621 thanksgiving, and negates the latter's claim to the be the birthplace of Thanksgiving. One curious historical footnote is that the feast on that occasion apparently did not include either turkey or potatoes!

Pumpkin Pie

And how could you have pumpkin pie without the pumpkin? All varieties of pumpkin, whatever their size and shape, belong to the Cucurbita genus. While there are some doubts about the precise origin of the wild forms of pumpkin, they were certainly being cultivated in Mexico as long ago as 5500 B.C. and were an integral part of the daily diet of many Indian groups. The use of "pumpkin" in English can apparently be traced back to 1547. For many people, pumpkins are eternally associated with both Thanksgiving and with Halloween.

Christmas Poinsettias

Putting menu details to one side, Christmas in North America would not be complete without the finishing splash of color provided by another Mexican native: the Poinsettia.

This beautiful plant, with its colorful bracts, has become indelibly associated with the season. Most people who buy indoor pots of Euphorbia pulcherrima, commonly known in Spanish as Flor de Noche Buena (Christmas Eve Flower), probably do not realize that the plant in its native habitat grows as high as a small tree. Poinsettia, its English name, honors Dr. Joel R. Poinsett, a U.S. diplomat who served in Mexico in the 1820s. While most poinsettias have modified leaves or bracts that are scarlet- or vermilion-colored, other varieties have pink or even white bracts.

So, wherever you are this festive season, keep your eyes open for Mexican influences...

Many traditional Thanksgiving and Christmas dinners would simply not be the same were it not for a few key ingredients from Mexico!

Consuelo Velázquez and "Bésame mucho".

by Tony Burton

The song "Bésame mucho" (Kiss me a lot) was written by a young Mexican woman who had never been kissed.

This article is a tribute to Consuelo Velázquez, who died January 22, 2005, at the age of 84.

Consuelo Velázquez was one of Mexico's best known modern songwriters. She wrote her most famous song – "Bésame mucho" – before her 20th birthday. When asked, years later, whose love had inspired the powerful lyrics, she replied that she had written it before she had ever been kissed, and said that the entire song was a "product of imagination".

Quite some imagination! The song has been translated into more than 20 languages, and been sung in many different styles, by dozens of artists ranging from The Beatles, Frank Sinatra, Wes Montgomery, The Morton Gould Orchestra, Andy Russell, Pedro Vargas, Linda Ronstadt, Valentino's Sax, Diana Krall and Plácido Domingo to Sammy Davis Jr., Magdalena Zárate, José Carreras, Joao Alberto, Elvis Presley and Mexican heart-throb Luis Miguel.

Words of "Bésame mucho" (Consuelo Velázquez)

Bésame, bésame mucho,
Como si fuera esta noche la última vez.
Bésame, bésame mucho,
Que tengo miedo perderte,
Perderte otra vez.

Quiero tenerte muy
Cerca, mirarme en tus
Ojos, verte junto a mí,
Piensa que tal vez

Mañana yo ya estaré
Lejos, muy lejos de ti.

Bésame, bésame mucho,
Como si fuera esta noche la última vez.
Bésame mucho,
Que tengo miedo perderte,
Perderte después.

Unofficial English translation:

Kiss me, Kiss me a lot,
As if tonight were the last time.
Kiss me, kiss me a lot,
Because I'm afraid of losing you,
To lose you again.

I want to have you very close
To see myself in your eyes,
To see you next to me,
Think that perhaps tomorrow
I already will be far,
very far from you.

Kiss me, Kiss me a lot,
As if tonight were the last time.
Kiss me, a lot,
because I'm afraid of losing you,
To lose you later.

Consuelo Velázquez was born in Ciudad Guzmán, Jalisco, on August 21, 1920, but grew up in Guadalajara. She began playing piano when she was 4, gave her first public recital at age 6, and moved to Mexico City in her teens to attend the National Conservatory and the Palace of Fine Arts. She became a concert pianist and started writing popular songs shortly afterwards, while overseeing classical music programs for the pioneering radio station XEQ.

"Bésame mucho"(Kiss me a lot) was first recorded in 1941 (by Emilio Tuero and Chela Campos) and became a huge Big Band hit during the Second World War. In 1999, the song, the only Mexican song ever to have topped the U.S. hit parade for 12 straight weeks, was declared the "Song of the Century" at a Univisión event in Miami, Florida.

In addition, "Bésame mucho" featured in several movies, including "A toda máquina" (1951), "The moon over Parador" (1988), "Sueños de Arizona" (1993), and "Moskva Slezam ne Verit", a Russian movie which won the 1980 Oscar for Best Foreign Film.

"Bésame mucho" brought fame and numerous awards to Consuelo Velázquez, including a Special Citation of Achievement Award from the U.S. Broadcast Music Incorporated. Invited to Hollywood to meet the legendary Walt Disney, she found him to be "nice, kind and respectful." Velázquez agreed to work in Disney's "The Three Caballeros". During the filming of this movie, Rita Hayworth stopped by and insisted on meeting Velázquez.

According to her close friends, Consuelo Velázquez remained a gentle, humble person throughout her life, often telling anecdotes about her life as if she was talking about someone else. She continued to play the piano most afternoons until well into her 80s.

Among other songs that she wrote that were popular in their day are "Yo no fui" (sung most famously by Pedro Infante), "Anoche", "Al nacer este día", "Aunque tengas razón", "Déjame quererte", "Pensará en mí", "Amar y vivir", "Que seas feliz" (interpreted recently by Luis Miguel), "No me pidas nunca", "Chiqui", "Volverás a mí", and "Cachito". When she died, she had only just finished another song – "Por el camino" – written especially for Luis Miguel's next album.

Consuelo Velázquez, "Consuelito", can rightfully be considered Mexico's greatest ever female composer. Her life and her songs will be remembered with great affection by music-lovers everywhere for years to come.

Que descansa en paz - May she rest in peace.

To contact Tony Burton, you can email him at: *tonyburton@pacificcoast.net*

17 Mexican and Yucatecan Holidays & Traditions

If you are building a life for yourself in Mérida, you are well advise to get to know a few of the holidays and traditions that make this such a special place. Let's start with food, and work our way to the special traditions in Mérida that are some of the pleasures of being down here.

Traditional Yucatecan Dishes

Yucatecan food has evolved from a wide range of influences, from Maya cuisine, to dishes from the Middle East, Spain and the Dutch. It is a unique style and is very different from what most people consider "Mexican" food. Some of the "regional" dishes that are popular all over the peninsula include:

Poc Chuc, a Maya version of a classic grilled pork dish.

Salbutes and Panuchos. Salbutes are soft, cooked tortillas with lettuce, tomato, turkey and avocado on top. Panuchos feature fried tortillas filled with black beans, and topped with turkey or chicken, lettuce, avocado and pickled onions. Habanero chiles accompany most dishes, either in solid or purée form, along with fresh limes and corn tortillas.

Queso Relleno is a "gourmet" dish featuring ground pork inside of a carved edam cheese ball served with tomato sauce.

Pavo en Relleno Negro (also known locally as Chilmole) is turkey meat stew cooked with a black paste made from roasted chiles, a local version of the mole de guajalote found throughout Mexico. The meat soaked in the black soup is also served in tacos, sandwiches and even in panuchos or salbutes.

Sopa de Lima is a lime soup with a chicken broth base often accompanied by shredded chicken or turkey and crispy tortilla.

Papadzules. Egg "tacos" bathed with pumpkin seed sauce and tomatoes. This is one of the few vegetarian Maya dishes.

Cochinita Pibil is a marinated pork dish and by far the most renowned from the Yucatecan food.

Bul keken (Mayan for "beans and pork") is a traditional black bean and pork soup. The soup is served in the home on Mondays in most homes. The soup is usually served with chopped onions, radishes, chilies, and tortillas.

Brazo de reina (Spanish for "The Queen's Arm") is a traditional tamal dish. A long, flat tamal is topped with ground pumpkin seeds and rolled up like a roll cake. The long roll is then cut into slices. The slices are topped with a tomato sauce and a pumpkin seed garnish.

Please note the one, quintessential spice found everywhere: ***Achiote!***
This is the most popular spice in the area. It is derived from the hard annatto seed found in the region. The whole seed is ground together with other spices and formed into a reddish seasoning paste, called *recado rojo*. The other ingredients in the paste include cinnamon, allspice berries, cloves, Mexican oregano, cumin seed, sea salt, mild black peppercorns, apple cider vinegar, and garlic. The most popular hot sauce, "El Yucateco," is made in Mérida, Yucatán. Hot sauces in Mérida are usually made from the indigenous chiles in the area which include: Chile Xcatik, Chile Seco de Yucatán, and Chile Habenero.

Día de los Muertos

Día de los Muertos, or **Day of the Dead,** throughout much of the Catholic world, especially in Latin America, is a time to celebrate life by remembering loved ones who have died. Friends and family members gather to clean and decorate graveyards and visit cemeteries offering prayers for the dead, set up devotional altars in their homes where they make offerings of food and drink to the deceased and gather to tell stories about ancestors, family lore, and recall loving anecdotes of friends and family who have died. Here's what you need to know to participate in this colorful and life-affirming tradition that honors those we've known and loved, but have passed from this life.

In Yucatán, Day of the Dead has a very distinct Maya sensibility to it that sets it apart from other celebrations around the country when it comes to food. "Hanal Pixán" in Yucatec Maya means "food of souls," and throughout the Yucatán, Day of the Dead is referred to as "Hanal Pixán" by the Maya. There are specific dishes associated with these festivities.

The quintessential dish is the "mucbipollo," which means "buried chicken." Very similar to tamales, it is made of corn dough and wrapped in banana leaves, but unlike regular tamales, it is prepared in a larger dish. In the countryside, it is baked in an underground pit. Many families in Mérida have place orders for their "mucbipollos" with local restaurants, and there always seems to be someone in the neighborhood who specializes in making them for friends and acquaintances.

Day of the Dead nomenclature:

Los angelitos: Young children who have died.

Calavera: Skulls. Often made out of sugar and placed on *ofrendas* (offering altars) or eaten as candy.

Ceras: Candles lit to guide the souls of the departed.

Ofrenda: Altars often decorated with flowers, photos, trinkets and food in honor of deceased souls.

Pan de muerto: Sweet bread often baked into buns shaped like bones and eaten with hot chocolate or set on ofrendas.

Papel picado: Paper cut into elaborate patterns and used for decorations or on ofrendas.

Retablos: Small devotional artwork.

Answer to the often-asked questions, **What's up with the skulls? Why are there so many skulls and skeletons?** Because that's these are iconography preferred by the First Peoples, which have been incorporated into mainstream Latin American societies.

Firecrackers

What a great tradition!

Yes, it can be startling at times to hear firecrackers going off in the distance – especially when so many people are on edge about "violence" in Mexico. And yes, I've been speaking with guests who jump thinking that there's gunfire in the distance, but rest assured it is all harmless.

In many parts of Mexico, it's customary for young men to propose engagement to their girlfriends at gatherings – family reunions, or when out with friends. And it's customary for the young man's friends to be ready for the moment when she says "Yes." How? With firecrackers nearby to celebrate the engagement!

It's also customary to have special events when there's a piñata – and the beaten up piñata, once it has been emptied of candy and treats, to be destroyed with firecrackers, as if to say good riddance. In fact, many Yucatecans celebrate New Year's Eve with a piñata in the shape of an old man, symbolizing the Old Year, and it really gets a thrashing since the Old Year never quite lived up to its promise. It's customary for the next day to destroy the piñata carcass on the sidewalk with firecrackers. So don't be surprised if on January 1st there are scores of old piñatas being blown up with firecrackers all over town by neighborhood youngsters. Good riddance to all the unmet expectations, right?!

Bombas!

In Spanish, "bomba" means an explosive, as in a car bomb; and it also means a pump, as in the pump for a well. In the Yucatán, "bomba," believe it or not, is also a naughty limerick!

Oh, yes, the Maya are culturally *very* randy, and double-entendres are part of everyday speech. So it only makes sense that, when they learned Spanish, they realized that Spanish is a very poetic language that lends itself to very naughty limericks. If you're not familiar with dirty poems, consider the Irish tradition of raunchy limericks. Here is one:

There once was a fellow McSweeny
Who spilled some gin on his weenie
Just to be couth
He added vermouth
Then slipped his girlfriend a martini

Normally, the Maya will tell their limericks during public dances, where, for instance, a man and a woman are dancing and they suddenly stop. He tells a limerick, the audience shouts, BOMBA amid laughter and then the dancing resumes. Bookstores around town sell small booklets with dozens of raunchy bombas, which is really a great way to impress friends with your "cultural immersion"!

Here are three popular, rather mild, limericks – and for those who don't speak Spanish, get someone in your Spanish class to help you!

Bomba!
Tienes la cara bonita,
Tus hombros estan muy bien,
Me gusta tu cinturita,
Y lo que sigue también!

Bomba!
Quisiera ser zapatito
Y estar en tu lindo pie
Para mirar un poquito
De lo que el zapatito ve!

Bomba!
La mujer de don Wilfrido
Anda buscando un buen socio
Porque dice que el marido
No le atiende su negocio!

Now you know the kinds of jokes you'd hear if you were able to eavesdrop in Mérida's central market – and you can imagine how scandalized the Spanish missionaries were centuries ago when they encountered such a magnificently bawdy society as that of the Yucatec Maya!

Mexico's Flag

In Mexico, as in most countries, the flag is revered. It is protected by law, not only the flag itself, but its imagery. While Americans may make a bikini out of their flag and parade around the beach, that never happens in Mexico. In fact, the flag, as well as the Coat of Arms, or *escudo nacional*, and the National Anthem are considered *símbolos patrios*, or patriotic symbols, of the nation, and it is against the law to desecrate them.

The flag itself consists of three vertical bands. One in green, the other in white and the last one is red. Mexican schoolchildren are taught to respect the "verde, blanco y colorado." Mexico's Coat of Arms, portraying an eagle resting on a pear cactus with a snake held in its beak and talons, which is based on an Aztec myth, is in the center of the white band. The proportions of the flag are 4:7.

The current flag was adopted in 1968, which is a slight variation of the flag first used in 1821. There have been few changes in the flag, principally reflecting changes in the Coat of Arms. The original meaning of the colors was that the green represented Independence, the white stood for religious faith, and the red was symbolic of the intermixing of the European and First Peoples of Mexico. This was changed by President Benito Juárez, whose was in office 1858 to 1872. His liberal government secularized Mexican society. Green today represents hope, white stands for unity and red is symbolic of the blood of fallen heroes who have defended the nation.

Mexico's Coat of Arms is the most distinctive feature of the Mexican flag. Legend has it that the Aztecs, a nomadic people from northern Mexico, established themselves in the Valley of Mexico when a prophecy was fulfilled. The Aztecs, who were also known as the "Mexica," pronounced "meh-shee-ka," believed that Huitzilopochtli, their God of War, had ordered them to build their city – Tenochtitlán – where they would come upon an eagle devouring a serpent while resting on a prickly pear cactus. Unfortunately for the Aztecs, they came upon such a scene in an inhospitable area of the Valley of Mexico, a series of swamps and marshes amid three lakes.

Holidays

January 1: New Year's Day

January 6: Founding of Mérida

February 7: Constitution Day

March 21: Birthday of Benito Juárez

March-April: Holy Week

April 30: Day of the Child

May 10: Mother's Day

September 16: Independence Day; Feast Day for Mérida's Christ of the Blisters

October: Festival of Fall

November 1: Day of the Innocents

November 2: Day of the Dead & Hanal Pixan

December 12: Day of the Virgin of Guadalupe

December 24: Christmas Eve (Nochebuena)

December 25: Navidad (Christmas Day)

But in fulfillment of their beliefs, they set about to dredge the swamps and lakes, and build a city in the center of the Valley of Mexico. The resulting metropolis, with pyramids and temples amid a series of canals would, centuries later, remind the Spanish of Venice.

Flag Day is February 24, a national holiday celebrated with civic ceremonies throughout the nation that are solemn and joyous. Viva Mexico!

Gremios

What are "Gremios"?

Each fall, beginning in September, there are a series of religious processions through the streets in all the neighborhoods throughout the Historic Center. These are known as "los gremios," or "the guilds." They trace their origin to Medieval Europe, and the first one is September 14 at the Cathedral on the Main Square. At 9 AM in the morning the Christ of the Blisters is removed from its sanctuary and there is a mass to commence the Guild Season at precisely 11 AM.

From September 27 through October 17 there will be scores of processions, with various saints and virgins honored through celebrations. The origin, of course, stems from the belief that different saints offered protection for various trades. There are patron saints who watch over bakers, market stall vendors, shoemakers, teachers, homemakers, taxi cab drivers, carpenters and so forth. Each profession, like a union, reserves a day and time when they will make a pilgrimage to honor their profession's patron saint.

The procession consists of pilgrims, usually accompanied by a small band, and young men with fireworks – holding banners and often times carrying their saint aloft. The women tend to wear impeccable Maya dresses – white huipiles with beautiful embroidery. The men often wear crisp guayabera shirts. So it goes for about three weeks until October 17, when at 11 AM a procession returns the Christ of the Blisters to its rightful spot, and mass is celebrated.

This tradition dates back to 1654 and is the longest, continuously celebrated Guilds in Mexico.

Here's a breakdown of the processions, by date and trade:

September processions:
27-28, Construction workers
28-29, Small business owners
29-30, Supplicants of Christ

30-1 October, Mirror, aluminum and glass workers

October processions:
1-2, Shoemakers
2-3, Seamstresses and embroiderers
3-4, Taxi drivers
4-5, Painters
5-6, Mechanics and ironworkers
6-7, Carpenters
7-8, Women
8-9, Business owners
9-10, Shop owners
10-11, Shop owners and workers
11-12, Teachers and students
12-13, Bakers
13-14, Train workers
14-15, Trinket stall owners and employees
15-16, Professionals
16-17, Market stall vendors

For more information call the Archdiocese: (999) 928-6131.

Mardi Gras – Carnaval

Mérida celebrates Mardi Gras to the fullest. It has, in fact, the third-largest Mardi Gras in the nation. (Only the ones in Veracruz and Mazatlán are bigger.) That said, be prepared for a week of festivities and parades, all leading up to a huge street party where revelers are out and about in full revelry.

Mardi Gras is held along Paseo de Montejo, and there still talk about moving it to a different location, simply because it has grown so large, and so popular and somewhat unruly. Compared with Mardi Gras in Rio de Janeiro, Brazil or New Orleans in the U.S., people in Mérida keep their wits about them – and there is a great deal less public drunkenness and disorderly conduct than one normally associates with such public displays of excess. But it still is a time when it seems the entire city goes a bit crazy – and that's crazy in a good way.

How popular is Mardi Gras? Consider this: The City maintains a full-time office to coordinate all activities associated with "el Carnaval." For more information, city government maintains a website dedicated exclusively to the Mardi Gras.

Here it is: *www.merida.gob.mx/carnaval/index.html*

Buen Provecho!

There will come a time when you will be sitting at a restaurant and someone you know will be across the room. If they approach you, either on their way in or their way out, or come directly to your table to say hello, they might very well say "Buen provecho," when they either pass by, or take their leave.

What does that mean? Two simple words, really, but they are loaded with meaning. It's easy to say it's the Spanish equivalent of "Bon Appetit," or "Guten Appetit," but these fall short in comparison. In Spanish it conveys the hope that the meal is pleasing and enjoyable – and that it is beneficial to your health.

It's such a gracious expression that sometimes complete strangers will say it to each other, when one is leaving a restaurant and passes by a table that is being served. Get in the habit of using it, since it's seen as mark of good breeding and civility.

18 Philanthropy & Non-Profit Organizations

If an organization solicits a donation from the public, but cannot provide an official receipt that is accepted by Mexico's federal tax and revenue agency, known as the Secretaria de Hacienda y Credito Público, or SHCP, it is violating the law. Mexican law is very clear that solicitation from the **public at large** can only be made by bona fide nonprofit organizations duly authorized to solicit donations and issue tax-deductible receipts. "Civil Associations," or "asociaciones civiles," can **receive** donations, but not through **public** fund-raising activities, and their receipts are not accepted as tax-deductible donations. Protect yourself from scams.

This is a list of bona fide non-profit organizations duly authorized by the SHCP to solicit donations **from the public** and issue tax-deductible receipts. The list may not be complete, so one way to make sure that an organization is authorized to solicit donations is to ask for an official receipt – "un recibo fiscal." **EVERY** organization authorized to solicit donations from the public **MUST** give you such a receipt, and if they cannot do so, then they are soliciting donations unlawfully!

Authorized Nonprofit Organizations Operating in the State of Yucatán

Albergue del Anciano en Progreso, A.C.

Albergue de San Vicente de Mérida, A.C.

Asilo de Ancianos, Señor de la Misericordia, A.C.

Alas al Vuelo, A.C.

Amanecer Nuevamente, A.C.

Amigos del Macay, A.C.

Apoyo a los Valores Humanos, A.C.

Aprendamos Juntos, A.C.

Asilo Brunet Celarain, A.C.

Asociación de Ayuda Alimenticia para Personas de Escasos Recursos Económicos, A.C

Asociación Cultural Teotepec, S.C.

Asociación para la Equinoterapia, A.C.

Asociación Hacia Todos los Caminos, A.C.

Asociación Mexicana de Ayuda a Niños con Cáncer Peninsular, A.C.

Asociación Mexicana para la Comunicación y Superación de las Personas con Discapacidad Auditiva, A.C.

Asociación Mexicana de Esclerosis Tuberosa, A.C.

Asociación Yucateca de Lucha contra el Autismo y Otros Transtornos del Desarrollo, A.C.

Asociación Yucateca de Padres de Familia Pro-Deficiente Mental, A.C.

Asociación Yucateca Pro-Deficiente Auditivo, A.C.

Avelino Montes Linaje, A.C.

Ayuda a la Mujer Embarazada, A.C.

Banco de Alimentos de Mérida, A.C.

Banco del Vestido, A.C.

Bien Cimentado, A.C.

Biocenosis, A.C.

Caballeros Kadosh, A.C.

Cáritas de Yucatán, A.C.

Casa para Ancianos Desamparados La Divina Providencia, A.C.

Casa Infantil El Roble, A.C.

Centro de Atención a Madres Solteras de Yucatán, A.C.

Colegio América de Mérida, A.C.

Centro Asistencial para la Superación de la Mujer en la Familia, A.C.

Comunidad Coox Meyaj, A.C.

Centro de Comunicación y Servicios Sociales, A.C.

Centro Comunitario Yutsil, A.C.

Comité de Desarrollo Integral, A.C.

Centro de Desarrollo Integral Enséñame a Caminar por la Vida, A.C.

Centro de Educación Especial La Luz de un Nuevo Amanecer, A.C.

Centro Escolar Miguel Alemán, A.C.

Centro de Investigación Científica de Yucatán, A.C.

Centro Loyola de Mérida, A.C.

Centro Social El Porvenir, A.C.

Centro Universitario Montejo, A.C.

Club Especial Ayelem, A.C.

Colegio Mérida, A.C.

Colegio Montejo, A.C.

Colegio Peninsular, A.C.

Colegio Teresa de Avila de Tizimín, A.C.

El Comienzo de un Nuevo Viaje, A.C.

Comunidad Vicentina de Mérida, A.C.

Convicción Social, A.C.

Cottolengo de Yucatán, A.C.

Daré de Mérida, A.C.

Dispensario María Soledad, A.C.

Educación Peninsular, A.C.

Educarte, A.C.

Escuela Jeanne de Matel, A.C.

Escuela Joaquín Peón, A.C.

Educación Profesional Peninsular, A.C.

Escuela Vasco de Quiroga, A.C.

Fundación Alborada, A.C.

Fundación de Apoyo Infantil Yucatán, A.C.

Fundación Banco del Vestido, A.C.

Fundación Bepensa, A.C.

Fundación para el Bienestar Natural, A.C.

Fundación CHI´K´AK´NAB para la Conservación de la Biodiversidad, el Desarrollo Sustentable y la Cultura, A.C.

Fundación Cultural Macay, A.C.

Fundación Emanuel de Mérida, A.C.

Fundación García Lavín, I.B.P.

Fundación Guadalupe Basteris de Molina, A.C.

Fundación Gruber Jez, A.C.

Fundación Grupo Abraham, A.C.

Fundación Kuri, A.C.

Fundación Mexicana para la Salud Capítulo Peninsular, A.C.

Fundación México-Libanesa, A.C.

Fundación Nicolás Urcelay, A.C.

Fundación Nicolás Xacur Slaimen, A.C.

Fundación de Orientación Holística, A.C.

Fundación Plan Estratégico de Mérida, A.C.

Fundación Progreso Yucatán, A.C.

Fundación Roche, A.C.

Fundación por la Salud en Yucatán, A.C.

Fundación Siqueff Millet, A.C.

Fundación de la Universidad Autónoma de Yucatán, A.C.

Fundación Valentina Arrigunaga Peón, A.C.

Fundación Yucatán, A.C.

Grupo de Apoyo a Pacientes Traumatizados y Ortopédicos, A.C.

Grupo Kerigma, A.C.

El Hombre sobre la Tierra, A.C.

Institución Asistencial, A.C.

Instituto José Pablo Rovalo Azcue, A.C.

Impulso Universitario, A.C.

Impulsora del Colegio Jenaro Rodríguez Correa, A.C.

Inter Universidad del Sureste, A.C.

Jesús de la Misericordia, A.C.

Joven Ballet de Mérida, A.C.

Luisa María Clar, A.C.

Mano Amiga Yucatán Conkal, A.C.

Mérida Itzáes Yucatán, A.C.

El Milagro de la Vejez, A.C.

Motolinía de Mérida, A.C.

Museo de la Canción Yucateca, A.C.

Niños y Crías, A.C.

Oasis de San Juan de Dios, A.C.

Organización de Servicios y Ayuda para la Navidad de los Enfermos, A.C.

Pastoral del Amor, A.C.

Patrimonio Peninsular, A.C.

Patronato de la Escuela de Educación Especial Roberto Solís Quiroga, A.C.

Patronato de Hogares Juveniles, A.C.

Patronato para la Orquesta Sinfónica de Yucatán, A.C.

Patronato Pro Historia Peninsular de Yucatán, A.C.

Patronato Peninsular Pro Niños con Deficiencia Mental, A.C.

Patronato Vida Humana Integral, A.C.

Pronatura Península de Yucatán, A.C.

Protección de la Joven María Suárez Molina, A.C.

Púrpura Plastika Fundación Cultural para el Desarrollo y la Expresión Artística, A.C.

Proyección Valor, A.C.

Red de Ecoturismo de Yucatán, A.C.

Refugio para Ancianos, A.C.

El Renacer del Mayab, A.C.

Serfam, A.C.

Sol y Luna, A.C.

Tras una Sonrisa, A.C.

Universidad del Mayab, S.C.

Universidad Marista de Mérida, A.C.

Ven Vive Convive, A.C.

Vida y Familia de Mérida, A.C.

Vive y Trasciende, A.C.

Voluntarias Vicentinas, A.C.

The Danger of the Hapless Altruist

This is a big country. This is an important country.

Far too many Americans make the mistake of thinking, when they move to Mexico, that they have moved to the same country as it was portrayed in the 1950s, that of a nation making the transition from an agricultural society to a modern, industrial one. If you think of Mexico as a backwards, unsophisticated nation, then you have to readjust your thinking.

Mexico is one of the most important nations in the world. It's a member of the G-20, which means that it is in top percentile of nations in the world. The World Bank, the International Monetary Fund and the CIA World Factbook each rank Mexico as the 14th largest economy on the planet.[6] When it comes to social programs, it has one of the most comprehensive social welfare systems anywhere in the hemisphere – only Canada has more social programs. Every conceivable concern is looked after, from an aggressive (and very successful) HIV education and prevention program, to a thorough and comprehensive health care system, to tough child-welfare programs, to pioneering environmental protection agencies. The peso, Mexico's currency, is one of the most stable in the world, often used in a basket of currencies by the IMF to support other central banks. (In 2011, the U.S. dollar has weakened considerably against a surging peso, a testament to Mexico's resilience and economic stability.[7]) This is a country that strives, albeit imperfectly and not always successfully, with providing for the general welfare.

Yes, given its resources and its population, many people fall between the cracks. Of Mexico's population of 110,000,000 people, just fewer than 80,000,000 are active participants in the nation's social welfare programs. That leaves 30,000,000 living in the "informal economy," as it is euphemistically called. For comparative purposes, 1 in 7 Americans rely on food stamps to feed their families, and in the largest American city, New York, 1 in 4 children live below the federal poverty line. No country addresses all of the needs of its people, but Mexico is diligent in at least working towards that end.

If you think that this is a country with no laws or legal institutions, a kind of place reminiscent of some Hollywood movie where it's the "Wild, Wild West," then you are in for a surprise. Mexico is one of the most bureaucratic nations in the hemisphere – it rivals France when it comes to official paperwork! And it rivals the Scandinavian countries when it comes to its aspirations for being a "nanny state." In fact, international agencies – from the World Bank to the International Monetary Fund – continue to remind Mexico that is has to "streamline" its bureaucracy if it wants to become more competitive in the global economy.

---

[6] See: en.wikipedia.org/wiki/List_of_countries_by_GDP_(nominal)
[7] See, "Peso's Gain on Dollar Pressures Mexican Exports," by Elisabeth Malkin, New York Times, February 8, 2011.

If you thought that the Instituto Nacional de Migración (INM) had a lot of paperwork for issuing an FM2 or FM3 visa, or that the Comision Federal de Electricidad (CFE) required lots of documentation before it opened an electric account in your name, that's a taste of the level of scrutiny applied to every facet of life in Mexico.

Mexico, in many ways, is a pioneering society. In December 2010, for instance, Yucatán State government announced the formation of an Office of Climatic Change (Oficina de Cambio Climático), with a $35 million peso budget, and which would work to coordinate efforts with the state governments of Campeche and Quintana Roo, in order to understand and mitigate the effects of climatic changes throughout the peninsula.[8] If this isn't a progressive and proactive place, than what is?

The reason it's important to understand this about Mexico is to prevent you from making mistakes that many English-speaking expats make: They look around, and since they can't speak the language, or understand how Mexcian society is organized, they presume that if they don't see it, it's not there. And then, with good intentions, they go about creating a *parallel* initiative, one without the political or societal foundation for enduring success.

It is always advisable to work within the **established** system. Become **informed**. Find out if there are organizations or government agencies already working on the issue about which you are passionate, and then see how you can contribute. Look at the breathtaking variety of nonprofit organizations already up and running in Yucatán

Warning about "Yucatan Today" magazine!

In Mérida, Yucatecans have a saying, "Una *gringada* no es una *gringada* si no cuenta con el apoyo de *Yucatan Today*."

This means, "A scam isn't a scam without the endorsement of *Yucatan Today*."

Sure enough, that magazine has been known to back some of the more dubious "charitable" initiatives of the expatriate community! Chances are that if it's endorsed by *Yucatan Today*, whether we're talking about an AIDS charity or a benefit for the scoff-law English-language library, there's some sort of sleazy angle to it.

You have been forewarned! If *Yucatn Today* endorses it, be very, very careful!

---

[8] See: www.yucatan.com.mx/20101225/nota-9/47065-firman-acuerdo-contra-el-cambio-climatico-los-gobernadores-de-la-peninsula.htm

State and you are sure to find something about which you are passionate.

You will be welcomed, but if you ignore the established groups, and launch an expatriate-led initiative that excludes the existing organizations, you will be marginalized. As with most charitable endeavors, a bit of soul-searching is always in order. Ask yourself this: Are you trying to give to the community around you, or are you attempting to ameliorate a disappointment in your life? The answer will determine the place from which you are coming when you reach out and those around you.

Five Organizations to Stay Away From! (in our opinion)

The following organizations have been known to solicit donations from the public, primarily targeting American expatriates, but do not appear on the official list compiled by the SHCP:

Amigos de Artesanos Nuevos de Yucatán (AANY)

This organization has been soliciting donations from the public since 2010. As of December 31, 2010, it has not been authorized to solicit donations from the public, or to issue tax-deductible receipts that are recognized as legitimate by Mexico's federal taxing authority, known as SHCP.

Brazos Abiertos, Inc.

For four years Brazos Abiertos, Inc., of Houston, Texas, engaged in fundraising activities in Mérida apparently without authorization of Mexican officials. It has never been authorized to solicit donations from the public in Mexico, or to issue tax-deductible receipts that are recognized as legitimate by Mexico's federal taxing authority, known as SHCP.

Fundación BAI, A.C.

This organization, an affiliate of Brazos Abiertos, Inc. of Houston, Texas, founded in April 2009 has not been authorized to solicit donations from the public, or to issue tax-deductible receipts that are recognized as legitimate by Mexico's federal taxing authority, known as SHCP.

Mérida English Language Library (MELL)

MELL claims to be a member of the American Library Association, which, as of December 31, 2010 it was not. It claims to be a "Mexican nonprofit institution," implying that it is authorized to solicit donations from the public, or to issue tax-deductible receipts that are recognized as legitimate by Mexico's federal taxing authority, known as SHCP, when this is not true. It is a "civil association," or an "asociacion civil," which is different from being a bona fide nonprofit organization authorized to solicit donations from the public and issue tax-deductible receipts.

MELL has a new director who has promised to get their papers in order, get its membership to the American Library Association current, and clean up the ethical mess left behind by the previous administration.

 ## Mérida Verde

Since 2008 this organization has been soliciting donations from the public. It was not incorporated as a "civil association," or "asociacion civil," by three American women until 2009. Why a group of Americans would come to Mérida and choose the name of an organization that has been working for almost a decade as its own is a mystery. ("Mérida Verde" is a long-standing nonprofit organization in Mérida, Venezuela.) That said, as of December 31, 2010, it has not been authorized to solicit donations from the public, or to issue tax-deductible receipts that are recognized as legitimate by Mexico's federal taxing authority, known as SHCP.

Part VI
Almost Paradise ...

19   Attorneys & Public Notaries

Dealing with a Mexican Attorney

When it comes to hiring an attorney, many of whom are also Public Notaries, the Mérida Consulate advises U.S. citizens:

How to Deal with Your Foreign Attorney:

a) Find out the attorney's qualifications and experience.
b) Find out how the attorney plans to represent you. Ask specific questions and expect the attorney to explain the legal process in the country concerned, as well as the legal activities planned on your behalf, in language that you can understand. Have your attorney analyze your case, giving you the positive and negative aspects and probable outcome. Be honest with your attorney. Tell the attorney every relevant fact in order to get the best representation of your interests. Do not fail to ask how much time the attorney anticipates the case may take to complete.
c) Find out what fees the country charges and what fees are expected. Some attorneys expect payment in advance; some demand payment after each action taken, refusing to proceed until they are paid. Others may take the case on a percentage basis, collecting a pre-arranged percentage of the monies awarded by a foreign court.
d) Ask that your attorney keep you advised of the progress your case according to a pre-established schedule. Remember your responsibility to keep your attorney informed of any new developments in your case. Request copies of all letters and documents prepared on your behalf.
e) Do not expect your attorney to give a simple answer to a complex legal problem. Be sure you understand the technical language contained in any contract or other legal document prepared by your attorney.

    In addition to the comments made by the U.S. Consulate there is also another consideration that is very, very important. As someone moving to Mérida, you are moving into an established community. Think what would happen if you, for instance, moved from New York to Cleveland. Arriving in Cleveland, you enter an established community where people know each other, often for several generations, and know "the lay of the land." As someone moving in, how long will you be here? Forever, or for a few years?

No one knows, but the people who are established in Cleveland are more likely to remain in Cleveland, whether you stay or go.

In other words, do you know the relationships that your attorney has with others in Mérida? Are you certain that, for instance, if you hire an attorney to represent you in purchasing a house that, in a what-a-small-world moment, it turns out that your attorney knows the seller's attorney, or the seller, or the seller's family?

Mérida is a city of a million people, but it can also resemble a small town. Be aware that there may be conflicts of interest arising from social, business or family relationships and connections. Be mindful that there may be conflicts of interest. Make sure that your attorney has *your* best interests at heart. Make sure that your attorney does not favor the other party – conscientiously or unconscientiously – because of existing relationships. If you have any doubts, it might be a good idea to hire a different attorney to look over the paperwork before you go forward.

These kinds of conflicts of interest are human, and more likely to occur when you are in a situation in which you are moving into an existing community where people have been here for generations.

Heed this advice: Never assume that the attorney you hire is exempt from a conflict of interest or unconscious bias that will undermine his or her ability to represent your interests fully.

With this in mind, here is a list of the attorneys in Mérida compiled by the State Department in Washington, D.C. for providing to American citizens in Mérida.

Please remember that choosing an attorney is a serious matter, and it is advisable that you consult with people you know and trust. Conversely, it is always a good idea to ask an attorney for two or three references from American or Canadian citizens for whom they have offered services.

In compiling this list, only attorneys who comply with State Department criteria are included here.

Mérida

Lic. Salvador Augusto Avila Arjona

Address: Calle 20 #203 by 29, Colonia García Ginerés, Mérida, Yucatán, 97070
Telephone: (999) 920-1133 (phone and fax)
Mobile: (999) 947-1727
Email: avila@racabogados.com.mx
Languages: Speaks Spanish and fluent English.
Specializes in: Contracts, corporations, criminal law, estates, foreign investments, immigration, marketing agreements, obtaining civil documents such as birth and death certificates, patents/trademarks/copyrights, theft/fraud/embezzlement. Masters Degree in corporate law at Anahuac University in 2005. Has practiced law for 20 years, experience in Yucatán, Campeche, Quintana Roo, Nuevo Leon, and Mexico City. Professional license number 4563411, issued on September 13, 2005.

Lic. Raúl Ballote Pantoja

Address: Calle 62 #313-A between Calle 35 and 37 Street, Centro, Mérida, Yucatán
Telephone: (999) 920-2011 ext.104
Mobile: (999) 947-1832
Email: raul@raulballote.com
Languages: Speaks Spanish and Full command of English. Limited French – Reading ability.
Specializes in: Contracts, corporations, foreign investments, immigration, real estate law. Certified legal Translator and Notary. Has practiced law for more than 20 years, experience in Yucatán, Campeche, and Quintana Roo. Professional license number 188243, issued on June 21, 1971. Lawyer registry number 3016, issued on March 6, 1996.

Lic. Luis Miguel Ceballos Capetillo

Address: Calle 20 #203-A by 29 Street, Colonia García Ginerés. Mérida, Yucatán, 97070
Phone and Fax: 999-920-1133
Mobile: 998-100-0873
Email: ceballos@racabogados.com.mx
Languages: Speaks Spanish and fluent English.
Specializes in: Contracts, corporations, criminal law, estates, foreign investments, investment, immigration, marketing agreements, obtaining civil documents such as birth and death certificates, patents/trademarks/copyrights, theft/fraud/embezzlement, notary law.

Notary and Translator. Has practiced law for 13 years, experience in Campeche, Yucatán, and Quintana Roo. Professional license number 2490012, issued on 1997.

Lic. Jaime Uriel Pacheco Torres

Address: Calle 58 #526-E between Calle 55 and 57 Street, Fracc. Las Granjas, Mérida, Yucatán, 97197
Telephone: (999) 941-2571
Mobile: (999)163-9602
Email: jaime0712@hotmail.com
Languages: Spanish, Limited English
Specializes in: Auto/accidents, banking/financial, contracts, corporations, criminal law, government relations, insurance, investment, patents/trademarks/copyrights, theft/fraud/embezzlement. Has practiced law for 8 years, experience in Yucatán, Campeche, Tabasco, and Quintana Roo. Professional license number 6024403, issued on June 24, 2009.

Lic. José Ignacio Puerto Gutiérrez

Address: Calle 25 #159 by 30 Street, Colonia García Ginerés, Mérida, Yucatán, 97100
Telephone: (999) 920-3050 (phone and fax)
Mobile: (999) 900-3260
Email: ipuerto@puertoypino.com
Languages: Speaks Spanish and fluent English.
Specializes in: Banking/financial, civil damages, collections, contracts, corporations, criminal law, estates, foreign investments, government relations, investment, immigration, labor relations, marketing agreements, marriage/divorce, patents/trademarks/copyrights, taxes, theft/fraud/embezzlement. Masters Degree in corporate law at Yale University in 1991. Has practiced law for 21 years, experience in New York City, Mexico City and Yucatán. Professional license number 1656658, issued on May 4, 1992. Lawyer registry number 2698, issued on August 17, 2000.

Lic. Mauricio Arturo Rojano Romero

Address: Calle 20 #203-A by 29 Street, Colonia García Ginerés, Mérida, Yucatán, 97070
Telephone: (999) 920-1133 (phone and fax)
Mobile: (999) 910-0464
Email: rojano@racabogados.com.mx
Languages: Speaks Spanish and fluent English.

Specializes in: Contracts, corporations, criminal law, estates, foreign investments, immigration, marketing agreements, investment, obtaining civil documents such as birth and death certificates, patents/trademarks/copyrights, theft/fraud/embezzlement, notary law. Has practiced law for 15 years, experience in Yucatán, Campeche and Quintana Roo. Professional license number 2170137, issued on September 26, 1995.

Valladolid

Lic. Salvador Augusto Avila Arjona

Address: Calle 20 #203 by 29 Street, Colonia García Ginerés, Mérida, Yucatán, 97070
Telephone: (999) 920-1133 (phone and fax)
Mobile: (999) 947-1727
Email: avila@racabogados.com.mx
Languages: Speaks Spanish and fluent English.
Specializes in: Contracts, corporations, criminal law, estates, foreign investments, immigration, marketing agreements, obtaining civil documents such as birth and death certificates, patents/trademarks/copyrights, theft/fraud/embezzlement. Masters Degree in corporate law at Anahuac University in 2005. Has practiced law for 20 years, experience in Yucatán, Campeche, Quintana Roo, Nuevo Leon, and Mexico City. Professional license number 4563411, issued on September 13, 2005.

Lic. Raúl Ballote Pantoja

Address: Calle 62 #313-A between Calle 35 and 37 Street, Centro, Mérida, Yucatán, 97000
Telephone: (999) 920-2011 ext.104
Mobile: (999) 947-1832
Email: raul@raulballote.com
Languages: Speaks Spanish and Full command of English. Limited French – Reading ability.
Specializes in: Contracts, corporations, foreign investments, immigration, real estate law. Certified legal Translator and Notary. Has practiced law for more than 20 years, experience in Yucatán, Campeche, and Quintana Roo. Professional license number 188243, issued on June 21, 1971. Lawyer registry number 3016, issued on March 6, 1996.

Lic. Jaime Uriel Pacheco Torres

Address: Calle 58 #526-E between Calle 55 and 57 Street, Fracc. Las Granjas, Mérida, Yucatán, 97197

Telephone: (999) 941-2571
Mobile: (999)163-9602
Email: jaime0712@hotmail.com
Languages: Spanish, Limited English
Specializes in: Auto/accidents, banking/financial, contracts, corporations, criminal law, government relations, insurance, investment, patents/trademarks/copyrights, theft/fraud/embezzlement. Has practiced law for 8 years, experience in Yucatán, Campeche, Tabasco, and Quintana Roo. Professional license number 6024403, issued on June 24, 2009.

Lic. José Ignacio Puerto Gutiérrez

Address: Calle 25 #159 by 30 Street, Colonia García Ginerés, Mérida, Yucatán, 97100
Telephone: (999) 920-3050 (phone and fax)
Mobile: (999) 900-3260
Email: ipuerto@puertoypino.com
Languages: Speaks Spanish and fluent English.
Specializes in: Banking/financial, civil damages, collections, contracts, corporations, criminal law, estates, foreign investments, government relations, investment, immigration, labor relations, marketing agreements, marriage/divorce, patents/trademarks/copyrights, taxes, theft/fraud/embezzlement. Masters Degree in corporate law at Yale University in 1991. Has practiced law for 21 years, experience in New York City, Mexico City and Yucatán. Professional license number 1656658, issued on May 4, 1992. Lawyer registry number 2698, issued on August 17, 2000.

Lic. Mauricio Arturo Rojano Romero

Address: Calle 20 #203-A by 29 Street, Colonia García Ginerés, Mérida, Yucatán, 97070
Telephone: (999) 920-1133 (phone and fax)
Mobile: (999) 910-0464
Email: rojano@racabogados.com.mx
Languages: Speaks Spanish and fluent English.
Specializes in: Contracts, corporations, criminal law, estates, foreign investments, immigration, marketing agreements, investment, obtaining civil documents such as birth and death certificates, patents/trademarks/copyrights, theft/fraud/embezzlement, notary law. Has practiced law for 15 years, experience in Yucatán, Campeche and Quintana Roo. Professional license number 2170137, issued on September 26, 1995.

ATTORNEYS & PUBLIC NOTARIES

Cozumel, Quintana Roo

Lic. Raúl Ballote Pantoja

Address: Calle 62 #313-A between Calle 35 and 37 Street, Centro, Mérida, Yucatán, 97000
Telephone: (999) 920-2011 ext.104
Mobile: (999) 947-1832
Email: raul@raulballote.com
Languages: Speaks Spanish and Full command of English. Limited French – Reading ability.
Specializes in: Contracts, corporations, foreign investments, immigration, real estate law. Certified legal Translator and Notary. Has practiced law for more than 20 years, experience in Yucatán, Campeche, and Quintana Roo. Professional license number 188243, issued on June 21, 1971. Lawyer registry number 3016, issued on March 6, 1996.

Lic. Patricio de la Peña Ruiz de Chávez

Address: Calle Granada #30, SM 2-A, Cancún, Quintana Roo
Phones: 998-887-9368
Mobile: 998-147-1603
Fax: 998-887-9368
Email: ppr@salasconsultores.com , ppr@dlpytrujillo.com
Languages: Speaks Spanish and good English
Specializes in: Civil damages, corporations, criminal law, labor relations, marriage/divorce, obtaining civil documents such as birth and death certificates. Has practiced law for nine years in Nuevo Leon and Quintana Roo. Professional license number 5311673, issued on October 24, 2007.

Lic. Angel Prieto Palmeros

Address: Retorno de la Paz #41, Super manzana 50, Manzana 20, Cancún, Quintana Roo, 77533
Telephone: 998-251-7010, 998-872-3732
Mobile: 998-137-8545
Fax: 998-848-0020
Email: prietoangel@yahoo.com
Languages: Speaks Spanish, fluent English, and limited Portuguese.
Specializes in: Adoptions, auto/accidents, banking/financial, child custody, civil damages, collections, contracts, corporations, criminal law, estates, foreign claims, foreign investments, government relations, insurance, investment, immigration, labor relations,

marketing agreements, marriage/divorce, obtaining civil documents such as birth and death certificates, patents/trademarks/copyrights, theft/fraud/embezzlement. Has practiced law for 19 years, experience in Philadelphia, Veracruz, and Quintana Roo. Professional license number 3619832, issued on August 14, 2002.

Lic. Javier Villalobos Castañeda

Address: Calle 17 Sur #1100, by Calle 20 Sur bis and Calle 20, Colonia Andres Quintana Roo II, Cancún, Quintana Roo
Phones: 987-869-7601, 987-872-1917
Mobile: 987-876-1747
Fax: 987-872-4033
Email: javiervillalobos@notariapublica15.com.mx
Languages: Speaks Spanish and fluent English
Specializes in: Civil damages, collections, contracts, corporations, criminal law, estates, foreign investments, investment, immigration, marketing agreements, marriage/divorce, obtaining civil documents such as birth and death certificates, patents/trademarks, copyrights, taxes, theft/fraud/embezzlement. Has practiced law since 2002 in Cozumel, Quintana Roo. Professional license number 2906420, issued on July 27, 1999.

Cancún, Quintana Roo

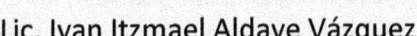

Lic. Ivan Itzmael Aldave Vázquez

Address: Boulevard Kukulkan, Manzana 52, Lote 18-12, Km. 12 J-2 Zona Hotelera, Cancún, Quintana Roo
Telephone: (998) 176-8180 / 82
Mobile: (998) 100-2007
Email: ialdave@aldaveabogados.com
Languages: Speaks Spanish and fluent English.
Specializes in: Banking/financial, civil damages, collections, contracts, corporations, foreign investments, insurance, investment, immigration, marketing agreements, marriage/divorce, patents/trademarks/copyrights, taxes. Has practiced law for 21 years, experience in Mexico City and Quintana Roo. Professional license number 1948644, issued on June 8, 1994.

Lic. Raúl Ballote Pantoja

Address: Calle 62 #313-A between Calle 35 and 37, Centro, Mérida, Yucatán, 97000
Telephone: (999) 920-2011 ext.104

Mobile: (999) 947-1832
Email: raul@raulballote.com
Languages: Speaks Spanish and full command of English. Limited French – Reading ability.
Specializes in: Contracts, corporations, foreign investments, immigration, real estate law. Certified legal Translator and Notary. Has practiced law for more than 20 years, experience in Yucatán, Campeche, and Quintana Roo. Professional license number 188243, issued on June 21, 1971. Lawyer registry number 3016, issued on March 6, 1996.

Lic. Humberto Baquedano Parra

Address: Real de Minas, Casa 8-A, Supermanzana 45, Manzana 2, lote 2, Cancún, Quintana Roo
Telephone: 998-843-5881, 998-848-0482
Mobile: 998-100-2737, 998-577-3250, 998-842-0639
Email: h_baquedano@hotmail.com
Languages: Speaks Spanish, fluent English, and French 80%.
Specializes in: Adoptions, auto/accidents, child custody, civil damages, collections, contracts, corporations, criminal law, government relations, marriage/divorce, narcotics, obtaining civil documents such as birth and death certificates, theft/fraud/embezzlement. Has practiced law for 20 years in all Yucatán Peninsula. Professional license number 2170143, issued on November 22, 2005.

Lic. Luis Miguel Ceballos Capetillo

Address: Calle 20 #203-A by 29 Street, Colonia García Ginerés, Mérida, Yucatán 97070
Phone and Fax: 999-920-1133
Mobile: 998-100-0873
Email: ceballos@racabogados.com.mx
Languages: Speaks Spanish and fluent English.
Specializes in: Contracts, corporations, criminal law, estates, foreign investments, investment, immigration, marketing agreements, obtaining civil documents such as birth and death certificates, patents/trademarks/copyrights, theft/fraud/embezzlement, notary law. Notary and Translator. Has practiced law for 13 years, experience in Campeche, Yucatán, and Quintana Roo. Professional license number 2490012, issued on 1997.

Lic. Juan José Corona Barssé

Address: Reno #45, Supermanzana 20, Manzana 20, Cancún, Quintana Roo
Telephone: 998-884-3437, 998-884-5717

Mobile: 998-100-2604
Fax: 998-884-5393
Email: jj@coronabarsse.com and jjcb@prodigy.net.mx
Languages: Speaks Spanish and fluent English.
Specializes in: Contracts, corporations, foreign investments, investment, immigration, and real estate. Notary and Translator. Has practiced law for 30 years, experience in Mexico City and Quintana Roo. Professional license number 978223, issued on May 3, 1985.

Lic. Fernando Doblado Rueda

Address: Avenida Nader #28-1, Primer Piso Edificio Popolna, Supermanzana 2, Cancún, Quintana Roo
Phone/Fax: (998) 898-0306, 998-898-1422
Email: fdr@asd.com.mx
Languages: Speaks Spanish and fluent English.
Specializes in: Aeronautical/Maritime, banking/financial, collections, contracts, corporations, foreign investments, government relations, investment, immigration, marketing agreements, patents/trademarks/copyrights, taxes, real estate. Has practiced law for 25 years in Quintana Roo. Professional license number 1402683, issued on October 9, 1989.

Lic. José Guillermo González Lomeli

Address: Seccion las Luciernagas, Supermanzana 17, Manzana 4, Lote 44, Avenida Contoy, Cancún, Quintana Roo
Telephone: (998) 884-4575
Fax: (998) 884-4531
Mobile: (998) 846-4921 and (998) 577-7398
Email: memolomeli2010@hotmail.com
Languages: Speaks Spanish, good English, and Italian.
Specializes in: Auto/accidents, child custody, contracts, corporations, criminal law, foreign investments, government relations, investment, immigration, labor relations, marriage/divorce, narcotics, obtaining civil documents such as birth and death certificates, patents/trademarks/copyrights, theft/fraud/embezzlement. Translator at court. Has practiced law for 13 years in Quintana Roo. Professional license number 4577834, issued on October 10, 2005.

Lic. Ernesto Che Gutiérrez Pérez

Address: Avenida Bonampak, Supermanzana 4, Manzana 6, lote 38-A, Office B, Cancún, Quintana Roo
Telephone: 998-892-7897
Mobile: 998-865-5999
Email: Cancun-lawyer@hotmail.com
Languages: Speaks Spanish, good English, and good French.
Specializes in: Adoptions, auto/accidents, child custody, collections, civil damages, contracts, corporations, criminal law, estates, foreign claims, foreign investments, government relations, insurance, investment, immigration, labor relations, marketing agreements, marriage/divorce, obtaining civil documents such as birth and death certificates, patents/trademarks/copyrights, taxes, theft/fraud/embezzlement, tourism law. Has practiced law for 27 years, experience in Mexico City, Puebla, Nayarit, Jalisco, Morelos, and Estado de Mexico. Professional license number 1958854, issued on July 12, 1994.

Lic. Andres Labarthe Sánchez

Address: Robalo #15, Supermanzana 3, Cancún, Quintana Roo
Telephone: 998-898-3547
Mobile: 998-100-1485
Email: alabarthe@gmail.com
Languages: Speaks Spanish and fluent English.
Specializes in: Child custody, contracts, corporations, estates, foreign claims, foreign investments, government relations, investment, immigration, labor relations, marriage/divorce, obtaining civil documents such as birth and death certificates, patents/trademarks/copyrights, taxes, trust and real estate consulting. Notary and Translator. Masters Degree in Corporate law. Has practiced law for 14 years, experience in Mexico City, San Luis Potosi, and Quintana Roo. Professional license number 2712797, issued on September 9, 1998.

Lic. José Roberto López Villa

Address: Ave. Nichupté 9 - C, Supermanzana 15, Cancún, Quintana Roo 77500
Phone/Fax: 998-884-9119
Mobile: 998-241-2879
Email: jrlopezvilla11@yahoo.com.mx
Languages: Speaks Spanish, fluent English.

Specializes in: Civil damages, contracts, corporations, criminal law, foreign investments, investment, marketing agreements, marriage/divorce, narcotics, taxes, theft/fraud/embezzlement. Can provide services as translator and notary. Has practiced law for 20 years, experience in Mexico and Panama. Professional license number 1535941, issued on January 25, 1991.

Lic. Francisco Javier Lozano Aceves

Address: Reno #34, Lote 13, Manzana 19, Supermanzana 20, Cancún, Quintana Roo, 77500
Telephone: 998-887-0350
Mobile: 998-577-2448
Email: lozanoab@prodigy.net.mx
Languages: Speaks Spanish and fluent English
Specializes in: Banking/financial, contracts, corporations, estates, foreign claims, foreign investments, government relations, investment, immigration, labor relations, marketing agreements, marriage/divorce, obtaining civil documents such as birth and death certificates, patents/trademarks/copyrights, real estate expert, time share contract cancelations. Masters Degree in Civil law. Has practiced law for 22 years, experience in Jalisco and Quintana Roo. Professional license number 1377263, issued on February 19, 1990.

Lic. Gabriel Marin González

Address: Robalo #15, Supermanzana 3, Cancún, Quintana Roo
Telephone: 998-898-3547
Mobile: 998-842-0022
Email: maringab@prodigy.net.mx
Languages: Speaks Spanish and good English.
Specializes in: Child custody, civil damages, contracts, corporations, estates, foreign claims, foreign investments, government relations, investment, immigration, labor relations, marriage/divorce, obtaining civil documents such as birth and death certificates, patents/trademarks/copyrights, taxes, trust and real estate consulting. Notary and Translator. Masters Degree in Corporate law. Has practiced law for 15 years, experience in Toluca and Quintana Roo. Professional license number 3010827, issued on July 12, 2007.

Lic. Jaime Uriel Pacheco Torres

Address: Calle 58 #526-E between Calle 55 and 57 Street, Fracc. Las Granjas, Mérida, Yucatán 97197
Telephone: (999) 941-2571

Mobile: (999)163-9602
Email: jaime0712@hotmail.com
Languages: Spanish, Limited English
Specializes in: Auto/accidents, banking/financial, contracts, corporations, criminal law, government relations, insurance, investment, patents/trademarks/copyrights, theft/fraud/embezzlement. Has practiced law for 8 years, experience in Yucatán, Campeche, Tabasco, and Quintana Roo. Professional license number 6024403, issued on June 24, 2009.

Lic. Angel Prieto Palmeros

Address: Retorno de la Paz #41, Super manzana 50, Manzana 20, Cancún, Quintana Roo 77533
Telephone: 998-251-7010, 998-872-3732
Mobile: 998-137-8545
Fax: 998-848-0020
Email: prietoangel@yahoo.com
Languages: Speaks Spanish, fluent English, and limited Portuguese.
Specializes in: Adoptions, auto/accidents, banking/financial, child custody, civil damages, collections, contracts, corporations, criminal law, estates, foreign claims, foreign investments, government relations, insurance, investment, immigration, labor relations, marketing agreements, marriage/divorce, obtaining civil documents such as birth and death certificates, patents/trademarks/copyrights, theft/fraud/embezzlement. Has practiced law for 19 years, experience in Philadelphia, Veracruz, and Quintana Roo. Professional license number 3619832, issued on August 14, 2002.

Lic. José Ignacio Puerto Gutiérrez

Address: Calle 25 #159 by 30, Colonia García Ginerés, Mérida, Yucatán 97100
Telephone: (999) 920-3050 (phone and fax)
Mobile: (999) 900-3260
Email: ipuerto@puertoypino.com
Languages: Speaks Spanish and fluent English.
Specializes in: Banking/financial, civil damages, collections, contracts, corporations, criminal law, estates, foreign investments, government relations, investment, immigration, labor relations, marketing agreements, marriage/divorce, patents/trademarks/copyrights, taxes, theft/fraud/embezzlement. Masters Degree in corporate law at Yale University in 1991. Has practiced law for 21 years in New York City, Mexico City and Yucatán. Professional license

number 1656658, issued on May 4, 1992. Lawyer registry number 2698, issued on August 17, 2000.

Lic. Mauricio Arturo Rojano Romero

Address: Super Manzana 27, Manzana 1, Lotes 7 and 8, Avenida Palenque by Xpuhil, Edificio Nerja, Apt. 11, Cancún, Quintana Roo
Telephone: (998) 884-8542
Fax: (998) 884-0678
Mobile: (999) 910-0464
Email: rojano@racabogados.com.mx
Languages: Speaks Spanish and fluent English.
Specializes in: Contracts, corporations, criminal law, estates, foreign investments, immigration, marketing agreements, investment, obtaining civil documents such as birth and death certificates, patents/trademarks/copyrights, theft/fraud/embezzlement, notary law. Has practiced law for 15 years in Yucatán, Campeche and Quintana Roo. Professional license number 2170137, issued on September 26, 1995.

Lic. Luis Alfredo Francisco Ramirez García

Address: Mojarra 2, Super Manzana 3, Cancún, Quintana Roo
Telephone: (998) 884-1406, 887-2416
Fax: (998) 884-1406
Mobile: (998) 897-1552
Email: luisalfredoramirez@hotmail.com
Languages: Speaks Spanish and good English.
Specializes in: Contracts, corporations, criminal law, investments, immigration, marriage/divorce, theft/fraud/embezzlement, time share contract cancelation. Has practiced law for more than 33 years in Mexico City and Quintana Roo. Professional license number 411355, issued on September 8, 1976.

Lic. Eutiquio Alejandro Salas Castillo

Address: Calle Venado #25, Supermanzana. 20-M, Manazana 19, Edif. 2, Planta Baja, Cancún, Quintana Roo
Telephone: (998) 887-7065, 887-8983
Fax: (998) 884-1053
Mobile: (998) 845-8841
Email: esalas@solissalasabogados.com

Languages: Speaks Spanish and good English.

Specializes in: Adoptions, banking/financial, child custody, civil damages, collections, contracts, corporations, criminal law, foreign claims, foreign investments, insurance, investment, immigration, labor relations, marriage/divorce, obtaining civil documents such as birth and death certificates, patents/trademarks/copyrights. Has practiced law for 14 years in Yucatán and Quintana Roo. Professional license number 2490031, issued on June 23, 1997.

Lic. Patricio de la Peña Ruiz de Chávez

Address: Calle Granada #30, SM 2-A, Cancún, Quintana Roo
Phone: 998-887-9368
Mobile: 998-147-1603
Fax: 998-887-9368
Email: ppr@salasconsultores.com, ppr@dlpytrujillo.com
Languages: Speaks Spanish and good English

Specializes in: Civil damages, corporations, criminal law, labor relations, marriage/divorce, obtaining civil documents such as birth and death certificates. Has practiced law for nine years in Nuevo Leon and Quintana Roo. Professional license number 5311673, issued on October 24, 2007.

Lic. Augusto Rivero Bolio

Address: AVENIDA Tulum #49 and #51, int. 101, SM.22, Centro. Cancún, Quintana Roo
Telephone: (998) 251-2553
Fax: (998) 251-2553
Mobile: (998) 136-3273
Email: augustorb@hotmail.com, *cancelyourtimeshare@hotmail.com*
Languages: Speaks Spanish and fluent English.

Specializes in: Auto/accidents, collections, contracts, corporations, criminal law, foreign claims, foreign investments, Government relations, insurance, investment, immigration, marketing agreements, obtaining civil documents such as birth and death certificates. Has practiced law for 12 years in Nuevo Leon and Quintana Roo. Professional license number 2770690, issued on November 24, 1998.

ATTORNEYS & PUBLIC NOTARIES

Playa del Carmen, Quintana Roo

Lic. Raúl Ballote Pantoja

Address: Calle 62 #313-A between Calle 35 and 37, Centro, Mérida, Yucatán, 97000
Telephone: (999) 920-2011 ext.104
Mobile: (999) 947-1832
Email: raul@raulballote.com
Languages: Speaks Spanish and Full command of English. Limited French – Reading ability.
Specializes in: Contracts, corporations, foreign investments, immigration, real estate law. Certified legal Translator and Notary. Has practiced law for more than 20 years, experience in Yucatán, Campeche, and Quintana Roo. Professional license number 188243, issued on June 21, 1971. Lawyer registry number 3016, issued on March 6, 1996.

Lic. Nadia Boone Oviedo

Address: Paseo Tulum, Manzana 19, Lote 8, Oficina 45. Playacar Fase II, Playa del Carmen, Quintana Roo
Phone and Fax: 984-879-3880
Mobile: 984-115-4162
Email: nadiaboone@hotmail.com
Languages: Speaks Spanish, fluent English, and French.
Specializes in: Auto/accidents, civil damages, collections, contracts, corporations, criminal law, estates, foreign investments, government relations, investment, immigration, labor relations, marketing agreements, marriage/divorce, obtaining civil documents such as birth and death certificates, theft/fraud/embezzlement. Has practiced law for 9 years, experience in Mexico City, Monterrey, and Quintana Roo. Professional license number 5089182, issued on March 12, 2007.

Lic. Javier Camou Bórquez

Address: Fuente de Los Angeles, Lote 20, Supermanzana 56, Manzana 1, Residencial Sante Fe del Carmen, Playa del Carmen, Quintana Roo, 77711
Telephone: 984-109-3430
Mobile: 984-876-2901
Fax: 984-109-1274
Email: javier.camou@quintanaroo.com
Languages: Speaks Spanish and fluent English.

Specializes in: Auto/accidents, civil damages, contracts, corporations, criminal law, foreign investments, investment, marriage/divorce, taxes, theft/fraud/embezzlement. Has practiced law for 11 years, experience in Sonora, Sinaloa, Chihuahua, and Quintana Roo. Professional license number 3300098, issued on March 5, 2001

Lic. Fernando Doblado Rueda

Address: Avenida 10 Norte #345, between Calle Calle 30 and 32 Street, Playa del Carmen, Quintana Roo
Phone/Fax: (984) 803-0326, 984-803-0133
Email: antonella@asd.com.mx
Languages: Speaks Spanish and fluent English.
Specializes in: Aeronautical/Maritime, banking/financial, collections, contracts, corporations, foreign investments, government relations, investment, immigration, marketing agreements, patents/trademarks/copyrights, taxes, real estate. Has practiced law for 25 years in Quintana Roo. Professional license number 1402683, issued on October 9, 1989.

Lic. José Antonio Faller Espinosa

Address: Calle 34 #36, by 20 Avenida Norte, Fraccionamiento Tohoku, Playa del Carmen, Quintana Roo
Telephone: 984-879-3307
Mobile: 998-116-4736
Fax: 984-879-3306
Email: faller58@prodigy.net.mx
Languages: Speaks Spanish and fluent English.
Specializes in: Banking/financial, contracts, corporations, estates, government relations, insurance, investment, immigration, labor relations, obtaining civil documents such as birth and death certificates, taxes, real estate law, title insurance. Has practiced law for 20 years, experience in Yucatán and Quintana Roo. Professional license number 2000355, issued on July 28, 1994.

Lic. José Enrique Faller Espinosa

Address: Calle 34 #36, by 20 Avenida Norte, Fraccionamiento Tohoku, Playa del Carmen, Quintana Roo
Telephone: 984-879-3307
Mobile: 984-115-0414
Fax: 984-879-3306

Email: faller58@prodigy.net.mx
Languages: Speaks Spanish and fluent English.
Specializes in: Adoptions, banking/financial, contracts, corporations, estates, foreign investments, government relations, insurance, investment, immigration, labor relations, obtaining civil documents such as birth and death certificates, taxes, real estate law, title insurance. Has practiced law for 20 years, experience in Yucatán and Quintana Roo. Professional license number 2000356, issued on July 28, 1994.

Lic. José Guillermo González Lomeli

Address: Seccion las Luciernagas, Supermanzana 17, Manzana 4, Lote 44, Avenida Contoy, Cancún, Quintana Roo
Telephone: (998) 884-4575
Fax: (998) 884-4531
Mobile: (998) 846-4921 and (998) 577-7398
Email: memolomeli2010@hotmail.com
Languages: Speaks Spanish, good English, and Italian.
Specializes in: Auto/accidents, child custody, contracts, corporations, criminal law, foreign investments, government relations, investment, immigration, labor relations, marriage/divorce, narcotics, obtaining civil documents such as birth and death certificates, patents/trademarks/copyrights, theft/fraud/embezzlement. Translator at court. Has practiced law for 13 years in Quintana Roo. Professional license number 4577834, issued on October 10, 2005.

Lic. Angel Prieto Palmeros

Address: Retorno de la Paz #41, Super manzana 50, Manzana 20, Cancún, Quintana Roo 77533
Telephone: 998-251-7010, 998-872-3732
Mobile: 998-137-8545
Fax: 998-848-0020
Email: prietoangel@yahoo.com
Languages: Speaks Spanish, fluent English, and limited Portuguese.
Specializes in: Adoptions, auto/accidents, banking/financial, child custody, civil damages, collections, contracts, corporations, criminal law, estates, foreign claims, foreign investments, government relations, insurance, investment, immigration, labor relations, marketing agreements, marriage/divorce, obtaining civil documents such as birth and death certificates, patents/trademarks/copyrights, theft/fraud/embezzlement. Has practiced law

for 19 years, experience in Philadelphia, Veracruz, and Quintana Roo. Professional license number 3619832, issued on August 14, 2002.

Lic. José Ignacio Puerto Gutiérrez

Address: Calle 25 #159 by 30, Colonia García Ginerés, Mérida, Yucatán 97100
Telephone: (999) 920-3050 (phone and fax)
Mobile: (999) 900-3260
Email: ipuerto@puertoypino.com
Languages: Speaks Spanish and fluent English.
Specializes in: Banking/financial, civil damages, collections, contracts, corporations, criminal law, estates, foreign investments, government relations, investment, immigration, labor relations, marketing agreements, marriage/divorce, patents/trademarks/copyrights, taxes, theft/fraud/embezzlement. Masters Degree in corporate law at Yale University in 1991. Has practiced law for 21 years in New York City, Mexico City and Yucatán. Professional license number 1656658, issued on May 4, 1992. Lawyer registry number 2698, issued on August 17, 2000.

Lic. Eutiquio Alejandro Salas Castillo

Address: 30 Avenida Norte s/n, by Calle 6 Norte, Altos #2, Playa del Carmen, Quintana Roo
Phone/Fax: (984) 803-2634
Mobile: (998) 845-8841
Email: esalas@solissalasabogados.com
Languages: Speaks Spanish and good English.
Specializes in: Adoptions, banking/financial, child custody, civil damages, collections, contracts, corporations, criminal law, foreign claims, foreign investments, insurance, investment, immigration, labor relations, marriage/divorce, obtaining civil documents such as birth and death certificates, patents/trademarks/copyrights. Has practiced law for 14 years in Yucatán and Quintana Roo. Professional license number 2490031, issued on June 23, 1997.

Lic. Patricio de la Peña Ruiz de Chávez

Address: Calle Granada #30, SM 2-A, Cancún, Quintana Roo
Phones: 998-887-9368
Mobile: 998-147-1603
Fax: 998-887-9368
Email: ppr@salasconsultores.com , ppr@dlpytrujillo.com

Languages: Speaks Spanish and good English
Specializes in: Civil damages, corporations, criminal law, labor relations, marriage/divorce, obtaining civil documents such as birth and death certificates. Has practiced law for nine years in Nuevo Leon and Quintana Roo. Professional license number 5311673, issued on October 24, 2007.

Chetumal, Quintana Roo

Lic. Raúl Ballote Pantoja

Address: Calle 62 #313-A between Calle 35 and 37 Street, Centro, Mérida, Yucatán 97000
Telephone: (999) 920-2011 ext.104
Mobile: (999) 947-1832
Email: raul@raulballote.com
Languages: Speaks Spanish and Full command of English. Limited French – Reading ability.
Specializes in: Contracts, corporations, foreign investments, immigration, real estate law. Certified legal Translator and Notary. Has practiced law for more than 20 years, experience in Yucatán, Campeche, and Quintana Roo. Professional license number 188243, issued on June 21, 1971. Lawyer registry number 3016, issued on March 6, 1996.

Lic. Humberto Baquedano Parra

Address: Real de Minas, Casa 8-A, Supermanzana 45, Manzana 2, lote 2, Cancún, Quintana Roo
Telephone: 998-843-5881, 998-848-0482
Mobile: 998-100-2737, 998-577-3250, 998-842-0639
Email: h_baquedano@hotmail.com
Languages: Speaks Spanish, fluent English, and French 80%.
Specializes in: Adoptions, auto/accidents, child custody, civil damages, collections, contracts, corporations, criminal law, government relations, marriage/divorce, narcotics, obtaining civil documents such as birth and death certificates, theft/fraud/embezzlement. Has practiced law for 20 years in all Yucatán Peninsula. Professional license number 2170143, issued on November 22, 2005.

Lic. José Guillermo González Lomeli

Address: Seccion las Luciernagas, Supermanzana 17, Manzana 4, Lote 44, Avenida Contoy, Cancún, Quintana Roo
Telephone: (998) 884-4575
Fax: (998) 884-4531

Mobile: (998) 846-4921 and (998) 577-7398
Email: memolomeli2010@hotmail.com
Languages: Speaks Spanish, good English, and Italian.
Specializes in: Auto/accidents, child custody, contracts, corporations, criminal law, foreign investments, government relations, investment, immigration, labor relations, marriage/divorce, narcotics, obtaining civil documents such as birth and death certificates, patents/trademarks/copyrights, theft/fraud/embezzlement. Translator at court. Has practiced law for 13 years in Quintana Roo. Professional license number 4577834, issued on October 10, 2005.

Campeche, Quintana Roo

Lic. Jaime Uriel Pacheco Torres

Address: Calle 58 #526-E between Calle 55 and 57 Street, Fracc. Las Granjas, Mérida, Yucatán 97197
Telephone: (999) 941-2571
Mobile: (999)163-9602
Email: jaime0712@hotmail.com
Languages: Spanish, Limited English
Specializes in: Auto/accidents, banking/financial, contracts, corporations, criminal law, government relations, insurance, investment, patents/trademarks/copyrights, theft/fraud/embezzlement. Has practiced law for 8 years, experience in Yucatán, Campeche, Tabasco, and Quintana Roo. Professional license number 6024403, issued on June 24, 2009.

Lic. José Ignacio Puerto Gutiérrez

Address: Calle 25 #159 by 30, Colonia García Ginerés, Mérida, Yucatán 97100
Telephone: (999) 920-3050 (phone and fax)
Mobile: (999) 900-3260
Email: ipuerto@puertoypino.com
Languages: Speaks Spanish and fluent English.
Specializes in: Banking/financial, civil damages, collections, contracts, corporations, criminal law, estates, foreign investments, government relations, investment, immigration, labor relations, marketing agreements, marriage/divorce, patents/trademarks/copyrights, taxes, theft/fraud/embezzlement. Masters Degree in corporate law at Yale University in 1991. Has practiced law for 21 years in New York City, Mexico City and Yucatán. Professional license

number 1656658, issued on May 4, 1992. Lawyer registry number 2698, issued on August 17, 2000.

If you have additional questions, contact the appropriate division of the Office of Citizens Services at:

Department of State
SA-29, Fourth
2201 C Street NW
Washington, D.C. 20520
Telephone: (202) 647-5226

Important Notice:

The Editor and authors assume no responsibility or liability for the professional ability or reputation of, or the quality of services provided by, the preceding persons or firms. The list above was made available by the U.S. State Department, which compiled it.

20   Doctors

As a new resident of Mérida, one of the great surprises you will find is the excellent number of doctors available. What's more, you will be taken aback at the "bedside" manner of Yucatecan physicians. The level of caring is astounding, and the level of human interaction is, for most Americans, exceptional. From my own experience, I can tell you that housecalls, follow-up visits and consultations by phone after an office visit are considered normal in Mexico. A physician will go out of his way to drop by your home to make sure you're doing fine, as a courtesy. A call in the middle of the night will be answered, and if necessary, the doctor will drive over to see you.

The professionalism and personal courtesies are sincere, and wonderful. Part of it, of course, is the nature of Latin American culture, where there is a greater emphasis on personal relationships. The other aspect, of course, is the pride and seriousness with which doctors and physicians view their profession in Latin America: They are here to provide an essential service to the community, and to do so honorably. Many Americans I know in town time and again tell me wonderful things about their doctors here, and my experience has been nothing short of exceptional.

This is a list of doctors and physicians that have complied with requirements set by the State Department in Washington, DC for being recommended to Americans living in Mérida. It is by no means exhaustive, and you are always well advised to ask others for recommendations, but here is a good starting list for your consideration.

Doctors listed by Specialties

GENERAL PRACTITIONERS

Dr. Humberto Angulo Cortés, (Eng 50% /Spa); **Telephone:** (999) 926-3078. CENTRO MÉDICO LAS AMÉRICAS. Calle 54 #365, by Avenida Pérez Ponce, Centro, Mérida

Dr. Eduardo Mena Arana, (No Eng); **Telephone:** (999) 925-8233. CLÍNICA DE MÉRIDA, Avenida Itzáes #242, Colonia García Ginerés, Mérida

ALLERGISTS

Dr. Jorge Carlos Bolaños Ancona, (Eng 50%); **Telephone:** (999) 925-8385. CLÍNICA DE MÉRIDA, Avenida Itzáes #242, Colonia García Ginerés, Mérida

CARDIOLOGISTS

Dr. Sergio A. Villareal Umana, (Eng / Spa); **Telephone:** (999) 926-6348. EDIFICIO ANEXO (CENTRO MÉDICO LAS AMÉRICAS). Calle 54 #365, by Avenida Pérez Ponce, First Floor C Room 9, Centro, Mérida

Dr. David Arjona Canto, (Eng / Spa); **Telephone:** (999) 925-4487. CLÍNICA DE MÉRIDA, Avenida Itzáes #242, Colonia García Ginerés, Mérida

Dr. Joaquin Jimenez Noh, (Eng / Spa); **Telephone:** (999) 925-4976. CLÍNICA DE MÉRIDA, Avenida Itzáes #242, Colonia García Ginerés, Mérida

Dr. Salvador Padilla Morales, (Eng / Spa); **Telephone:** (999) 926-2367. CENTRO MÉDICO LAS AMÉRICAS. Calle 54 #365, by Avenida Pérez Ponce, Centro, Mérida

Dr. Carlos Wabi Dogre, (Eng / Spa); **Telephone:** (999) 925-6255. CLÍNICA DE MÉRIDA, Avenida Itzáes #242, Colonia García Ginerés, Mérida

DERMATOLOGISTS

Dr. Roger Enrique Pérez Pérez, (Eng / Spa); **Telephone:** (999) 925-9976. CLÍNICA DE MÉRIDA, Avenida Itzáes #242, Colonia García Ginerés, Mérida

Dra. María Rosa Rivero Vallado, (No Eng); **Telephone:** (999) 925-8406. CLÍNICA DE MÉRIDA, Avenida Itzáes #242, Colonia García Ginerés, Mérida

DENTISTS

Dr. Carlos Alayola Montañez Orthodontics Specialist, (Eng / Spa); **Telephone:** (999) 923-5380 928-5939. Calle 60 #387-B by Calle 43, Centro, Mérida

Dr. Javier Cámara Patrón, (Eng / Spa); **Telephone:** (999) 925-3399. Calle 17 #170 by Calle 8 and 10 Street, Colonia García Ginerés, Mérida

Dr. Rolando Peniche Marcín, (Eng / Spa); **Telephone:** (999) 926-4434. CENTRO MÉDICO LAS AMÉRICAS. Calle 54 #365, by Avenida Pérez Ponce, Centro, Mérida

Dra. Ana Leticia Morales Vera, (Eng / Spa); **Telephone:** (999) 928-6810. Calle 6 #489 by Calle 17 and 19 Street, Colonia GARCÍA GINERÉS, Mérida

DOCTORS

Dr. Rafael Alonso Dominguez, (Eng / Spa); **Telephone:** (999) 920-2461. CENTRO ESTETICO ODONTOLOGICO. Avenida Cupules #74. POR 6 & 8 Colonia García Ginerés, Mérida

ENDOCRINOLOGISTS

Dr. Hugo Laviada Molina, (Eng / Spa); **Telephone:** (999) 925-8233. CLÍNICA DE MÉRIDA, Avenida Itzáes #242, Colonia García Ginerés, Mérida

Dr. Mario Barrero Estrada, (No Eng); **Telephone:** (999) 920-1037. CENTRO MÉDICO PENSIONES, AVENIDA BARRERA VÁZQUEZ #215-A, Colonia Pensiones, Mérida

GASTROENTEROLOGISTS

Dr. Francisco Rivero Maldonado, (No Eng); **Telephone:** (999) 925-4776. CLÍNICA DE MÉRIDA, Avenida Itzáes #242, Colonia García Ginerés, Mérida

GENERAL SURGERY

Dr. Miguel Fernandez Martínez, (Eng / Spa); **Telephone:** (999) 943-7070. STAR MÉDICA, Calle 26 #199 between Calle 15 and 7 Street, FRACC. Altabrisa. 404, Mérida

Dr. Luis Alberto Navarrete Jaimes, (Eng / Spa); **Telephone:** (999) 920-0949. CLÍNICA DE MÉRIDA, Avenida Itzáes #242, Colonia García Ginerés, Mérida

GYNECOLOGISTS

Dra. Catalina Aldana de Mendez, (Eng / Spa); **Telephone:** (999) 943-2694. STAR MÉDICA, Calle 26 #199 between Calle 15 and 7 Street, FRACC. Altrabrisa. Mérida

Dr. Manuel Mendez Arceo, (Eng / Spa); **Telephone:** (999) 943-1344. STAR MÉDICA, Calle 26 #199 between Calle 15 and 7 Street, FRACC. Altabrisa, Mérida

Dr. José Pereira Carcano, (Eng / Spa); **Telephone:** (999) 925-6819. CLÍNICA DE MÉRIDA, Avenida Itzáes #242, Colonia García Ginerés, Mérida

Dr. Luis Jesús Rodriguez Bolio, (Eng / Spa); **Telephone:** (999) 925-3998. CLÍNICA DE MÉRIDA, Avenida Itzáes #242, Colonia García Ginerés, Mérida

INTERNAL MEDICINE

Dr. Sergio A. Villareal Umana, (Eng / Spa); **Telephone:** (999) 926-6348. EDIFICIO ANEXO (CENTRO MÉDICO LAS AMÉRICAS). Calle 54 #365, by Avenida Pérez Ponce, Centro, Mérida

Dr. Antonio Briceño Vargas, (Eng / Spa); **Telephone:** (999) 925-0868. CLÍNICA DE MÉRIDA, Avenida Itzáes #242, Colonia García Ginerés, Mérida

NEUROLOGISTS

Dr. Ruben Dario Vargas García, (Eng / Spa); **Telephone:** (999) 925-7508. CLÍNICA DE MÉRIDA, Avenida Itzáes #242, Colonia García Ginerés, Mérida

ONCOLOGISTS

Dr. Delio Ceballos Bojorquez, (Eng / Spa); **Telephone:** (999) 925-8333 and (999) 925-5499. CLÍNICA DE MÉRIDA, Avenida Itzáes #242, Colonia García Ginerés, Mérida

OPHTHALMOLOGISTS

Dr. Adolfo Baqueiro Díaz, (Eng /Spa); **Telephone:** (999) 925-3253. CLÍNICA DE MÉRIDA, Avenida Itzáes #242, Colonia García Ginerés, Mérida

Dr. Alberto Cáceres Peniche, (Eng /Spa); **Telephone:** (999) 925-4152. CLÍNICA DE MÉRIDA, Avenida Itzáes #242, Colonia García Ginerés, Mérida

Dr. Alejandro Millet Molina, (Eng /Spa); **Telephone:** (999) 925-6944. CLÍNICA DE MÉRIDA, Avenida Itzáes #242, Colonia García Ginerés, Mérida

ORTHOPEDISTS

Dr. Luis Mario Baeza Mezquita, (Eng /Spa); **Telephone:** (999) 926-2154. CENTRO MÉDICO LAS AMÉRICAS. Calle 54 #365, by Avenida Pérez Ponce, Centro, Mérida

Dr. Felipe Eduardo Camara Arrigunaga, (Eng / Spa); **Telephone:** (999) 943-6202 and (999) 43-7202. STAR MÉDICA, Calle 26 #199 between Calle 15 and 7 Street, FRACC. Altabrisa, Mérida

Dr. Herbe Rivero Maldonado, (Eng / Spa); **Telephone:** (999) 920-1658. CLÍNICA DE MÉRIDA, Avenida Itzáes #242, Colonia García Ginerés, Mérida

Dr. Eduardo Muñoz Menéndez, (Eng / Spa); **Telephone:** (999) 925-4865. CLÍNICA DE MÉRIDA, Avenida Itzáes #242, Colonia García Ginerés, Mérida

Dr. Javier Pasos Novelo, (Eng / Spa); **Telephone:** (999) 926-2009. CENTRO MÉDICO LAS AMÉRICAS. Calle 54 #365, by Avenida Pérez Ponce, Centro, Mérida

OTORRINOLARINGOLOGISTS

Dr. Miguel Baquedano Sauri, (Eng / Spa); **Telephone:** (999) 925-5034. CENTRO ESPECIALIDADES MEDICAS, Calle 60 #329-B by Calle 35 and Avenida Colón, Mérida

Dr. Juan José Castellanos Dorbecker, (Eng / Spa); **Telephone:** (999) 943-2991. STAR MÉDICA, Calle 26 #199 between Calle 15 and 17 Street, FRACC. Altabrisa, Mérida

Dr. Sergio Ivan Díaz Esquivel, (No Eng); **Telephone:** (999) 926-4278. CENTRO MÉDICO LAS AMÉRICAS. Calle 54 #365, by Avenida Pérez Ponce, Centro, Mérida

PEDIATRICIANS

Dr. Gregorio Cetina Sauri, (Eng / Spa); **Telephone:** (999) 925-7056. MEDICA ITZÁES ESPECIALIDADES, Avenida Itzáes #252 by Calle 29, Mérida

Dr. Carlos Lara Navarrete, (No Eng); **Telephone:** (999) 926-2920. CENTRO MÉDICO LAS AMÉRICAS. Calle 54 #365, by Avenida Pérez Ponce, Centro, Mérida

Dr. Enrique Ortegón Ruiz, (Eng / Spa); **Telephone:** (999) 925-9944. CLÍNICA DE MÉRIDA, Avenida Itzáes #242, Colonia García Ginerés, Mérida

PNEUMOLOGISTS

Dr. Nicolas Hernandez Flores, (Eng / Spa); **Telephone:** (999) 925-8218. CLÍNICA DE MÉRIDA, Avenida Itzáes #242, Colonia García Ginerés, Mérida

Dr. Javier Torre Bolio, (Eng / Spa); **Telephone:** (999) 926-8589. CENTRO MÉDICO LAS AMÉRICAS. Calle 54 #365, by Avenida Pérez Ponce, Centro, Mérida

PSYCHIATRISTS

Dr. Roberto Carrillo Ruiz, (Eng / Spa); **Telephone:** (999) 944-7347. Calle 15 #251-1 between Calle 36 and 38 Street, FRACC. Campestre. Mérida

Dr. Arsenio Rosado Franco, (Eng / Spa); **Telephone:** (999) 920-1644. Avenida Colón #199A by Calle 24, Colonia García Ginerés, Mérida

UROLOGISTS

Dr. Jorge Carlos Aviles Rosado, (Eng / Spa); **Telephone:** (999) 926-2745. CENTRO MÉDICO LAS AMÉRICAS. Calle 54 #365, by Avenida Pérez Ponce, Centro, Mérida

Dr. Jorge Navarrete Fernandez, (Eng / Spa); **Telephone:** (999) 920-1986. CLÍNICA DE MÉRIDA, Avenida Itzáes #242, Colonia García Ginerés, Mérida

MEDICAL EMERGENCIES

Dr. Juan José Falcón Arias, (Eng 50% /Spa); **Telephone:** (999) 920-4040, EXT 116. CENTRO ESPECIALIDADES MEDICAS, Calle 60 #329-B by Calle35 and Avenida Colón, Colonia García Ginerés, Mérida

> **Important Notice:**
> The Editor and authors assume no responsibility or liability for the professional ability or reputation of, or the quality of services provided by, the preceding doctors and physicians. The list above was made available by the U.S. State Department, which compiled it.

> From the State Department, general overview of health insurance questions for Americans overseas:
>
> **Where can I find a list of physicians in the country I plan to visit?**
>
> - For detailed information on physicians abroad, the authoritative reference is The Official ABMS Directory of Board Certified Medical Specialists, published for the American Board of Medical Specialists and its certifying member boards.
> - U.S. embassies and consulates abroad maintain lists of hospitals and physicians, many of which are posted on the embassy or consulate web site.

21 Schools, Colleges, Universities and Research Centers

The city of Mérida has 244 preschool institutions, 395 elementary, 136 Junior High School (2 years middle school, 1 high), 97 High Schools and 26 Universities/Higher Education facilities and research centers.

As a result, Mérida has emerged as an educational powerhouse in southeastern Mexico. It's not uncommon to find students from other states, particularly from neighboring Quintana Roo, but also foreign countries enrolled in schools here. There are students from Cuba, Costa Rica, Venezuela, Belize as well as post-graduate research students from the United States, Canada, the United Kingdom, Spain, Italy and Korea enrolled in the city's schools.

An increasing number of American and Canadian expatriates are moving to Mérida with their school-age children, or are having children (American-Mexicans!) here. And, of course, a good number of young adults are pursuing college and graduate-level courses, which is a phenomenon that is contributing to the diversity of campus life in Mérida. What follows is a list of schools that have expatriate students enrolled.

Schools, Kindergarten through High School (Preparatorias)

American School

Phone: (999) 941-9371
Address: Calle 3B #244, between Calle 20 and 18 Street
Colonia Xcumpich
Levels: Kinder and Primaria

Centro Educativo Palmerston

Phone: (999) 944-5457
Address: Calle 21 #144
Levels: Kinder, Primaria

Centro Educativo Renacimiento (CER)

Phone: (999) 944-4808
Address: Calle 33 #468, between Calle 10 and 14 Street
Fraccionamiento Montebello
Levels: Primaria, Secundaria and Preparatoria
Website:
www.cerenacimiento.edu.mx

Colegio Americano

Phone: (999) 928-5509

Address: Calle 72 #499, between Calle 59 and 61 Street
Centro
Levels: Primaria, Secundaria and Preparatoria
Website: www.americanomerida.edu.mx

Colegio Iberoamericano de Mérida, A.C.

Phone: (999) 925-2712 and (999) 925-3112
Address: Avenida Colón #196-A, between Calle 12 and 14 Street
Colonia García Ginerés
Levels: Kinder, Primaria, Secundaria, Preparatoria
Website: www.iberoMérida.com

Colegio Peninsular Roger's Hall

Phone: (999) 944-5364
Address: Calle 21 #131 (a short distance street from Office Depot)
Levels: Kinder, Primaria, Secundaria, Preparatoria

Educrea

Phone: (999) 925-7931
Address: Calle 23 #209, between Calle 30 Street and Avenida Itzáes
Levels: Kinder, Primaria, Secundaria, Preparatoria
Website: www.educrea.com.mx

Escuela Modelo

Phone: (999) 927-9833 and (999) 927-9944
Address: Calle 56-A #444 (Paseo de Montejo)
Levels: Primaria, Secundaria and Preparatoria
Website: www.modelo.edu.mx

Instituto Cumbres (for Boys)

Phone: (999) 944-4090
Address: Calle 5 by Calle 18 S/N ("S/N" stands for "Sin Número," or "without a number") Glorieta Cumbres
Levels: Primaria, Secundaria, Preparatoria

M.J. International

Phone: (999) 984-3939
Address: Calle 66 #618-C, between Calle 77 and 79 Street
Levels: Kinder, Primaria

Saint Patrick's

Phone: (999) 948-0985
Address: Calle 31 #144
Colonia Mexico
Levels: Kinder

Centro Educativo Piaget, A.C.

Calle 33 #140, between Calle 20 and 22 Street
Colonia Chuburná.
Levels: Kinder, Primaria, Secundaria and Preparatoria
Website: www.piaget.edu.mx/index2.htm

SCHOOLS, COLLEGES, UNIVERSITIES AND RESEARCH CENTERS

These are state institutions offering higher education

Universidad Autónoma de Yucatán (UADY)
Escuela Superior de Artes de Yucatán (ESAY)
Instituto Tecnológico de Mérida (ITM)
Universidad Tecnológica Metropolitana (UTM)
Universidad Pedagógica Nacional
Escuela Normal Superior de Yucatán (ENSY)
Universidad Nacional Autónoma de México (UNAM)

These are the more important private institutions for higher education

Centro de Estudios Superiores CTM (CESCTM)
Colegio de Negocios Internacionales (CNI)
Universidad Anáhuac Mayab
Universidad Marista
Universidad Modelo
Universidad Interemericana para el Desarrollo (UNID)
Centro Educativo Latino (CEL)
Universidad Interamericana del Norte
Centro Universitario Interamericano(Inter)
Universidad Mesoamericana de San Agustin (UMSA)
Centro de Estudios de las Américas, A.C. (CELA)
Universidad del Valle de Mexico (UVM)
Instituto de Ciencias Sociales de Mérida (ICSMAC)
Universidad Popular Autónoma de Puebla, Plantel Mérida (UPAEP Mérida)

Mérida has several national research centers of renown. They include—

Centro de Investigacíón Científica de Yucatán (CICY)
Centro de Investigaciones Regionales Dr. Hideyo Noguchi, dependent on the UADY, which conducts biological and biomedical research.

SCHOOLS, COLLEGES, UNIVERSITIES AND RESEARCH CENTERS

Centro INAH Yucatán, dedicated to anthropological, archaeological and historical research and preservation.
Centro de Investigacion y de Estudios Avanzados CINVESTAV/IPN

22   Nutrition, Yoga & Personal Trainers

Do you recall that it was mentioned that the median temperature in the Yucatán peninsula was hotter than it is in the Arabian peninsula?

If you don't, then think about it now. It can be hot, and that means that your diet and nutrition needs to reflect the reality of living in the tropics. Unless you are moving to Mérida from Hawaii, the Desert cities near Death Valley in California, the American Southwest or South Florida, there is no place in the United States that compares with the heat in this part of the world.

This is simply the way it is, and it probably requires a few lifestyle changes for you, from being more conscious of drinking more fluids, to changing your exercise regime to early morning or late afternoons, evenings or nights. It also means you have to eat more fruits and vegetables, and refrain from indulging in as much alcohol, tobacco and fatty foods as you might otherwise be used to consuming.

A good recommendation, of course, is to have a complete physical once a year, and to tell your regular physician of the

Acclimatization

Acclimatization is the physiologic and psychological adjustment to a new environment. In terms of heat acclimatization, this can be something as dramatic as moving from a cool, dry climate to a hot, humid one, or simply adjusting from spring to summer.

Some of the physiologic adaptations during heat acclimatization include: reduced heart rate, core temperature, and utilization of muscle glycogen, as well as increased blood flow to the skin, plasma volume, and work time until exhaustion. Well-conditioned athletes have a higher heat tolerance than sedentary people, as regular exercise creates "internal heat stress" and thus pre-acclimatizes athletes to some degree.

Heat acclimatization usually takes 10 to 14 days, although 75% of the adaptations are believed to occur within the first five days. Exercise sessions during the acclimatization process should be shorter and less intense, gradually building up to normal by the end of the two week period.

Source: www.personalbestnutrition.com

heat in Mérida, so he or she can make any necessary adjustments to the medications, if any, that you take.

In recent years, "wellness retreats" in Yucatán have focused on nutrition and improving one's quality of eating and lifestyle choices. "Boot camp" retreats that help to detoxify the body and teach you how to eat again have grown in popularity. One leading American nutritionist from San Diego conducts intensive two-week retreats where participants learn to become reacquainted with their bodies, food, think about nutrition as part of their daily lives and adopt habits that improve one's health, well-being and psychological outlook on life.

As a new resident of Mérida, in addition to that what has been discussed, there's something to be said for following the advice offered by the U.S. government to U.S. citizens. If you are not familiar with the MyPyramid program, here is nutritional advice from the U.S. Government:

MyPyramid Tracker

MyPyramid Tracker is an online dietary and physical activity assessment tool that provides information on your diet quality, physical activity status, related nutrition messages, and links to nutrient and physical activity information. The Food Calories/Energy Balance feature automatically calculates your energy balance by subtracting the energy you expend from physical activity from your food calories/energy intake. Use of this tool helps you better understand your energy balance status and enhances the link between good nutrition and regular physical activity. Keep track of your energy balance history and view it up to one year. MyPyramid Tracker translates the principles of the 2005 Dietary Guidelines for Americans and other nutrition standards developed by the U.S. Departments of Agriculture and Health and Human Services.

Go to the website listed below for a tutorial on MyPyramid Tracker:
www.mypyramid.gov/tracker/trackertutorial.html

Assess Your Food Intake

The online dietary assessment provides information on your diet quality, related nutrition messages, and links to nutrient information. After providing a day's worth of dietary information, you will receive an overall evaluation by comparing the amounts of food you ate to current nutritional guidance. To give you a better understanding of your diet over time, you can track what you eat up to a year.

Go to the website listed below to assess your food intake:
www.mypyramidtracker.gov/Default.aspx?Module=3

Assess your physical activity

The physical activity assessment evaluates your physical activity status and provides related energy expenditure information and educational messages. After providing a day's worth of physical activity information, you will receive an overall "score" for your physical activities that looks at the types and duration of each physical activity you did and then compares this score to the physical activity recommendation for health. A score over several days or up to a year gives a better picture of your physical activity lifestyle over time.

Go to the website listed below to assess your food intake:
www.mypyramidtracker.gov/Default.aspx?Module=4

Once you have an idea of where you stand on the MyPyramid stands, you will be in a better position to think about your nutrition and what you need to do to be healthy.

The great thing about Mérida is that if offers a wide variety of gyms, from a no-frills place with antiquated equipment, something straight out of a movie about boxers and boxing in the 1950s, to state-of-the-art facilities that offer cappuccinos and espresso bar at the coffee station, along with yoga and massage services. A good number of expatriates were members of gyms back home, and many others find that joining now is not only much more affordable, but less intimidating that the health clubs in the U.S.

Gyms and Health Clubs

Here is a list of gyms and health clubs around town that count on expatriates as members.

Boscos

Calle 61 #550, between Calle 70 and 72 Street, Centro
Telephone: (999) 928-1380

This place is a relic from the 1950s. What a mess, but a charming, no-frills mess. Concentrating on free weights and ancient weight machines, this place is *mixto*, meaning co-ed. (There's a women's area on the second floor.) The gym has lockers and showers, and a good number of muscle-bound body builders are always hanging around. You have to remind yourself that you get what you pay for: $20 pesos for a day pass; $200 pesos for a month membership.

Hours:
Monday-Friday: 5:30 AM to 9:30 PM
Saturday: 5:30 AM to 3:00 PM
Sunday: 7:00 AM to 12 PM

Exersite Fitness Center

Plaza Altabrisa
Calle 7 #451, Local 73
Fracc. Altabrisa
Telephone: (999) 167-9257
Website: *www.exersite.com.mx*

At the other extreme is this state-of-the art health club that rivals anything you could expect either in Los Angeles or Miami. This mixto health club also has quite a number of activities for children, who are well supervised. The facilities include squash courts, a swimming pool, yoga, Pilates, and training for everything from men's cycling to children's Jazzercise classes. There are steam rooms, sauna and rooms set aside for varied classes as aerobics to ballroom dancing to boxing classes. Their website is astounding at the number of activities that are offered, and its membership reflects the solidly middle- and upper middle-class of Yucatecan society.

Hours:
Monday-Friday: 6:00 AM to 10:00 PM
Saturday-Sunday: 8:00 AM to 3:00 PM

Mérida Sports Center

Kilometro 12 Carretera Mérida – Progreso, Residencia Xcanatun

To say this is a state-of-the-art health club does not do it justice. This is, by far, a world class facility, a health club and sports center so large, comprehensive and with all the modern amenities, that it has its own full-service spa. It could be beamed to Los Angeles or Miami and it would rival anything anywhere in the world. That it is on the highway to Progreso itself tells you much: it caters to an exclusive clientele that can spend just over $100 USD a month for basic membership. There are more classes that can be listed in this description, and the best recommendation is to visit their website, and then drive on over. If you are serious about health clubs, and just as serious about sweating in the company of the city's privileged and elite, than this is the club for you. Their facilities rival anything you've every seen that's available today – except for one small detail: It doesn't have a heliport, like a certain health club in Sao Paulo, Brazil has!

Hours:
Monday-Thursday: 6:00 AM to 11:00 PM
Friday: 6:00 AM to 10:00 PM
Saturday: 8:00 AM to 6:00 PM
Sunday: 9:00 AM to 4:00 PM
Website: *www.meridasportcenter.net*

North Gym Center

Calle 56 #496, between Calle 59 and 61 Street, Centro

This is a modern facility, with free weights, weight and resistance machines and a good number of cardio equipment and treadmills. A *mixto* health club, it attracts women because of its spinning and cardio classes, as well as the popular dance courses that range from salsa to Jazzercise. There is a sunning lounge on the roof, but this is for women only.

Hours:
Monday-Friday: 6:30 AM to 9:00 PM
Saturday: 7:00 AM to 3:00 PM
Closed Sunday

SporTec Muscle Factory

Calle 22 #113, between Calle 13 and 15 Street
Colonia San Antonio Cinta
Telephone: (999) 948-4640

With a high-tech name like this, you have certain expectations, but these are mistaken if you presume it's a place for body builders. On the contrary, it is a modern, *mixto* facility with as much cardio equipment as weight training machines and free weights. The place features modern locker rooms, a studio for aerobics, Pilates and spinning classes. There is a snack bar featuring healthful beverages and juices, and the place is fully air conditioned.

Hours:
Monday-Friday: 6:00 AM to 10:00 PM
Saturday: 7:00 AM to 3:00 PM
Closed Sunday

WW Gym

Calle 30 #99, between Calle 19 and 21 Street
Colonia Mexico
Telephone: (999) 944-4739

This *mixto* facility is the only one in Mérida that features an Olympic-size swimming pool. It is enormous, with studios dedicated exclusively to certain activities: one studio for spinning classes, another for yoga, and another for aerobics. The cardio room has two dozen treadmills, and the weight training room has state-of-the-art machines. The free weight room has a good number of weights, but it is the least frequented room, which indicates that while a *mixto* facility, more women then men are members. The health club offers a dizzying array of dance classes from Salsa to traditional Latin. A good number of members are women whose children attend the Roger's Hall school across the street, and they work out with their friends before school lets out for the day, meaning that lunch is being prepared back home by their cooks. Yes, its membership comes from the more privileged segment of Yucatecan society.

Hours:
Monday-Friday: 6:00 AM to 10:00 PM

Saturday: 7:30 AM to 2:00 pm.
Closed Sunday

Xtreme Body Gym

Calle 50 #55, Local 10
Plaza Montejo
Fracc. Francisco de Montejo

Located in a middle-class neighborhood, this is a small facility, with minimal cardiovascular equipment, but a respectable selection of weight resistance equipment. A mixto facility as well, it does not currently have yoga or Pilates classes. Its membership reflects the neighborhood, and there are few expatriates as members, apart from a number of Cuban and Lebanese expatriates.

Hours:
Monday-Friday: 7:30 AM to 9:00 PM
Saturday: 8:00 AM to 2:00 PM
Closed Sunday

Personal Trainer

There are several personal trainers and martial arts instructor in Mérida, but the one who is American is Philip Geerts. If you are not confident in your Spanish, you might prefer a native English-speaking trainer.

Philip Geerts
Telephone: (999) 151-9734
Website: *www.meridatrainer.com*
Email: *phil.geerts@yahoo.com*

Massages

There are a good number of masseurs and masseuses in Mérida, but the one who is an American is Lane Gallagher. If you are not confident in your Spanish, you might prefer a native English-speaking masseur.

Lane Gallagher
Masseur
Telephone: (999) 928-2027
Email: *islalane@hotmail.com*

Yoga

There are a good number of yogis in Mérida, and Mérida is emerging as a yoga retreat destination in its own right. Clauda Guerrero of Semilla Yoga is completely fluent in English and Spanish and she has trained and taught throughout Mexico and in the United States. Emily Navar is an American, but she is located in Izamal, a nearby city an hour or so northeast of Mérida. There are other yoga centers, but the clients are primarily Yucatecans and Mexicans, and the classes are primarily conducted in Spanish.

Semilla Yoga

Claudia Guerrero
Calle 15 #210 between Calle 24 and 26 Street
Colonia García Ginerés
Telephone: (999) 920-5361
Website: *www.semillayoga.com.mx*

Centro VIRYA 2011

Calle 14 #85 by Calle 5
Colonia San Antonio Cinta
Telephone: (999) 127-9810
www.meridayoga.com

Yoga Para Ti

Calle 26-A #313, between Calle 43 and 45 Street,
Fracc. Montealban
Telephone: (999) 444-166

Hotel Macan Ché

Emily Navar and Alfred Rordame
Izamal, Yucatán
Telephone: (988) 954-0287
Email: *macanche@gmail.com*
Web: *www.macanche.com*

23 Health Care & Health Insurance

The careful reader will have noticed that one of the complaints about Mérida is that it is brutally hot in the summer. For expatriates who are living in Mérida year-round, this is a serious concern. It can wear on your physical being, and heat exhaustion is not uncommon. As we age, our bodies are more sensitive to the heat, and more care is required. In the subtropics and tropics alike, plenty of fluids, a good night's sleep, eating healthful foods and moderate exercise are the key ingredients to remaining healthy.

From the State Department, general overview of health insurance questions for Americans overseas:

Can the U.S. government assist me if I become disabled overseas?

- If an American becomes ill or is seriously injured abroad, a U.S. consular officer can assist in locating appropriate medical services and informing family or friends.
- If necessary a consular officer can also assist in the transfer of funds from the United States.
- Payment of hospital and other expenses is the responsibility of the traveler.

It's no wonder that healthy Yucatecans are up bright and early (some before the crack of dawn!) and walking briskly in the parks and sports stadiums, getting in their cardiovascular workouts before the sun rises. It's also common to see them in the fruit markets, buying whatever happens to be in season for a healthful breakfast that is nutritious – while being environmentally responsible. What does that mean? That it makes sense to enjoy a ripe mango that was harvested from someone's backyard for breakfast, than it is to buy imported strawberries that were picked – when not fully ripe! – and then flown thousands of miles to end up in a grocery store.

HEALTH CARE & HEALTH INSURANCE

One of the great things about Mérida is that, if you set your mind to it, it is possible to have one of the healthiest and most nutritious diets you can possibly imagine, where fruits and vegetables are grown in small towns, outside the industrial agricultural business, and the same goes for the fish, poultry and pork that are sold in the commercial local neighborhood *mercados*. Almost everything is free range and raised without vaccines, growth hormones and humanely.

With that in mind, it's a good time to begin to assess your health, since this will determine how best you go about staying healthy – and in some cases, becoming healthy. If you are unfamiliar with how to assess where you stand, so to speak, when it comes to your own health, the best thing to do, of course, is to get a physical.

It is also a good idea to find a local doctor with whom you feel comfortable. The chapter on doctors has a list of exceptional physicians in Mérida, as well as dentists. It's also important to find a hospital that is close to your home, or with which you are satisfied. You can be confident in the world-class medical facilities in town. Mérida has a good number of regional hospitals and medical centers. All of them offer full services for the residents of Mérida. The Regional Hospitals provide services for residents of outlying communities of Yucatán State, as well as patients from neighboring states of Campeche and Quintana Roo.

From the State Department, general overview of health insurance questions for Americans overseas:

Why should I be concerned about medical coverage abroad?

- The Social Security Medicare Program does not provide coverage for hospital or medical costs outside the United States.
- Many health insurance plans do not provide coverage overseas. Those that provide "customary and reasonable" hospital costs abroad may not pay for your medical evacuation back to the United States which can cost $10,000.00 and up depending on your location and medical condition.
- Many foreign doctors and hospitals require payment in cash prior to providing service.
- Uninsured patients may be refused service.
- Countries with socialized medicine may not provide full services to non-residents.
- Payment of hospital and other expenses abroad is the responsibility of the traveler.
- Some countries require tourists to carry accident or travel insurance. Check the Country Specific Information for the countries you plan to visit for detailed information.

Mérida has one of the most prestigious medical faculties in Mexico under the direction of the Universidad Autónoma de Yucatán. Mérida's proximity to U.S. cities of Miami and Houston allow local doctors to cross-train and practice in both countries. As a result Mérida is one of the best cities in Mexico in terms of health services availability, and there is a rapidly-expanding "medical" tourism industry, where foreigners are coming to Mérida for medical and dental treatment at significantly lower prices that are available in their home countries. It is an important regional health care center, one that rivals Miami in its facilities and attention to patients. Indeed, Mérida is emerging as an important "medical tourism" destination for people from the U.S. and Canada who wish to have medical treatment, procedures and dental work done at reasonable costs, and at world-class facilities. There are several companies that now cater specifically to this niche market, and can take are of all the details necessary for medical treatment to be performed here. There are several health clubs dedicated to seniors, and a good number of assisted living centers with bilingual staff. In addition there are tour companies that specialize in trips for the "over 50" crowd, with itineraries that accommodate specific needs of elder travelers.

But for resident expatriates, you really aren't tourists since you live here. It's nevertheless important to be current on medical facilities available, healthy living and the kinds of insurance that are available to you. First, it's always good to know the hospitals in town, private and public.

 Private Hospitals

Clínica de Mérida

Avenida Itzáes #242
Colonia García Ginerés
Telephone: (999) 942-1800
Emergencies - Adults: Ext. 1141 & 1142, **Children:** Ext. 1123
Intensive Care - Adults: Ext. 1122, **Children:** Extx 1235
Website: www.clinicademerida.com.mx/DEP.html

Star Médica

Calle 26 #199 by Calle 15 and 17 Street
Colonia Altabrisa
Telephone: (999) 930-2880, **Emergencies:** Ext. 5
Website: www.starmedica.com/default.asp?seccion=150

Centro de Especialidades Médicas (CEM)

Calle 60 #329-B by Calle 35 and
Avenida Colón
Colonia Alcalá Martín
Telephone: (999) 920-4040
Emergencies: Ext. 111
Website:
www.cemsureste.com/cem_index.htm

Centro Médico de las Américas (CMA)

Calle 54 #365
Centro
Telephone: (999) 926-2111
Emergencies - Adults: Ext. 127 or phone 927-2199, **Children:** Ext. 512
Website:
www.centromedicodelasamericas.com.mx/directorio.php?Offset=0

Centro Médico Pensiones (CMP)

Calle 7 #215-A
Colonia Pensiones
Telephone: (999) 925-8019,
Emergencies: Ext. 106
Website:
www.hospitalcmp.com/index.htm

Hospital Santelena

Calle 14 #81, by Calle 5 and 7 Street
Colonia San Antonio Cinta
Telephone: (999) 943-1333,
Emergencies: Ext. 135
Website:
www.hosantme.medicosmerida.com

From the State Department, general overview of health insurance questions for Americans overseas:

What questions should I ask my health insurance company?

- Does this insurance policy cover emergency expenses abroad such as returning me to the United States for treatment if I become seriously ill?
- Does this insurance cover high-risk activities such as parasailing, mountain climbing, scuba diving and off-roading?
- Does this policy cover pre-existing conditions?
- Does the insurance company require pre-authorizations or second opinions before emergency treatment can begin?
- Does the insurance company guarantee medical payments abroad?
- Will the insurance company pay foreign hospitals and foreign doctors directly?
- Does the insurance company have a 24-hour physician-backed support

HEALTH CARE & HEALTH INSURANCE

Public Hospitals:

Hospital Agustin O'Horán

Avenida Itzáes by Avenida Jacinto Canek
Centro
Telephone: (999) 924-0749
Director: Dr. José Rafael Pacheco

Cruz Roja Mexicana

Avenida Quetzacoalt #104
Centro
Telephone: (999) 983- 0233

Centro de Salud Pública

Calle 72 #463, between Calle 53 and 55 Street
Centro
Telephone: (999) 928-6185

Clínica Materno-Infantil "María José"

Calle 53 #484 by Calle 54 and 56 Street
Centro
Telephone: (999) 928 5325

IMSS (Instituto Mexicano de Seguro Social, or Mexican Institute of Social Security)

H. G. P. Torre de Especialidades Mérida CMN Yucatán
Calle 34 by 41 #439, Ex-Terrenos El Fénix
Colonia Industrial
Telephone: (999) 922-56-0601, and for emergencies (999) 922-5656 Ext. 4102

Hospital Benito Juárez IMSS

Avenida Colón by Avenida Itzáes
Colonia García Ginerés
Telephone: (999)925-0831 and for emergencies (999) 925-0866 ext. 2553

Whether private or public, all hospitals are required by law to treat people in the emergency room regardless of what, if any, insurance they have, or their legal status in the country. No one can be turned away. Additionally, the Hospital O'Horan has state-of-the-art facilities for treating people living with HIV and AIDS.

Personal Health Insurance

In addition, you will need to have some sort of health insurance – unless you are prepared to self-insure. Be aware that Americans citizens and permanent aliens who are enrolled in Medicaid and Medicare in the United States will find that neither program pays for health coverage while in Mexico. There are a few trial programs and exchange pilot initiatives but these tend to be concentrated on the U.S.-Mexico border, such one between San Diego and Tijuana. The U.S. military has also been working on administering healthcare coverage for U.S. veterans living in Mexico.

Here is how the American Association of Retired Persons (AARP) addresses the current situation:

"Experience has been gained in Mexico, however, showing that a less ambitious program, the military's Tricare Standard coverage, can operate there and ensure reasonable coverage for retirees living there and delivery of medical and hospitalization services at a cost saving compared to scheduled Medicare costs in the USA. The experimental program there was administered by the Wisconsin Physicians Service. It was not only effective; it has encouraged the adoption of medical standards recognized as meeting Medicare criteria, in Mexico."

It is expected that sometime in the course of this new decade, some Medicare programs will be available in Mexico.

In the meantime, there are three general approaches to securing health insurance in Mexico. First is to secure private insurance, either from an U.S. company that offers health insurance to Americans living overseas. The second is to secure health coverage from a private Mexican health insurance company. The third is to enroll in Mexico's public health program, which allows foreigners in Mexico with an FM2 or FM3 visa to participate in the national healthcare program available nationwide.

From the State Department, general overview of health insurance questions for Americans overseas:

What insurance information should I carry with me abroad?

- Carry both your insurance policy identity card as proof of your insurance and a claim form.

305

Health Insurance from American and Canadian Companies

Expat Global Medical

This is from their Mission Statement:
Since 1992 our companies have been insuring people all over the globe. Affordable, comprehensive health and medical insurance coverage for expatriates. If you are planning to live abroad, outside your country of normal residence, your government or regular health insurance plan will not cover you. The Expatriate health insurance plan is designed for Expatriates who are no longer covered under a basic health insurance plan, or individuals who are awaiting other insurance coverage in the country in which they intend to reside.

J.W. McGee & Associates

J.W. McGee & Associates
106 Keswick Drive, 1st Floor
Advance, NC 27006
Telephone: (336) 998-9583 (This is a U.S. area code)
Email: *john@expatglobalmedical.com*
Website: *www.expatglobalmedical.com*

American Express (Aetna Global Benefits)

This is from their Mission Statement:
If you are looking for a first-class expatriate health insurance product with excellent service, contact American Express worldwide health insurance. We have a wide range of health insurance programmes that have been developed specifically for expatriates over many years. Our expat health insurance products can provide you with some of the best cover available - as one of our policyholders, you can rest assured that we will always be at hand to help if you have an accident or fall ill while you are overseas

American Express

American Express Goodhealth Worldwide (Global) Limited
c/o Aetna Global Benefits
4630 Woodland Corporate Blvd.
Tampa, FL 33614
Telephone: (866) 545-3252 (Toll-free, inside USA only) or (813) 775-0220
Email: *AmericasServices@aetna.com*
Website: *www.worldwidehealthplan.com/Expatriate_health_insurance.asp*

Expat Financial

This is from their Mission Statement:
Expat Financial offers several different international health insurance plans for expatriates of any nationality across the world. We offer plans from several different insurance companies that are designed for foreign nationals (expats) living outside the country for which they hold a passport or any local national living outside US or Canada. We also offer excellent service before and after you purchase your international health insurance plan.

Expat Financial

Expat Financial
c/o TFG Global Insurance Solutions Ltd.,
#216 - 2438 Marine Drive
West Vancouver, BC V7V 1L2
Canada
Telephone: (800) 232-9415 (Toll-free, inside the USA and Canada)
Email: *info@tfgglobal.com*
Website: *www.expatfinancial.com*

Health Insurance from Mexican Companies

In Mérida, there are several Mexican companies that offer health insurance plans for expatriates. These have a wide selection of plans, and once you know what is available from companies in the U.S. and Canada for expatriates in Mexico, you will have a good idea of what you can expect to pay.

Here are three, two with offices in Mérida, and Met Life Mexico, the largest insurer in the country.

GE Seguros (in the process of becoming HDI Seguros)

Calle 60 #289, between Calle 23 and 25 Street, Colonia Alcalá Martín
Telephone: (999) 920-7215
For health insurance, ask for Julileta Morales
Website: *www.hdi.com.mx*

La Peninsular Seguros

Calle 58-A #499, between Calle 29 and 33 Street, Centro
Telephone: (999) 920-2329
For health insurance, ask for María Esquivel
Website: *www.lapeninsular.com.mx*

Met Life Mexico

Manuel Ávila Camacho 32
Pisos SKY, 14 al 20 y PH
Colonia Lomas de Chapultepec, C.P. 11000
Delegación Miguel Hidalgo
México, D.F.
Telephone: (555) 328-7000
Email: *contacto@metlife.com.mx*
Website: *www.metlife.com.mx*

Health Insurance from the Mexican Government

The final option is to sign up for Mexico's national health care program. The **Instituto Mexicano del Seguro Social**, known as **IMSS**, now offers a program that allows foreign residents to join the national health care system. IMSS is the largest health care system in the Spanish-speaking world and it offers medical services for everyone at reasonable rates.

IMSS has established two offices where foreigners can sign up for health insurance. Depending on the coverage you choose, the premiums range from $1,000 pesos to $3,000 pesos annually – that's $80 USD to $250 USD!

> This is from their Mission Statement:
> The Mexican Sociay Security (Health Care) Institute has a legal mandate derived from Article 123 of the Political Constitution of the United States of Mexico. Its mission is to be the basic instrument of social security (health care), established as a public service of national nature for all workers and their families. This means that the increase in the population coverage is pursued as a constitutional mandate, with a social approach.

If you live north of Calle 59, you have to apply in person with your FM2 or FM3, and three copies of the entire passport:

IMSS (Pensiones)

Calle 7 #432, between Calle 32 and 34 Street
Colonia Pensiones

If you live south of Calle 59, you have to apply in person with your FM2 or FM3, and three copies of the entire passport:

IMSS (Serapio Rendon)

Calle 42 Sur #999, between Calle 127-A and 131 Street
Colonia Serapio Rendon

Once the paperwork has been processed, you will be assigned to a "primary" IMSS clinic. At that time you will be issued your Carnet, which is a small booklet, which is a record of your visits. Upon your first visit, you will be assigned a general practioner, who will be your primary care physician. Normally, you will then be scheduled for a complete physical, just to have a record of your health, medical history and the medications you are currently taking. At that time, your primary care physician may refer you to specialists within the IMSS system.

Going forward, all visits to the IMSS clinic are free, since they are covered by your premium. The good news is that you now have affordable health care. The bad news is that Mexico's IMSS does not allow you the choice in doctors assigned to you. Hundreds of American expatriates, however, have taken advantage of this program, and most report that they are pleased with the services they receive and the care offered to them.

For more information, visit the website for IMSS: *www.imss.gob.mx/English*.

Beyond Health Care

There's more health care than eating right, a list of hospitals and health insurance. There's also the pursuit of happiness. So here are a few ways expatriates are pursuing better health through the pursuit of happiness.

Gym for Seniors

Right in the heart of the "north" part of Mérida one finds a state-of-the-art gym designed for people over the age of 50. Now you have no excuses that gyms are filled with young ladies listening to Beyonce on the treadmills, or muscle-building young men dropping weights on the floor!

American Refugees from Obamacare?

IMSS is so popular that the cable network Comedy Central has, on "The Daily Show," mocked American "refugees" fleeing to Mexico for affordable health care. In one report, Wyatt Cenac came to Mérida to report on the popularity of IMSS among American and Canadian retirees. The piece, titled "American Refugees Seek Health Care in Mexico," is available at:

www.thedailyshow.com/watch/mon-november-30-2009/american-refugees-seek-health-care-in-mexico

Seniors Gym

Calle 19 #88, by Calle 32
Colonia Campestre
Telephone: (999) 944-5427
Website: *www.fisiocare.com.mx*

Adventure Travel and the Elder Expat

It's good to know that Mexico's culture of respect for age extends to expatriates! There are few places that where a travel tour company does wonderful business designing adventure travel for those who are active and retired. **Aguilar & Lord** is a travel agency that specializes in mature travelers.

This is from their Mission Statement:

"Aguilar & Lord — and the December 2010 trip to the Yucatán — came about as a result of our own experience traveling though the Yucatán with an older family member; someone who loves learning about new places and people, but who wasn't looking for a rugged trek through the jungle. It was the beginning of March. She had escaped the cold of a New England winter and come to spend a little time with us in Mexico to get the chill out of her bones. After a couple of days of relaxing by the beach, we packed our bags and set out to explore."

Set out to explore by contacting them at their **Website:** *www.aguilarandlord.com*.

Sex and the Expat

We all know that a healthy sex life is an integral part of a healthy lifestyle, right? Fortunately, many expatriates are married, or have partners, a fact that solves the question of sex (or not!).

But that's not the case for everyone, of course. Many widows, widowers, divorced people or singles end up becoming expatriates in Mérida. There are several scenarios that play themselves out. First, for some reason, a disproportionate number of gay men end up relocating to Mérida. Some joke that since there is so much remodeling and redecorating to be done in the city's Historic Center, they flock down here to be "creative." Of course this plays to stereotypes, but it can't be denied that there are lots of gay expatriates in town.

Gay men in Mérida have their own culture, insular and self-affirming, which may or may not be a good thing, depending on one's perspective. A disproportionate number of gay men, for example, are clients of male hustlers in town, and they often fall victim to the kind of crimes familiar with that kind of lifestyle. (Gringo Gultch is filled with boring gossip about the misadventures of expatriate gays and local hustlers, which in many ways is a throwback to the 1940s and 1950s when "rough trade" dominated gay life in the United States. But, hey, who knew so many S&M orgies ended up in police reports?) Gay women, on the other hand, have always been more circumspect and sophisticated in their community, and it is often the case that they make a much more easy transition to the woman-centered community of Mérida's lesbians.

The world being what it is, straight men are the most fortunate: There are plenty of single, straight expatriate women and local women who covet foreigners, giving them ample choices. (Again, stereotypes prevail, and Yucatecan and Mexican women think, rightly or wrongly, that foreign men are more willing to be "equals" in their relationships.) Whether this is true or not, it is astounding to see how many American and Canadian men in town, well into their 50s and 60s, are with Mexican and Yucatecan women, decades younger, and starting new families.

Straight female expatriates, on the other hand, have the most difficult time finding their groove. They are simply not enough straight expatriates around, and most are not sufficiently fluent in Spanish to carry on romantic relationships with Mexican or Yucatecan men. That isn't to say that there is an emerging "subculture" of Latin Lovers out there – Mexican and Yucatecan men who fancy themselves Casanovas, and who enjoy seducing expatriate women. Oh, yes, word has gotten out to the point that there is an expression in Mérida for the Single Expatriate Woman: "Gringas muertas por pingas." It may sound unkind – "Gringas dying

---

 *From the State Department, general overview of health insurance questions for Americans overseas:*

You can't assume your insurance will go with you when you travel. It's very important to find out **before** you leave. You should ask your insurance company two questions:

1. **Does my policy apply when I'm outside the United States?**
2. **Will it cover emergencies like a trip to a foreign hospital or an evacuation?**

In many places, doctors and hospitals still expect payment in cash at the time of service. You can't simply give them your insurance card and expect it will go through. If your policy doesn't go with you when you travel, it's a very good idea to purchase a separate policy for your trip.

The Social Security Medicare Program does not provide coverage for hospital or medical costs outside the United States.

for dick" – but that's the perception out there. And this leads to a warning: **Beware the Gigolo**, regardless of nationality, since there have been cases of wonderful middle-aged women being taken advantage of by men with ulterior motives. In one notorious case, one expatriate found herself waking up alone one morning – the love of her life gone back to Philadelphia, after he empited her bank account of almost $50,000 USD. If it weren't bad enough that a good number have had their bank accounts emptied, what can mend a broken heart? For women of all ages, "Sex and the Single Female Expat" requires constant vigilance!

Plastic Surgery

As part of the growing medical tourism industry in Mérida, there are now a number of plastic surgeons. Whether it is liposuction or breast augmentation, Botox or rhinoplasty, Mérida is becoming an important destination for affordable surgery.

Clínica Colón

Dr. Fernandez Muñoz
Avenida Colón #199, by Calle 26
Colonia García Ginerés
Telephone: (999) 920-2121
Website: *www.clinicacolon.com*

A Friend of Bill W?

There are three English-language AA meetings. The Mérida English Library hosts one on Tuesdays at 5:30 PM, Thursdays at 7:00 PM, and on Sundays at 5:30 PM. Casa Catherwood, located on Calle 59 #572, between Calle 72 and 74 Street, hosts one Tuesdays at 6 PM. In addition, the Mérida English Language Library hosts an Al-Anon meeting on Wednesdays at 5:30 PM.

Sports Facilities

Mérida has a good number of sports facilities and nationally-ranked professional teams in baseball, soccer and basketball. There are wonderful opportunities to enjoy these facilities, to join informal leagues and to make life-long friends in pick-up basketball games, participating in baseball matches, and finding a friend to play a court sport. In the early mornings, many of these parks are filled with avid "brisk" walkers getting in their cardio exercise first thing in the morning before the heat of the day arrives.

Sports facilities include:

- **Estadio Salvador Alvarado** in the north
- **Unidad Deportiva Kukulcán** (with the major Soccer Stadium Carlos Iturralde, Kukulcán BaseBall Park and Polifórum Zamná multipurpose arena)

- **La Inalambrica Sports Complex**, in the west (with archery facilities that held a world series championship)
- **Unidad deportiva Benito Juárez García**, in the northeast.
- **Gimnasio Polifuncional**, where professional basketball team Mayas de Yucatán plays for the Liga Nacional de Baloncesto Profesional de México (LNBP) representing Yucatán.

Nationally-Ranked Teams

Team Name/Sport	League
Leones de Yucatán, Baseball	Liga Mexicana de Béisbo
F.C. Itzáes, Soccer Mérida F.C., Soccer	l Segunda División de México Liga de Ascenso de México
Mayas de Yucatán, Basketball	Liga Nacional de Baloncesto Profesional de México

24   Gay and Lesbian Mérida

It can be safely said that the vast majority of expatriates moving to Mérida come from societies whose principle religious traditions derive from the three Abrahamic faiths: Judaism, Christianity and Islam. These three religions take dim views of same-sex relations. In the Torah, Leviticus (18:22) call same-sex relations an "abomination." Leviticus is also one of the books in the Christian Bible. In the Qu'ran (Koran), we find, "The Prophet, peace and blessings of Allaah be upon him, said: 'If a man has sexual relations with another man, they are both guilty of zina (adultery), and if a woman has sexual relations with another woman they are both guilty of zina (adultery).'"

Other religious traditions also take dim views of homosexuality. The three major faiths of Indian origin – Hinduism, Buddhism and Sikhism – discourage or forbid engaging in same-sex relations.[9] Further East, the same biases are found. In the Taoic religions, homosexuality is not viewed as being a path to human fulfillment, and it is

>
>
> **The Maya Moon Goddess: Sexual Libertine**
>
> "The story of the Moon Goddess was replete with important codes for Maya Society. It provided the nobles with legitimacy, developed an important story about the mother, inspired moral stories related to deception, gave one ethnic group a symbol to colonize others, and suggested a story if not a method of resistance. It was a tale of colonialism and an anticolonial struggle, all rolled up into one, and all centered around particular concepts of gendered performance and sexual desire.
>
> As the story goes, the Moon Goddess reproduced Maya lineages which were associated with her own community, a group among the Itzá, perhaps the people of Cozumel From this base, the Moon Goddess was to her geopolitical power. By engaging in many sexual acts with the other gods the Moon Goddess was able to reproduce many lineages and assert control over other communities. These acts, in fact, increased the Moon's power over the various Maya peoples. For peoples so concerned with lineage, any of the Moon Goddess's reproductive sexual acts became a primary element in an Itzá colonialism. But how did she convince the other gods to engage in sexual acts with her?" Pete Sigal, *From Moon Goddess to Virgins*

---

[9] See: Gyatso, Janet (2003). *One Plus One Makes Three: Buddhist Gender Conceptions and the Law of the Non-Excluded Middle*, History of Religions. 2003, no. 2. University of Chicago Press.

discouraged as vacuous. (As recently as the 1970s Maoist China condemned homosexuality as a form or mental illness.)

This religious disapproval has also shaped secular views of homosexuality, the point being that gays and lesbians encounter various forms and degrees of biases and bigotries, and the struggle for acceptance is a continuing one.

That said, many expatriates look at Mexico, realize that it is a deeply Catholic society, and make the assumption that the dim views of homosexuality that inform Catholic teachings dominate.

Yes, and no.

Officially, Mexicans are taught that homosexuality is to be frowned upon, and that it violates Biblical teachings. But in practice, there are two trends that mitigate homophobia in society at large. The first is secular: the Mexican belief that one should mind one's own business. "Uno no se debe meter en vidas ajenas," meaning "One should not meddle into other people's affairs," is a saying that often-repeated in Mérida's homes – just as one is about to dish gossip about somebody. As a result there is a very strong cultural aversion to passing judgment on others, one of the traits that makes Yucatecans such good neighbors, and it promotes a healthy "live and let live" attitude.

The other factor is cultural: the ambivalence about same-sex relationships among the Maya. This is consistent with the worldviews of the First Peoples throughout the continent, where gay and lesbian sexual relations are not normally condemned. In recent years, much scholarly work has been undertaken to explore the view of homosexuals as being "two-spirited" people throughout the pre-Columbian societies of the Americas, especially among North American First Peoples.

 **Two-Spirit People**

"Multigendered adult people at Mescalero are usually presumed to be people of power. Because they have both maleness and femaleness totally entwined in one body, they are known to be able to 'see' with the eyes of both proper men and proper women. They are often called upon to be healers, or mediators, or interpreters of dreams, or expected to become singers or others whose lives are devoted to the welfare of the group. If they do extraordinary things in any aspect of life, it is assumed that they have the license and power to do so and, therefore, they are not questioned," Claire R. Farrer

Among the Maya, for instance, some deities, such as God K, are bisexual, depicted as having relations with women in some places, and with men in others. The Moon Goddess, which became closely associated with the Virgin Mary during the Colonial period, was represented as bisexual![10]

The social organization of homosexuality is vastly different among the Maya, and these cultural views offer greater acceptance than what normally finds in other areas of Mexico. It's not often appreciated by foreigners, but **throughout Mexico, the Yucatán is seen as a place – whether one admires it or ridicules it – where there is a kind of hedonism that encourages libertine sexual expression**. While certain cultural norms prevail for everyone – *public displays of overt sexuality are frowned upon regardless of sexual preference* – it's possible to see age-appropriate couples if not walking hand-in-hand, then at least arm-in-arm, without raising eyebrows.

With this background, it's not difficult to imagine why Mérida is a place where gays and lesbians let their guards down and enjoy greater social acceptance and freedoms.

Gay Mérida

If many associate "Mexico" with "macho," then Mérida is perhaps the least "macho" city in the entire country, and this is meant as a compliment, regardless of sexual orientation. There are few places in the world where one sees men holding their children, fathers kissing their kids, men helping women with the grocery shopping, or assisting their elderly parents at restaurants in such loving and unselfconscious ways.

The cultural gentleness of the Maya, which is evidenced in any small town you visit, where people gather around a baseball field, or the local market, is remarkable. And this gender-neutral division of social responsibilities extends to tolerance for gay and bisexual men. It would be misleading to say that there is no social stigma to being gay in Mérida, but there is far less hostility than foreigners tend to presume. Yes, a slightly inebriated man dressed in high heels pretending to be Tina Turner walking down the street will get looks, and a few chuckles, but he is almost likely to be left alone, by passersby or the local police alike.

And if you have any doubts about the tolerance in Mérida for gays and lesbians, then Mérida's Carnival should put anxieties to rest, since the number of gays on the floats resembles a

---

[10] For more information, see: *From Moon Goddesses to Virgins: The Colonization of Yucatecan Maya* Sexual Desire, by Pete Sigal, University of Texas Press, 2000; and *The Construction of Homosexuality*, by David Greenberg, University of Chicago Press, 1990.

cross between Mardi Gras in New Orleans and Folsom Street Fair in San Francisco. If you are curious, there are a dozen or so videos on YouTube depicting various Gay an d Lesbian marchers during Pride in Mérida. (Go to YouTube.com and search "Marcha Lésbico Gay Mérida Yucatán – 2009" to see the video clips.)

And Mexico itself is very progressive. In recent years same-sex marriage has been legalized (in Mexico City) and so have same-sex adoptions. Mexico's Supreme Court ruled in August 2010 that gays and lesbians in Mexico must afforded the same rights as heterosexuals. As a result, there's now a new confidence among gays and lesbians.[11] The ascendance of the homophile community in Mexico, interestingly, coincides with the influx of gay and lesbian expatriates not only from the U.S. and Canada, but Europe and South America, meaning that over the past decade the GLBTQ communities have grown more diverse and disparate.

Gay Pride Mérida

Gay Pride is celebrated the last week in June.

Still, several observations can be made to offer guidance. As is often the case, gay men are more visible in the community than are lesbians, and Mérida is no exception. From the Main Square (Zócalo) north along Calle 60 to the Peón Contreras Theater, the Cafés, parks and outdoor restaurants are favorites among gay men. Other places that remain popular are the Internet cafés along Calle 61. Mérida, however, being a city of almost a million people, not everyone cares to frequent a four-city block area, and the scores of places in the Colonias where local gay men gather. In the past decade a more popular way of connecting is through social networking.

"Gay Mérida" on Facebook has almost 500 "Likes", and it's quite possible to connect with people before you arrive. Other websites, which are primarily for encounters other than social, are popular, including Manhunt and Bear411. Increasingly one finds posts on Craigslist.org for people who are visiting from outside Mérida. There is also an important GLBTQ magazine called MID-OPEN, for and by the local community (see the end of the chapter).

Places to stay

Casa Mexilio

Calle 68 #495, between Calle 57 and 59 Street

---

[11] In August 2010, Mexico became the 11th country in the world to provide LGBT people equal access to marriage, joining the Netherlands, Belgium, Portugal, Spain, Canada, South Africa, Iceland, Norway, Sweden, and Argentina.

Centro
Website: www.casamexilio.com

Los Arcos B&B

Calle 66 #408-B, between Calle 49 and 51 Street
Centro
Website: www.lorarcosmerida.com

Casa Lorenzo

Calle 41 #516-A, between Calle 62 and 64 Street
Centro
Website: www.lacasalorenzo.com

Bars

Gay bars and discos are located along the highway that encircles the city. If you don't have a car, they are a short cab ride from downtown.

Pride Disco

Anillo Periferico Mérida-Campeche
(200 meters from the Uman Bridge near the airport)
Telephone: (999) 947-9874
Open: Thursday - Sunday
Website: www.pridedisco.com
The bar opens at 10 PM, has a drag show every night, caters primarily to gay men, but is frequented by a good number of lesbians.

Scalibur

Calle 4-B #308, by 39-A Street
Colonia San Camilio II
Telephone: (999) 108-2046
Open: Thursday - Sunday
Website: www.myspace.com/scalibur_cabare_Mérida
The bar opens at 11 PM, has a drag show every night. There is a Tea Dance on Saturday and Sunday, beginning at 2 PM

Milk Gay Club

Kilometro 0.3, Carretera Mérida-Cancún

Telephone: (999) 101-0492
Open: Thursday - Sunday
Website: www.milkgayclub.com
The bar opens at 10 PM, has both a stripper show and a drag show every night. Straight women also attend, most of whom arrive with their girlfriends, since they like to see muscle boys stripping on stage. Features Sunday Tea Dances.

Angel Luz Club

This club has two locations.
Anillo Periferico Mérida-Campeche, Kilometro 7
Open: Thursday - Sunday
Website: www.angeluzclub.com.mx
The bar opens at 10 PM, has a drag show every night.
The other location, which opened in 2011, across from the Post Office in Itzimná, Colonia Itzimná

Foxxy's

Periferico Oriente, 30 meters towards Tixkokob
Telephone: (999) 988-1466
Open: Wednesday - Sunday
Website: www.foxxys.mx
The bar opens at 8 PM, has both a stripper show and a drag show every night.

Cafés and Scenes

Café La Habana

Calle 59 #511-A, between Calle 60 and 62 Street
Centro

Café Chocolate

Calle 60 #442, by 49 Street
Centro

Café El Hoyo

Calle 62 #491, between Calle 59 and 61 Street
Centro

Amaro Restaurant

Calle 59 #507, between Calle 60 and 62 Street
Centro

Gran Hotel Café

Calle 60 #496, between Calle 59 and 61 Street
Centro

| Sorbeteria Colón | North side of the Main Square (Calle 61, between Calle 60 and 62 Street) |

Places Favored by Gay Men

La 68 Cinema

Open air cinema and restaurant showcasing international documentaries and films, quite a scene, depending on what's showing, Thursdays, Fridays and Saturdays. To check out schedule:
la68.com/casa-de-cultura-merida/cartelera-documentales.html

Address: Calle 68 #470-A, corner of 55 Street
Centro

Mérida Gay Facebook Community

www.facebook.com/pages/GAY-MERIDA/94476241897

Mérida Gay Websites

The following websites are popular among gay men in Mérida:

Bear 411: *www.bear411.com*
Gay Dating: *www.gay.com*
Gaydar: *www.gaydar.co.uk*

Lesbian Mérida

What can you say about a Mexican city of a million people that elected a lesbian mayor over a decade ago?

You go, girl!

> ## A Message from the Mérida Bed & Breakfast Association
>
> The governor of Yucatán State is a woman, Ivonne Ortega. The Mayor of Mérida, Mexico's fifth largest city, is a woman, Angélica Araujo. Not only is there is a long, distinguished tradition of female politicians, but also lesbians and bisexual women play an important role in the Yucatan's society. A former Mayor of Mérida, Ana Rosa Payán, was a woman-directed woman. And one of the city's leading businesswomen, Carmen Barbachano, the owner of the "Casa del Balam" Hotel, is openly a lesbian. A former governor, Dulce María Sauri, not only heads the country's largest political party on a national level, the Institutional Revolutionary Party, known as the PRI, but is often mentioned as a potential presidential candidate.
>
> Indeed, it is difficult to envision a more open, welcoming place for bisexual women and lesbians to vacation than the Yucatán. And to a large degree this has to do with the influence of the Maya people, who have a very fluid understanding of human sexuality. The Maya created a breathtaking rainforest civilization, whose vast city-centers were graced with pyramids and temples, and they had no problem with powerful female rulers, such as Lady Xox who governed in the city of Yaxchilán centuries ago.
>
> Where else can you climb pyramids; enjoy the charm of a colonial city; eat terrific food; relax by the beach; go on expeditions into the jungle on horseback; scuba, snorkel or swim in a *cenote* (freshwater sink hole); enjoy the wonder of nature by visiting reserves; and do it all in a city where women hold positions of authority, and society is welcoming of bisexual women, bestowing the highest compliment: A welcoming, knowing smile.
>
> As you plan your holiday in the Yucatan, be mindful of the women-owned Bed & Breakfast that caters to women. And, in keeping with the progressive sense of place, there is a woman-owned travel agency that specializes on trips for women, designed for and by women.
>
> Welcome to the Yucatán, where the daughters of Sappho are out and about.
>
> *www.meridabedandbreakfast.org/visitorguidance/womendirectedwomen.html*

As is often the case around the world, lesbians are more discreet and have lower visibility compared to gay men. All it takes, however, is a simply a stroll around town to notice that female energy that abounds. But, it's one thing to see Packers and Princesses everywhere, and quite another to make contact with them. That there are no lesbian bars, however, should not discourage you: kitty punchers and vagitarians abound in the cafés around town, and there are three time-tested ways of making contact.

For casual interactions, it's best to frequent one of the cafés, galleries and museums favored by the lesbian community, as well as getting recommendations on events about town from the women who are the owners of Casa Ana.

The other defining characteristic of Mérida's lesbian community, as is seen by the high profiles women have in the political life of the Yucatán, is to reach out to certain groups that are non-profit organizations headed by, or staffed with, a high number of distinguished and accomplished lesbians. It is refreshing to see half a dozen or so very high-profile and active nonprofit organizations, which work in environmental, special education, women's health and child welfare organizations that are run by lesbians. Whenever these organizations have events, scores of attendees are lesbians. In fact, in the same way that gay men dominant events such as the opening night of a symphony concert or an opera, lesbians figure prominently in the city's nonprofit sector, where they are executive directors, program directors and managers of some of the city's most important NGOs working in the fields of health, education and environment.

As a matter of discretion, if you are interested in a list of nonprofit organizations that are led by lesbians, and which might be having social or fundraising events while you are in town, you can send an email to *info@meridabedandbreakfast.org*.

Then there are online resources. More than 225 Mérida lesbians are "friends" of "Solteras Less Mérida," meaning "Mérida Single Lesbians." It wouldn't hurt to become a friend and make contact with a few women before your visit. Obviously, if you know some Spanish that will help. But bear in mind that there is no shortage of Mexicans who want to improve their English by practicing with a native-English speaker! The benefit of this online community is that it allows you to establish contact with as many self-identified Mérida lesbians as you'd like to, and there's no reason why you can't set up to meet for coffee, or drinks, or a meal before you arrive – or once you are in town. As is the case with just about everyone else, Yucatecans are very proud of their city, of the Maya civilization and of their history. Most welcome nothing more than the opportunity to be gracious and helpful and to show you around town. And what could be better than having a new friend show you around town? Go ahead, there's absolutely nothing wrong with flowmancing via Facebook in Mérida!

If, on the other hand, you are more interested in meeting other lesbians who are part of Mérida's expat community, or are also visiting Mérida, there are two ways of doing this. The first is to make a visit to the Mérida English Language Library. Although it often resembles a daycare center for American and Canadian senior citizens (nothing wrong with that), they do have events that which are popular and draw a good number of lesbians who live in town. The monthly "expat" social is very popular, and you can easily meet other women with similar interests.

For hanging out with other women who are traveling through the Yucatán, the best resource is the only woman-owned tour company, MexicaChica Tours. In 2011 they launched several day trips, the most popular one being a day trip to the Cacao Plantation about twenty minutes from the ruins of Uxmal. Not only is this an adventure – and very butch one at that – it is a unique experience: A women's day trip into the rainforest to see cacao trees, learn all about the history of chocolate and embark on a grand adventure in the company of other women: It's Xena, Warrior Princess meets chocolate!

It bears repeating: Without having to spend time drinking in bars, it's quite possible to become part of Mérida's lesbian community rather easily. From making a few introductions casually over Facebook, hanging out at some of the cafés and coffee shops where local lesbians hang out, or making an effort to reach out to some of the prominent and socially active lesbians heading important NGOs in town, one thing you will find is that this is a very nonjudgmental society, where women face few obstacles and little discrimination in living their lives on their own terms.

> ### Pink Choice Says:
>
> For the gay and lesbian traveler, the good news is that Mérida is fairly safe place to visit because it is a close knit community and there simply isn't any place to run. It has the lowest crime rate in the whole of Mexico. Traffic is chaotic, particularly downtown and as most of the streets are one way, getting around by car is definitely challenging. ... Mérida is nothing like Cancún or Playa del Carmen. If you want to experience Mexican culture while staying relatively close to the Caribbean Sea then Mérida is a great place to go. The city is a wonderful blend of a colonial city and a cosmopolitan destination. The central main plaza of Mérida is a great base, from where you can visit cathedrals and churches, Mayan ruins, museums, haciendas and *cenotes*, shops and the local theaters.

The following are lesbian-owned businesses, or are places where local lesbians frequent.

Places to Stay

Casa Ana
Calle 52 #469, between Calle 51 and 53 Street

Centro
Website: www.casaana.com

Hotel Casa del Balam

Calle 60 #488, by 57 Street

Centro
www.casadelbalam.com

Bars

Pride Disco

Anillo Periferico Mérida-Campeche
(200 meters from the Uman Bridge near the airport)
Telephone: (999) 947-9874
Website: www.pridedisco.com
The bar opens at 10 PM, has a drag show every night, caters primarily to gay men, but is frequented by a good number of lesbians.

Cafés and Hangouts

Café Chocolate

Calle 60 #442, by Calle 49 Street
Centro

Café Organico

Centro Comercial Colón, Local 1-C
Calle 33-D and Reforma Avenue
Colonia García Ginerés

La Boheme

Paseo de Montejo #470-B, between Calle 37 and 39 Street
Colonia Santa Ana (Paseo de Montejo)

Amaro Restaurant

Calle 59 #507, between Calle 60 and 62 Street
Centro

Gran Hotel Café

Calle 60 #496, between Calle 59 and 61 Street
Centro

Sorbeteria Colón

North side of the Main Square (Calle 61, between Calle 60 and 62 Street)

Places Favored by Lesbians

Museum of the City

Calle 56, between Calle 65 and 65-A Street
Hours: Tuesday – Saturday, 9 AM to 8 PM
Sundays, 9 a.m to 2 PM
Free admission

La 68 Cinema

Open air cinema and restaurant showcasing international documentaries and films, quite a scene, depending on what's showing, Thursdays, Fridays and Saturdays. To check out schedule:
www.la68.com/casa-de-cultura-Mérida/cartelera-documentales.html
Address: Calle 68 #470-A, corner of 55 Street, Centro

Day Trips

MexicaChica Tours

Website: www.MexicaChica.com

Mérida Lesbian Blog

www.lesgaradio.blogspot.com

Mérida Lesbian Facebook Community

www.facebook.com/pages/Solteras-Less-merida/106226992763453

Mérida GLBTQ Community Resources

Mérida has a gay and lesbian magazine called MID-OPEN. "MID" is the airport code for the city, and OPEN is about openly affirming one's identity. The magazine's motto is "In Mérida Things Change." The Facebook page has almost 3,000 "Likes," from the spectrum of Mérida's GLBTQ communities. The Facebook's Wall has everything from public endorsements from Mérida's mayor to the GLBTQ community to information on upcoming drag shows.

Website: www.mid-open.com
Facebook: www.facebook.com/pages/MID-OPEN/100808197394

Fighting Homophobia

Although Mérida is a very tolerant town, that doesn't mean there aren't bigots. "Yucatan Today" published a book in 2008 that implied that gays and lesbians are more likely to tolerate pedophilia than straights.

This is what they published:

"There are some things you should know about gay [and lesbian] life in Mérida... [t]he authorities are very protective of their teens. If you consider a tryst with a younger person, be sure that person is 18 or older."

Mesoamerica Foundation spoke out against this hate speech and declared a boycott of **Yucatan Today** magazine. We respectfully request that you take a stand and boycott Yucatan Today and their advertisers, whether it is in their monthly magazine or on their website: Yucatantoday.com

For more information on the boycott, go to:
www.mesoamerica-foundation.org/keepingthemhonest/homophobia.html

25 U.S. Taxes and Voting

If you are an American citizen or a resident alien who is living in Mérida, you still have to comply with both your legal obligations to the IRS and (for citizens) your civic duty to vote. Yes, Uncle Sam wants you to file a tax return, and your mother wants you to vote!

Taxes for U.S. Citizens and Resident Aliens Abroad

If you are a U.S. citizen or resident alien, the rules for filing income, estate, and gift tax returns and paying estimated tax are generally the same whether you are in the United States or abroad. Your worldwide income is subject to U.S. income tax, regardless of where you reside.

When to File

If you reside overseas, or are in the military on duty outside the U.S., you are allowed an automatic 2-month extension to file your return until June 15. However, any tax due must be paid by the original return due date (April 15) to avoid interest charges. If you are unable to file your return by the due date, you can request an additional extension to October 15 by filing Form 4868 before the return due date. However, any payments made after June 15 would be subject to both interest charges and failure to pay penalties.

Where to File

If you are a U.S. citizen or resident alien (Green Card Holder), and you live in a foreign country or you are a non resident alien, mail your U.S. tax return to:

Department of the Treasury
Internal Revenue Service Center
Austin, TX 73301-0215
USA

Estimated tax payments should be mailed with form 1040-ES to:

Internal Revenue Service
P.O. Box 660406
Dallas, TX 75266-0406
USA

Taxpayer Identification Number

Each taxpayer who files, or is claimed as a dependent on, a U.S. tax return will need a social security number (SSN) or individual taxpayer identification number (ITIN). To obtain a SSN, use form SS-5, Application for a Social Security Card. To get form SS-5, or to find out if you are eligible for a social security card, contact a Social Security Office or visit Social Security International Operations. If you, or your spouse, are not eligible for a SSN, you can obtain an ITIN by filing form W-7 along with appropriate documentation.

Exchange Rates

You must express the amounts you report on your U.S. tax return in U.S. dollars. If you receive all or part of your income or pay some or all of your expenses in foreign currency, you must translate the foreign currency into U.S. dollars. Taxpayers generally use the yearly average exchange rate to report foreign-earned income that was received regularly throughout the year. However, if you had foreign transactions on specific days, you may also use the exchange rates for those days. Exchange rates can be found at www.oanda.com. Yearly average currency exchange rates for most countries can be found at Yearly Average Currency Exchange Rates.

How to Get Tax Help

The IRS Office in Philadelphia provides international tax assistance. This office is open Monday through Friday from 6:00 AM to 11:00 PM EST and can be contacted by:

Telephone: (215) 516-2000 (not toll-free)
Fax: (215) 516-2555

Mail: Internal Revenue Service
P.O. Box 920
Bensalem, PA 19020
USA

U.S. TAXES AND VOTING

 ## Voter Registration & Voting for American Citizens in Mérida

This information is provided by the State Department, Washington, D.C. for American citizens in Mérida:

"U.S. citizens overseas are eligible to participate in primary, run-off, and special elections that occur throughout the year, as well as the general elections in November. A calendar of election dates is available on the Internet at www.fvap.gov/pubs/primarycal.html. You should register to vote and/or request absentee ballots as early in the year as possible to ensure that you will receive all ballots for which you are eligible.

The following is the basic absentee voting process:

1. You complete an application form, available from any U.S. Consulate, and send it to local election officials in the U.S.
2. The local official approves your request, or contacts you for further information
3. The local official sends you an absentee ballot
4. You vote the ballot and send it back in time to meet your state's deadline

If the ballot receipt deadline is drawing near, and you have not yet received the blank ballot from local officials, you can download an emergency ballot, write in the names of the candidates and the offices for which they are running, and send it back in time to meet your state's ballot receipt deadline. Registration and ballot request procedures and deadlines vary by state.

There may be late changes to your state's voting calendar, procedures or deadlines. When these occur, the Federal Voting Assistance Program (FVAP) will issue a News Release.

The official US Government website for overseas absentee voting assistance is the Federal Voting Assistance Program website at www.fvap.gov/. It has a wealth of information about absentee voting, including the downloadable absentee ballot application (SF-76, Federal Post Card Application, or FPCA), state-specific instructions for completing the form, links to or contact numbers for state and local officials, and the downloadable emergency ballot.

To register to vote and to request an absentee ballot, download the Federal Post Card Application at *www.fvap.gov/pubs/ofwab.pdf*. You can also obtain this form from overseas American citizens groups or from the U.S. Embassy/Consulate. Fill it out and send it in, following the guidelines for your state. A postage-paid envelope template, valid if you are using the U.S. postal system, is available at *www.fvap.gov/pubs/returnenvelope.pdf*.

Each state has different voting procedures. Information about your state's procedures is available at *www.fvap.gov/links/statelinks.html*. Information about your state's deadlines to register and vote, as well as calendar of election dates, is available at *www.fvap.gov/pubs/primarycal.html*.

States sometimes make last-minute changes. There may be late changes to your state's voting calendar, procedures or deadlines. When these occur, the Federal Voting Assistance Program (FVAP) will issue a News Release. News Releases are available at *www.fvap.gov/pubs/releases.html*.

Be an educated voter. Non-partisan information about candidates, their voting records, and their positions on issues is widely available and easy to obtain via the Internet. Use the links appearing on the Federal Voting Assistance Program website at *www.fvap.gov/links/electionlinks.html*, or choose any one of several search engines to locate articles and information.

The Voting Assistance Officer at the U.S. Embassy in Mexico City is available to answer questions about absentee voting. To contact the Voting Assistance Officer, call (55) 5080-2000 x 4131 or send an email to *ccs@usembassy.net.mx*.

Overseas Americans may contact Democrats Abroad, Republicans Abroad or other American citizens groups or organizations for absentee voting information, or for assistance in registering to vote or to request absentee ballots. Additionally, the Voting Assistance Officer at the U.S. Consulate in Mérida is available to answer questions about absentee voting. To contact the Voting Assistance Officer, send an email to: *Meridacons@state.gov*.

Again, we strongly encourage you to begin this process as soon as possible. Should questions or problems occur, you would still be able to address them in time to vote in your state's primary and general elections."

If you want to be informed of changes in tax or voting laws, be advised that several times a year officials from the U.S. Embassy in Mexico City travel to Mérida to conduct public awareness seminars and consult with American citizens and resident aliens. The Consulate in Mérida has a schedule for upcoming visits.

General Services: Emergency, Police, Fire, Post Offices & More

General Contact Numbers

General Emergency Numbers

General Emergency: 066 from land line, or 113 from a cell phone
Mérida Police Department: (999) 942-0060
Mérida Federal Police Department: (999) 946-1203
Mérida Fire Department: (999) 924-9242 or (999) 923-2971
Red Cross (Cruz Roja): (999) 924-9813
Green Angel Roadside Assistance: (999) 983-1184
Consumer Protection Agency: (999) 923-2323
Federal Consumer Protection Agency: 01-800-468-8722 (ask to speak to an English language operator, or visit their **Website:** www.profeco.gob.mx/english.htm)Immigration (Instituto Nacional de Migracion): (999) 925-5009

Utilities

JAPAY (Water): (999) 930-3450
CE (Electricity): 071
Telmex (Phone): 01-800-123-0000

Hospitals

CEM Hospital, Calle 60 and Avenida Colón (across from Hyatt Hotel): (999) 920-4040
Clínica de Mérida, Avenida Itzáes #242, (near the Donde factory): (999) 925-4508
CMA, Calle 54 & Pérez Ponce, (near Wal-Mart) (Emergency room and Hospital): (999) 926-2111
Star Médica Hospital, Calle 26 #199 and 15 Street, Colonia Altabrisa: (999) 930-2880, (Ext. 5 for emergencies)

Ambulances

Red Cross (Cruz Roja) Free Ambulance: 065, or (999) 924-9813
Alfa Ambulance Service (serves Star Médica): (999) 924-1322
Sami Ambulance Service (serves Star Médica): (999) 925-4048

Taxis

EconoTaxi: (999) 945 0000
Taxi Santa Ana: (999) 928-5600
TaxiMetro: (999) 922-7575

Animal Rescue

Animal Rescue (AFAD): 044 (999) 947-6319 (This is a cell phone)

Visitor Information

For a comprehensive listing of current events, pick up a copy of "**Explore Yucatán**," readily available at most hotels, car rental and tourist agencies. It's free of charge and has the most comprehensive, objective and useful visitor information, along with a comprehensive guide to monthly events. It is also available online at *www.yucatan.revistaexplore.com*.

The **Mérida Bed & Breakfast Association** (MBBA) provides a good service of listing lots of useful information, with no commercial advertising, for everything from bus schedules to exchange rates, weather forecasts to day trips.

The website is: *www.meridabedandbreakfast.org*. (Note: The Editor of this book manages the MBBA.)

Post Offices

Mérida Post Offices

Calle 53 #468, between Calle 52 and 54 Street, Centro
Telephone: (999) 928-5404

Calle 65 by Calle 56 Street, Centro
Telephone: (999) 928-5404

Calle 72 #389 (Avenida Reforma) by Calle 37 Street, Centro
Telephone: (999) 920-2106

Calle 20 #99-G, between Calle 19 and 21 Street, Colonia Chuburná de Hidalgo
Telephone: (999) 981-3833

Calle 59 #300 by 50 Street, Colonia Cordemex
Telephone: (999) 944-1112

Calle 95 #504 by Calle 62 Colonia Delio Moreno Canton
Telephone: (999) 928-5225

EMERGENCY, POLICE, FIRE, POST OFFICES & MORE

Calle 28 #224 (Avenida Pérez Ponce), between Calle 21-A and 26 Street, Colonia Itzimná
Telephone: (999) 927-1323

Calle 24 #440, between Calle 41 and 43 Street, Colonia Las Brisas
Telephone: (999) 986-3048

Calle 5 #432 by 48 Street, Colonia Pensiones
Telephone: (999) 987-0840

Calle 50 #441, between Calle 57 and 59 Street, Colonia Pacabtun
Telephone: (999) 982-1826

Progreso Post Office

Calle 81 #150, between Calle 78 and 80 Street
Telephone: (969) 935-0565

Postal Service Website: *www.sepomexyuc.gob.mx/oficinas.html*

General Information about Yucatán

Population (2010)
 Total 1,945,840
 Rank 21st
 Density 49.1/km2 (127.2/sq mi)
 Density rank 17th
Time zone
 Central Standard Time, (UTC-6)
 Summer (DST) CDT (UTC-5)
Postal code 97000
Telephone Area Codes
 • 969 • 985 • 986 • 988 • 991 • 997 • 999
Elevation
 10 m (33 ft)
Major Airport:
 Manuel Crescencio Rejón International Airport
 IATA Code: MID
Internet Access:
 All public parks and squares are equipped with free Wi-Fi. Most in the Historic Center also have kiosks with electrical outlets for recharging batteries for laptops and cellphones.

EMERGENCY, POLICE, FIRE, POST OFFICES & MORE

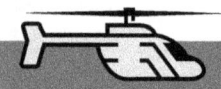

Air Ambulance & Med-Evac Companies

U.S.-based Companies

STAT AIR INTERNATIONAL - AIR AMBULANCE

Telephone: (800) 557-5911 or (619) 754-6550
Fax: (619) 754-6153
www.statair.com

TRINITY AIR AMBULANCE INTERNATIONAL

Lauderdale by the Sea, FL 33308
Telephone: (954) 771-7911
Fax: (954) 771-4882
www.trinityairambulance.com

AIR COMPASSION

(866) 270-9198
001- (883)-270-9198
www.aircompassionamerica.org

ADVANCED AIR AMBULANCE

Miami, FL
(800) 633-3590 / (305) 232-7700
www.flyambu.com

AIRMD AIR AMBULANCE SERVICES

Clearwater, FL
(800) 282-6878 / (727) 530-7972
www.airmd.net

AIR AMBULANCE PROFESSIONALS

Fort Lauderdale, FL
(800) 752-4195 / (954) 491-0555
www.airambulanceprof.com

AIR RESPONSE

Orlando, FL
(800) 631-6565 / (303) 858-9967
www.airresponse.net

CRITICAL AIR MEDICINE

San Diego, CA
(800) 247-8326 / (619) 571-0482

U.S. Embassy, Consulates and Consular Agencies in Mexico:

Embassy Location:
The U.S. Embassy is located in Mexico City at Paseo de la Reforma 305, Colonia Cuauhtemoc.
Telephone from the United States: 011-52-55-5080-2000
Telephone within Mexico City: 5080-2000
Telephone long distance within Mexico 01-55-5080-2000
Website: mexico.usembassy.gov/eng/main.html

U.S. Consulates

Ciudad Juárez:
Paseo de la Victoria 3650
Telephone: (656) 227-3000

Guadalajara:
Progreso 175, Colonia Americana
Telephone: (333) 268-2100

Hermosillo:
Calle Monterrey 141 Poniente, Colonia Esqueda
Telephone: (662) 289-3500

Matamoros:
Avenida Primera 2002 and Azaleas
Telephone: (868) 812-4402

Mérida:
Calle 60 #338 K between Calle 29 and 31 Street, Colonia Alcalá Martín
Telephone: (999) 942-5700

Monterrey:
Avenida Constitución 411 Poniente
Telephone: (818) 047-3100

Nogales:
Calle San José, Fraccionamiento "Los Alamos"
Telephone: (631) 311-8150

Nuevo Laredo:
Calle Allende 3330, Colonia Jardin
Telephone: (867) 714-0512

Tijuana:
Avenida Tapachula 96, Colonia Hipodromo
Telephone: (664) 622-7400

Consular Agencies

Acapulco:
Hotel Continental Emporio, Costera Miguel Alemán 121 - Local 14
Telephone: (744) 484-0300 or (744) 469-0556

Cabo San Lucas:
Blvd. Marina Local C-4, Plaza Nautica, Centro
Telephone: (624) 143-3566

Cancún:
Blvd. Kukulcán Km 13 ZH Torre La Europea, Despacho 301
Telephone: (998) 883-0272

Cozumel:
Plaza Villa Mar en El Centro, Plaza Principal, 2nd floor, Locales 8 and 9
Telephone: (987) 872-4574

Ixtapa/Zihuatanejo:
Hotel Fontan, Blvd. Ixtapa
Telephone: (755) 553-2100

Mazatlán:

Hotel Playa Mazatlán, Playa Gaviotas 202, Zona Dorada
Telephone: (669) 916-5889

Oaxaca:

Macedonio Alcalá #407, Interior 20
Telephone: (951) 514-3054 or (951) 516-2853

Piedras Negras:

Abasolo 211, Local 3, Centro
Telephone (878) 782-5586 or (878) 782-8664.

Playa del Carmen:

The Palapa, Calle 1 Sur, between Avenida 15 and Avenida 20
Telephone: (984) 873-0303

Puerto Vallarta:

Paseo de Los Cocoteros 85 Sur, Paradise Plaza – Local L-7, Nuevo Vallarta, Nayarit
Telephone: (322) 222-0069

Reynosa:

Calle Monterrey 390, Esq. Sinaloa, Colonia Rodríguez
Telephone: (899) 923-9331

San Luis Potosi:

Edificio "Las Terrazas", Avenida Venustiano Carranza 2076-41, Colonia Polanco
Telephone: (444) 811-7802 or (444) 811-7803

San Miguel de Allende:

Dr. Hernandez Macias 72
Telephone: (415) 152-2357

Veterinary Services

If it's true that "you can judge a country by the way they treat their animals," there's something to be said about Mérida. The Autonomous University of Yucatán, or UADY, will open its new world-class, state-of-the-art veterinary hospital in September 2011 at a cost of $1.1 million USD. Located in Colonia of San José Vergel, minutes from downtown, this facility will rival any veterinary hospital in Latin America or the U.S. In addition, it is great to know that there are government facilities dedicated to protecting animal welfare. There are also private nonprofit organizations that work to find homes for pets, as well as conduct workshops to provide free services to pets.

Bilingual Veterinarians:

Pets & Company

Sandra Milena Leguizamón
José Encarnación Muñoz
Address: Calle 17 #222, Suite 2, by Calle 20, Colonia Jardines del Norte, Mérida, Yucatán
Telephone: (999) 943-7787
Email: *info@petsandcompany.com*
Website:
www.petsandcompany.com

Veterinary Association

For expatriates, the Asociación de Médicos Veterinarios Especialistas en Pequeñas Especies de Yucatán, A. C. (AMVEPEY), is a nonprofit organization that can direct you to a bilingual veterinary doctor close to you. For more information, you can contact the AMVEPEY:

AMVEPEY

Website: *www.amvepey.com*

Adopt-a-Pet:

To adopt a pet, Silvia Cortés operates a sanctuary for dogs in need of a loving home. Her organization, Evolución Yucatán, continues to win praise from the expatriates.
Silvia Cortés, Director
Evolución Yucatán
Email: *slv_cc@hotmail.com*
Website: *evolucionyucatan.com*

Responsible Dog Breeders

Mérida is home to Criadora Itaboca, a world-class dog breeding company, that exports dogs all over Mexico, the U.S. and as far away as Russia and Malaysia. Trained in Brazil, Felipe Xacur Baeza, complies with the norms established by the American Kennel Club and aims to preserve and improve the breeds to which he is dedicated.

Criadora Itaboca

Felipe Xacur Baeza, Director
Calle 16 #213 by Calle 13, Fracc. Vista Alegre, Mérida, Yucatán
Telephone: (999) 943-0148
Email: *faxcur@itaboca.com*
Website: *www.itaboca.com*

27 If There Were a "Better Business Bureau" in Mérida ...

There is no "Better Business Bureau" in Mexico as it is understood in the United States. By that we mean a non-governmental organization that receives complaints from the public and advocates on behalf of the aggrieved consumer, and offers ratings on local businesses.

Mexico, however, does have a federal agency to protect consumers. It does not rank companies on the basis of complaints filed against them. But it is a proactive federal agency that receives praise from the Mexican public as being diligent, honest and effective. If you encounter any consumer problem, PROFECO may be the place to go to file a complaint if you have exhausted your recourse by contacting the company directly. PROFECO's services are free of charge, they operate a national toll-free number and have a very comprehensive website.

Mexico's Procuduria Federal del Consumidor, or PROFECO, has an English-language website designed to help individuals, regardless of nationalities, protect their rights as consumers. PROFECO's website offers this advice:

WELCOME

Welcome to the Federal Attorney's Office of Consumer (PROFECO) web site. This portal contains basic information on the PROFECO in English. ... Mexico is the second Latin-American country with a Federal Law of Protection to the Consumer and the first one in creating an Attorney's office. The Mexican experience is important, especially for the countries that [are beginning to employ] protection of the rights of the consumers. On February 5, 1976, the Federal Law of Protection to the Consumer enriches the social rights of the Mexican people, which for the first time established rights for the consuming population and believes a specialized agency in the proxy of justice in the sphere of the consumption. There were conceived from the National Institute of the Consumer and the Federal Attorney's office of the Consumer, this one as [an] organism decentralized of social service, juridical personality and own patrimony with functions of administrative authority entrusted to promote and protect the interests of the consuming public.

MISSION

To promote and to protect the rights of the consumer, to foment intelligent consumption and to arbitrate the equity and juridical safety in the relations between suppliers and consumers.

VISION

To be an effective institution in the promotion of a culture of intelligent consumption and in the application of the law.

AIMS OF THE PROFECO

To protect the rights of the consumer.

To promote the rights of the consumer.

To foment a culture of intelligent consumption.

To arbitrate the equity in the relations of consumption.

To arbitrate the juridical safety in the relations of consumption.

For more information, their website is: *www.profeco.gob.mx/english.htm*

If there were a "Better Business Bureau" in Mérida!

But what if there were a Better Business Bureau? What follows is a list of companies in Mérida that have been known to have complaints filed about them with consumer agencies and they have been known to leave their customers unsatisfied. In the opinion of contributors to this book, these are companies that have shown poor judgment in how they treat their customers and the public at large. When you consider that this is a city of almost a million people, you'll find that the list is rather short, a testament to the integrity of shopkeepers who live and work here.

Based on years of experience living in Mérida, all we are saying is **CONSUMER BEWARE**!

Architects

Henry Ponce

IF THERE WERE A "BETTER BUSINESS BUREAU"

Bars & Pubs
Hennessey's

Bed & Breakfasts
Cascadas de Mérida

City Tours
Mérida English Language Library (MELL) House & Garden Tours

Cooking Schools
Los Dos

Expatriate Services
Yucatán Expatriate Services (YES)

Gardening/Landscaping
Selva y Jardin

Hotels
Hotel Caribe

Property Managers
Rubén Ballote
Urbano Rentals

Real Estate Companies
Hacienda Mexico
Mexico International
Tierra Yucatán

Restaurants
El Cangregito

Shops
Mundo Maya

IF THERE WERE A "BETTER BUSINESS BUREAU"

Tour Companies

Iluminado Tours

Tourist Information

Yucatán Today

Web-Hosting Companies

Eclectec, S.A. de C.V. (YucatanLiving.com)

> More detailed information appears at:
> *www.meridabedandbreakfast.org/touristadvisories.html*

28 End of Life Issues: Wills, Assisted Living Options & Caring for an Elderly Parent

In Samuel Butler's classic, *The Way of All Flesh*, the reader is reminded of each person's mortality, since that is part of the cycle of life. It is a masterful work, one that traces four generations of a family that attempts, often in vain, to find happiness. The novel does ask readers to contemplate the nature of mortality, and end of life issues. It would be easy to point out that none of the characters lived in Mérida! No wonder they're miserable! So it is for expatriates in Mérida. There will come a time when an important decision will have to be made: To remain in Mérida, or to return home.

Traditionally, there have been two scenarios played out. There are expatriates who, once they reach a certain stage in life and can no longer comfortably or capably live on their own, avail themselves to their adult children, siblings or other relatives back home. Often times, arrangements are made for them to return to assisted living centers in the U.S., or to nursing homes. When this happens, the chapter of their lives living in Mérida is meticulously closed up, and they leave for the twilight of their time back in their home country. The other is to make arrangements to remain in Mexico, through a network of friends and institutional relationships forged during their time living in Mérida. There are some who, for lack of family, or the desire to remain far removed from the travesties of the elder healthcare industry in the U.S., decide to remain in Mérida.

Whichever course is right for you – should I stay or should I go? – it's important to have a will and written instructions that clearly, legally and *bilingually* spell out your wishes. Just because you live in Mérida doesn't mean you won't get hit by the proverbial bus!

There's another point to consider: Since 2000 there has been rapid and strong growth of assisted living communities in Mérida, as well as nursing homes. Many are a fraction of the costs back in the U.S. or Canada, and they offer far superior person-to-person individualized care, from both physicians and staff. This is fast-becoming a popular option. How popular? Consider this:

To assist the expatriate community, the State of Yucatán commissioned an opinion poll to help determine if government-assistance is required in creating a retirement community for Americans citizens living in Mérida, which would include an assisted living center.

That said, if you have a will in English, and you should, it is well worth having a summary of it translated and notarized by either a Mexican Public Notary or the U.S. Consulate public notary services, just in case. Quick! If the proverbial bus *were* to hit you now, do you want your body shipped back to your home country, or do you want to be cremated in Mérida? How would the coroner's office know your wishes?

With this in mind, the following is excerpted from a set of guidelines prepared by the U.S. State Department on caring for elderly parents who are overseas for members of the Foreign Service. After this account, the procedures for handling a death in Mérida are discussed.

Caring for Elderly Parents

The following is a set of recommendations for caring for elderly parents for Foreign Families overseas. It is included here because these are sound recommendations that can benefit many families who have members living as expatriates in Mérida.

State Department Recommendations:

How to care for elderly parents is a major concern of many Foreign Service families. Our concerns mirror those of other American families, but how to ensure good health care, find the right living situation, and handle legal questions is often complicated for Foreign Service families by being posted abroad. The distance involved makes it harder to get information and help so contingency planning is essential.

Often Foreign Service families only have short visits during R & R or on home leave and hate to spend the precious time with their parents talking about serious business or unpleasant possibilities. While it is difficult to discuss the issues of aging, the family who has discussed the options and agreed on plans will be better able to handle whatever happens. It will be worth the time taken, if there is an emergency.

The ideal situation is when the parents take control of their own situations and make decisions in advance of an emergency. They should investigate the types of retirement options and decide which is most appropriate, make informed decisions about life-sustaining medical care, and make sure that documents, instructions, and powers of attorney are available to those who must take responsibility in an emergency. The American Association of Retired Persons recommends that elderly people use a document locator list to make sure their papers are in order. This list can then be given to the person(s) who will be responsible for them should an emergency arise. Going through the list with your parents should ensure that their wishes are understood.

Communicating with Elderly Parents

Talking with our elderly parents about their living situations and the possible need for change is not always easy. A successful conversation depends to an extent upon the relationship we have with the parent, as well, of course, as on the parent's mental, emotional and physical condition. To the extent possible, talk with your elderly parents gently and honestly about their wishes, their abilities and their options. The following are suggestions for conversations with your elderly parent:

- Share your own feelings, and reassure the parent that you will support them and can be depended upon to help them solve their problems.
- Help the parent to retain whatever control is possible in making his or her own decisions. Respect and try to honor their wishes wherever feasible.
- Encourage the smallest change possible at each step, so that the parent is more able to adjust to the change.
- Educate yourself on legal, financial and medical matters that pertain to your parent as background for your conversations, including current knowledge on the aging process.
- Respect your own needs - be honest with your parents about your time and energy limits.

If this kind of conversation seems impossible or the situation and relationship with the elderly parent become overwhelming, professional counseling may be very helpful.

When a Lifestyle Change May Be Necessary

Physicians and geriatric social workers warn that there are a number of danger signs that indicate an elderly person needs extra help or a change in living arrangement. Any marked change in personality or behavior should be heeded. However, no change in lifestyle should be made without discussions with the elderly person, other family members, and health professionals.

Danger Signals

- Sudden weight loss could be an indication that the elderly person is simply not eating or not preparing foods.
- Failure to take medication or over-dosing may indicate confusion, forgetfulness, or a misunderstanding of the doctor's instructions.
- Burns or injury marks may indicate physical problems involving general weakness, forgetfulness, or a possible misuse of alcohol.

- Deterioration of personal habits such as infrequent bathing and shampooing, not shaving, or not wearing dentures could be the result of either mental or physical problems.
- Increased car accidents can indicate slowed reflexes, poor vision, physical weakness, or general inability to handle a vehicle.
- General forgetfulness such as not paying bills, missing appointments, or consistently forgetting name, address, phone number, and meal times could be a signal.
- Extreme suspiciousness could indicate some thought disorder. Your parents thinking that their neighbors, friends, family, doctor, and lawyer are all conspiring against them would be an example. Intense ungrounded fears about dire consequences may be a danger signal.
- A series of small fires could be caused by dozing off, forgetting to turn off the stove or appliances, or carelessness with matches. They may indicate blackouts or dizzy spells.
- Bizarre behavior of any kind could be a warning sign. This behavior could be dressing in heavy gloves and overcoat in 90 degree weather or going outside without shoes when it's snowing. Watch for uncharacteristic actions or speech.
- Disorientation of a consistent nature may indicate a need for help. Examples include not knowing who one is, where one is, who the family is, or talking to people who are not there.

Elder Care Options

If you see danger signals in your parent's behavior, it is important to discuss the changes and do some research. (See IQ: Information Quest below for information about the Department of State's free resource referral service.) There are many housing options available to the elderly. Choosing the best one will depend on the elderly person's preference, age, health, and financial condition.

Aging in Place

Under this option, the elderly person continues to live in his/her own apartment. Many elderly people live in Naturally Occurring Retirement Communities (NORCs), apartment buildings, condominiums, or cooperatives not designed as retirement communities but where at least 50 percent of the residents are 62 years old or older.

- Home care services are available in many communities, providing appropriate, supervised personnel to help older persons with either health care (giving medications, changing dressings, catheter care, etc.) or personal care (bathing, dressing, and grooming).
- Meals and transportation are available to older people to help them retain some independence.
- Adult day care is similar to child day care. The elderly person goes to a community facility daily or 2 or 3 days per week. Activities include exercise programs, singing, guest lectures, and current events discussions. Cost varies and there are often long waiting lists at such centers.
- Respite care brings a trained person into the home to give the full-time caregiver time off or take a vacation. Service is generally offered through area Departments of Social Services and is based on a sliding fee scale.

Other Housing Options

There are several types of retirement communities that provide living arrangements and services to meet the needs of both independent seniors and those who need assistance. It is important when investigating these housing options to understand completely the services provided and the cost.

- Adult congregate communities are designed for the fully able-bodied, 55 and older. Residents buy co-ops or condominiums and pay a monthly fee for grass mowing, leaf raking, and snow shoveling. A pay-as-you-go medical center is on site and a nurse is on duty 24 hours a day to make home visits in emergencies. Leisure World is the most famous example of an adult congregate community.
- Assisted living communities are rental retirement communities for independent seniors who need some assistance. A homelike atmosphere, three meals a day, maid, linen, and laundry service, availability of a registered nurse, and many personal care services are provided in the all-inclusive rent.
- Rental retirement communities with fee-for-service nursing units charge residents an entrance fee plus a substantial monthly rent. When the need for nursing care arises, residents pay an extra daily fee and stay in a nursing unit, usually located on site or nearby.
- Life care or continuing care communities provide a continuum of care from independent living to nursing home care on the premises. The individual must be independent when s/he enters the community. These communities require a substantial entrance fee and monthly service fee. Residents get one meal a day in a dining room, maid service, linen service, maintenance, transportation to shopping and cultural events, travel planning, and a pull cord to an emergency nurse. If nursing care is needed, it is provided at no extra cost.
- Personal care homes (board and care) are licensed in many communities to provide shelter, supervision, meals, and personal care to a small number of residents.
- Subsidized housing for the elderly is an option for the elderly poor in reasonably good health. Subsidized by Department of Housing and Urban Development, income limits apply. No round-the-clock care is provided but nurses come in to check blood pressure and assess a resident's functioning. Residents take meals in a dining room and may have use of a library, recreation area, or beauty shop.

Nursing Facilities

If the elderly person is not capable of independent living, a nursing home may be the appropriate option. Nursing homes offer two levels of care - skilled nursing and intermediate care - depending on the patient's needs. Most nursing homes offer both levels of care on a single site.

- Skilled nursing facilities provide 24-hour nursing services for people who have serious health care needs but do not require the intense level of care provided in a hospital. Rehabilitation services may also be provided.
- Intermediate care facilities provide less extensive health care than skilled nursing facilities. Nursing and rehabilitation services are provided but not on a 24-hour basis.

These facilities are for people who cannot live alone but need a minimum of medical assistance and help with personal and/or social care.

Paying for Long-Term Care

It is important to understand the different types of insurance that are available to older people. Many people believe that Medicare will cover long-term care needs. It will not.

Medicare

Medicare is a Federal health insurance program which helps defray many of the medical expenses of most Americans over the age of 65. Medicare has two parts:

(Part A) Hospital Insurance helps pay the cost of inpatient hospital care. The number of days in the hospital paid for by Medicare is governed by a system based upon patient diagnosis and medical necessity for hospital care. Once it is no longer medically necessary for the person to remain in the hospital, the physician will begin the discharge process. If the person or the family disagrees with this decision, they may appeal to the state's Peer Review Organization.

Medicare does not pay for custodial care or nursing home care. It will, however, cover up to 60 days in a nursing home as part of convalescence after hospitalization. (Part B) Medical Insurance pays for many medically necessary doctors' services, outpatient services, and some other medical services. Enrollees pay a monthly premium.

Medicaid

Medicaid is a joint federal-state health care program for people with a low income. The program is administered by each state and the type of services covered differs. There are strict income requirements so it is necessary for the person to "spend down" all income and assets to poverty levels before becoming eligible. Medicaid is the major payer of nursing home care. The Medicaid requirement to "spend down" all income and assets created a great hardship for the spouse of a person needing nursing home care. Changes in the Medicaid rules now allow the spouse to keep a monthly income and some assets, including the primary residence.

Other Insurance

Medigap is the name given to privately-purchased supplemental health insurance. It is designed to help cover some of the gaps in Medicare coverage but does not cover long-term care. Long-Term Care Insurance is a private insurance that is usually either an indemnity policy or part of an individual life insurance policy.

Information about other long-term insurance policies are available from:

The American Foreign Service
 Association (AFSA)
Retiree Liaison
2101 E Street, NW
Washington, DC 20037
Telephone: 202-338-4045, ext. 528
Fax: 202-338-6820
Email: afsa@afsa.org
http://www.afsa.org

American Foreign Service Protective
 Association (AFSPA)
1716 N Street, NW
Washington, DC 20036
Telephone: 202-833-4910
Fax: 202-883-4918
http://www.afspa.org

As with Medigap health insurance, it is important to read the policy carefully and understand its restrictions before purchasing.

The Final *Adios*

Every expatriate who decides to remain in Mérida until death do you part, would be wise to:

1. Have an original and a copy of his or her birth certificate on hand, along with an official, notarized, translation of that birth certificate.

2. Have an official translation of your will, notarized, and on hand.

These two documents will save those taking care of the final details of your affairs much easier, especially when navigating through the bureaucracy that surrounds death.

The first step in all of this, of course, requires that you take the initiative and, how shall we put it? Yes, you need to die. Having done that, your part is done. But what of those who now have to deal with your physical remains and disposing of your worldly possessions?

Here is a breakdown of what happens:

If you died at a clinic, or hospital, or at the scene of an accident, or at home with others by your bedside, chances are that a doctor is involved in the matter. If you died in your sleep, alone, then someone will have to find your body.

Once you die and your body is found, whoever is present, notifies a doctor. If you are an American citizen, someone should also contact the U.S. Consulate to report the death of an American in Mexico.

The doctor confirms the death and fills out one document: Certificado de Defunción which is an official document from the Secretaria de Salud del Estado de Yucatán, which confirms that the person died in the State of Yucatán.

This certificate, along with an original and notarized translation of the birth certificate, is taken to a funeral home. If the death occurred in a medical facility, the staff calls a funeral home ahead of time.

The staff at the funeral home examines the birth certificate, the notarized translation and the Certificado de Defunción to make sure everything is in order. Arrangements are made for the body to be picked up.

The funeral home will assign a staff member to assist you in going to the Registro Civil, on Calle 65 between Calle 64 and 66 Street, to register the death. Once the information is entered into the Registro Civil's computer, an Official Death Certificate is issued. This grants the funeral home the legal authority to make arrangements for the disposal of the body – cremation, burial in Mexico, or arrangements to ship the body overseas. Ask for at least three copies of the Official Death Certificate since it will expedite things along the way.

The funeral home will then notify the Municipal Crematorium, the cemetery or the next of kin for instructions. If the body is to be cremated or buried in Mexico, there will paperwork associated, along with the fees (and payment of those fees), for either cremation or opening and closing of the tomb. If the body is to be shipped overseas, airlines have their own offices that are in charge of shipping human remains.

The final step is filling out forms at the U.S. Consulate, and returning the passport to consular personnel. The U.S. Consulate will issue a "Report of the Death of an American Citizen Abroad," which, in essence, confirms the legality of all the Mexican paperwork, which is necessary for the next of kin to be able to execute the will, and handle legal matters in the United States. The Consulate will automatically inform all U.S. agencies, such as the Social Security Administration, Veterans Affairs, and so forth, of your death.

Have a wonderful afterlife, or reincarnation!

29 Mexican Embassies and Consulates in the U.S. and Canada

USA

Alaska

Anchorage

610 "C" Street Suite A-7, Anchorage, Alaska 99501
Telephone: Tel (907) 334-9573 * Fax (907) 334-9673
Email: *consulmexalaska@hotmail.com*

Arkansas

Little Rock

3500 South University Avenue, Little Rock, AR, 72204
Telephone: (501) 372-6933 * **Fax:** (501) 372-6109
Email: *consulmexlir@comcast.net*

Arizona

Douglas

1201 F Avenue, Douglas, AZ 85607
Telephone: (520) 364-3142 * **Fax:** (520) 364-1379
Email: *douglas@sre.gob.mx*

Nogales

571 N. Grand Ave., Nogales, AZ 85621
Telephone: (520) 287-2521 * **Fax:** (520) 287-3175
Email: *consulmex2@mchsi.com*

Phoenix

1990 W. Camelback, Suite 110, Phoenix, AZ 85015
Telephone: (602) 242-7398 * **Fax:** 242-2957
Email: *contactenos@consulmexphoenix.phxcocmail.com*

Tucson

553 S. Stone Ave., Tucson, AZ 85701
Telephone: (520) 882-5595 * **Fax:** (520) 882-8959
Email: *contucmx@sre.gob.mx*

Yuma

298 S. Main Street, Yuma, AZ 85364
Telephone: (928) 343-0066 * **Fax:** (928) 343-0077
Email: *contucmx@sre.gob.mx*

California

Calexico

408 Herber Ave., Calexico, CA 92231
Telephone: (760) 357-4132 * **Fax:** (760) 357-6284
Email: *informacion@concalexio.org*

Fresno

2409 Merced Street, Fresno, CA 93721
Telephone: (559) 233-3065 * **Fax:** (559) 233-6156
Email: *consulado@consulmexfresno.net*

Los Angeles

2401 W. Sixth Street, Los Angeles, CA 90057
Telephone: (213) 351-6800 * **Fax:** (213) 351-2114
Email: *consulado@sre.gob.mx*

Oxnard

3151 West Fifth Street, Oxnard, CA 93030
Telephone: (805) 984-8738* **Fax:** (805) 984-8747
Email: *consul@consulmexoxnard.com*

Sacramento

1010 8th Street, Sacramento, CA 95814
Telephone: (916) 441-3287 * **Fax:** (916) 441-3146
Email: *sacramento@sre.gob.mx*

San Bernardino

293 North "D" Street, San Bernardino, CA 92401
Telephone: (909) 889-9836 * **Fax:** (909) 889-8285
Email: *conmexbe@hotmail.com*

San Diego

1549 India Street, San Diego, CA 92101
Telephone: (619) 231-8414 * **Fax:** (619) 231-4802
Email: *info@consulmexsd.org*

San Francisco

532 Folsom Street, San Francisco, CA 94105
Telephone: (415) 354-1700 * **Fax:** (415) 495-3971
Email: *confrancisco@sre.gob.mx*

San José

540 North First Street, San José, CA 95112
Telephone: (408) 294-3414 * **Fax:** (408) 294-4506
Email: *consjose@sre.gob.mx*

Santa Ana

828 N. Broadway Street, Santa Ana, CA 92701-3424
Telephone: (714) 835-3069 * **Fax:** (714) 835-3472
Email: *consana@sre.gob.mx*

Colorado

Denver

5350 Leetsdale Drive, Suite 100, Denver, CO 80246
Telephone: (303) 331-1110 * **Fax:** (303) 331-1872
Email: *infodenver@sre.gob.mx*

District of Columbia

Washington (Embassy of Mexico)

1911 Pennsylvania Ave., N.W., Washington, D.C., 20006
Telephone: (202) 736-1000 * **Fax:** (202) 234-4498
Email: *consulwas@aol.com*

District of Columbia (Consulate)

2827 16th. Street N.W., Washington D.C., 20009-4260
Telephone: (202) 736-1000 * **Fax:** (202) 2344498
Email: *consultas@aol.com*

Florida

Miami

5975 S.W. 72nd Street, Miami, Florida 33143
Telephone: (786) 268-4900 * **Fax:** (786) 268-4895
Email: *info@mexicomiami.org*

Orlando

100 W. Washington Street, Orlando, FL 32801
Telephone: (407) 422-0514 * **Fax:** (407) 422-9633
Email: *consulado@conorlando.net*

Georgia

Atlanta

2600 Apple Valley Rd, Atlanta, GA 30319
Telephone: (404) 266-2233 * **Fax:** (404) 266-2302
Email: *informacion@consulmexatlanta.org*

Idaho

Boise

720 Park Boulevard, Suite 260, Boise, Idaho, 83712
Telephone:(208) 343-6228 343-6237 * **Fax:** (208) 343-6237

Indiana

Indianapolis

39 west Jackson Place, Suite 103, Indianapolis, IN 46225
Telephone:(317) 951-0005 * **Fax:** (317) 951-0006
Email: *indianapolis@sre.gob.mx*

Illinois

Chicago

204 S. Ashland Ave., Chicago, IL 60607
Telephone: (312) 738-2383 * **Fax:** 312-491-9072
Email: *Info@consulmexchicago.com*

Louisiana

New Orleans

901 Convection Center Boulevard, Suite 119, New Orleans, LA 70130
Telephone: (504) 528-3722
Email: *connorleans@sre.gob.mx*

Massachusetts

Boston

20 Park Plaza, Suite 506, Boston, MA 02116
Telephone: (617) 426-4181 * **Fax:** (617) 695-1957
Email: *cmxboston@sre.gob.mx*

Michigan

Detroit

645 Griswold Ave. Suite 1700, Detroit, MI 48226
Telephone: (313) 964-4515 * **Fax:** (313) 964-4522
Email: *detroit@sre.gob.mx*

Minnesota

Saint Paul

797 East 7th Street, Saint Paul, MN 55106
Telephone: (651) 771-5494 * **Fax:** (651) 772-4419
Email: *contacto@consulmexstpaul.com*

Missouri

Kansas City

1600 Baltimore, Suite 100, Kansas City, MO 64108
Telephone: (816) 556-0800 * **Fax:** (816) 556-0900
Email: *conkansas@sre.gob*

Nebraska

Omaha

3552 Dodge Street, Omaha, NE 6811
Telephone: (402) 595-1841-44 * **Fax:** (402) 595-1845
Email: *info@consuladoomaha.org*

Nevada

Las Vegas

330 S. 4th Street, Las Vegas, Nevada 89101
Telephone: (702) 383-0623 * **Fax:** (702) 383-0683
Email: *conlvegas@sre.gob.mx*

New Mexico

Albuquerque

1610 4th Street NW, Albuquerque, NM 87102
Telephone: (505) 247-4177 * **Fax:** (505) 842-9490
Email: *consulmexalb@qwestoffice.net*

New York

New York

27 East 39th. Street, New York, NY 10016
Telephone: (212) 217-6400 * **Fax:** (212) 217-6493
Email: *titularny@sre.gob.mx*

North Carolina

Charlotte

P.O. Box 19627, Charlotte, NC 28219
Telephone: (704) 394-2190

Raleigh

336 E. Six Forks Rd, Raleigh, NC 27609
Telephone: (919) 754-0046 * **Fax:** (919) 754-1729
Email: *conraleigh@sre.gob.mx*

Oregon

Portland

1234 S.W. Morrison, Portland, OR 97205
Telephone: (503) 274-1450 * **Fax:** (503) 274-1540
Email: *portland@sre.gob.mx*

Pennsylvania

Philadelphia

111 S. Independence Mall E, Suite 310, Bourse Building, Philadelphia, PA 19106
Telephone: (215) 922-4262/3834 * **Fax:** (215) 923-7281
Email: *buzon@consulmexphila.gob.mx*

Texas

Austin

200 E. Sixth Street, Suite 200, Austin, TX 78701
Telephone: (512) 478-2866 * **Fax:** (512) 478-8008
Email: *austin@sre.gob.mx*

Brownsville

724 E. Elizabeth Street, Brownsville, TX 78520
Telephone: (956) 542-4431 * **Fax:** (956) 542-7267
Email: *conbrownsville@sre.gob.mx*

Corpus Christi

800 N. Shoreline Blvd. Suite 410, North Tower, Corpus Christi, TX 78401
Telephone: (512) 882-3375 * **Fax:** (512) 882-9324

Dallas

8855 N Stemmons Freeway, Dallas, TX 75247
Telephone: (214) 252-9250 ext. 123 * **Fax:** (214) 630-3511
Email: *info@consulmexdallas.com*

Del Rio

2398 Spur, Del Rio, TX 78840
Telephone: (830) 775-2352 * **Fax:** (830) 774-6497
Email: *consulmexdel.titular@wcsonline.net*

Eagle Pass

2252 E. Garrison Street. Eagle Pass, TX 78852
Telephone: (830) 773-9255 * **Fax:** (830) 773-9397
Email: *consulmxeag@sbcglobal.net*

El Paso

910 E. San Antonio Street, El Paso, TX 79901
Telephone: (915) 533-3644 * **Fax:** (915) 532-7163
Email: *consulmexepa@elp.rr.com*

Houston

4507 San Jacinto Street, Houston, TX 77004
Telephone: (713) 271-6800 ext 1400 * **Fax:** (713) 271-3201
Email: *conhouston@wt.net*

Laredo

1612 Farragut Street, Laredo, TX 78040
Telephone: (956) 723-6369 * **Fax:** (956) 723-1741
Email: *consul@srelaredo.org*

McAllen

600 S. Broadway Ave., McAllen, TX 78501
Telephone: (956) 686-0243 * **Fax:** (956) 686-4901
Email: *consumexmc@aol.com*

Presidio

Juárez Ave.Y 21 de Marzo Street, Presidio, TX 79845
Telephone: (423) 229-2788 * **Fax:** (423) 229-2792
Email: *conpresidio@bigbend.net*

San Antonio

127 Navarro Street, San Antonio, TX 78205
Telephone: (210) 271-9728 * **Fax:** (210) 227-7518
Email: *info@consulmexsat.org*

Utah

Salt Lake City

155 South 300 West 3rd floor, Salt Lake City, Utah 84101
Telephone: (801) 521-8503 * **Fax:** (801) 521-0534
Email: *consuladoslc@consulmexslc.org*

Washington

Seattle

2132 Third Ave., Seattle, WA 98121
Telephone: (206) 448-3526 * **Fax:** (206) 448-4771
Email: *conseattle@sre.gob.mx*

CANADA

Alberta

Calgary

Suite 1100-833 4th Avenue SW
Calgary, Alberta T2P 3T5
Telephone: (403) 264-4819 * **Fax:** (403) 264-1527
Email: *concalgary@sre.gob.mx*

British Columbia

Vancouver

Suite 411-1177 West Hastings Street, 4th Floor

Vancouver, B.C. V6E 2K3
Telephone: (604) 684-1859 * **Fax:** (604) 684-2485
Email: *mexico@consulmexvan.com*

Ontario

Ottawa (Embassy of Mexico)

45 O'Connor Suite 1500
Ottawa, Ontario K1P 1A4
Telephone: (613) 233 8988 * **Fax:** (613) 235 9123
Email: *info@embamexcan.com*

Toronto

199 Bay Street, Suite 4440, Commerce Court West
Toronto, Ontarip M5L 1E9
Telephone: (416) 368-1847 * **Fax:** (416) 368-8141
Email:*cgmtoronto@consulmex.com*

Quebec

Montreal

2055 rue Peel, Suite 1000,
Montreal, Québec, H3A 1V4
Telephone: (514) 288 2502 y (514) 288 2707 * **Fax:** (514) 288 8287
Email:*comexmt@consulmex.qc.ca*

www.ingramcontent.com/pod-product-compliance
Lightning Source LLC
Chambersburg PA
CBHW080528170426
43195CB00016B/2505